# A DIVERSITY OF WOMEN: ONTARIO, 1945–1980

Edited by Joy Parr

Our perception of women s roles has changed dramatically since 1945. In this collection Joy Parr has brought together ten studies from a variety of disciplines examining changing ideas about women.

Mariana Valverde writes about teenage girls in the immediate postwar years and finds that stereotypes of a supposedly simple, secure, politically quiescent, and sexually conformist life do not really hold. Joy Parr follows women shoppers of the early 1950s, in their sometimes comical encounters with male designers, manufacturers, and retailers, in search of the tools and totems of modernity for their homes. Increasingly these homes were in suburban subdivisions, whose pleasures and possibilities for women Veronica Strong-Boag reconsiders. Joan Sangster reminds us that wage-earning mothers were numerous in the 1950s and 1960s, and through a juxtaposition of their own stories with contemporary studies tells much about these self-denying women's lives. Franca Iacovetta discusses the experiences of immigrant and refugee women in northwestern and south-central Ontario, experiences that were interpreted through their starkly different European wartime memories. Based on her work among the rural women of south-western Ontario, E.A. (Nora) Cebotarev charts the changes that transformed farm families and finances from the 1960s to the 1980s. Ester Reiter compares the recollections of women who had worked together during the 1960s in an auto parts plant in the Niagara Peninsula with contemporary newspaper accounts of a strike, and leads us into a complex narrative of gender and militancy. Nancy Adamson reconsiders the diversity of feminist organizing within the province over the decades since second-wave feminism began; she tracks the different needs and paths that brought women to the women's liberation movement and the ways in which their feminist analysis arose from their experience as community activists. Linda Cardinal writes about Franco-Ontarian women, charting the ways in which feminist activists challenged and were challenged as they worked with traditional farm and church-based women's groups in northern and eastern Ontario. Marlene Brant Castellano and Janice Hill introduce us to four aboriginal women: Edna Manitowabi, Jeannette Corbière Lavell, Sylvia Maracle, and Emily Faries, whose work has been to reclaim and build upon the knowledge and responsibilities long entrusted to the women of Ontario's First Nations.

JOY PARR is a professor in the Department of History, Simon Fraser University.

EDITED BY JOY PARR

# A Diversity of Women:
# Ontario, 1945–1980

UNIVERSITY OF TORONTO PRESS
Toronto Buffalo London

© University of Toronto Press Incorporated 1995
Toronto Buffalo London
Printed in Canada

ISBN 0-8020-2615-x (cloth)
ISBN 0-8020-7695-5 (paper)

Printed on acid-free paper

---

**Canadian Cataloguing in Publication Data**

Main entry under title:

A Diversity of women : Ontario, 1945–1980

Includes index.
ISBN 0-8020-2615-x (bound) ISBN 0-8020-7695-5 (pbk.)

1. Women – Ontario – History – 20th century.
I. Parr, Joy, 1949–      .

HQ1459.06D58  1995          305.4'09713          C95-930243-3

---

Major funding provided by the Government of Ontario through the Ministry of
Culture, Tourism and Recreation, which acknowledges the role of the Ontario
Historical Studies Series in initiating this project.

University of Toronto Press acknowledges the financial assistance to its publishing
program of the  Canada Council and the Ontario Arts Council.

# Contents

vi   Contents

# Contributors

NANCY ADAMSON is a long-time feminist activist. The holder of a PhD in early modern English history as well as a degree in nursing, she has taught at the University of Toronto and at Carleton University. She is currently the status of women coordinator at Carleton.

LINDA CARDINAL is professor in the Department of Sociology at the University of Ottawa, where she also teaches in the Women's Studies Program. Her areas of specialization are social movements, francophone minority groups, and sociological theories. She co-authored 'L'Etat de la recherche sur les communautés francophone vivant à l'extérieur du Québec' with Yvon Theriault (CRCCF/CRPFO) in 1994. She is also editor of *Une langue qui pense* (University of Ottawa Press 1993).

MARLENE BRANT CASTELLANO is a Mohawk from the Bay of Quinte. Her first career was in social work, before she took time out from professional activities to marry and have four sons. In 1973 she joined the Department of Native Studies at Trent University and has acted as chair of the department for several terms. In 1992 she took leave from Trent to become co-director of research for the Royal Commission on Aboriginal Peoples.

E.A. (NORA) CEBOTAREV is a feminist rural sociologist and a University Professor Emerita in the Department of Sociology and Anthropology at the University of Guelph. She has been teaching and researching on rural issues, particularly farm women and families, since the early 1970s. She has published research and reflections on farm women and families in Canada, Latin America, and the Caribbean, in English, Spanish, and Portuguese.

JANICE HILL is a Mohawk from the Bay of Quinte. She has served her home community as education counsellor and the larger Aboriginal community as president of the Ontario Native Education Counselling Association. From 1989 to 1992 she was a member of the team developing an Aboriginal education program at Queen's University. She is completing her Bachelor of Arts degree at Trent University, along with requirements for her Bachelor of Education through the community-based program delivered by Queen's University.

FRANCA IACOVETTA teaches history at the University of Toronto. Her publications include *Such Hardworking People: Italian Immigrants in Postwar Ontario* (McGill-Queen's University Press 1992), winner of the Floyd S. Chalmers Award in Ontario History and a Toronto Historical Board Award of Merit. She also co-edited *Gender Conflicts: New Essays in Women's History* (University of Toronto Press 1992).

JOY PARR is Farley Professor of History at Simon Fraser University. Her earlier writing in Ontario history includes *Labouring Children: British Immigrant Apprentices to Canada, 1869–1924* (1980, second edition University of Toronto Press 1994) and *The Gender of Breadwinners: Women, Men and Change in Two Industrial Towns, 1880–1950* (University of Toronto Press 1990). She is studying the gender politics of consumer policies, goods, and practices in postwar Canada and Sweden.

ESTER REITER teaches Social Science and Women's Studies at Atkinson College, York University. She is interested in women and unions as both a scholar and an activist.

JOAN SANGSTER, professor of history at Trent University, is the author of *Dreams of Equality: Women on the Canadian Left, 1920–50* (McClelland and Stewart 1989), and co-editor of *Beyond the Vote: Canadian Women and Politics* (University of Toronto Press 1989). Her forthcoming book, *Earning Respect: The Lives of Working Women in Small-Town Ontario, 1920–1960,* will be published by University of Toronto Press.

VERONICA STRONG-BOAG is director of the Centre for Research in Women's Studies and Gender Relations at the University of British Columbia. She is author or editor of numerous books and articles on Canadian women's history, including *The New Day Recalled: Lives of Girls and Women in English*

*Canada, 1919–1939* (Copp Clark 1988), which won the John A. Macdonald Prize from the Canadian Historical Association.

MARIANA VALVERDE is the author of *The Age of Light, Soap and Water: Moral Reform in English Canada, 1885–1925* (McClelland and Stewart 1991) and *Sex, Power and Pleasure* (Women's Press 1985), as well as co-editor of *Gender Conflicts: New Essays in Women's History* (University of Toronto Press 1992). She is currently undertaking a historical sociology of the category 'vice,' with special focus on the regulation of alcohol sales and gambling. She is at the Centre of Criminology, University of Toronto.

# Acknowledgments

We are grateful to Nancy Kiefer and her colleagues at the Ontario Ministry of Culture, Tourism and Recreation for their interest in this project and to Linda Clippingdale, Caroline Andrew, and their colleagues at the Canadian Research Institute for the Advancement of Women for their advice and support. Nancy Adamson, Constance Backhouse, Linda Cardinal, Franca Iacovetta, and Mariana Valverde provided astute commentaries on an earlier draft. At the University of Toronto Press we are particularly thankful for the skilful work of Gerry Hallowell and Karen Boersma, and of Rosemary Shipton, who both edited and named our book. Annette Lorek prepared the index.

All royalties from this volume will be used to support the Canadian Research Institute for the Advancement of Women (CRIAW).

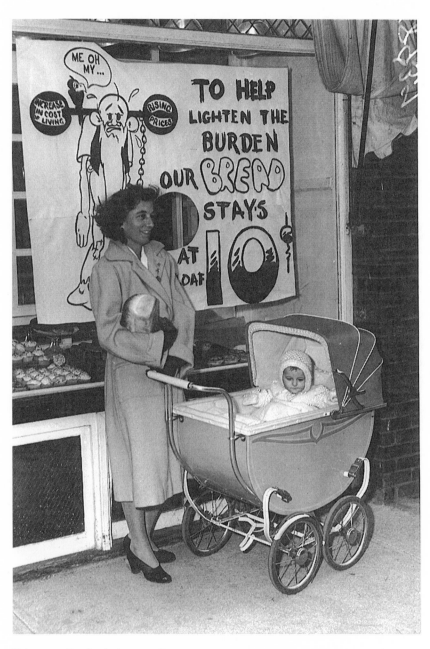

Bakery on Danforth Avenue, Toronto, 1947

High school cheer-leader, 1947

The 'New Look' fashion reaction to wartime austerity

Modern Canadian living-room, 1956

Young Greek women in ethnic costume at the International Institute of
Metropolitan Toronto

Woman staff worker with the International Institute of Metropolitan Toronto
advertising activities intended to attract 'new' and 'old' Canadians

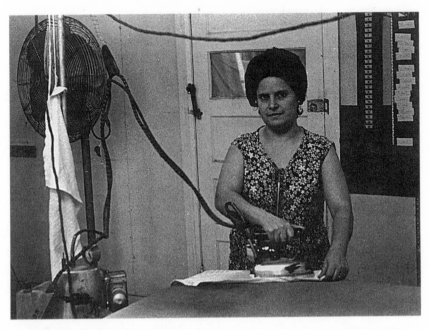

Pressing shirts in a Toronto laundry. European immigrant women, like the Italian woman above, filled the ranks of Ontario postwar female industrial workers.

Gerda Frieberg, Holocaust survivor and prominent Jewish community activist

Sisters-in-law together, 1957

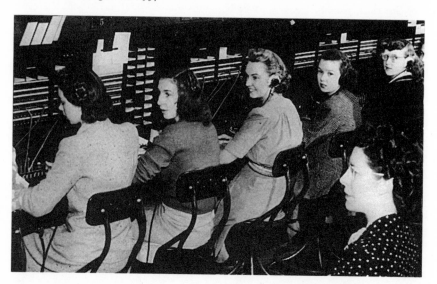

Bell Canada operators at #3 Combined Dial Switchboard, Peterborough

Westclox clock assembly, *c.* 1950, Peterborough

Lanark strikers at the provincial legislature, Queen's Park, Toronto

Yvette Ward addressing the Lanark strikers in Dunnville, 1964

October 1991 reunion of Lanark strikers convened by Yvette Ward, Millie Trufal, and Ester Reiter

Farm family at work, early 1980s

Women leaders, 1980s

Woman farmer working, 1980s

Woman working with farm machine, 1980s

Women painting a sign

The Brown Breast Brigade

The Women's Place, Kitchener-Waterloo

International Women's Day celebration, Toronto, March 1973

Cover of The Other Woman newspaper, July–August 1973

A DIVERSITY OF WOMEN

JOY PARR

# Introduction

For the first generation of Canadian feminists in the early twentieth century, women were defined starkly by what they were not. They were not men, and therefore they were not voters, candidates for public office, professionals, or soldiers. Reform-minded women and men relied on a single unifying equation of womanhood with motherhood, and worked to create new rights and roles for women by expanding the definition of the mother role. Their philosophical discussions were of the 'woman question' and their political campaigns centred on the struggle for 'woman suffrage.'

Today the search to know women through their common womanhood, and the assumed common distinctiveness of woman from man, seems a distant and troubled project, at once utopian and fraught with sorrow. A century after the woman question first rose to public prominence in Ontario, the differences between women and men no longer seem so settled and defining. As the goal of gender equity remains before us, commanding and critical, the differences among women, and among men, insistently draw our attention.

The thirty-five years following 1945 were a time of great change in Ontario. During the Second World War the majority of Canadians surveyed dreamed of a peace in which unemployment was eliminated, the standard of living improved, and all citizens shared in a more equitable division of wealth. Seared by the Depression and heartened by government accomplishments during the war, Ontarians looked forward to the possibility of a coordinated rationalization of the economic system. The provincial Conservative, Liberal, and CCF parties alike promised planning as the magical path towards better times.[1]

Uncertainty, however, was mixed with expectation. In the late 1940s marriage rates in Ontario rose to new heights, a third greater each year than they had been in the interwar years, but many marriages made in wartime did not weather the peace. Between 1946 and 1948 divorces were more common than ever in the province, more than 84 per 100,000 population in 1947 alone. As a massive new highway system was proposed at Queen's Park and the citizens of Stratford planned for an international Shakespearean festival in their town, a rural woman could still be refused her request for one electrical wall socket for operating a washing machine and an iron. In 1947 more than half of Ontario urban households, better provisioned than those in the country-side, relied on ice boxes rather than mechanical refrigeration, one in four was not equipped with an electrical washing machine, and 13 per cent were still cooking with wood or coal.[2]

In this time of 'Home Dreams,' of yearning for a settled domesticity after the disruption of depression and war, the different circumstances in which Ontarians found themselves were starkly apparent in their dwell-ings. The nearly twenty years during which residential construction had been deferred, and the resources for ordinary upkeep had been the luxury of the few, had exacerbated long-standing inequalities in housing in the province. In 1951 more than one in ten Ontario homes had a sagging foun-dation, a faulty roof or chimney, unsafe stairs, or an interior with large chunks of plaster missing from the ceiling or walls. Two-thirds more rent-ers than owners lived in dwellings in need of major repair. While homes in the south were in relatively good shape, those in the east and the north commonly had serious structural problems. In Prescott County 44 per cent of dwellings and in Cochrane, 24 per cent were in need of major repair. While overall in the province 12 per cent of households sheltered more than one person per room, here again the regional differences were acute. Toronto was at about the provincial average, but in the northern mining city of Sudbury more than a third of households were overcrowded in the census-takers' term in 1951. The 'compassionate landscape' young archi-tects and planners were imagining for their generation was still a distant feature on the horizon of many Ontarians.[3]

Through the decade of the 1950s the population of the province grew by 35 per cent, from 4.5 million in 1951 to 6.2 million in 1961. These were the baby-boom years. Birth rates were more than twenty-six per thousand Ontarians during most years in the 1950s. And European immigration into the province was large, accounting for a third of Ontario's population growth. Public interest in international affairs was keen. As George Woodcock has suggested, there was a shift in national tone during the 1950s 'from the bucolic to the urbane.' It was a decade of megaprojects – power developments along the St Lawrence, the Burlington Skyway, the four-lane divided highway from Windsor to the Quebec border – a time when provincial activity in housing widened and the foundation for medicare was laid.4

From this time of triumphant modernity, whose masculine heroes were diplomats and engineers, the image of womanhood that has come down to us is eerily quiescent. The legacy of the preceding decades' suffering and hostilities spoke loudly through this willful quiet, in the fears of the Cold War and the bomb, the urgency to make up for depression and wartime losses, the wish to be settled after so much change, to conform if conforming would bring predictability, to accept sameness in material goods and settings if these would allow a modest social minimum. The conformity and consensus prized in these years was forged in denial, which fostered a steady current of anxiety. We see this anxiety in this volume among working mothers, immigrant wives, school girls, shoppers, and women immersed in male-dominated political work.5

Domestic metaphors, which in the late 1940s and early 1950s proclaimed the promise of the peace, cloaked all women's activities. In contemporary National Film Board depictions, 'women were the object of a complex and confused series of double messages. Flattered and assured of their immense, if undefined power, women were simultaneously trivialised at every opportunity. The primary message that a young woman growing up in the 1950s received was that no undertaking which deflected her energies from her primary task as wife and mother was to be taken seriously. Careers outside the home were made to seem subtly abnormal; homemaking was magnified so that it appeared to demand a woman's entire waking attention.' In the Ontario neighbourhood he and his colleagues renamed Crestwood Heights, John Seeley found classrooms where boys were urged to plan for careers, while girls learned that 'the full stamp of social approval was given' only to women who achieved marriage and motherhood. Women university graduates bridled their academic ambitions in the belief that the real work of their adult life should be marriage.6

For southern Ontario lesbian women, the clubs of Buffalo offered weekend escapes from the strict 1950s codes of compulsory heterosexuality. In these clubs young working-class women found relatively safe places in which to meet other lesbians and, despite harassment from the border patrols, to retain some of the greater liberty wartime had allowed for women socializing together, spaces rare for any 1950s women where female sexual desires were explored and expressed.7

Both for individual women and for women attempting to work together in organizations, the common emphasis on domestic activities and aspirations created harsh conflicts. The insistance on shared womanly pleasures and pursuits often underlined women's differences. In Sudbury the full-time house-wives who joined the Ladies Auxiliary of the Mine Mill and Smelter Union to work within domestic 'definitions of women's sphere' – catering dinners, raising money through cookbook sales, sustaining the voluntary welfare services of their city – had difficulty accepting that the women who worked full-time for the mine were not 'violating traditional women's roles and therefore untrustworthy.' The Women's Committee of the Ontario CCF, founded in 1947 to forward women's issues and increase women's involvement in all levels of the party, sensibly decided to recruit membership widely by appealing to women 'where they were rather than where you thought they should be.' But the committee foundered on internal disputes and conflicts with the party hierarchy when it tried to move beyond price-monitoring and fund-raising to press for daycare and equal pay. The Ontario Female Employees Fair Remuneration Act, which on its passage in 1951 seemed to hold such promise for protecting women in the workforce, had the effect of dividing women's jobs more categorically from men's, leaving the possibility of a woman's life outside the domestic sphere almost as difficult as it had been before.[8]

Though the circumstances in which Ontario women and girls found themselves in the 1950s were diverse and conflicting, the beliefs with which they were urged to make sense of themselves drew on a myth of generalized, peaceable affluence. John Porter wrote of 'an image of middle-level classless-ness' forged to make the province's burgeoning cities seem as coherent and unified as the countryside had been imagined two generations before.[9]

By the mid-1960s the standards of living in Ontario were far higher than for any previous generation of Canadians. The province gloried in its position as Canada's industrial heartland. In constant dollars, both manufacturing production and personal income more than doubled from 1950 to 1965. Personal income per capita rose by 42 per cent. Except for the years 1958–62, yearly unemployment rates in the province through the 1950s and 1960s remained securely below 4 per cent. The number of women in the labour force grew by 56 per cent between 1951 and 1961, and 73 per cent between 1961 and 1971, as the proportion of jobs in the service sector burgeoned while employment in primary and secondary manufacturing relatively declined.[10]

This prosperity, the golden age of capitalism in Ontario, created the demand and the possibility for higher standards of social service than had been provided previously in the province. The aspirations for a modest suffi-ciency of the early postwar years were surpassed in the 1960s by a 'new age of affluence, bigness, specialization, professionalisation and bureaucracy,' by modern hospitals, new and growing universities, regional governments, school boards, and police forces designed to provide all the citizens of the province with a range and quality of service available previously only to wealthy urban residents.[11]

Except for the founding of the Ontario Women's Bureau in 1963,[12] little of this expanding state action in the 1960s explicitly addressed women's concerns. Yet the demographics of the decade show stark changes in women's circumstances. While in 1941 average female life expectancy in Ontario was seventy years, by 1971 women were surviving into their late 1970s, an average of seven years longer than men. Even before the legislative changes of 1968, the divorce rate in the province had begun to climb. By 1970 seventy-six of every thousand births in the province were to unmarried mothers, a stark increase from thirty-two per thousand a decade before. The age at which women first married, which had declined yearly since the war, rose steadily after 1968. The 1950s myth of affluent familialism and domesticity was fractured. 'Family life' had become 'less continuous, sandwiched between premarital and post marital independence,' but the implications of this independence were ambiguous. Through a variety of circumstances, more of the women of Ontario were spending more of their lives outside marriage; more were raising children alone; more were caring for elders at the same time that they had young children at home; and more of them, with more confined employment opportunities and lower rates of pay than men, were poor.[13]

Within this conjuncture arose the second wave of feminism, facets of which Nancy Adamson and Linda Cardinal discuss in this volume. The years from 1968 to 1972 have been described as 'a permissive moment' in the North Atlantic world. The biographer of Conservative premier John Robarts described them as years when 'much of the old moral order in Ontario was passing, [when] many of the young abandoned the puritanism, the discipline and order and hierarchy underlying so many aspects of their parents' lifestyles ... wanted to liberalize the censorship standards, liberalize the drinking laws, liberalize education, grow their hair long and smoke some marijuana.' Access to divorce was widened considerably in 1968. Access to medically supervised abortions was possible within confined circumstances after 1969, and the display and selling of contraceptives was no longer illegal. By 1979 there were 256 divorces for every 100,000 population in the province, and twenty-five abortions for every hundred live births. Yet as the 'permissive moment' passed, women of Ontario could be forgiven for reflecting, 'permissive for whom?' While these legislative enactments changed women's circumstances, they were not in the 1970s supported by the broader political change that would have readjusted 'the appropriate balance between the state's responsibility for family life, through social programs, and women's need to control their own lives.' And the levers through which this broader political change might be achieved remained elusive. More women presented themselves as candidates for political office. In the 1977 Ontario election 35 per cent of candidates were female, a marked increase from the 15 per cent of contenders in 1971, but only six of these these women candidates assumed seats in Queen's Park. The detailed research and policy proposals drafted by women's groups across the province for equal pay and day-care reform, for transformations in the school system and the provision of health care did not result in legislative change.[14]

Through the 1970s, inflation began to erode the prosperity achieved in the 1960s. The cost of food, which in Ontario cities had risen about 17 per cent between 1965 and 1971, rose 228 per cent between 1971 and 1979 in both Toronto and Thunder Bay. Housing costs, which had risen by 20 per cent between 1965 and 1971, climbed by more than 80 per cent between 1971 and 1979. The proportion of Canadian low-income families who lived in Ontario rose through the decade. Reliance on provincial assistance was greatest in the east and in the north, and was especially high in the counties of Frontenac, Haliburton, and Manitoulin, but the need in southern cities was also great. Social service expenditures rose by 80 per cent in Metropolitan Toronto and 85 per cent in Hamilton-Wentworth between 1974 and 1979. The 54 per cent rise in provincial social service expenditure in these years met some of the pressure on real incomes. But through the 1970s 'the significant factor in preventing family income from declining in real dollars' was the income of wives.[15]

By the 1970s, the last decade this volume treats, wage-earning women in Ontario were entitled through the federal unemployment insurance program to eleven weeks of paid maternity leave and reinstatement at the same level of pay and seniority when they returned to work. Although the dilemmas concerning childcare which Joan Sangster addresses remained, and remain, acute, this change in the Canada Labour (Standards) Code was a clear acknowledgment that 'the employment cost of child-bearing ... was a community responsibility rather than an individual woman's burden.'[16]

A study of women in Ontario's more recent history will need to analyse a vital transformation in the composition of Ontario's female population which was just beginning to become apparent in the 1970s. The proportion of Ontarians of Asian and West Indian descent trebled in the decade. Especially in the cities of southern Ontario, immigrant women were now facing discrimination on the basis of race as well as gender. They were additionally disadvantaged because they had been allowed to come to Canada only as 'family class' rather than 'independent' residents, or with temporary work permits under the Foreign Domestic Worker program rather than immigrant status. For these women the protections of the modern industrial state, steadily amplified over the postwar years, were often ephemeral or inaccessible. The promise of prosperity, that steady theme in the political and social culture of the province through the preceding three decades, was by the 1970s generally challenged by inflation and especially elusive for those most recently arrived.[17]

In this book we explore the diversity of women's lives in Ontario in the years 1945–1980. We seek to understand how the beliefs about women were formed in these years, both what others expected of them and how women came to understand their own predicaments; how the distinctive circumstances in which they found themselves framed their experiences; and how they, in interpreting these experiences, made sense of their lives. Some of us are Ontario born, some are immigrants to the province. Some of us were already adults when the period we study began, more of us are writing about years we cannot remember, or about the decades when we ourselves were girls learning to read the curious and conflicting signals about how to be women. We have come from diverse rural and urban girlhoods and heterogeneous class and ethnic backgrounds to similar adult circumstances, as teachers and writers trained in the social sciences.

The articles in this volume are presented in roughly chronological order, beginning with Mariana Valverde's study of teenage girls in the years immediately following the Second World War. Although the images of these years which have come down to us through popular culture suggest an uncomplicated sociability and a certain naivete and innocence, Valverde finds deep uneasiness and sharp anxiety. She links the recurring episodes of moral panic in the cities to a fear that basic social values were being threatened by the postwar transition. Using the examples of a young woman who had died following abortions and another who had killed a child left in her care, Valverde shows how press coverage conflated 'morally deviant' women with all women by portraying female sexual desire and maternal feeling as urges so powerful they were scarcely civilly contained. Reports about girls who were members of gangs emphasized their sexual deviance and suggested that distinctive fashions favoured by young women seen in the company of zoot-suited young men were precursors to defiant and thus deviant behaviour of other sorts. The distinctive education in civics of the period – for boys citizenship training, for girls consumer education – arose from a worry about the frailty of democratic institutions and a particular concern in the case of girls to create feminine desires compatible with free-market consumer culture. Whether formulated in psychiatric or environmental terms, contemporary analyses figured decadent youth as 'the enemy within.'

The theme of wartime influence carrying over into the peace continues in Veronica Strong-Boag's portrait of Ontario suburbs, drawn through the eyes of women who welcomed their wide lawns and soundly built new dwellings after the deprivations of the thirties and forties. Like the girls in 1940s gangs, suburban women of the 1950s were objects of scrutiny by psychological experts and were found wanting for their deviation from appropriate feminine roles. In social scientific studies and the popular press, suburbs were 'symbolically constructed as pre-eminently female space.' This pre-eminence, once asserted, was labelled pathological, the automony and resourcefulness of suburban women diagnosed not as healthy adaptations to their new responsibilities and circumstances, but featured as troubling mutations that compromised both the femininity of wives and the manliness of their husbands. Here, too, the rigid sexual roles that have come to us as characteristic of 1950s social relationships emerge more as prescriptions driven by the disquiet of observers than as descriptions of behaviour they actually observed. The women with whom Strong-Boag has worked want to be remembered for the diversity of their contributions to their families and communities and for the pride and resilience with which they held up their end of the marital partnership. She asks us to ponder why both feminist and non-feminist critics should have singled out suburban women for their complicity in forming a mass culture of their time; why they in particular should be pilloried for their 'meaningless parasitism' in, for example, Betty Friedan's widely read *The Feminine Mystique*. Joanne Meyerowitz, writing about postwar mass culture in the United States,[18] suggests that Friedan was not really the prescient critic of suburban women's blind delusions she featured herself to be. Rather, *The Feminine Mystique* was popular because the book captured dilemmas women of the 1950s consciously were struggling to resolve, dilemmas Strong-Boag's informants construed as challenges, not barriers. To be sure, the commitment to family which led couples to the suburbs, and which was strengthened there by the apparent absence of alternatives to heterosexual nuclear family life, made suburban women at the time disparage wage-earning mothers as irresponsible. But Strong-Boag argues that from their frustrations and accomplishments in the suburbs many Ontario women developed a consciousness and confidence that made them part of the liberal, essentialist feminism in the 1960s.

Shopping, like the suburb, was defined as a feminine sphere in the postwar years. Women had played an important role, both as bureaucrats and as home-makers, in helping the wartime rationing system to work effectively.

As Valverde notes, the polemics about democratic citizenship after the war emphasized women's continuing civic responsibilities as consumers. But the conception of the modern state which cast men as producers and women as consumers, and which removed men from the suburbs by day and left women to manage the household, featured women as the leading actors in a part of social life over which they actually had very limited influence. The design, manufacturing, and retailing of the tools women needed to do their domestic work remained in the sphere of male engineers and marketing executives. Earnings from the production of domestic appliances and the refining of the metals from which they were made were crucial to the health of the Ontario economy, but the productivity of work in the homes of the province was neither measured nor weighed in any consideration of the province's wealth. Joy Parr's paper sketches the predicament of women shopping for stoves in Ontario in the early 1950s; it tells the story of one attempt by a group of consumers to have what they believed would be a more efficiently stove manufactured and sold, and to exercise some control over this sphere so frequently described as their own. Their noble failure to realign the gender politics of the market economy tells us a good deal about the rapid changes that were remaking relationships between women and men as mass production and mass consumption came to define the prosperity of the province through the 1950s.

If men's position in consumer relationships in the 1950s and 1960s was masked, women's place in the labour force was equally obscured by contemporary beliefs about gender roles. As Joan Sangster notes, by 1965 40 per cent of the Canadian female labour force worked in Ontario, a female participation higher than that in any other province. Most married women wage-earners came from lower-income groups and were drawn into the workforce by economic need. Couples who had lived through the deprivations of the Depression and the war shared in the aspirations for a rising standard of consumption, particularly in the hope they could provide better educational opportunities for their children than they themselves had been able to enjoy. But as Sangster shows, married women's wage work was not discussed in these terms. Mothers who went out to work encountered and absorbed a strong measure of social censure. Through the 1960s their employment was featured in popular and policy discussions as a child welfare issue, in a way that marginalized the importance of both family needs and women's rights. Yet as the Ontario economy boomed in the later 1960s, the practical pressure to draw women into the labour force became clear. The Ontario Women's Bureau was established by the Conservative government in 1963 explicitly to facilitate this change. The legislation that emerged from the bureau to create the right to maternity leaves, end the advertising of jobs by sex, and prohibit dismissal on marriage or pregnancy made married women's work a matter of productivity and equity. But as rapid inflation eroded incomes during the early 1970s, and more women were compelled to take up paid employment, the fallacy of acknowledging the economy's need for women workers while refusing to acknowledge day-care as a social responsibility remained unresolved. Sangster argues that, in this irresolution, the traditional sexual division of labour and images of innate sex differences persisted as morally regulated barriers to women's right to paid work.

The rapid growth in the Ontario economy in the 1950s and 1960s was fuelled and faciliated by substantial European immigration. Franca Iacovetta's article focuses on the foreign-born women who entered early postwar Ontario. She shows that these women, grouped by contemporaries under the singular rubric 'New Canadians,' came from widely different class and vocational backgrounds, framed in European settings that gave them starkly contrasting perspectives on Cold War politics. By analysing the reaction of longer-settled Ontario residents to these newcomers, Iacovetta clarifies the roots of the familialism by which suburban women measured themselves, and against which working mothers and teenaged girls were appraised. She argues that conformity in feminine behaviour took on political urgency as adherence to common family values came within Cold War rhetoric to define the superiority of the Western democracies. Because these 'traditional' values were more part of a shared national mythology than a shared lived experience, they were anxiously elusive goals, often most readily defined by contrast with immigrant families. First in anticipation and then by ascription, immigrant women came to symbolize a generalized uncertainty about 'what a normal family life was.' Iacovetta traces the activities of early postwar immigrant women in their families and in paid work, as well as in their encounters with shopkeepers, teachers, and the staff of social welfare institutions. Her account shows us the adjustments of immigrant women as a series of mutual accommodations between newcomers and old-timers, among diverse newcomers, and among family, neighbours, and friends.

The identity 'woman' in postwar Ontario was never settled or unitary, but was constantly being remade as individual women and groups of women learned more about themselves and appraised and assimilated what others said about them. Sometimes, in fact often, there has been a good deal of slippage between what they came to know through their relationships with other women and with men and what we retrospectively think we know about them. As immigrant women on entry to Canada were classified by federal regulations as dependants of their husbands, and thereafter by extension characterized as passive rather than active in their families and workplaces, so the rhetoric of brotherly solidarity and the highly visible male leadership, which for many defined Ontario unionism right through the 1970s, sustained problematical inferences about the gender politics of labour militancy. Ester Reiter's article re-examines these inferences by situating a single 1964 strike in a Niagara Penninsula auto plant within the context of growing internationalization in mass-production industries and the worsening bargaining conditions this change created for women workers and their unions. The young women who dominated the labour force of the Lanark Manufacturing plant in Dunnville, Ontario, were in their own way parrying with contemporary definitions of femininity and familialism. The plant was a place where they could claim some reprieve from their often onerous domestic responsibilities as daughters, where they could find sociability with other younger women and support from older workers more experienced in dealing with the class and sexual politics of the shop floor. The Lanark workers remember using expectations of their feminine vulnerability as tactical resources during the strike, as ways to outwit strike breakers and unsettle the police, and to leaven long tense days with practical jokes at the expense of the male union organizers made solemn and circumspect by their attention to sexual propriety. Reiter's portrait of the strike through the eyes of the strikers challenges generalizations about male-dominated industrial unions and their lack of support for women workers; rather, it directs attention to the complexities of gender and class politics in labour solidarity.

Ontario changed radically between 1945 and 1980, but the implications of these changes for women were often contradictory and confusing. The effects of recession or inflation on incomes and job prospects were rapid and forceful. But social and cultural values, and beliefs about gender roles, marched to different drummers, tied to loyalties, traditions, and hierarchies over which economic influence was contingent and indirect. While flexibility in adapting to economic change was generally praiseworthy in men, women's accommodations to alterations in their material circumstances evoked more contradictory responses. Urban wives who needed or chose to go out to work were left to resolve individually and uncomfortably the practical difficulties and social disapproval that surrounded placing their children in day-care. Nora Cebotarev sees similar dilemmas arising among the rural women of southwestern Ontario. As the agricultural economy changed, farm women were both drawn to and compelled to take on new roles and responsibilities that substantially changed the sexual division of labour on the farm. As agricultural incomes declined, more women and men took off-farm jobs. At the same time, more farms had to be worked by family members without the aid

of hired help. Farm debt loads grew and farmers became increasingly dependent on bankers rather than family and neighbours for credit. For the first
time sizeable numbers of women took on farms of their own, instead of or in
addition to working with their husbands. By talking with farm women and
analysing their organizations, Cebotarev charts the different ways mothers
and daughters raised in the countryside and women who married onto the
land negotiated these changes, reconsidering their sense of themselves and of
their place within the rural community.

For the First Nations women Marlene Brant Castellano and Janice Hill
interviewed, adaption to the sweeping changes in Ontario Aboriginal communities since the Second World War has been a struggle to reclaim traditional
cultural resources. The four women whose personal stories they tell describe
their relationships with their parents and grandparents and their roles in guiding their own children. They see these relationships as the context for their
work of nurturing their own Aboriginal identities and healing the wounds created in their communities by the residential schools, the Christian church, and
the provincial child welfare system. They see women's work of teaching
Aboriginal languages, regenerating Aboriginal spiritual traditions, and healing through traditional practices as ways to sustain their communities through
roles that were formerly the domain of women. Their discussions are not of
their changing gender identities, but of the ways in which being a First Nations
person has framed their responsibilities as Aboriginal women.

Nancy Adamson's paper is a province-wide survey of the ideology and
activities of the feminist movement in Ontario and the changes in feminist
activism and analysis through the 1970s. Through accounts of the theatrical
public confrontations that were their tactics of choice in the early days, she
recaptures the mix of enthusiasm and anger which brought women from the
New Left into the Women's Liberation Movement in the late 1960s. Already
by 1971, however, she suggests that the movement had become less focused
on doctrine than on experience, as women turned their attention to women's
centres, writing, publishing, and issue-specific campaigns through which
women could create spaces for themselves and events that reflected their own
needs. From this emphasis on personal experience came a recognition of
shared experience and a will to take concerted action to address common
problems. Among the fruits of these actions was a broadening and more systematic analysis of the conditions that had forged women's common experiences. Yet, Adamson suggests, these years left an unintended and unresolved
legacy to the 1980s, because the rhetoric of sisterhood, by emphasizing how
gender united women, made it difficult to integrate an understanding of how
race, class, sexual orientation, and ability separated them.

This sense of separation is palpable in Linda Cardinal's discussion of the experience of Franco-Ontarian women working within provincial and national feminist organizations. Historically, Franco-Ontarians were predominantly agriculturalists, and many of the challenges Cebotarev described confronting the farm women of southwestern Ontario were shared by francophone women in the east and the north. Cardinal sketches the history of women's organizations in Franco-Ontario and introduces a remarkable group of feminist animators, led by Carmen Paquette of Ottawa. From the late 1960s, Paquette and her colleagues used their experience in the New Left and the adult education movement to guide their work for women's organizations of francophone Ontario. Although the way was often uncertain and contested, Cardinal argues that through their publications, conferences, and animation work, feminists helped to revitalise these established organizations and to transform them from organizations of helpers to organizations that could help their members recognize and secure their rights as individuals and as citizens. But the problem for Franco-Ontario feminists was not only to break from the definition within their own community of woman as mother, farm-wife, and servant, but to tackle the multiple discrimination that existed where ethnicity, language, regionalism, and gender inequality met. For Franco-Ontarians, Cardinal argues, labour-force participation and job training, domestic violence and single motherhood, were class and language as well as women's issues – issues that tokenism in the anglophone-dominated women's movement left the women of Franco-Ontario to tackle alone.

This book is not a comprehensive history of women in Ontario in the 1950s, 1960s, and 1970s. For such a work we will probably have to wait some decades more. Rather, these essays are first attempts to distinguish the chronological contours of the period which most influenced the lives of Ontario women, and the social settings, identities, and organizations which most characteristically gave meaning to their lives as women. There are wonderful women to meet in these pages. We hope that, as you read, you find them well met.

NOTES

1 Mariana Valverde, 'Building Anti-Delinquent Communities: Morality, Gender, and Generation in the City,' this volume; Jane Ursel, *Private Lives, Public Policy: 100 Years of State Intervention in the Family* (Toronto: Women's Press 1992), 209; Robert Bothwell, *A Short History of Ontario* (Edmonton: Hurtig, 1986), 164.
2 Douglas Owram, 'Home and Family at Mid-century,' paper presented at the annual meeting of the Canadian Historical Association, Charlottetown, 1992, 28;

Paul Litt, *The Muses, the Masses, and the Massey Commission* (Toronto: University of Toronto Press 1992), 17–8; Dominion Bureau of Statistics, *Vital Statistics: Marriages and Divorces, 1921–49*; Canadian Daily Newspapers Association, *Canadian Consumer Survey 1947*, 146–50.

3  Veronica Strong-Boag, 'Home Dreams: Women and the Suburban Experiment in Canada, 1945–60,' *Canadian Historical Review* 72, 4 (1991): 470–504; *Census of Canada 1951*, vol. 3, tables 17, 86, and 87; John Miron, *Housing in Postwar Canada: Demographic Change, Household Formation and Housing Demand* (Kingston and Montreal: McGill-Queen's University Press 1988), chapter 7; Humphrey Carver, *Compassionate Landscape* (Toronto: University of Toronto Press 1975).

4  K.J. Rea, *The Prosperous Years: The Economic History of Ontario, 1939–1975* (Toronto: University of Toronto Press 1985), 27, 29; Canada, *Vital Statistics, 1971–5*, 68; Robert Bothwell, John English, and Ian Drummond, *Canada since 1945: Power, Politics, and Provincialism* (Toronto: University of Toronto Press 1981), 168. The most thorough treatment of state activity in Ontario during the 1950s is Roger Graham, *Old Man Ontario: Leslie M. Frost, 1895–1973* (Toronto: University of Toronto Press 1990).

5  See the articles in this volume by Joan Sangster, Franca Iacovetta, Veronica Strong-Boag, Mariana Valverde, and Nancy Adamson.

6  On the film prescriptions for 1950s women, see Yvonne Matthews-Klein, 'How They Saw Us: Images of Women in National Film Board Films of the 1940s and 1950s,' *Atlantis* 4, 2 (1979): 26, and Susannah J. Wilson, 'The Changing Image of Women in Canadian Mass Circulation Magazines, 1930–1970,' *Atlantis* 2, 2 (1977): 33–44; John R. Seeley, Alexander Sim, and E.W. Loosley, *Crestwood Heights: A Study of the Culture of Suburban Life* (Toronto: University of Toronto Press 1956); Elspeth Wallace Baugh, 'A Slow Awakening,' in Joy Parr, ed. *Still Running: Personal Stories by Queen's Women Celebrating the Fiftieth Anniversary of the Marty Scholarship* (Kingston: Queen's University Alumnae Association 1987), 101.

7  See Elizabeth Lapovsky Kennedy and Madeline D. Davis, *Boots of Leather, Slippers of Gold: The History of a Lesbian Community* (New York: Routledge, Chapman, Hall 1993), 71, 74, 132, 374. The Ontario commentary in this volume is most readily followed through references in the narrator index to Whitney. See also the 1992 National Film Board film, 'Forbidden Love.'

8  Meg Luxton, 'From Ladies Auxiliaries to Wives' Committees,' in Linda Briskin and Lynda Yanz, eds., *Union Sisters: Women in the Labour Movement* (Toronto: Women's Press 1983), 338, 342; Dean Beeby, 'Women in the Ontario CCF, 1940–50,' *Ontario History* 74, 4 (1982): 258–83; Joan Sangster, *Dreams of Equality: Women on the Canadian Left, 1920–1950* (Toronto: McClelland & Stewart 1989), 215–22; Sylvia Bashevkin, *Toeing the Lines: Women and Party Politics in English*

*Canada* (Toronto: University of Toronto Press 1985) 23, 109–10; Dan Azoulay, '"Winning Women for Socialism": The CCF and Women, 1947–1961,' paper presented at the annual meeting of the Canadian Historical Association, Ottawa, 1993, 17; Shirley Tillotson, 'Human Rights as Prism: Women's Organizations, Unions, and Ontario's Female Employees Fair Remuneration Act, 1951,' *Canadian Historical Review* 72, 4 (1991): 532–57.

9 John Porter, *The Vertical Mosaic: An Analysis of Social Class and Power in Canada* (Toronto: University of Toronto Press 1965), 4, 129, 132; for the United States see Wini Breines, *Young, White and Miserable: Growing Up Female in the Fifties* (Boston: Beacon 1992), 8, 12, 23, 35; for England see Birmingham Feminist History Group, 'Feminism as Femininity in the Nineteen-fifties?' *Feminist Review* 3 (1979).

10 A.K. McDougall, *John P. Robarts: His Life and Government* (Toronto: University of Toronto Press 1986), 205; Rea, *Prosperous Years*, 83, 84, 194; F.H. Leacy, ed., *Historical Statistics of Canada*, 2nd edition (Ottawa: Statistics Canada 1983), F95, D494, D517.

11. McDougall, *Robarts*, 205–6.

12 See Joan Sangster, 'Doing Two Jobs: The Wage-earning Mother, 1945–70,' this volume.

13 Canada, *Vital Statistics: Briths, Marriages and Divorces*, 1971–5, 1971–9; Monica Boyd, 'Changing Canadian Family Forms: Issues for Women,' in Nancy Mandell and Ann Duffy, *Reconstructing the Canadian Family: Feminist Perspectives* (Toronto: Butterworths 1988), 86, 92.

14 McDougall, *Robarts*, 205–6; Jane Lewis, *Women in Britain since 1945* (Oxford: Blackwell 1992), chapter 2; Canada, *Vital Statistics: Births, Marriages and Divorces* 1979; Jane Jenson, 'Getting to Morganthaler: From One Representation to Another,' in Janine Brody, Shelley Gavigan, and Jane Jenson, *The Politics of Abortion* (Toronto: Oxford University Press 1992), 20, 36; Bashevkin, *Toeing the Lines*, 73, 75, 29–30; *Ontario Legislators and Legislatures* (Toronto: Ontario Legislative Library 1984).

15 *Ontario Statistics*, 1980 (Toronto: Ministry of Treasury and Economics), tables 13.1, 12.7, 4.10, and 4.11; Pat Armstrong and Hugh Armstrong, 'Women Family and Economy,' in Mandell and Duffy, *Reconstructing the Canadian Family*, 161–2, using figures from Edward T. Pryor, 'Canadian Husband-Wife Families: Labour Force Participation and Income Trends 1971–81,' in *The Labour Force* (Ottawa: Supply and Services, May 1984).

16 Sandra Burt, 'The Changing Patterns of Public Policy,' in Sandra Burt, Lorraine Code, and Lindsay Dorney, *Changing Patterns: Women in Canada*, 2nd edition (Toronto: McClelland & Stewart 1993), 222.

17 *Ontario Statistics*, 1980, table 2.19, and 1984, table 3:16; Roxanna Ng, 'Racism,

Sexism, and Immigrant Women,' in Burt, Code, and Dorney, *Changing Patterns*, 279–308; Laura C. Johnson, *The Seam Allowance: Industrial Home Sewing in Canada* (Toronto: Women's Press 1982), 117; Roxanna Ng, 'The Social Construction of Immigrant Women in Canada,' in Michelle Barrett and Roberta Hamilton, *Politics of Diversity* (Montreal: Book Centre 1987), 280–2.

18 Joanne Meyerowitz, 'Beyond the Feminine Mystique: A Reassessment of Postwar Mass Culture, 1946–1958,' *Journal of American History* 80, 2 (1993): 1455–82.

MARIANA VALVERDE

# Building Anti-Delinquent Communities: Morality, Gender, and Generation in the City

Most of us think of the postwar period as one of exceptional moral, social, and political conformity. We know that Canadians were getting married in larger numbers, at younger ages, and in more lasting unions than the generations before and after.[1] We also know that this period saw the building of massive suburbs planned for middle-class couples to bring up nearly identical children in nearly identical houses, away from the moral corruption of the inner city. But we don't choose to know that the number of women in the labour force, though temporarily falling in 1945–6, continued to rise all through the postwar period;[2] we also ignore the fact that for a small number of Canadians, the postwar period offered for the first time in history a distinct homosexual subculture in major urban centres.[3]

Perhaps more importantly, we often make assumptions about what people felt, about what a particular woman meant when she married, bought an appliance, or moved to the suburbs. This article, like others in this collection, questions the view that we already know what the baby boom and the suburban explosion meant to those directly involved. It begins by asking whether our preconceived view of the postwar period is not to some extent the product of our psychological need to imagine an immediate collective past – often coinciding with our personal childhood – in which life was simple and secure, if boring. The baby-boom era has come to represent a lost age of social naivety, political quiescence, and sexual conformity, an age in which – we imagine – women's worst fear was getting a bad perm.

The research done for this article did not bear out the stereotypes. On the contrary, it revealed that a surprisingly high level of anxiety about basic social values pervaded the supposedly naive and innocent postwar period. For example, Dr Cecil Goldring, Toronto's director of education and a respected leader of public opinion on many social issues, reacted to the end of the war not with joy but with fear. 'A few months ago we were asking anxiously each day, "How goes the war?" Should we not now ask with equal anxiety, "How goes the peace?" and "What of the future of Canada?"'[4] This article is an attempt to understand what the Toronto Young Woman's Christian Association (YWCA) called 'a growing uneasiness regarding all phases of the post-war life,' specifically the fears expressed in postwar discussions about 'deviant' morality among urban young people.[5]

At the height of the baby boom, at a time when few couples were divorcing, Princess Elizabeth (age twenty-two, but already married, like so many of her contemporaries) broke with protocol to make an impassioned speech warning her subjects that the moral fabric of civilization was in danger: 'We live in an age of growing self-indulgence, of hardening materialism and of falling moral standards,' she reportedly said.[6] Her speech was quoted and praised in the highest terms by Toronto's clergy, and the *Globe and Mail* saw fit to add that 'her concern was based on statistics. These show that the ratio of divorces to marriages in England and Wales last year was almost one to eight.'[7]

With hindsight, one could say the soon-to-be queen's fears were unjustified, but that was not obvious at the time. Contemporaries felt a sense of social and moral crisis, perhaps due to the fact that some key values were undergoing rapid change. On the gender front, even though there was a concerted effort to return to an altogether mythical prewar state of gender stability, the wartime experience of women working at men's jobs or raising families on their own could not be erased. In 1948 the respectable social workers and educators making up the Canadian Youth Commission stated that employment 'made some women better mothers,'[8] while the post-marriage employment of women teachers was defended vigorously in both articles and letters to the editor in Toronto postwar papers.[9]

In terms of race and ethnicity, prewar social reformers had on the whole felt sure that a good dose of Anglo-Saxon Protestantism would make Canadian citizens out of immigrants. By 1945, however, there was a new discourse on democratic respect for other cultures and for individual choices which made it difficult for social experts to orient their work. The YWCA of Toronto, while committed to Anglo-Protestant values, defended the right to vote of its own Japanese-Canadian members and was reluctantly led into political action against racial discrimination. Generational differences, a source of anxiety in their own right, compounded the difficulty of doing anti-discrimination work from within a traditional Anglo-Protestant organization: some 'ladies' of the board said that the younger members' street picketing of a racist skating rink was 'undignified.'[10] These women (mainly married volunteers) preferred to send a delegation to the Police Commission, and forbade the 'girls' (young, single working women) from using the YWCA name when they attended street demonstrations.

In their work with women of colour and single European women from displaced persons' camps, the YWCA was unambiguously committed to justice, publicly complaining about discrimination against Black women in nursing schools and other forms of racism; yet it was very uneasy about extending its work to non-Protestants.[11] Young women of colour were accepted even in leadership positions as long as they were Protestant, and as long as they did not fuel generational anxieties by insisting on 'undignified' actions.

Toronto delinquency expert Hugo Wolter faced a similar dilemma. Like the YWCA women, he was at heart an old-fashioned moralist; but, making explicit what in YWCA discussions was only implicit, he noted that the content of moral values was open to some discussion, given the postwar emphasis on democracy: 'it is therefore necessary to define moral responsibility in such universal terms that all people, all religions, and all nationalities can be included.' Groping for a definition of morality, he equated it with 'social' (as opposed to antisocial) behaviour; but finding himself at a loss to define 'social' behaviour, his text suddenly turned to psychiatry: 'social behaviour as outlined is almost synonymous with mental health.'[12]

Wolter's confused text demonstrates the difficulties of moral regulation in a pluralist society and helps to explain the popularity of 'mental hygiene' and other psychiatric practices in the period. Traditional moral and social values were being increasingly perceived as ethnocentric (although the word was not yet in use), and as the clergy and other traditional agencies of moral regulation lost ground, psychiatry – regarded as scientific and hence as unbiased – rose in standing.[13]

Wolter's dilemma concerning ways to respect and yet regulate all religions and all nationalities was typical of the period. Immigrants had suddenly become New Canadians, a term presaging the multicultural values of the late 1960s.[14] Racism was alive and well in postwar Toronto, but the firm consensus regarding the essential Anglo-Saxon and Protestant character of Ontario was now shaken by a vague and yet sincere commitment to 'democracy' and, within very narrow boundaries, cultural difference. A large-scale survey of Canadian youth done in the last year of the war revealed that while those surveyed thought that immigrants should learn English and adopt Canadian customs, they were keenly indignant about racial slurs and overt discrimination, especially against Jews.[15] Provided with only a shapeless notion of democracy,[16] social experts of the time sighed that citizenship education was difficult because the concept of Canada was 'still something much too blurred to be a compelling object of national feeling.'[17]

Some progressive social experts tried to use the victory against fascism and the subsequent enthusiasm about parliamentary democracy to critique and reform gender and family relations. The Canadian Youth Commission argued that the prewar 'patriarchal' family was being replaced by a new 'democratic' family. European family forms were more patriarchal, but, the commission pointed out, 'frontier conditions' in Canada 'introduced no small measure of democracy': 'The family became more equalitarian [sic]; the authority of the husband declined and the rights and wishes of the wife and children received greater consideration. In the relationship of husband and wife more emphasis was placed on partnership and less on ownership.'[18] Needless to say, this concept of democratic family life was at odds with most other official and popular pronouncements on gender, sex, and family, but the Youth Commission members were not alone in their attempt to make the prevailing political ideas perform more progressive work.

'Democracy' also figured prominently in the political discourse of the YWCA, often in connection with attempts to legitimize women's participation in public economic and political activities. The North Toronto branch of the YWCA expressed a common sentiment when it promoted women's political involvement, saying that 'having in mind the importance of women's place in shaping the future of our world, we are building leaders and better citizens for democracy.'[19]

The Canadian Youth Commission introduced its pro–social security, gender-progressive reports with an elaborate analogy between seventeenth-century New France and 1945 Canada, in which both societies were presented as similar because of their postwar status and their need for social planning. The granting of 'family allowances' by the colonial French government to habitants was noted in an implicit defence of the baby bonus. Colonial French authorities had a youth program to settle ex-soldiers on the land and to encourage a baby boom, but the difference was democracy: whereas both the government and the sexual politics of the *ancien régime* were feudal, 'our youth programme must be designed to produce democratic and responsible men and women.'[20]

Elaine Tyler May has provided an insightful analysis for the United States of the ways in which political fears – about the atomic bomb, communism, and the apparent fragility of democracy – were simultaneously addressed and repressed in the postwar period through sexual and familial discourses. She documents the way major social and political questions (national security, the Cold War) were displaced onto the sexual arena, in part by the conflation of spies with homosexuals and in part by a peculiar sexualization and femininization of political danger: government pamphlets explaining the dangers of radioactivity portrayed each type of ray as a femme fatale, and the safety of the nation was invariably symbolized by a white nuclear family huddling in a nuclear shelter.[21]

Similar phenomena took place in Canada, as seen in the RCMP-led moral panic about homosexuals in the civil service[22] and in the notorious case of the alleged hooker-cum-spy Gerda Munsinger, cases that have not yet received sufficient scholarly attention. But homosexuals and voluptuous female spies were not the only characters threatening to break the contradictory and anxi-ety-ridden moral and political consensus of the postwar years. This article seeks to reveal some of the links between political and sexual order by exam-ining the claims that inappropriate gender and sexual conduct among urban young women and among members of 'street gangs' posed a challenge to 'democracy' as well as to morality. First, two notorious events involving mor-ally deviant young women will be considered; second, fears about gender deviance in street youth will be looked at; finally, the positive moral and social reform programs advocated and put in place by a variety of institutions, from school boards to welfare agencies to training schools, will be examined. Throughout, emphasis will be placed as much on the everyday practices designed to produce and reproduce 'respectable' and properly gendered youth as on the easily sensationalized events involving the small minority of moral outcasts. This dual approach is to highlight the fact that moral regulation involves routine processes affecting everyone, not just coercive measures affecting the few.

## YOUNG URBAN WOMEN AND MORAL DEVIANCE

On 9 April 1948 huge banner headlines shocked Torontonians: a young upper-middle-class woman described by the *Globe* as an 'attractive brunette' and by the *Star* as 'pretty [and] dark-haired,' had been found dead by the side of a road near Yonge and York Mills, and all indications were that she had died of an illegal abortion. Unlike the demure *Globe*, the *Star* bluntly stated in its headline 'Operation Killed Girl,' and both papers mentioned that the dead woman's purse contained $500 in $50 bills. The police were quoted as saying that the illegal abortionist (who was obviously so frightened as to neglect to collect the cash) had undoubtedly driven the body to a spot near but not too close to the clinic to 'hide the evidence.'[23]

What had led this upper-middle-class woman in her mid-twenties to such a pass? Both papers presented a series of 'facts' from which the reader could draw only one conclusion – that this unfortunate woman was reaping the reward of her unnatural acts. The woman, whom we shall call Jane, had married in 1942; her husband had served in the army and, on his return home, a combination of marital difficulties and the Toronto housing shortage had caused a separation. Jane, employed as a downtown stenographer, had placed her five-year-old daughter in a boarding nursery school and saw her only once every two weeks (as was the nursery's policy). Jane's husband, a professional in a high-status municipal job, was portrayed as a good father who, after the separation, walked his daughter to school every day. He was unwilling to stigmatize his estranged wife, saying, 'It's all a mystery to me. She never skylarked. She had only a few select friends.'

These 'select friends' included a Leaside real estate salesman (the only person involved not named by the newspapers), who admitted giving Jane the $500 the morning before her death. He claimed he was not responsible for Jane's 'condition,' but the implication was clear, especially since the *Star* mentioned that his wife had been undergoing a nervous breakdown.

The abortionist responsible for Jane's death was thought to have been responsible for the similar death of a single, young woman from York Township. Police questioned a North York doctor at length, but no charges were subsequently laid.

The story contained all the elements for a patriarchal morality play about fallen womanhood: the separation, the job downtown, the neglect of the daughter, the seducer, the evil doctor – and, last but perhaps most important, the 'nice' and apparently forgiving husband. The fate inherent in a tragic childhood, a key element in social melodrama generally, was explored in a substory about Jane's father, a prominent professional who had burned to death in an accident apparently linked to alcohol.

Jane's life, including her death, was turned into a lesson warning women that marriage, moral respectability, and middle-class status had to be actively maintained, not taken for granted. This narrative was so tightly written that it would have been impossible to insert an alternative moral of the story – for instance regarding the lack of safe and legal abortions. In the newspapers, fact followed fact with seeming inevitability: Jane's death was the 'natural' conclusion to her fall from moral respectability.

If women who sought to control their sexual and social lives by seeking abortions or rejecting motherhood in other ways were stigmatized and even demonized by the media, there was at least one young woman whose extreme violent behaviour was ascribed to an excess desire to become a mother, a desire that supposedly led her to violent jealousy and resentment. In 1952 a twenty-two-year-old Toronto woman was charged with the murder of a three-year-old child whom she was babysitting.[24] The police stated that the babysitter had had 'an operation' (possibly a hysterectomy) and, presumably as a result, did not go out with boys or engage in approved heterosexual behaviour. She apparently knitted and read a great deal, and the police did not fail to mention to the press two titles in her collection: *Lust for Love* and *Sinful Bargain*. The young woman's own sinful bargain was reportedly described in a note found in the child's crib, reading, 'If I can't have children, you can't have them either.'

A jury found the babysitter guilty of manslaughter, not murder, and the judge sentenced her to ten years in custody, with a recommendation for psychiatric treatment. The judge's admonition, reported at length in the *Star*, gave the public the impression that the category of criminal sexual psychopath becoming common at this time could include women as well as men.[25] In the case of this woman, however, it was not so much sexual lust as the desire to have children that seemed to have caused a homicidal rage. Reading this and the Jane story together, a female reader might conclude that urban women had to walk a difficult tightrope in managing their gender-specific desires, for an excess of maternal zeal could be as dangerous as a deficiency of it. And in both stories, there was a constant slippage between mothering and sexual desire; discussions of mothering practices and desires turned into comments on 'lust for love.'

May has suggested that the postwar period saw a decline in Victorian ideas about female lack of passion and a rise in the belief that women of all classes had strong sexual desires. These desires could not be eliminated, but they needed to be 'contained,' partly through monogamous marriage and partly through the discipline imposed by mothering. Her analogy between 'sexual containment' and the idea prevalent in US government circles about the 'containment' of communism and of the nuclear threat is useful in understanding the newspaper coverage of both of these cases.[26] Rather than preaching less passion or celibacy, the newspapers suggested that these women went astray because their sexual passions were not properly contained: the abortion-clinic victim because she had left her husband and her child, and the babysitter because of a physiological inability to channel her sexuality into childbearing.

CITY STREETS AND CITY CLOTHES: THE 'PROBLEM' OF GANGS

If young women's psychosexual development was perceived as a potential danger not only to themselves and those around them but also to the sexual and political order of the city generally, male gender formation was by no means without problems too. This can be seen by a study of middle-class fears about deviant gender formation among boys and girls involved in unsupervised inner-city street activity.

The postwar concern about working-class children and youth in the inner city was, in Toronto, the continuation of a wartime concern about parental absence or neglect and the consequent emergence of 'latchkey kids.' In 1943 City Council asked the Toronto Welfare Council to study 'widespread public concern over the increase in juvenile delinquency.'[27] The employment of mothers in war work and the absence of fathers in the forces were ritually deplored in the subsequent report; but, interestingly, parental absence was not stressed as much as in other writings of the period. Other factors were highlighted. One of the problems contributing to sexual offences among Toronto girls was the sexual allure of uniforms: 'The glamour which is cast over adolescent girls by young men in uniform has contributed to the increase in delinquency ... Irresponsible sexual relations arise more frequently than before, with the consequent rise in unprepared and irresponsible parenthood.'[28] But the main explanation of delinquency, and one that would loom large in the Welfare Council's postwar work with urban youth, was the inherently deviant character of certain neighbourhoods. The report claimed that successive waves of immigration did not seem to affect the moral character of some 'notorious' Toronto neighbourhoods: 'The new residents, frequently of a different origin, with different religions and cultural backgrounds, may be said to have inherited the evil conditions of the area into which they moved. It seems proper to assume that, in such a case, delinquency is primarily a problem of neighbourhood relationships, standards and traditions, as well as one of conditions in individual families.'[29]

This analysis prompted a collaborative effort between the Welfare Council and the city Department of Public Welfare known as 'area projects,' involving community work to improve morals in the east-end neighbourhoods extending from Cabbagetown, through Moss Park and Regent Park, to South Riverdale. (It should be noted that, then as now, these districts, though containing some immigrants, were the primary home of Toronto's Canadian-born, English-speaking poor, by contrast to the predominantly immigrant districts west of Spadina.)

A 1944 report on the work of area projects laid the rationale for continuing neighbourhood-based (as opposed to family-based) social work after the war by stating that juvenile delinquency 'is not a wartime phenomenon' but a long-term problem due to a variety of psychological and environmental causes. As of the end of 1944, efforts had been made to organize the leisure time of young people in Cabbagetown by using two schools as evening and weekend community centres offering 'loom weaving, clay modelling and folk dancing,' activities presumably designed to lure girls away from unsupervised outings with men in uniform.[30]

The area project was not the only effort made to deal with the perceived problem of deviant use of leisure time. The YWCA sponsored weekend dances and teenage 'hang-outs' at its various branches, as well as Sunday tea-dances that drew up to four hundred people to its central branch, many of them men in uniform willing to engage in non-alcoholic heterosexual flirting under the moral auspices of the YWCA.[31] On its part, the City Parks department was involved in setting up park facilities and community centres which, while not designed as sites for social work, were regarded as part of the broader network of institutions contributing to the prevention of juvenile delinquency. Like the YWCA Sunday teas, supervised sports and recreation were perceived as preventing respectable youth from being lured by rougher forms of leisure activity. The area projects were specifically aimed at the poorer classes, and intervened not only in class relations and property crime but also in gender and sexual training.

The supposedly natural aggressiveness of young working-class boys, for instance, was channelled into the Regent Athletic Association, a boxing club on Gerrard Street, while youthful heterosexuality was given a supervised outlet through a series of summer dances, each attended by around 350 Cabbagetown teenagers. Masculine aggression and heterosexual desire were thus not to be suppressed but rather channelled into morally and socially appropriate settings supervised by representatives of the middle class. The social worker in charge of area projects was particularly proud of having persuaded an alleged boys' gang, the Flying Aces, to turn itself into a 'club' supervised by the east-end settlement Central Neighbourhood House.[32]

The general assumption behind these efforts to replace spontaneous street activity by supervised recreation was that proper sexual behaviour and correct gender roles would not be learned by young people from either their parents or their peers. Rather, they could be stimulated under the supervision of middle-class men and women whose morals and gender identities were beyond reproach.

It is probable that few Torontonians knew of the community work done with inner-city youth by municipal and private agency workers. In fact, by 1949 the average Toronto newspaper reader would have thought that urban youths were becoming more dangerous rather than less, since in that year there were half a dozen well-publicized news stories portraying the activities of dangerous street gangs. These gangs were distinguished from their predecessors by the 'zoot suits' worn by the young men.[33] ('Zoot suits,' adopted from Mexican-American urban culture, had large padded shoulders, wide pegged legs, and came in loud colours such as purple and green.)

The 'gang' activities described in the stories were often of a very petty character, but the flashy clothing and defiant attitudes of the young people involved seemed to magnify their misconduct and turn it into a major crime. For example, in July 1949 a group of thirteen young 'zoot suiters' responded quite aggressively 'when passersby made uncomplimentary remarks about their flashy clothing'; but as one reads further into the story it appears that even if some physical fighting was involved, their major crime was to have boarded the Bathurst streetcar with expired transit transfers.[34] A few weeks later, a woman was robbed of four dollars, a crime that would not have been reported in the press except that 'she said one of the pair was wearing green strides [pants] and the other had wine-colored trousers.'[35]

It would seem that any misbehaviour, however petty, was newsworthy if connected to zooters, or to other deviant clothing styles. The Toronto Welfare Council opined that Toronto was not 'a gang-ridden community,' and that 'too much publicity had been given gangs ... the gang situation would appear to be no worse than in previous years.'[36] But the press was keen to create the impression that great dangers lurked in city streets and that young people wearing 'flashy clothing' were serious criminals.

Some girls participated in zoot-suit gangs, although they were a small minority; other girls struck out on their own and engaged in single-sex crime. A story in the *Globe* recounted the misdeeds of three teenage girls who stole $500 worth of dresses from a downtown store and drove away in a cab in broad daylight.[37] One of the nineteen-year-old women involved in the robbery, incidentally, was apparently not reformed by whatever sentence she served; in 1953 she was thought to be the leader of a street gang with nine boys located on Dundas Street East.[38]

The connection between abnormal desires in the sphere of fashion – for loud zoot suits, for stolen dresses – was so firmly connected in the public mind with the perceived rise of serious street crime that city controller Leslie Saunders suggested to the Welfare Council that 'manufacture of those silly colored zoot suits' be banned as a measure to prevent juvenile delinquency. Council secretary Florence Philpott disagreed with the focus on the zoot suit, in keeping with the council's sceptical view of sensationalist coverage of gangs.[39] But for several months the papers persisted in highlighting the role of zoot suits in youth crime.[40]

Although the zoot suit was worn by men only, the *Star* carried an interesting article describing a minor assault on two west-end youths by two zoot-suited boys and a girl, with the lurid headline, 'Stride-clothed Girls Cheer as Teen-agers Beat Youth Insensible.'[41] It is unclear exactly what kind of trousers were indicated by the term 'strides,' and so it is difficult to say whether the girl (turned into several by the inaccurate headline) was newsworthy because she was cross-dressing or because she was wearing a zoot suit. But the general point about deviant behaviour arising out of deviant dressing was unmistakeable.

Another story highlighted the role of 'an attractive 16-year-old girl' in provoking a west-end youth gang into going to the east end and starting 'a zoot-suiters' fight.' In this incident the fighting was fairly minor, but seven boys and one girl were charged and the *Star* gave the story the headline, 'Pape Avenue Riot.'[42] The girl's clothing was not described, however.

The newspaper stories make it clear that the girls involved in gang activity, whether actually committing crimes such as stealing or simply 'cheering' fighting boys from the sideline, were deviating from accepted feminine norms. Just as working-class boys were thought to be always at risk of developing deviant masculine identities (criminals instead of breadwinners, street fighters instead of disciplined boxers), girls from poor neighbourhoods were suspected of deviant gender identities, generally linked to sexual misbehaviour.

The urgent need to contain youthful female sexuality was eloquently articulated in a press account of the Welfare Council's special report on juvenile delinquency. The council, it was reported, found that 'girls buy their way into gangs, frequently becoming supporters of the boys ... Common [sexual] property of the gangs, the girls lean heavily upon their financial influence for entry.' The girls, the *Star* said, were 'practised prostitutes by the time boy members of the gang are mending their ways. And we find that when a boy does find a girl he likes, he never brings her near the gang.'[43]

Female sexual deviance was thus thought to be a necessary attribute of 'the girls in the gang.' And because sexual deviance was thought to be more indelible and less subject to reform than traditionally male deviant activities such as fighting and petty stealing, girls belonging to gangs, even if a minority, were perceived as more of a problem than boys. The girls' sexual offences were compounded by the fact that the male-breadwinner model was reversed in youth gangs, with girls earning the bigger wages, supposedly through prostitution, and boys being financially subordinate. The postwar suspicion about women who 'took men's jobs,' whether in gangs or in corporations, was clearly connected to, and fuelled by, fears about sexual and gender role reversals.

Countless postwar films and novels gave dire warnings about the link between female sexual wiles and monetary greed, so the comments just cited about girls buying their way into gangs are not unexpected.[44] What is more remarkable about the zoot-suit moral panic is that the press chose to highlight what the boys and men were wearing: male clothing is not generally subject to the same level of moral regulation as female clothing. Nevertheless, during the war, Mexican-American zoot-suiters had been physically attacked in Los Angeles by sailors and soldiers on leave, in interracial strife known as 'zoot-suit riots.' There does not seem to be any indication that Toronto zoot-suiters were members of racial minorities, but the zoot suit was a counter uniform, the badge of a defiant working-class masculinity that led to an inversion of the correct financial and sexual relationship between the two genders. Just as feminine sexual and social morality has throughout history been structured, among other factors, by the binary opposition between the hooker's finery and the lady's dress,[45] so here we see masculinity being regulated through the binary opposition between two kinds of clothes: in wartime, the zoot suit versus the uniform, and, after the war, the loudly coloured zoot suit versus the organization man's grey suit.[46]

It would be inaccurate, however, to conclude that the moral panic about zoot-suit gangs was created solely by the newspapers. Early in 1949, before most of the newspaper stories were published, Toronto mayor H.E. McCallum appointed a high-level committee to study the problem of juvenile delinquency, chaired by Cecil Goldring and involving dozens of moral and social experts. The Toronto Welfare Council, which already had its own reports on the matter, seems to have taken the major leadership role in the comittee, and in fact some of the final recommendations repeated verbatim parts of the Welfare Council's reports. An initial meeting was held in the council chamber on 14 March, and later on the large group divided itself into working subcommittees that eventually came up with an extensive list of recommendations.

These recommendations provide a good summary of the kinds of analyses and practices that were widely accepted by social workers, educationists, and other public and private officials with jurisdiction over inner-city youth.[47] Clearly trying to dissociate themselves from media exposés of zoot-suit gangs (the word 'zoot suit' does not appear in the document), the committee spent some time considering repressive measures for the small group actually charged with crimes, but on the whole put much more emphasis on preventive measures aimed at the entire youth population. The emphasis on positive moral regulation – on programs aimed at creating the right sort of habits in the whole population rather than merely punishing deviants – was very much in keeping with Goldring's total environmental approach, designed, in his words, to 'build anti-delinquent communities.'[48]

The report began by suggesting improvements in the correctional services provided for delinquent youth, as well as an expansion of the psychiatric services provided through the school system by the Toronto Board of

Health. The old-fashioned moralism of some committee members dove-tailed with the modern psychological regulation favoured by others, or by the same people when they utilized newer discourses. A major part of the document focused on the 'breakdown of moral fibre' that was thought to be typical of the postwar period. The list of 'home conditions contributing to delinquency' began with divorce, followed by drunkenness and other domestic vices, 'lack of spiritual background,' the breakdown of traditional values, and 'lack of guidance at an early age in the techniques of living a well-adjusted life.' The phrase 'well-adjusted' reflects the eruption of modern psychiatric-social work discourse (in which 'adjustment' was everything) into an otherwise old-fashioned moral analysis. Poverty and poor housing were named in sixth and seventh place, respectively, and these structural factors, unlike the moral and psychological ones, did not receive commentary.)

To deal with parental responsibility for delinquency, the committee made a number of recommendations. One, in keeping with the general trend towards expert advice on everyday life, was to mount courses in parent education, voluntary courses for 'normal' parents and compulsory courses for parents of delinquent children. But the older moral concerns with alcohol as demon rum and with parental moral example were equally prominent. It was thought that 'insobriety, especially on the mother's part,' was a major cause of juvenile delinquency. (Male insobriety was probably thought to be less threatening to gender roles.)

It is difficult to judge whether the moralistic and pro-temperance recommendations had more weight than the 'modern' ones, since the report was clearly a compromise document. Nevertheless, it may be significant that the Welfare Council's more modern, enviromentalist approach was reflected in the very first recommendation. In it, City Council was urged to eliminate slum areas by 'erecting new housing developments similar to Regent Park,' a huge public-housing project in east-end Toronto.

The modernizing dreams of postwar social and urban reformers, whether in the area of expressway design or crime prevention, were to come to grief from the late 1960s onward, owing to growing scepticism about large-scale planning, whether architectural or social. And yet, perhaps precisely because of the contemporary strength of scepticism about social engineering and planning in general, it is worthwhile taking time to describe the positive vision of a socially planned future that animated postwar reformers. Their faith in social and moral reform techniques, from psychiatry to supervised playgrounds, is often ridiculed in our own era, yet it deserves to be sympathetically analysed.

*Training schools*

The discourse of a world in crisis pervaded even the relatively isolated world of the convents serving as correctional institutions for girls.[49] In 1949, the head of St Mary's training school breathlessly mixed her metaphors to proclaim: 'To all whose task it is to form citizenship in the rising generation the past year has been of severe challenge. It has beheld amongst the youth of our province large groups in organized array riding the offensive on a seething tide of serious delinquency.'[50]

It is interesting that the nuns at St Mary's (Sisters of the Good Shepherd, an order that had also run the Catholic voluntary shelter for penitent prostitutes for many decades) saw their task as involving more than simply repairing the moral and sexual defects of their charges: they took the larger political goal of democratic 'citizenship' quite seriously. The head of the Protestant training school for girls echoed these feelings: 'We felt that perhaps the most important thing for these girls to have acquired at the school was some appreciation of the ideals of our democratic society.'[51]

And yet, while the boys' training schools undertook the political training of male youth by instituting 'Police Days' with visits by local officers, as well as trips to meet with the RCMP in Ottawa,[52] in the girls' schools the vague goal of training for citizenship and democracy was implemented mainly by focusing on the girls' sexual practices and feminine skills. The girls' sexuality seemed to be scrutinized more closely than the boys': while the medical reports for boys' training schools do not mention venereal disease tests, hundreds of syphilis and gonorrhea tests were carried out annually in the girls' schools. Very few girls were listed as receiving treatment, so one can conclude that the routine tests were more reflective of the authorities' assumptions about girl delinquents than of any actual symptoms. This is corroborated by a statement in the introduction to the 1948 report on girls' training schools: 'One of the great differences in problems of delinquencies between boys and girls is the predominance of sex offences in regard to the latter.'[53] The report goes on to argue that, precisely because of the sexual character of girls' offences, 'we are inclined to favour the longer stay, as at St Mary's School.'[54]

Until 1951 young people in training schools could be kept there at the discretion of the authorities until the age of twenty-one. In that year, indeterminate sentences were shortened when a new top age limit of eighteen was introduced. Although budgetary and space problems undoubtedly created pressures on the managers to release inmates they would have preferred to keep, it is clear that, even after the 1951 reform, a year or more were not thought too long for reforming sexuality and gender. Given the fact that the vast majority of girls in training schools had no court appearances at all prior to commitment (or to 'admission,' an extrajudicial form of commitment), one suspects that many of the girls were the victims of processes on the margins of the legal system. It would seem that girls were more subject to the opinions of social workers, parents, and other authorities than to the letter of the law.[55] The delegation of power from the courts to non-legal social and psychiatric authorities seemed often to conflict with the ideas of working-class parents, who apparently believed that their children were in for a fixed time of six months and did not understand the principle of the indeterminate sentence. (In 1948, two years was the most common time served, which is about the same that many men served for rape.)[56]

Girls and young women thus arrived at the school through a number of possible channels, from judicial sentence to decisions by extralegal juvenile authorities sometimes based simply on claims about 'parental neglect' or 'parental vice.'[57] Once there, the two hundred or so girls found at any one time in training schools were given regular school classes in addition to feminine training in sewing and home economics, together with a little music. The sewing, however, seems to have doubled as a means of rehabilitation and as an income-generating activity for the institution: the 1948 report for the Cobourg school states that the 102 inmates made almost one thousand garments and mended another 800.[58] In addition, a great deal of farm work, including much pickling and canning, was also performed, especially at St Mary's. Some efforts were made to teach girls marketable but still feminine skills, such as typing, office skills, and hairdressing: but these were small and sporadic classes. 'Homemaking,' together with a minimum level of schooling, seemed to be the main focus, and it is possible that girls quickly discovered the superintendent's preferences and made a show of proficiency in domesticity: 'The special homemaking class maintained its prestige throughout the year, the girls according it a true feminine preference.'[59] This activity was portrayed not as imposed from above but as arising directly from girls' own nature: 'The homemaking instinct has always been strong in our girls, in whose eyes the charge of even a small culinary, sewing or cleaning project is a coveted assignment.'[60]

In their more optimistic moments, the authorities probably imagined a happily married, domestic future for their girls. But the reality was that upon release most of the girls and young women, unless so young that they had to return to school, had to make their own living. The training they had received fitted them for nothing better than domestic service or unskilled sales, service, or factory work. Over the six years from 1947 to 1952, the figures on the situation of girls and women leaving the training schools are as follows:

Back to school      264
Domestic service  248
Factory work         198
Sales/service        145
Office jobs            57

Although most of the features of training-school life listed thus far were gender- and class-specific, one feature was common to both boys' and girls' schools – namely 'mental hygiene' intervention by counsellors, psychologists, and occasionally psychiatrists. IQ tests were administered to the inmate/students, and on that basis a large proportion – sometimes larger for boys, interestingly – were judged to be intellectually below normal.[61] A counselling program initiated at the Cobourg school in 1948 was designed to adjust the girls to the school rather than to validate their feelings, since its goals were 'to interpret the aims and system of the school and, when necessary, the reason for committal.'[62] In addition, all the schools had arrangements with psychiatric institutions in Kingston and in Toronto for occasional consulting.

Although the reports about mental illness and low IQ scores indicate that the training-school population was rife with mental problems, in fact the inmates did not include those clearly labelled as 'feeble-minded' or, in 1950s' language, as 'mentally defective.' Those inmates, if female, were sent to a special institution in Orillia even if they were judged to be delinquent. The significant presence of psychologists, counsellors, and psychiatrists at the schools can thus be regarded as part of a general trend in work with youth – the increasing emphasis on psychiatry not only among 'deviants,' but among youth in general.

*Citizenship and Consumption*

Training schools affected a small minority of children. Moral regulation, however, did not affect only those singled out as 'bad'; there were a number of programs aimed at all school children that promoted a combination of gender, moral, and political values. Two will be examined here: first, citizenship education, and, second, homemaking and 'consumer education.' The latter was meant only for girls and was completely linked to prevailing ideas about femininity; the former was largely aimed at boys, but included some recognition that women too could and should be patriotic in their own non-militaristic way. Both programs seemed to arise out of adults' anxiety that the postwar generation – especially if poor, but even if middle class – was in some danger of failing to reproduce the nation's moral fibre, the combined moral and patriotic capital carefully accumulated by the war generation.

As usual, Goldring was particularly eloquent in formulating the national anxiety about the vulnerability of a self-regulating moral economy and the consequent need for moral and social planning as well as economic planning: 'In the future, possession of things may not be so important as the possession of qualities ... strong character, good personality, outstanding skill in one's profession, a disciplined mind – in short, assets that are an inseparable part of oneself ... [T]he present need is for each man to invest in himself, to build up personal assets of permanent worth.'[63]

The moral resources of youth could only be developed if parents, teachers, and other adults were themselves rich in moral capital: Goldring warned teachers that they should devote their spare time to doing war work, joining clubs, and other activities ensuring that they would continue to 'invest heavily' in themselves. This concern with the teachers' own moral capital as a precondition for proper instruction was also found in the report of the 1950 Royal Commission on Education, which stated: 'In the final analysis, the responsibility for education in citizenship in the individual school rests with the teacher; his personality, his methods of teaching, indeed his way of life, will exert a powerful influence.'[64]

This 'education for citizenship' was one of the strategies for reconstructing the moral and political capital of the nation, as embodied in the souls of its young citizens. Citizenship in a democracy, the commission claimed, involved work and effort: it 'not only carries rights but also imposes obligations.' The home and the church were seen as important sites for citizenship education, but the school held pride of place.[65] Specific classes on 'civics' were of course important, and history, at least Canadian history, was also regarded as conducive to lessons in democratic citizenship.[66]

Citizenship was regarded not simply as part of the curriculum, but as a kind of ether floating through all school activities. Young people were to learn the practical applications of democratic citizenship by watching the example set by their teachers and by participating in student councils and other school activities. In a statement tending to disguise the conflicts between democracy and efficiency, Goldring stated: 'When the machinery of the school works in a precise, efficient manner, many children will acquire from such procedures a valuable lesson in citizenship.'[67] The Canadian Youth

Commission reiterated the need for students to practise democracy and not merely hear about it: 'Education for citizenship is not merely a course in civics or a history of ancient conquests. It should consist of activities which make the student a free and responsible agent, making decisions and accepting consequences.'[68]

That the burden of democratic citizenship was to be borne by men both literally and symbolically was made clear in a speech Goldring gave to Commonwealth teachers in 1955. He praised two products of Toronto public schools, British MP Sir Beverley Baxter and industrialist Garfield Weston, stating they had helped to bring Canada out of its boyhood and into a period of independent manhood. At the beginning of the Second World War, Goldring continued, Canada was a 'gangling adolescent boy,' but in the intervening years it has reached maturity. 'The adolescent is now a confident young man in his twenties.'[69] (The portrayal of Canada as male went against the newspaper cartoonists' tradition of showing a maidenly 'Miss Canada,' more often than not being threatened by the advances of Uncle Sam.)

Goldring's own contribution to the virility of Canada as well as that of individual boys was to organize interprovincial exchanges in which boys (not girls) from Toronto schools travelled to get a sense of Canada as a whole, and, on their return, spoke to their schoolmates. The Canadian Education Association, of which Goldring was president for a time, sought to inspire school inspectors and superintendents with nationalist ideals through national meetings; these were apparently all-male gatherings. In Goldring's vision of patriotism, women were mentioned only once and then briefly; their contribution to nationalism and democracy was described as limited to setting a good example in the virtues of 'loyalty to one's family' and, in second place, one's country.[70]

Even if women played a marginal role both in representing and in demonstrating citizenship, however, girls were undoubtedly expected to be avid consumers of the kind of patriotic school spectacle favoured by Goldring for Empire Day and other occasions. Decrying the teaching of civics as a dry subject, Goldring said that 'greater use of pageantry in teaching citizenship might be made'; he was also keen on the use of national media, especially radio, to reach broad audiences and 'appeal to the emotions.'[71]

Goldring argued that Canadian ideals, as differentiated from both communism and fascism, emphasized 'the ancient British tradition of freedom of the individual under the law, the dignity of the individual'; but then he went on to add, without noticing the contradiction, that citizenship programs in schools should also teach the opposite of individual freedom – respect for the law and for local authorities such as police, firemen, health inspectors, and school authorities.[72] This contradictory view of Canadian citizenship was endorsed by the Royal Commission on Education in Ontario, which saw the 'balance' of autonomy (democracy) and obedience as the key to citizenship education.[73] Pointing out that intelligence alone had not prevented citizens of other countries from choosing nefarious political systems, the commission stated that there were two parts to education, one intellectual and one moral, and that the latter was more important than the former. Education in morality would make young Canadian citizens (imagined as male) less likely to follow questionable leaders; without such education, 'we may expect continued dependence and weakness in moral fibre.'[74] Canadian citizens clearly had to be masculine and avoid falling into the feminized state of dependence and weakness. How independence was to be reconciled with the need for obedience to authority was not explained.

*Feminine Citizenship and the Education of Desire*

Just as many youth experts thought that classes in civics were not sufficient to train the largely male active citizens of postwar democracy, so classes in such feminine subjects as home economics were deemed insufficient to create the necessary sexual and political identity in girls. As far back as 1934 a speech by Goldring to the home economics teachers' association decried classroom study for home economics: 'Domesticity should be taught in some ideal home building by a kind of laboratory method ... There should be a general course in pedagogy, another in child study, and finally a course in maternity during the last year.' The very epistemology of home economics classes needed to be suited to the feminine brain: rather than dealing with facts and testing students through examination, 'everything should be as suggestive and germinal as possible.'[75]

In Ontario postwar schools, home economics was usually taught in grades 7 to 10, but only as an option; furthermore, only large urban schools had the facilities needed for actual rather than theoretical cooking and sewing. The Royal Commission on Education thought this lack of facilities was deplorable and recommended making home economics compulsory in grades 9 and 10 and optional in grades 11 and 12. It was obvious to the commission that 'the future welfare of the home and family will depend in large measure on the training received by girls in the home and in the school.'[76] Given the concerns about female sexual independence and urban youth deviance, it is clear that the 'welfare of home and family' was perceived as a key social and political objective as well as women's sexual destiny.

The sexual and gender politics involved in the postwar vision of domesticity were not unique to the period, but these years added a new twist to the old tale of 'the angel in the house' – specifically, a consumerist twist. Along with less time-specific fears about sexual deviance, the postwar period saw a profound economic anxiety about a possible relapse into the prewar Depression. Fuelling consumption by convincing women, especially housewives, to buy more goods would guarantee economic prosperity as well as social and sexual conformity. Because the war had promoted an ethic of austerity, the new ethic of consumption had to be promoted, especially among women. This is clearly seen in Goldring's plan to introduce an additional school subject in Toronto, 'consumer education,' aimed specifically at girls.[77]

Goldring's speech on the new subject began with the 'fact' that 80 per cent of the buying in stores was done by women. Since shopping was obviously a female pursuit, Goldring continued, 'it should be part of [a woman's] vocational education.' This specifically feminine training for shopping consisted of two aspects: first, of providing girls with information about 'buying wisely,' and, second of the grander goal of reforming the girls' subjectivities through 'the formation of tastes,' a process 'more important than the actual buying.' Taste, then – what the sociologist of culture, Pierre Bordieu, later called 'habitus'[78] – is the real objective of the gendered process of consumer education. Young women should not merely buy economical goods because someone told them how to budget, but should be taught to desire the right objects. 'Behind the decision as to what article is to be bought, there are a set of desires and a scale of values, and our education should play a large part in helping to form those desires.'

Like the citizenship education aimed primarily at boys, consumer education ought not to be considered as a special subject: it should be integrated throughout the curriculum, presumably because training in gender-appropriate desires was such a vast task. Some curricular suggestions followed for teachers in various subjects: commercial teachers could teach business law, English teachers could analyse advertising, and other teachers could warn future consumers against the postwar phenomenon of buying in instalments. The primary purpose of this all-pervasive education in desire was to create the right kind of femininity for postwar consumer society; but, as usual with gender/sexual politics, the interests of politics, in this case free enterprise, were regarded as inseparable from moral and gender regulation. Goldring dissasociated his plan from those of some consumer groups – possibly the communist-inspired 'housewives against rising prices' – which had 'taken an extreme point of view' in criticizing business. Toronto's school-based consumer education, Goldring warned, should stay away from consumer groups 'affiliated with radical groups, [and] opposed to private interests.' Free enterprise and 'correct' femininity were thus associated and linked in ways that would haunt consumer culture down to our own day.

## CONCLUSION

Postwar discussions of gender ideology reveal a tension between upholding a mythical prewar patriarchy and an effort to expand the wartime slogans of democracy and freedom into the realm of the family. The advocates of democracy in the home were, however, attempting to modernize the institution of the family, not questioning its hegemony. Neither the newspaper readers who defended married women teachers nor the social workers who decried overly patriarchal 'European' family forms carried their critique of old moral systems so far as to sympathize with the women who had illegal abortions, the girls in training schools, or the young women who stole dresses or simply chose to wear 'strides' in the street.

Thus, while arguing with each other about the relative merits of older and newer gender identities, progressives and conservatives were united against perceived threats to the dominant moral system. The siege mentality documented both in the research for this article and in Elaine Tyler May's book on the postwar US family seemed to prevent even the more progressive social actors from questioning the universal validity of married heterosexuality and the male-headed nuclear family. Extra-familial sex, masculine deviance in dress and in employment, and feminine deviance in sexual and economic status were not alternative lifestyles but, rather, the enemy within.

The perceived attack on 'the' family and on 'morality' was ascribed to specific individuals such as homosexuals and juvenile delinquents, but it was also blamed – and in this lies the 'modernity' of postwar moral regulation – on amorphous social and moral forces working for decadence rather than reconstruction. Therefore, approaches focusing exclusively on individual psychology were not regarded as sufficient, at least by 'progressives' in the YWCA, the Toronto Welfare Council, and the Board of Education. These reformers promoted an environmental approach, seen for instance in the attempt to reform youth through the moral and physical cleansing of inner-city neighbourhoods in 'area projects.' In this approach, gender, sexual, and moral identities were envisaged as created or at least stimulated by educational, psychological, and recreational programs, but also by particular architectural and urban planning innovations.

Neither individual nor environmental techniques of moral regulation were aimed solely at the morally deviant or at the poor. Postwar social intervention involved the much larger task of constantly monitoring and encouraging proper moral, gender, and political habits among respectable youth. The large-scale building projects of postwar Toronto clearly played a role in the postwar economic boom, but they were also regarded as key tools for the social and moral engineering of 'anti-delinquent communities' based on married heterosexuality, dependent wives, and male breadwinners. Now that, in the postmodern 1990s, the Gardiner Expressway is universally regarded as a monstrous eyesore that should be buried underground, and Regent Park is synonymous in the eyes of middle-class white Toronto with Black single mothers and crack addiction, it is time for a new appraisal of the anxiety-filled faith in modernity of the social and moral engineers of the postwar city.

NOTES

1  On the marriage boom see Doug Owram, 'Home and Family at Mid-Century,' paper given at the Canadian Historical Association, Charlottetown, June 1992, 8–16, and Ruth Roach Pierson, *They're Still Women After All: The Second World War and Canadian Womanhood* (Toronto: McClelland & Stewart 1986), 215–16.
2  For the short-term dip in women's employment see Pierson, *They're Still Women After All*, 215, and for the long-term trend see Veronica Strong-Boag, 'Women with a Choice: Canada's Wage-earning Wives and the Construction of a Middle Class, 1945–1960,' paper given at the Canadian Historical Association, Charlottetown, June 1992. Strong-Boag's figures rely in turn on B. Spencer and D. Featherstone, *Married Female Labour Force Participation: A Micro Study* (Ottawa: Dominion Bureau of Statistics 1970).
3  See Gary Kinsman, *The Regulation of Desire: Sexuality in Canada* (Montreal: Black Rose 1987), 116–20.
4  C.C. Goldring, 'Toward National Unity by Means of Education,' Sept. 1945 speech, box 2, unnumbered file, Goldring Papers, Toronto Board of Education Archives (TBE).
5  Annual Report of Toronto YWCA, 1944, series B-1, box 11, Archives of Ontario (AO).
6  'Elizabeth Scolds Britain,' *Globe and Mail*, 19 Oct. 1949.
7  'Princess' Speech on Morals Praised,' ibid.
8  Canadian Youth Commission, *Youth, Marriage, and the Family* (Toronto: Ryerson 1948), 46.
9  This is clear from a perusal of the newspaper clippings file for 1946–50, TBE.
10  YWCA of Toronto, Minutes, special meeting, 11 Feb. 1947. See also the policy on use of the YW name, Minutes, Meeting, 20 March 1947, series A, box 5, AO.
11  YWCA of Toronto, Minutes and Annual Reports, 1944–9. The YW supported a variety of civil liberties initiatives but never seemed wholehearted about them,

perhaps because many of them were spearheaded by Jewish groups. For a resolution against discrimination against Black women in nursing schools see Annual Report, 1948. The same year, however, the YW decided to limit its important work with single women from DP camps in Europe to 'Protestant girls.'

12  Hugo Wolter, Brief on Delinquency [to Toronto Welfare Council Conference on Gangs], March 1949, City of Toronto Archives, RG 283, file 1.

13  The YWCA of Toronto ran a popular personal counselling service (see Minutes and Annual Reports, 1944–9); this service seems to have been run in a more progressive, less medicalized fashion than other mental-health services of the day. Social-work students were the primary counsellors, and vocational testing was carried out by psychologists. Psychiatrists were subtly denigrated through stories showing how young women who thought they needed a psychiatrist were quickly 'set right' by the YW's friendly counsellors (1949 Annual Report; see also 1947 Annual Report). More research needs to be done in the history of social work and mental-health services in this period; see Franca Iacovetta, 'Making "New Canadians": Social Workers, Women and the Reshaping of Immigrant Families,' in Franca Iacovetta and Mariana Valverde, eds, Gender Conflicts: New Essays in Women's History (Toronto: University of Toronto Press 1992).

14  The postwar use of the term 'New Canadian' is documented in Franca Iacovetta, Such Hardworking People: Italian Immigrants in Postwar Toronto (Montreal: McGill-Queen's University Press 1992). The Toronto YWCA began to use the term in 1947, as well as 'newcomer.' These were clearly more user-friendly terms than 'alien' and 'foreigner.'

15  Canadian Youth Commission, Youth Speaks Out on Citizenship (Toronto: Ryerson Press 1948). The survey results are on pages 121–40.

16  The Canadian Youth Commission provided a typically flowery and yet empty paean to 'democracy' in their summary of the various youth studies done at the end of the war. They stated that because of the war, 'we have a new faith in democratic beliefs,' and they noted that democracy is not simply the franchise but is a 'ferment' deep down inside each citizen, a 'core of light' within the individual. Canadian Youth Commission, Youth Speaks Its Mind (Toronto: Ryerson 1948), 13–16.

17  Canadian Youth Commission, Youth Speaks Out on Citizenship, 96–7. On earlier social and moral reform movements founded on a more militant view of Anglo-Saxon Protestantism see Mariana Valverde, The Age of Light, Soap and Water: Moral Reform in English Canada, 1880s–1920s (Toronto: McClelland & Stewart 1990).

18  Canadian Youth Commission, Youth, Marriage and the Family (Toronto: Ryerson 1948), 1 and 25.

19  YWCA of Toronto, Annual Report, 1947.

20  Canadian Youth Commission, *Youth Speaks Its Mind*, 3–6.

21  Elaine Tyler May, *Homeward Bound: American Families in the Cold War Era* (New York: Basic Books 1988).

22  See Kinsman, *The Regulation of Desire*, chapter 8, and Philip Girard, 'From Subversion to Liberation: Homosexuals and the Immigration Act 1952–1977,' *Canadian Journal of Law and Society* 2 (1987): 1–27. Kinsman is currently working on the RCMP's witch hunt of homosexuals in the civil service.

23  'Operation Killed Girl'; *Toronto Star* 9 April 1948; 'Girl Slain, Body Thrown from Car,' *Globe*, 9 April 1948. Information also taken from subsequent stories in the *Star*, 10, 12, and 15 April 1948.

24  'Charge Sitter, 22, Tied Baby, 3, Bludgeoned Her to Death in Crib,' *Star*, 7 Feb. 1952.

25  'Babysitter Killer Gets Ten Years,' *Star*, 9 May 1952.

26  May, *Homeward Bound*, 14–15.

27  Welfare Council of Toronto, *A Plan for the Reduction of Juvenile Delinquency in Toronto*, 15 November 1943, files of the Social Planning Council of Metropolitan Toronto (SPC).

28  Ibid., 5.

29  Ibid., 25.

30  Progress Report in Respect to Organization and Development of Area Project, November 1944, Welfare Committee Report, no.18); Metro Archives, RG 5.1, box 153, file 73.1, vol. 3.

31  For teen 'hang-out,' see Minutes of Toronto YWCA, 20 Jan. 1944, and many subsequent followups. The Sunday teas at the central branch are also regularly reported and continued into the late 1940s.

32  Memo from E. Bishop, area projects coordinator, to R.J. Morris, director of social services, Department of Public Welfare (DPW), 10 Oct. 1947, Metro Archives, RG 5.1, box 154, file 73.1.

33  A survey of the Toronto Star, the paper with most coverage of youth gangs, shows no stories about zoot-suit gangs in 1948, six in 1949, one in 1950, one in 1951, none in 1952, and one in 1953.

34  '13 Zoot-suiters Fight on Tram, Hold up Traffic,' ibid., 9 July 1949.

35  'Two in Zoot Suits Rob Woman of $4,' ibid., 10 Aug. 1949.

36  Memo from W.A. Turnbull to commissioner of DPW, 30 March 1949 [Report of an inter-agency meeting held at the Board of Education], Metro Archives, RG 5.1, box 153, file 5.

37  'Three Girls, Youth Held in Robbery of Dress Store,' *Globe & Mail*, 12 Oct. 1949.

38  'Girl Held as Gang Leader,' *Star*, 9 March 1953.

39  'Ban Making of Zoot Suits Asked to Curb Gangs,' ibid., 5 Oct. 1949.

40  'Zoot Suiters Invade Village of Ayr,' ibid., 9 Aug. 1949; 'Spring-knife Zooters Take Car, Leave Driver at Mosquitoes' mercy,' ibid., 10 June 1950.

41  *Star*, 17 Oct. 1949.

42  'Pape Avenue Riot' ibid., 6 July 1949.

43  'Recreation No Answer, Study of Gangs Shows Streamline Campaign,' ibid., 9 July 1949. None of the documents on this Welfare Council study found in the Metro Archives contains the lurid passages about girl delinquents, however; in fact the committee doing the study expressed scepticism about the dangerousness of gangs on a number of occasions in the spring of 1949. See memo from W.A. Turnbull to Commissioner of public Welfare, 30 March 1949; Minutes of Mayor's Conference on juvenile delinquency, 14 March 1949; and letter from commissioner of public welfare to P.G. Alapan, 4 March 1949, all in Metro Archives, RG 5.1, box 153, file 5.

44  One thinks here of the Marilyn Monroe characters in the classic films *Gentlemen Prefer Blondes* and *How to Catch a Millionaire*.

45  For one study of this opposition see Mariana Valverde, 'The Love of Finery: Fashion and the Fallen Woman in Victorian Social Discourses,' *Victorian Studies* 32, 2 (1989): 169–88.

46  On zoot-suit riots in the United States see Stuart Cosgrove, 'The Zoot-suit and Style Warfare,' *History Workshop* 18 (autumn 1984): 77–91.

47  The recommendations, with a preamble on the development of the committee, is found in the Minutes of Proceedings of the Council of the Corporation of the City of Toronto, 12 Jan. 1950, Appendix A.

48  'We live in troubled and difficult times and we should try to reduce these uncertainties, tensions and hostilities and thus, by attacking the major causes of juvenile delinquency, help to build anti-delinquent communities.' C.C. Goldring, Address to the Empire Club, 1954; Goldring Papers, box 1, unnumbered file.

49  The case files of training schools, as well as any records that might survive from the juvenile courts, are closed for 100 years to protect the privacy of people who may still be alive. Thus the only documents available in this area are annual reports of training schools, as well as newspaper accounts.

50  St Mary's Training School Report, 1949, in Report of the Department of Reform Institutions, AO.

51  Report of the Cobourg Training School for Girls, 1947, ibid., 26.

52  See for example, Report of St Joseph's School for Boys, 1949, ibid., 50–1.

53  Annual Report of the Department of Reform Institutions, 1948, 8.

54  Length of time served is provided only in the 1954 report, through which it becomes clear that girls unfortunate enough to be Catholic ended up serving much longer time than Protestant girls: the average stay at St Mary's was one year and ten months, compared with one year at Galt (formerly Cobourg). Ibid., 1954, 42.

55  More than half of the boys were also 'committed' or 'admitted' without any court appearance, but the proportion of girls without court appearance is much higher.

56  Annual Report of the Deptartment of Reform Institutions, 1948, 8. The comment about parents' mistaken belief is also found in the 1947 report.

57  The exact figures for girls admitted through a fault of their parents is not available, but one report mentions that some of the girls in the 'admitted' rather than 'committed' category are there owing to parental neglect, desertion, or vice. Report of St Mary's Training School for Girls, 1947, ibid., 53.

58  Report of the Cobourg Training School for Girls, 1948, ibid., 40.

59  Report of St Mary's Training School for Girls, 1947, ibid., 36.

60  Ibid., 1952, 34.

61  IQ reports are not found in every annual report. In 1947, however, 36 out of 88 girls at St Mary's were found to have below-normal IQs, compared with 39 out of 54 boys at St Joseph's. In 1949, out of 190 girls in both training schools, 69 were thought to be below normal intellectually. Annual Reports of the Department of Reform Institutions, 1947, 52, and 1949, 40 and 50.

62  Report of the Cobourg Training School for Girls, 1949, ibid., 38.

63  C. Goldring, 1941 Address to Assistant Schoolmasters, Goldring Papers, box 1, unnumbered file.

64  Report of the Royal Commission on Education in Ontario (RCEO), 1950, 165.

65  Ibid., 38–9 and 161–73.

66  The Ontario curriculum had British and imperial history in grades 8 and 9, and Canadian history only in grade 10; civics, however, was apparently combined not just with history but with geography. See Canadian Youth Commission, *Youth Speaks Out on Citizenship*, especially 163.

67  C. Goldring, Address to Commonwealth Teachers' Conference, Feb. 1955, Goldring Papers, box 1, unnumbered file.

68  Canadian Youth Commission, *Youth Speaks Its Mind*, 212.

69  Goldring, Address to Commonwealth Teachers' Conference.

70  Ibid. See also an article written by Goldring for the National Home and School publication, 1945, 'Education – A Factor in Building Canadian Citizenship.'

71  C. Goldring, 'Toward National Unity by Means of Education,' Sept. 1945, ibid., box 2, unnumbered file.

72  C. Goldring, 'Canadian Citizenship,' speech to Canadian School Trustees' Association, Sept. 1952, ibid., box 2, unnumbered file.

73  Report of the Royal Commission on Education, 28–31.

74  Ibid., 27.

75  C. Goldring, 'Education of Adolescent Girls,' Address to household science teachers, 1934, Goldring Papers, box 1, unnumbered file.

76  Royal Commission on Education, 136–7.

77  C. Goldring, 'Consumer Education,' Goldring Papers, box 1, unnumbered file.

78  Pierre Bordieu, *Distinction: A Social Critique of the Judgement of Taste* (Cam-

bridge, Mass.: Harvard University Press 1984). Bordieu's analysis of the formation of what he calls 'cultural capital' indicates that, unlike economic capital, cultural capital is not made up of the art objects or cultural performances one has or consumes; rather, it consists of a certain way of doing things, a style, a 'habitus,' only partially reflected in commodities. This reflects Goldring's view that the nation needed human qualities, not material things. See his views on consumer training, as well as note 71.

VERONICA STRONG-BOAG

# 'Their Side of the Story': Women's Voices from Ontario Suburbs, 1945–60

Released from the uncertainty and despair of the Great Depression and the Second World War, Canadians in the 1940s and 1950s dreamed of better times. At the centre of such aspirations for many thousands of women and men lay a suburban landscape where a non-wage-earning wife/mother presided over a home removed from both urban chaos and rural poverty. Ontario, the richest of the provinces, led the nation in experimenting with the suburban settings desired by an estimated 42.9 per cent of prospective house buyers in 1945.[1] Towns and cities, especially larger centres like Toronto, soon struggled to cope with the equivalent of a land rush as Queen's Park saw applications for subdivision planning approval jump from 100 to 1200 between 1945 and 1953 alone.[2] By 1956 the one-millionth Canadian house constructed since VE Day took shape as a three-bedroom bungalow in Scarborough's Wishing Well Acres.[3] Three years later, Etobicoke celebrated the construction of the *Star Weekly Magazine*'s first 'All-Canadian Home,' 'the pride' of its subdivision. The purchase of more than 1800 sets of plans of this one model and viewing by some 100,000 curious visitors offered further proof of suburbia's many attractions.[4]

As 'the trek to the suburbs turned into a stampede in the '50's,'[5] thousands of Ontario families purchased residences in communities like North York, where the population jumped 914 per cent from 1945 to 1962.[6] By the 1960s the suburbs, as Franca Iacovetta notes in her study of Toronto's Italian community, appealed to a wide range of the province's inhabitants.[7] Settled on the outskirts of cities, thousands of women and men experimented daily with an ideal that Humphrey Carver, a leading planner of the day, called 'the middle-class home-owning family ... detached ... self-contained and self-reliant, looking in upon itself and inhabiting a completely equipped autonomous dwelling.'[8] Ensconced in residences that offered unprecedented levels of comfort, suburbanites hoped to get on with the lives that the regimentation and deprivation of the 1930s and 1940s had derailed for so many. In the process, Ontario residents from a range of ethnic and class backgrounds attempted to attain the ideal of a nuclear family supervised on a daily basis by a wife and mother and financially maintained by a male breadwinner.

Despite their subsequent reputation for radicalism, the 1960s saw large numbers of Canadians continue to search for order and security, the good life, on the suburban frontier. Like many of my generation, some of my vividest memories of this decade spring from having joined Sunday crowds of home-seekers in touring open houses in new developments around Toronto. My family could never, however, afford to exchange the reality of cramped city apartments for expansive suburban dreams.[9] While it became fashionable in the 1970s to gentrify older areas and, not incidentally, displace poorer residents, suburbia has remained the option of choice for many householders in Ontario as elsewhere in Canada – its appeal, rooted in lower initial costs, larger lots, newer accommodation, and an idealized familism overseen by a mother/wife.[10]

## SUBURBIA'S CRITICS

Despite or perhaps because of this popularity, a baleful mythology has grown up around postwar suburban expansion.[11] Just as they stood at the centre of many families' suburban ambitions, women, or certain views of women, have rested at the core of much criticism. Indeed, as the commonplace designation 'bedroom' or 'dormitory' suburb suggested, the suburban landscape was symbolically constructed as pre-eminently female space. Men, creatures more it seemed of the centre city, farm, or resource frontier, were likely to appear almost as sojourners or even intruders on female terrain. This gendered landscape, pejoratively nicknamed Babbitt Bluffs, Herd Hollow, Pecksniff Properties, Hidebound Acres, Apathy Acres, Matriarchy Mills,[12] has proved an easy target. Suburban women in real places such as Don Mills, Oakridge Acres, Wishing Well Acres, Alta Vista, and Thorncrest have regularly become objects of casual scorn and dismissal. In particular, in the minds of most critics of mass society who flourished in the years after the Second World War,[13] the suburb emerged as the residential and female expression of the moral bankruptcy of the modern age, otherwise exemplified by giant corporations, big governments, and grey-clad 'organization men.'

Non-feminist critics have routinely targeted female suburbanites. In *The Mechanical Bride*, Marshall McLuhan dismissed 'millions of women who live isolated lives from 8:00 to 6:00 p.m.'[14] as constituting little more than millstones for their more industrious and interesting husbands. In 1956 in 'You Take the Suburbs, I Don't Want Them,' Toronto novelist Hugh Garner savaged a world in which his sex could not make all the rules.[15] Suburbia's psychological failings were typically diagnosed by the assistant director of Montreal's Mental Hygiene Institute. In 1958 Dr Alastair MacLeod warned Canadians that 'the suburbs give children fresh air, but take away their fathers. They give women efficient kitchens, but are hard on their femininity and gentleness. They give men pride in providing so handsomely, but drive many of them to drink to make up for their watered-down maleness.' This Canadian psychiatrist damned suburbs as 'matriarchies, manless territories where women cannot be feminine because expediency demands that they control the finances and fix drains and where night-returning men cannot be masculine because their traditional function of ruler and protector has been usurped.'[16] Such updating of the longstanding misogyny of much Freudian theory made female suburbanites simultaneously victims of modern urban development and self-serving predators on helpless husbands.

The indictment of Canadian social critics was elaborated most fully in a 1956 best-seller, *Crestwood Heights*, a case study of Toronto's Forest Hill, an 'inner suburb' built before the Second World War.[18] Dissecting the family lives of an upper-class sample of WASP (white, Anglo-Saxon Protestant) and Jewish Torontonians, the authors revealed what many opponents of mass society feared. Dissatisfied women wielded power in a community where they were the dominant adults for the daylight hours. Mothers were overly preoccupied with their offspring, to the detriment of themselves and their children. Both sexes were overly focused on material success, and their contributions to the wider society were intrinsically limited. For all its miscasting as a representative postwar community, upper-class Crestwood Heights rapidly became the measure by which suburbia as a whole was judged.[18]

To be sure, elements of this orthodoxy were occasionally challenged. In 1968 sociologist Samuel Clark produced an impressive study, *The Suburban Society*, which in its comparison of a wide range of communities all around Toronto countered presumed conformity with ethnic, class, and morphological diversity. Yet for all his stress on variety, Clark ultimately joined other critics of the modern landscape in casually stereotyping women residents as 'seeking amusement or instruction in light reading,' lonely and miserable, and a 'social waste.'[19] Rich or poor, Catholic or Protestant, British in origin or not, female suburbanites emerged again as a homogeneously sorry lot, deserving little serious attention from scholars or others.

Feminists have also joined in this condemnation of women's lives on the urban periphery. The most famous indictment of the day came from Betty

Friedan in *The Feminist Mystique.*[20] This soon-to-be classic identification of 'The Problem That Has No Name' captured the imagination of a generation and more of readers. More than anyone else, Friedan helped middle-class women challenge the egalitarian claim of North American abundance. Ultimately, she argued, and many readers agreed, the gendered experience of suburbia betrayed women, consigning them to subordination and frustration within society at large and unhappiness within the nuclear family. Limited options for women also meant an immeasurably poorer 'Free World,' a critical point when winning the Cold War was all important. In Canada, Friedan's dismissal of modern housekeeping as neither sufficiently dignified nor time-consuming to require full-time dedication by wives and mothers was matched by a barrage of popular articles in the 1950s.[21] Such disapproval has proved persistent. In the last decade of the twentieth century, postmodern feminists like Margaret Atwood, daughters of the 1950s generation, are still inclined to emphasize suburban women's complicity in society's overall failings.[22] Ultimately, Friedan and her successors, for all their support for broader interpretations and expressions of female ability, have had something in common with other, often misogynous, social commentators in their failure to credit suburban women with either sense or sensibility. The prevalence of this targeting from such a range of critics merits attention from today's feminist scholars, who ought to be only too familiar with how women frequently become the scapegoats for society's perceived failings.

THE VOICES OF SUBURBAN WOMEN

That women should be allowed to speak for themselves is a good guiding principle for this and other investigations. In 1959 *Chatelaine*'s readers responded passionately to attacks on suburban women. In more than 300 letters they captured the complexity of women's lives. In all, 42 per cent defended women, men, and suburbia itself, one critic bluntly summing up her assessment of misogynist attacks as 'Bunk.' A further 11 per cent of respondents blamed the problems of modern life on something other than suburbia, while 8 per cent gave it mixed reviews. The remaining 39 per cent agreed with much criticism of suburban women, but pointed out how social roles in general often limited women's opportunities, how lives were constructed out of a series of restricted options. Taken together, the tenor of the letters suggested a diversity of opinion and experience that was not as easily summed up as critics would have us believe.[23]

In the 1990s, as part of a larger project on Canadian suburbs, I am conducting interviews, circulating questionnaires, and receiving correspondence from veterans of Canadian suburbs in the years 1945–60. So far my sample includes twenty-six women and one man from Ontario. This small group is far from representative, produced as it from advertisements in the *Globe and Mail*, an interview with the CBC, and a developing word-of-mouth network. The bias is inevitably in favour of articulate, middle-class commentators.[24] The material is nevertheless suggestive in its introduction to women's own views of what happened in postwar Ontario. These voices, so long ignored, deserve a hearing before we can reconstruct in its totality, and not merely caricature, the suburban landscape that figured so large in the history of postwar Ontario.

The suburban veterans who contacted me in the 1990s have tried to make sense of what occurred in the day-to-day life of the 1940s and 1950s. They tell stories constructed through the uncertainties of human memory, the outcomes they live today, and the criticism and support that suburban sites have received both in the present and in the past. The demands of class, race, sexual orientation, and gender, among other identities, have been and are charted by women who, while they have never had absolutely free choice, have never been entirely passive. They have struggled to understand and manage prevailing ideologies and institutions in ways that make personal sense, offer a reasonable expectation of reward, and appear 'doable' given their resources.

Inevitably, some unknowable degree of self-silencing and silencing of others informs each narrative. While the reality of class is acknowledged in a number of accounts, chiefly through a sense of accomplishment rather than entitlement, racial and especially heterosexual advantage appears in contrast largely taken for granted. The apparently unproblematized nature of much privilege is a striking feature of what women are willing to tell. Ultimately, most seem exponents, and of course beneficiaries, of a view of Canada which makes the middle-class, the white, and the heterosexual citizen the measure of normality. Other experiences are for the most part ignored. These women cannot provide all the truths or describe all the consequences of the choice of suburban residences after 1945. Nevertheless, for all the limitations of these accounts, they offer a largely untold story. Their stress on the 'situatedness' and the context of women's choices tells careful listeners much more than many feminist and non-feminist critics of mass society have about why postwar Ontario committed so heavily to a suburban landscape.

WHY THE SUBURBS?

The choice of suburban sites was fundamentally shaped by the absence of realistic housing alternatives for many families after the Second World War.

Across the country, Canadians found little to rent or to buy at prices they could afford. Ottawa, provinces like Ontario, and a host of private builders and developers responded to the housing crisis with suburban solutions.[25] Only urban fringes commonly offered land cheap enough to tempt public policy-makers and to profit private interests. City centres, where space was frequently limited, expensive, and crowded, could rarely compete. Support from the Canadian Mortgage and Housing Corporation made mortgages on new suburban homes much more affordable than those available on older residences. While the Wartime Housing Corporation initially seemed to promise a high level of direct government involvement, real estate developers and private builders soon dominated the suburban housing market, offering home-hungry Canadians the opportunity to take on CMHC mortgages in communities like E.P. Taylor's Don Mills.[26]

Immigrants to the urban periphery in the 1940s and 1950s were desperate to exchange unsatisfactory accommodation for the promise of one-and-a-half store models, bungalows, and split-levels around Ontario's cities.[27] Many, like Gordon and Barbara, *Chatelaine*'s 1950 choice of Canada's typical bride and groom, had existed uncomfortably before their move. In their case they spent their first years together on the top floor of his family's house, sharing both a kitchen and a bathroom.[28] One correspondent told the happy story of leaving her RCAF veteran husband's parents' house, where they had lived from 1945 to 1949, for North York. Like many others, she stressed, 'we had no choice, we needed a house & had very little money.' Another commentator described financial constraints equally matter-of-factly: 'We could get more for our money living in the suburbs.' One woman explained a common experience in detail: 'The day we found our house there were three new subdivisions advertised in the *Toronto Star*. These were the first we had seen in our price-range. Good friends loaned us their car and minded our children while we drove out to see the house. We chose the first one we looked at because it had the largest lot, was close to a public school, and we much preferred the house plan. There were several houses in various stages of completion and the rest of the lots were just holes in the ground. We chose the next lot to be built on – this was early in Oct. and we moved in Dec. 29/50.'[29] For such Ontario families, the suburbs offered the most house at the least price.

Suburban choices were especially prized because Canadians had strong memories of bad times in the 1930s and 1940s. A writer explained: 'We were very poor in the depression – 8 people in a 4 room one storey house. So when we bought our home in 1951 – I was really excited to have a 5 room brick bungalow for the two of us. Such luxury!!'[30] These suburbanites had reason to feel good about substantially improving their living conditions in the

1950s. While they did not know it at the time, they were benefiting from the century's greatest gains in purchasing power.[31] The growth of suburban communities was a direct consequence of better times for wage-earners.

In recounting their experiences, women often communicated a particular sense of personal accomplishment. Unlike Friedan's enervated and privileged subjects who appeared to take little responsibility for the comforts around them, these women helped on the construction site, stretched pennies and dollars, and raised down-payments and monthly mortgages. They remembered full well making things happen for their families. Right after the purchase, money was likely to be especially tight, as couples caught up in childbearing and child-rearing struggled to match obligations with resources. No wonder housewives were self-conscious about overseeing budgets that 'were carefully crafted and followed to the letter.'[32] Suburbia's veterans had no hesitation in defending themselves as full partners, not parasites, in the construction of a fulfilling way of life. Their sacrifices and commitment help explain subsequent pride in suburban homes.

## FAMILISM

Central to almost all explanations of suburban choices was a dedication to what has been termed 'familism,' a life-style placing 'a high valuation on family living, marriage at young ages, a short childless time span after marriage, child-centeredness.'[33] Years of stress and fear made survivors desperate to get family lives on track again. As they remembered: 'After the depression, then a war, things seemed pretty good ... We were happy because the war was just over & we could settle down together & start our families.' Without exception, women stressed the high value they placed on family-centredness and child-rearing. The duties of her sex were typically summed up by one mother of three: 'My job was my home and family. This was our reason for marrying.' In an age where 'having a child' was often 'the thing to do,'[34] growing families made better accommodation an urgent priority. Initial choices, and occasionally later moves to bigger premises, met pressing life-cycle needs for the parents of what would become the 'baby boom.'

Couples often came to the suburbs in their late twenties or early thirties with at least one child; almost all added to their families while there. A better life for daughters and sons in the form of educational and recreational opportunities supplied the chief justification for remaining. A part-time clerical worker living in a 940-square-foot house in North York explained: 'My poor husband tried to ignore the 3 hours per day, 6 days a week, he would have to spend on public transportation, and we concentrated on the benefits for our children – the larger backyard, safe streets, and nearby school and playmates – and no more moves.' Calling on the suburbs in 1955, *Chatelaine* endeavoured to sum up a consensus: 'This is a land concerned with youth, for the majority of families who buy a home in the suburbs do so to provide free growing space for their children.'[35]

## CHILDBIRTH AND CHILD-REARING

In the suburbs women found acceptance of their commitment to family. Pregnancy, for example, seemed publicly taken for granted. Contemporary experts like Dr Marion Hilliard, chief of obstetrics and gynaecology at Toronto's Women's College Hospital, who hailed childbirth as her sex's 'highest fulfillment,' updated an older romanticism to include a new openness about the discussion and revelation of pregnancy. Women in Don Mills and other developments were encouraged to take pregnancy in stride. The fashion industry contributed the same message, encouraging mothers-to-be to dress 'in the modish maternity clothes of today and look proud and happy.'[36] Shyness and embarrassment, so much a feature of the past, were no longer deemed appropriate or necessary in settings liberated from traditional prejudices. Canada's suburban women, the epitome of modern freedoms, were expected to experience both personal fulfilment and social approval in pregnancy and child-rearing.

The postwar landscape, shunned by critics as boring and undifferentiated, produced major advantages for mothers of pre-schoolers. As a defender recalled, 'We baby sat for each other. The houses were identical so the babies didn't make strange. Everyone knew where the bathroom was. We rigged intercoms across the driveways. We reported fast delivery trucks.' The pioneering days of developments were especially likely to produce happy memories of shared predicaments: 'Nearly all of us had small children and it was a daylong job keeping them out of the mud and excavated house sites ... It was like a small village and we knew almost everyone.'[37] While a few reported finding such proximity intrusive, a majority of women's accounts suggested that the sense of community that developed in new locations reassured uncertain parents.

Echoing the conclusions of child-care experts of the day, many women were convinced that mothers were the best and most suitable persons to raise children. They alone had the interest and dedication needed to care for and guide daughters and sons. When instinct proved insufficient, correspondents consulted Dr Spock to deal matter of factly with emergencies. Some also remembered reading John Bowlby on maternal deprivation and

William Blatz on security, both authors likely to reinforce notions of maternal responsibility. Aid from community and relatives was cited less often. As one British newcomer recollected, however, neighbours sometimes proved invaluable: 'I was 13 years married before becoming a mother, so I had a lot to learn from my neighbours who were tried and true parents, and I would have been lost without them ... My neighbours were helpful to me in giving me the Canadian viewpoint and this did influence me, especially in school situations.' Women who worried about their 'ability to do a good job of mothering without any training in parenting,' and often far from relatives, believed they were helped by observing and discussing parenting with neighbours.[38] Such sentiments were understandable not only among Ontario's immigrant families but also among those who had torn up Canadian roots to seek new opportunities in the expanding suburban community.

The ages and numbers of children combined to supply the fundamental dynamic of many household routines. Children occupied mothers almost constantly. Babies and pre-schoolers in particular made substantial demands on maternal time and energy. The contemporary enthusiasm for maternal 'naturalness' in matters ranging from childbirth to feeding was made possible by and justified women staying at home.[39] For all their baby boom, new communities made little or no formal provision for 'under-sixes,' who were presumed the sole responsibility of stay-at-home mothers. Pre-school groups, organized largely by volunteer mums, remained unusual.

Suburban settings most obviously served girls and boys aged roughly six to thirteen. They were the particular clientele of both the public schools that rested at the heart of many developments and the Brownies, Cubs, Scouts, Guides, and other programs supported by churches and community centres. School-aged children, more than their younger siblings, put mothers into active contact with their neighbourhood. In discussing their experiences with me, women overwhelmingly credited the school as a major influence in their family lives, followed at some considerable distance by the church. The church, while critical in a few cases, was not rated as very important by most of my sample. As class 'mothers' and members of the Parent-Teacher Association, however, many women felt like active and knowledgeable members of  their community. For the most part, too, they to believed their contribution to elementary schools helped to make the suburbs a success for their generation.

In contrast, teenagers and high schools appear to have been less critical in integrating mothers into neighbourhoods. Indeed, the suburbs seem to have made little effort to respond to children once they left the primary system.

Like the schedules of pre-schoolers, those of teens were largely left up to individual parents. Mothers looked beyond their communities' borders to discover options for their older children, whose energies were preferably applied to educational, recreational, and cultural activities. Although adolescents are rarely credited with performing any significant work around the home, their subsequent success was evidently considered sufficient repayment for maternal labours.

While new settlements were seen as easening women's passage to motherhood, their children were often perceived as the chief beneficiaries. Larger houses, which often included individual bedrooms, plumbing and heating systems superior to any previously experienced, and an abundance of green space, were praised as 'an idyllic place for children.' Parents, who made sacrifices to get to the suburbs, today remain largely convinced that their offspring were happier and healthier than they would have been elsewhere. It was also believed that children were generally safer. From the perspective of the 1990s, with all the intervening recognition and publicity given child abuse, the immediate postwar years frequently seem 'a wondrous age of innocence for children with no adult predators, no speeding vehicles and very few non-local vehicles. We locked our homes only when we left ... Because stay-at-home moms were outside so much and visited often their protection for their own and others in an emergency was automatic. There were no street lights or sidewalks and children were not out alone at night.' In summing up the peacefulness of that time, a writer concluded, 'I never heard of a child molester until recently. Believe me, times have changed. Everywhere!' Such nostalgia, for whatever reason, ignored recurring evidence in the years following the Second World War of abuse by strangers, as well as by family and supposed friends.[40]

Survivors of the post-1945 years took it for granted that women would reap fulfilment in directing children from the cockpit of the private home while men fuelled the family enterprise with wages. They now treasure family stories, worn much in the telling, which provide humourous but telling illustrations of maternal stress. Such was the case with a suburban veteran who recalled: 'Shopping was a chore with three small children, and on one occasion my daughter let all of the budgies and canaries out of their cages in a Woolworth's store as I paid a clerk.'[41] It was hard to miss the message here that good mothering required patience, effort, and an abundance of good temper: it was, in other words, hard and demanding work. From the perspective of the 1990s, almost all women seemed preoccupied and largely satisfied with a female role firmly located in the nuclear family and centred on the raising of young children.

HUSBANDS

Children were especially important because wage-earning spouses were frequently away, either on a long day of work, which regularly stretched from 7 a.m. to 7 p.m., or on longer trips that required absences of days or weeks. The spectre of 'weekend husbands' surfaced constantly in female narratives of the suburbs.[42] Whatever domestic problems they created, male jobs of the day were viewed as extremely demanding. Female commentators would have sympathized with the Ontario businessman who complained to his doctor: 'I try to forget my problems when I leave the office. I want a leisurely dinner with my family and a quiet evening among pleasant friends. I want my home to relieve the tensions of the working day. But when I prepare for bed ... by the time my head hits the pills I've relieved every crisis of the day.'[43] As wives explained matter-of-factly:

I did the childrearing because my husband travelled a great deal.

He was never truly in the suburbs that much ...

My husband had long hours and a day off when the children would be in school, so I was in charge most of the time.

My husband was a typical 50s husband – his job was everything – and needed to be in order to make it.[44]

In postwar Ontario such conclusions were in keeping with the functionalist sociology of the day, which naturalized women's services as the home's expressive centre and men's instrumental role in the marketplace.[45]

In contrast to routine acceptance of men's work lives, some women like the author of 'An Open Letter to My Husband's Boss' rejected the corporate policies that intruded on the family.[46] Critics among the women writing to me also concluded that children in particular were shortchanged by 'workaholic' fathers. As two wives, whose husbands commuted into Toronto, the 'home of the Canadian brand of Organization Man,' recalled:

'My husband had nothing to do with the children. He didn't particularly want them, and told me if I did, they were MINE. And they are.'

My husband found the three children messy & boisterous & spent most of his time at the office.[47]

Such stories confirm not only the gendered but the contested nature of parenting in the 1940s and 1950s. In any case, whether absent by design or necessity, husbands were rarely regarded as the core of family life.

Nevertheless, while commonplace, the story of the absent and sometimes neglectful husband/father was not universal. A few men were presented as its antithesis. A working-class housewife remembered gratefully: 'My husband was very good with the children & had lots of patience. Every Sunday he'd take them to the park or the museum, so that I could have some time to myself.' And a well-to-do contemporary in London also championed her partner: 'My husband was a caring, sensitive wonderful father who skied, sailed, swam, made special trips back home for birthdays – was great fun! – changed diapers – cooked – cleaned – shared everything. He could teach some young fellows a few things even now. What a great guy!'[48] Such observations point to the difficulty of distinguishing what exactly generated good feelings about the suburban years: Was it good marriages that would have succeeded in many settings, or did the suburbs contribute something important to making these relationships work well? In any case, it is clear that some suburban fathers did participate actively and happily in child-rearing. The fact that it was structurally often difficult for them to do so, given the nature of their jobs, clearly made their wives appreciative of their 'voluntary' contribution to women's domestic realm.

With the exception of outdoor work, such as painting and lawn-mowing, fathers normally escaped regular responsibility for household labour. While a number of correspondents have changed their minds since the 1940s and 1950s, women in those days assumed that domestic tasks were ultimately theirs. There was also a strong sense from many commentators, as one librarian revealed, that the house was a privileged domain over which women relinquished rule with some reluctance:

Despite the fact that I was working full time I did most of the indoor work. Saturday mornings was housecleaning, laundry etc. while my husband played golf. I always liked to do the housework myself as it was done quickly without interruption. These were normal patterns for our household. I have never had a cleaning lady, though many of my neighbours had paid help. I never felt the need for it, nor did I feel I could let someone else come into my house and look after it for me.[49]

Paid assistance varied dramatically from one community to another, reflecting not so much individual inclination as relative financial resources. Most women reported no 'cleaning ladies' for themselves or their neighbours; they had perforce to take pride in their own work.

Wives who counted themselves fortunate, even if husbands did little child-rearing, commonly emphasized a strong sense of partnership and joint deci-sion-making. Buoyed up by a belief that men too were working hard for the family, albeit in a different setting, they remained confident of their subur-ban choices. These sentiments were summed up by one woman who remem-bered 'good years for us. My husband was getting ahead and I saw myself as a helpmate.' Another stated firmly in the same vein: 'We were all "regular folk" with various backgrounds and levels of education and knew that our fortunes would improve with our husbands' promotions.' Such confidence was rooted in many Canadians' experience of steadily increasing earning power and entry into the property-owning urban middle class in these years.[50]

### NEIGHBOURS

In communities where women were often the only adult inhabitants during the daylight hours, neighbours frequently emerged as a positive feature of the landscape. Nearby householders were described as being in much the same boat financially, and, less explicitly, of much the same general back-ground. Their familiarity was generally viewed as a good thing, enhancing opportunities for mutual aid and friendship, not to mention reinforcing prop-erty values. During a period in their life cycle when women were concentrat-ing on children, uncertainty in terms of neighbourhood dynamics was rarely regarded as an advantage. It made life a great deal less disturbing if those nearby, and their youngsters, could be predicted to respond in a familiar fash-ion, whether standards in discipline, cleanliness, or consumption be in ques-tion.

Relationships among women often formed quickly after the move. An inclusive sense of community was described by a long-time resident of Wil-lowdale: 'We all had lawns and gardens to put in so there was much visiting back and forth, and as new houses were built, and new occupants came, we added them to our group.' The importance of other wives in providing a foot-hold in the new environment was suggested in another account:

The first winter about a dozen of us met weekly in each other's homes, taking our pre-schoolers of course. We had tea and cookies, exchanged recipes, discussed the school, teachers, shopping facilities or lack of the same and other topics women always find to discuss. We formed a little club and paid in 25 cents each meeting and in the spring we all went out for dinner one night and left our husbands to cope with dinner and chil-dren. We had such a good time we made it an annual event for several years.[51]

The informality of most arrangements was illustrated by the apparent contradiction found in another reminiscence: 'We borrowed and lent and gave assistance needed, covering for absent Moms and taking children home to meals or off to picnics or hockey games. I knew of no co-op[erative] activity.'[52] Interaction was important, but it was also largely taken for granted as a logical extension of proximity among women. Such experiences, repeated a thousand times over in suburbs from one part of the province to another, fuelled memories of happy times.

The bridge games, coffee-klatching, and joint shopping expeditions routinely recalled by commentators on the postwar years served many purposes. Their real value was not always obvious, as a participant reminded sceptics: 'Women did get together separately, it was the only escape from household and child rearing chores. We used to call around and see who was ready to go to the shopping centre, not just for [the] sake of buying things, but to talk over any problems or concerns we had.'[53] Women similarly remembered visits from Avon 'ladies' meaning much more than an opportunity to purchase cosmetics. On their rounds, often of their own neighbourhoods, such saleswomen made their own contribution to sociability and information exchange. To be sure, relationships incorporated clients into patterns of mass consumption, but their success also occurred because they meant much more than sales.[54]

Testimonials to the significance of female networks were not universal. A small number of those contacting me lamented that 'with small children who had much social life?' Still more negative was the assessment, shared by several women, that 'the suburbs put blinders on women and separated them from other groups of women.' One woman criticized what she saw to be relentless pressure to consume, a competition fostered in gatherings from children's parties to baby showers.[55] Nevertheless, while not every commentator placed equal value on women getting together, it seems clear that opportunities for mixing did much to contribute to good feelings about the suburbs. Despite the symbolic and real isolation of single-family homes, pioneering, whether with children or in a landscape, fostered initial communication among women. In time the intensity of relationships often waned, but many suburban veterans reported continuing levels of interaction that several found meaningful and rewarding.

Although contentment with neighbours stemmed often from shared experience, such homogeneity could also sometimes be a source of concern. One critic voiced her unhappiness about the makeup of her suburban community: 'No poor people. No rich. No bachelors, or spinsters, or sharing singles. Not even grandmothers and grandfathers.'[56] While lack of diversity also often meant an absence of neighbours from different racial and religious groups, this at least was hardly new to Ontario settlements. Discrimination had long been the order of the day. Not until 1960 did Ottawa pass an order-in-council amending the National Housing Loan Regulations 'to prevent discrimination by merchant builders and rental entrepreneurs against any person on the grounds of race, colour, religion or origin.'[57] Even then, many postwar communities discouraged integration by the coolness, sometimes hostility, to suspect newcomers.

In the 1990s some suburban veterans were self-conscious about charges of uniformity. A resident of a community just west of Toronto defended herself and her neighbours in citing a spectacular, although undeniably unusual, case:

Our enclave was neither purely WASP nor dull. Our next-door neighbour was Olga, Grand Duchess of Russia, sister of Czar Nicholas. She moved as freely through the area as the children, knowing everyone and insisting that we all called her Olga. She had no interest in housework. One morning as 'dreary' I was on my knees waxing and polishing our precious hardwood floors, an obligatory duty each Friday, Olga opened the unlocked front door and arrived to visit. Her Russian military-issue rubber boots were wet and mud-caked. As droplets and drying particles fell, I wonder how one told a Grand Duchess to take off her dirty old boots.[58]

This story acknowledged the reality that postwar suburbs were not merely British enclaves. At least as clearly, it also reinforced the speaker's faith that her choice of residence was further legitimated by exotic arrivals who presumably had other housing options. The only other veteran to mention ethnic diversity referred positively to the cheerful activities of her blue-collar Italian neighbours in Cooksville, just west of Toronto. To those concerned by such matters, the entry of 'ethnic strangers' seemed proof that Ontario really did offer equal opportunity to all citizens and that suburban residence was largely determined by self-sacrifice and industry, not by privilege.

Nevertheless, despite some real tolerance, many women took comfort in the similarity of those around them. Ultimately, in dealing with the day-to-day of suburban life, they depended on a certain amount of shared experience and outlook. The need for support and assistance were likely to be especially urgent in the early days of settlement and for those with young families. Above all, female neighbours were resources to be called on in times of emergency. Their availability, unlike that of husbands, might well help women cope with strange environments and growing families. Neighbours whose habits and views could not be readily predicted, and trusted, were not as likely to be helpful. This practical reality reinforced the racism that few Canadian communities have escaped.

HOUSEWORK

Neighbourhoods changed over the years as repairs and renovations transformed houses to suit evolving family requirements. Women occasionally participated in exterior alterations, especially in gardens, but sometimes too with everything from building extensions to fences. More commonly, however, they assumed responsibility for the interior chores that kept homes running smoothly. These duties shifted in response to individual needs, product availability, and family finances. Over time, new furniture and appliances, especially washing machines, electric refrigerators, and wall-to-wall broadloom, changed the nature and amount of the domestic work women expected to perform. The wife of a tool-and-dye maker described what this meant in the 1950s: 'Housework took a long time because I had no vacuum cleaner; a wringer washer was finally purchased so that was a great help.'[59] The benefits of up-to-date appliances were self-evident to women who had waxed hardwood floors, stored food in an ice box, or struggled to wash clothing by hand.

Yet, in reflecting on their lives, women also recognized that expectations of cleanliness and tidiness grew with each technological addition to the home. Working with new domestic technologies, women implemented on a daily, time-consuming basis the improvements in families' standard of living which signified the passage from the more difficult times of early marriage and home-building. Notably, only one woman, who had waged employment, sent any cleaning out – her husband's shirts to a local laundry. For the most part significant family investments in consumer durables such as washing machines merely reinforced the long-standing view that work in the home was women's responsibility.[60]

Although women were unanimous in their positive response to new domestic technologies, they were acutely aware of the technical shortcomings of the wider environment. In particular, like many other suburbanites, they were extremely dissatisfied with their access to transportation.[61] Few suburban developments were served by regular public transit. Few families boasted two cars; indeed some at least initially had none. Getting to stores, with its routine lugging of children and groceries, loomed as the detested bugbear of many days. Despite the hyperbole accompanying the opening of commercial centres like Etobicoke's Humbertown in 1954,[62] not one correspondent claimed to enjoy shopping – a stark contrast to today's car sticker 'Born to

Shop.' The contrast between then and now was summed up in a bitter comment: 'I was homesick, bored, lonely, isolated and miserable. There was nothing to do and nowhere to go. The shopping centres were not enclosed then as they are today so when it got cold I had to remain indoors. I frequently thought death would be preferable to another Ottawa winter.' An English immigrant testified to commonplace frustration: 'Walked & pushed baby carriage to most places. Never had a second car – poor bus service especially with 3 children! ... Traffic was hazardous on highway & only route to major shopping centre.'[63]

Given such transportation problems, house-to-house delivery was welcomed. In addition to the convenience, these visits offered other advantages: 'We liked to see a vegetable man come along the street. Ice, milk and bread were delivered as were beer and pop. The Avon lady and the Fuller Brush man provided some new faces.' Such itinerant retailers connected households throughout the neighbourhood, offering one defence against isolation. No wonder *Chatelaine* found an enthusiastic audience when it took a fashion show to Don Mills in 1959; as spectators explained, 'it's practically impossible to get to the stores.'[64] Such difficulties encouraged the purchase of second cars, and, in the 1960s, the move of retailers to suburban locations. Even then, suburban sprawl continued to penalize women endeavouring to meet family needs.

The 'tight' finances that characterized the early years in many suburban homes meant that many women made considerable effort to stretch the dollar. Women routinely passed on baby clothes, bought cheap cuts of meat, sewed their own and children's outfits, and improvised for furniture. As one person fondly indicated, women got 'together, exchanging ideas to make things go further.' Not all such strategies seemed merely a matter of necessity. Women prided themselves on being thrifty housewives and good managers of happy households. Slip-covering aging furniture, not to mention painting and carpentry, were causes of pride. In reflecting on their diversity of skills, women stressed their contribution to the marital partnership. They 'found cooking, cleaning, washing, gardening and children filled' their days. 'Suffice to say,' insisted one commentator, 'the day just went on 'til bedtime!' These women wanted to be remembered as holding up their end of a marital partnership. For the most part, suburban veterans did not require waged work in order to feel a sense of accomplishment.[65]

Not surprisingly, satisfaction with the gendered division of labour was especially marked among women who were able to make time for themselves. They might work hard, but they reaped substantial rewards. So at least concluded two veterans of Toronto and London:

The satisfaction gained from keeping a happy family well cared for was sufficient for us. After all with small homes and regular schedules, we had hours each day to read, write, study, parent, do handwork, or anything we wished to improve ourselves. These new or improved skills could be used later when children no longer came from school for lunch or lived at home.

I was well organized & did all the housework before noon, including dinner preparation. I spent, then, most of the afternoon, drawing, painting or reading.[66]

Such experiences suggested an optimal outcome, far removed from the struggle of day-long work remembered by some and the meaningless parasitism pilloried by *The Feminine Mystique*. These women gained significant personal advantages from their investment in the gendered and class politics of the day. From their point of view, postwar Ontario provided ample rewards for intelligence, efficiency, and industry in its citizens. Only those without these qualities were in trouble.

PAID WORK

The sense of unlimited opportunity conveyed by these accounts was not, however, universal even among my contacts. Many commentators felt pressed to fulfil all their obligations. In addition, many searched for jobs, frequently part-time, which could accommodate urgent family demands.[67] Money-making was on many women's minds. Typing skills were regularly put to use, as one entrepreneurial account suggests: 'A friend asked me if I would do secretary work at home if they supplied me with a Dictaphone. I agreed, typed for several companies and had enough work that I hired a couple of neighbours to help.'[68] Such suburbanites often enjoyed their part-time jobs, finding new stimulation and company. Teachers, librarians, and other professionals appeared especially satisfied, no doubt reflecting their relative privilege in the labour market.

Yet, for most, drudgery was rarely far off. As one veteran remembered, only the prospect of cash justified some initiatives: 'All my friends tried to earn a little extra money, to re-finish the cupboards, to get a new light fixture or put a folding door on the dining room. One typed envelopes for a mail-order place. I typed up a 3 x 5 card for every dry-cleaners listed in the Yellow Pages.'[69] In more than a few cases, suburbia's better life, the difference between mere survival and the comfort of holidays, new furniture, and better education for the children, was secured by the waged work of middle-class women outside the home.[70] Since they also remained responsible for managing happy households, most woman had little leisure to invest in self-improvement activities.

A second shift for wives and mothers required continuing support and negotiation, all the more so as many husbands were embarrassed by spouses toting pay cheques. Men's practical help was rarely mentioned by wage-earning women. Existing community networks seemed more likely to be put to use and solutions to child-care dilemmas continued to be sought locally:

The first women who went out to work in our suburb were the two school teachers who had access to the family car. My next door neighbour and myself each minded their two babies for the next few years until they became pregnant again ... As years went by and transportation improved and the children grew older, many of the women with only 1 or 2 children did go back to work – usually arranging for after-school care with neighbours.

Aside from child care, hired domestic assistance was commonly sought outside the suburb itself. 'Cleaning ladies' normally came in once a week by bus or streetcar, though there were exceptions: 'My cleaning lady was my neighbour across the street, whose husband had left her to bring up their two boys on her own and her only marketable skill was housework so she was pleased to have a job once a week so close to home.' For the most part, however, women performed their own domestic tasks, taking pride in their accomplishment and with limited funds or willingness to pay substitutes to do 'their' work.

Attitudes to so-called working wives and mothers varied among the correspondents. One former resident of Rexdale said straightforwardly: 'We saw working mothers as selfish – putting themselves ahead of the children they brought into this world.' Much the same observation was made by a housewife from Willowdale, albeit with an important caveat: 'No neighbour did paid work within the home that I can remember, and I didn't. Money seemed sufficient. We were generally pretty financially secure – not rich but could manage. Working mothers tended to be looked down on – but never by me if the money was needed and the children were well looked after.' For some women the issue was never a matter of debate. After the arrival of children the matter was effectively settled: 'It was felt that if you had children it was your responsibility to stay home and look after them. We never had money to spare, but were happy just to have a place of our own.'[72] This last speaker's stress on economy was typical of those who felt that at least some women worked for wages when 'real' need did not exist. From this point of view, it was far better to be satisfied with fewer material possessions and to keep mothers at home.

At least as often, the highly personal nature of the decision to take employment was stressed. One employed wife and mother described her anger at criticism:

Working mothers were accepted as part of life, it was considered a very personal decision to go back to work. My own experience when I went back to work after the birth of my first child, was heightened by the fact that one of the women in my department took it upon herself to lecture me in front of the whole staff, about leaving my son at home while I went back to work. I always resented that invasion of what was to my husband and I a joint decision that I go back to work for a while to help out with finances.

*good*

Another relatively well-off contemporary who did not return to the paid labour force, although she was an active volunteer, also concluded that the decision to take a job was ultimately practical and personal: ˙

I honestly don't think there were debates about working mothers. Women who worked in services, factories or baby-sitting did so because their husbands were blue-collar workers and that was understood. My physician was a woman with four children matching mine in age. She was also a good friend, and I don't think anyone ever felt negative about her role, i.e., that she was neglecting her family.

The same respondent, nevertheless, could not entirely ignore the reality of discrimination, admitting revealingly: 'Most of the women professors I knew were single in those days.'[73] As this respondent hinted, employment in male-dominated professions was rarely a realistic option for wives wherever they lived.

Making sense of memories about working wives and mothers some thirty and forty years after the fact is not easy. Naturally, women have been informed by the outcome of their own choices and those of their daughters' generation, not to mention feminist reassessments. What does seem clear is these suburbanites' pre-eminent commitment to home and family, to the ideology of familism. They had initially chosen suburbs because of their promise for family life and child-rearing, and to a large extent this reason still seemed valid. Whether they planned or even loved to work outside the home had not been key to setting up house in new neighbourhoods. Indeed, in most cases, paid labour was made additionally difficult. As one woman observed ironically: 'My husband's occupation was THE determining factor of where we'd live, and always has been. In fact, any jobs I had after marriage were simply found somewhere along his route from home to work, so that he could drop me off and pick me up. Otherwise, how would I have been home on time to cook his dinner?'[74] An essentially familialist position still dominates memories. It largely explains the commonplace ambivalence about wage-earning mothers. Children, and the maintenance of the home, were women's overriding responsibilities.

## MAKING PERSONAL SENSE OF THE SUBURBS

In thinking about their days in Ontario's suburbs, women in my survey were also asked about feminism, particularly with respect to women's organizations of the day and Friedan's *The Feminine Mystique*. Most observed that explicit feminism was rarely visible in the 1940s and 1950s. With the exception of work for the Home and School or Parent-Teacher Association, women's 'involvement' in lobbying or activist organization was, they agreed, 'more a social role ... often a behind-the-scenes role.' One contributor elaborated, 'Women were helpmates to their men in public life, playing low-key roles in hospitality and behind the scenes. "Behind every good man is a good woman" covered the subject perfectly.'[75] Not surprisingly, no female politicians or activists were singled out for comment by contributors.

During the decades after the Second World War, the women I contacted were at stages in the family life cycle which required heavy commitments of time and energy. None, with the possible exception of two active in the YWCA, appear to have been known publicly beyond their own community. Their generally low profile was explained several times: 'I was not a group-activity person and was pretty much preoccupied with my young family and responsibilities.' Another commented, 'I have been quite content as a homemaker and after marriage expected to be home and raising a family.' Such women also often admitted being relatively sheltered, both in a fulfilling marriage and from economic hardship. It appeared fairly easy for them to be 'pretty happy with the status quo,'[76] which left them heavily committed to child care and family life.

While some commentators did not recall either reading Friedan or being aware of feminism in general, a few remembered being disturbed but powerless. 'I knew it; but there was no energy or time to do anything about it,' summed up some feelings. Other women were hesitant to espouse feminist issues for fear of retribution or ridicule: 'I was intrigued by feminist things but was hesitant about agreeing with them in public. I was afraid of being laughed at by both women and men. I am a feminist now.' Another woman commented:

I was afraid of that book [*The Feminine Mystique*]. I read it in very small snatches, because it stirred me greatly, and I couldn't see any purpose to that. There I was, a relatively uneducated woman with two small children to raise – hardly in a position to stick a flag in my navel and to lead the parade. I would get myself into a quiet internal resentful rage, and then it would take me a whole day to calm down and stop banging the pots and pans around.[77]

Such frustration appears to have found few outlets in suburban communities. For the most part, the residents of these communities found satisfaction and rewards in their commitment to a domestic bargain that left women primarily responsible for family life and their husbands for bread-winning. For such women the organized feminism of the day, with its concentration on issues of the paid workplace,[78] was especially uninteresting.

For all the lack of interest in collective analysis and action by women, many insisted that they had found satisfactory ways of asserting their own individuality. They had not felt powerless or oppressed in their choices as women. Some women even considered themselves feminists in postwar Ontario and today:

I've always been a feminist. To reconcile that with my acceptance of my role as a wife/mother may be difficult to others, but logical to me. I believe each of us should be the best we can be, and equal pay for equal valued work must surely come soon. In the years my husband spent weekdays away and I was responsible for the children and home alone, I was quite confident I could do that. If I went away for a weekend my husband could cover equally well. I could chair a Home and School meeting, plan a fun fair, anniversary party or write to the editor of a newspaper. It is mild compared to today's feminism but it was worthwhile then.

As an artist, I work alone – most of my friends were back at university – we weren't typical – all of us had plans for what we would do when our children were grown. We looked ahead to freer days. We assumed responsibility for ourselves – we disliked any sort of grants or handouts. We were very bright independent women – We were all quite fascinated by 'The Feminine Mystique' but, we were already in charge of our lives & didn't feel abused ... Child-rearing was just one delightful aspect of life – in such a big wonderful world I foresaw numerous avenues open to me in the future – work, travel, etc. ... I was always a feminist. I always said, pleasantly to men, 'Why of course, my dears' and then went on & did exactly as I pleased. Poor things, what do men know. As a little girl, aged 6 or so, growing up with grandparents, father, & aunts & uncles at home before they married, I observed, that the men made a great deal of noise about nothing & the women smiled & did as they pleased. I had wonderful women role-models.[79]

Characteristic of such accounts is a strong sense of individual competence, but also a distinct failure to acknowledge privilege. In large measure such women appear to have accepted both the ideology of innate differences between women and men, with the attendant division of interests and duties, and the liberal faith that capitalism, except for some anomalies that afflicted women, offered effective equality of opportunity. This optimistic vision was sustained by the economic growth of these years which saw unprecedented gains in the standard of living of many citizens.

Their essential liberalism, as much as their heavy domestic duties, helps explain why my correspondents rarely expressed their remembered feminism in collective action or assistance to other women in less comfortable circumstances. Sometimes only a traumatic experience, such as a neighbour who in loneliness and despair murdered her own children, could move relatively privileged women to action, in this case to the founding of mothers' support groups.[80] Unless such an event occurred, most women, whether content with their lot or intimidated by the world around them, worked quietly on the home front to realize more personal aspirations. By sustaining happy families and cohesive neighbourhoods, most believed they had done their share of the world's work. Such women felt little need to assume roles beyond the local school or church. Still more they felt no need to apologize to feminist critics or to take second place to their husbands in the world's estimation.

This sample of female voices from Ontario's suburban past helps us to understand women, an age, and a place which have often been discredited – in matters ranging from equality rights to the environment. Some survivors shared that conclusion. More often, however, women tried to contextualize their experience of the suburbs in terms of their commitment to familism. Children and the family were their first and most satisfying priorities. Many claimed to find no contradiction between equality for the sexes and a gendered division of labour within marriage. Revealingly, not one indicated that alternatives, either to suburbia or to wife-hood and motherhood, were apparent. When they looked around them, especially in comparison with their parents' generation, they felt satisfied with the middle-class lives they had largely attained. Today, as these suburban veterans observe their daughters, both their successes in finding good jobs and egalitarian spouses and their failures in ending labour market discrimination and solving child-care dilemmas, they often label themselves feminist too. Such feminism nevertheless appears to be, as it was for most of them in the decades after the Second World War, essentially liberal and essentialist. Such a perspective, coincident as it was with many of the dominant values

of modern Canada, empowered many women who were abl.
suburbia's gendered landscape.

From these accounts, postwar suburbia emerges as a relatively quiet
moment in the twentieth century, when some fortunate citizens experimented with constructing domestic worlds safe from depression and war.
That 'nesting' impulse seems little different from the 'cocooning' that some
observers noted in the conservative 1980s. Veterans of both experiments conscientiously devoted themselves to private rather than public pursuits. The
recovery of women's voices from the 1940s and 1950s helps tell us why this
was so.

NOTES

My thanks to Joy Parr and other authors in this volume for their thoughtful comments on an earlier draft. This discussion of the 1940s and 1950s has also benefited from conversations with friends and colleagues in sociology, Gillian Creese,
Jane Gaskell, and Arlene Tigar McLaren.

1 Maclean-Hunter, *The Housing Plans of Canada* (Toronto 1945), 15.

2 'Analysis of Planning Survey Material,' *Ontario Planning*, March 1955, 8.

3 'Million Mark Reached,' *Canadian Builder*, Oct. 1956, 41.

4 'First All-Canadian Home Completed in Etobicoke,' *Star Weekly Magazine*, 12
Sept. 1959; 14–18. See also 'A Runaway Best-Seller ... that Was Last Year's All-
Canadian Home,' ibid., 9 April 1960, special section, 15.

5 David Macdonald, 'Farewell to the Fifties,' ibid., 2 Jan. 1960, 24.

6 H.J.A. Reitsman, 'North York. The Development of a Suburb' (MA thesis, University of Toronto 1962), 44.

7 See Franca Iacovetta, *Such Hardworking People: Italian Immigrants in Postwar
Ontario* (Montreal and Kingston 1992), 56–7.

8 Humphrey Carver, *Cities in the Suburbs* (Toronto 1962), 99.

9 Carver estimated that, in 1961, 30–40 per cent of Canada's urban families lacked
the minimum annual income of $4000 necessary for them to purchase 'a new
N.H.A. home in the suburbs.' Ibid., 105.

10 On the continuation of suburbia's appeal into the last half of the twentieth century
see, for the United States, Kenneth T. Jackson, *Crabgrass Frontier: The Suburban-
ization of the United States* (New York and Oxford 1985).

11 For discussion of this myth see Peter McGahan, *Urban Sociology in Canada* (Toronto 1986), 216–22.

12 'Odds and Ends,' *Canadian Architect*, Nov.–Dec. 1955, 13.

13 For one of the rare discussions of these critics in Canada see Paul Rutherford,
*When Television Was Young: Primetime Canada, 1952–1967* (Toronto 1990),

especially chapter 1. For a provocative and convincing assessment of the connection between fears about mass society and the maintenance of masculinity see Barbara Ehrenreich, *The Hearts of Men* (Garden City, NY 1983).

14 Marshall McLuhan, *The Mechanical Bride: Folklore of Industrial Man* (New York 1951), 76.

15 *Maclean's*, 10 Nov. 1956, 3.

16 'The Sickness of Our Suburbs,' *Chatelaine*, Oct. 1958, 23, 94–5.

17 John Seeley, A.A. Sim, and E.W. Loosley, *Crestwood Heights: A Study of the Culture of Suburban Life* (Toronto 1956).

18 See Robert Olson, 'What Happened to the Suburb They Called Crestwood Heights?' *Maclean's*, 12 Oct. 1956, 24–5, 34–6, 38. The strength of this legacy can be seen in the incorrect identification of Crestwood Heights as Don Mills in McGahaw, *Urban Sociology*, 187.

19 Samuel D. Clark, *The Suburban Society* (Toronto 1968), 4.

20 (New York 1963).

21 See Richard Roe, 'I'm Sending My Wife Back to Work,' *Canadian Home Journal*, April 1954, 4–5, 93; Jean Pringle, 'How I Broke Out of Solitary Confinement,' *Chatelaine*, May 1948, 34; Beverly Gray, 'Housewives Are a Sorry Lot,' *Chatelaine*, March 1950, 26–7, 37; Isabel T. Dingman, 'A Widow Writes an Open Letter to Wives,' *Chatelaine*, June 1954, 20–1, 34–5, 37; Dr Marion Hilliard, 'Stop Being Just a Housewife,' *Chatelaine*, Sept. 1956, 11, 90; Patricia Clark, 'Stop Pitying the Underworked Housewife,' *Maclean's*, 19 July 1958, 8, 37–8; James Hamilton, 'Housewives Are Self-Centred Bores,' *Star Weekly Magazine*, 22 Aug. 1959, 38, 45.

22 Margaret Atwood, 'There Was Once,' *This Magazine* 26, 3 (1992): 21. On Atwood and postmodernism see Linda Hutcheon, *The Canadian Postmodern: A Study of Contemporary English-Canadian Fiction* (Toronto 1988), chapter 7.

23 See Strong-Boag, '"Home Dreams": Women and the Suburban Experiment in Canada, 1945–60,' *Canadian Historical Review* 72, 4 (1991): 501–4.

24 Nor did all contacts provide the same amount of information. Twenty completed detailed forms with questions ranging from house design to family background, division of labour, and childrearing views. Three gave extensive interviews to accompany the seventeen-page questionnaire. Six women and one man communicated only by letter, with these contributions ranging in length from one to four pages.
    The twenty-seven individuals represented many of Ontario's major urban centres: what is now Metropolitan Toronto (22), London (3), Ottawa (3), Niagara Fall (1), and Hamilton (1). Eight began suburban living in the 1940s, and twenty in the 1950s. While data were not sufficient to assess everyone fully, and thus numbers don't add up to twenty-seven, a relatively clear picture emerged of this group. In

terms of country of birth, seventeen were Canadian-born, four from the British Isles, three from the United States, and one from Europe. The women were also relatively well educated. Ten had some or all high school; two had business college; four had some university; eight had a BA or better. Most women had some experience in the paid workforce before marriage: eleven as clerical/sales workers, four as teachers, two in social work, and two as librarians. Thirteen worked, often part-time, at some point after marriage, usually as clerical workers and, less frequently, as teachers. A substantial majority, or twenty, could generally be judged as in receipt of a middle-class family income by virtue of the male bread-winner's employment as a white-collar business employee or a professional. Only two families seemed clearly working class, with one husband a tool-and-die maker and the other a low-paid employee in an industrial operation. In the last two cases, one wife found paid employment after her children were older and one remained at home. The numbers of children varied from one to four, including one case of two adopted offspring. Only six women reported any paid help with home and child-care, and five of these women worked outside the home. In contrast, most correspondents didn't know anyone with a 'cleaning lady' or paid household help of any kind. They were also similar in that twenty-one reported supporting their local home-and-school or parent-teacher organization, both through attendance at meetings and, frequently, in undertaking executive duties. In addition, four women did regular volunteer work in their children's classrooms, and five assisted with Sunday schools, Cubs and Scouts, and Brownies and Guides through their churches. Four or so also volunteered elsewhere as well, notably with hospital auxiliaries. With few exceptions, however, most found domestic work and child care a heavy responsibility that provided little opportunity for other sustained endeavours. Today, most remain married to the same person. Several are widowed, and several more are divorced or separated. In reflecting on their lives, twenty of the female commentators were substantially positive about their experience, while seven concluded that they, and others, were sometimes losers. The women who answered the questionnaire asked to specify how they wished to be identified, whether anonymously with reference to their community or by name, and their choice is reflected in the notes to this article.

25 See Albert Rose, *Canadian Housing Policies, 1935-1980* (Toronto 1980).

26 On Don Mills see Joan Simon, 'Don Mills – Idealism and Speculation,' *Dimensions of Canadian Architecture: Society for the Study of Architecture in Canada: Selected Papers* 6 (1983): 31–3, and John Saywell, 'Don Mills: E.P. Taylor and Canada's First Corporate Suburb,' *City Magazine* 2, 3 (1977): 28–38.

27 This crisis is vividly portrayed in the newspapers of the day. See 'No Home, Six Live in Tent "Feel Just Like Animals,"' *Toronto Star*, 8 April 1946; 'Over 100 in Trailer Camps Ready to Resist Eviction,' ibid., 24 April 1947; 'Rent Jump Over

100 P.C. Profiteers – Fishleigh 5,000 Facing Eviction,' ibid. 24 April 1949; 'Proceed with Disputed Homes,' *Scarboro Mail*, 11 Aug. 1949; '3 Families Face Eviction with No Place To Go – Fenning,' *Etobicoke Press*, 2 Oct. 1947; 'Scarboro Has Growing Pains,' *The Enterprise*, 28 April 1949; John Clare, 'Where Are the Houses?' *Star Weekly Magazine*, 8 June 1946.

28 See Wilma Tait, 'Bride with A Future,' *Chatelaine*, April 1950, 31, 44, and J.C. Smith, 'First Home – Doll Size,' ibid., 53.

29 North York respondent 2, 'Canadian Women and the Suburban Experience 1945–60: Questionnaire for Residents' (henceforth Questionnaire), to author (1991–2), 16; Toronto respondent 2, Questionnaire, 4; North York respondent 1, Questionnaire, 4.

30 Hazel Boneham, Questionnaire, 5.

31 See 'Seven Decades of Wages Changes' (Statistics Canada), as cited in 'Big Gains Gone with the Big Bopper: '90s Are a Wipe Out,' *Vancouver Sun*, 9 June 1993.

32 Lois Margaret Strong, Questionnaire, 15.

33 Wendell Bell, 'The City, the Suburb, and a Theory of Social Choice,' as quoted in McGahan, *Urban Sociology*, 219–20, and Richard Harris, '"Canada's All Right": The Lives and Loyalties of Immigrant Families in a Toronto Suburb, 1900–1945,' *Canadian Geographer/Le Géographe canadien* 36, 1 (1992): 13–30.

34 North York respondent 2, Questionnaire, 17; Lois Strong, Questionnaire, 16; Max Braithwaite, 'New Baby – A Cure for Middle Age,' *Chatelaine*, Nov. 1950, 60.

35 North York respondent 1, Questionnaire, 2; 'How Chatelaine Went Calling on the Suburbs,' *Chatelaine*, March 1955, 1.

36 Marion Hilliard, *A Woman Doctor Looks at Love and Life* (Toronto 1957), 20; Frank Moritsugu, 'The Amazing Don Mills,' *Canadian Homes and Gardens*, Dec. 1954, 56.

37 Toronto respondent 2, Questionnaire, 10; personal correspondence, Anne Lapp to author, 19 May 1991.

38 On maternal deprivation see Dr Alastair MacLeod, *Chatelaine*, June 1957, 11, 44–6, 48–9, and Phyllis Lee Peterson, 'Letter to My Daughter-in-Law,' ibid., Oct. 1957, 18, 40–3; Jocelyn Raymond, *The Nursery World of Dr. Blatz* (Toronto 1991), and, on Bowlby, Bob Mullan, *Are Mothers Really Necessary?* (London 1987); Don Mills respondent 2, Questionnaire, 8; West Toronto respondent 1, Questionnaire, 18.

39 See, for example, Anna-Marie Klinkenberg, 'I Had My Baby at Home,' *Star Weekly*, 19 Sept. 1959, 46.

40 London respondent 3, Questionnaire, 5; Strong, Questionnaire, 10; Kathleen Cobban, Questionnaire, 10; on strangers, see Lotta Demsey, 'We the People vs. the Sex Criminal,' *Chatelaine*, Jan. 1948, 6, and, on the family, Sylvia Fraser, *My Father's House: A Memoir of Incest and Healing* (Toronto: Doubleday, 1987). For

an important discussion of the misleading preoccupation with strangers see Karen Dubinsky, *Improper Advances: Rape and Heterosexual Conflict in Ontario, 1880–1929* (Chicago and London: University of Chicago Press, 1993).

41 Alaine Barrett Baines, Questionnaire, 13.

42 Ibid., 16.

43 Patricia Lamong, 'Why You Can't Sleep,' *Canadian Homes and Gardens*, Jan. 1955, 19. See also Isabel T. Dingman, 'A Widow Writes an Open Letter to Wives,' *Chatelaine*, June 1954, 20–1, 34–5, 37; Bruce Lee, 'Does Your Husband Work Longer than You?' *Star Weekly*, 11 Aug. 1956, 9 and Jean Libman Block, 'Husbands Should Not Do Housework,' ibid., 16 Nov. 1957, 6, 33.

44 Toronto respondent 2, Questionnaire, 8; Baines, Questionnaire, 6; Lapp, Questionnaire, 8; West Toronto respondent 2, Questionnaire, 8.

45 See Strong-Boag, 'Home Dreams,' 476–9.

46 Mrs John Doe, 'An Open Letter to My Husband's Boss,' *Canadian Home Journal*, May 1954, 10–11, 93, 93.

47 Carver, *Cities in the Suburbs*, 21; Toronto respondent 4, Questionnaire, 16.; Personal correspondence, Don Mills respondent 1 to author, 6 April 1991.

48 Hazel Boneham, Questionnaire, 8; London respondent 3, Questionnaire, 8;

49 Don Mills respondent 2, Questionnaire, 6.

50 Toronto respondent 2, Questionnaire, 17; Strong, Questionnaire, 16; see 'Seven Decades of Wages Changes' (Statistics Canada)' and Strong-Boag, 'Canada's Wage-earning Wives and the Construction of the Middle Class, 1945–60,' *Journal of Canadian Studies*, forthcoming.

51 Lapp, Questionnaire, 7; North York respondent 2, Questionnaire, 7.

52 Strong, Questionnaire, 7.

53 Don Mills respondent 2, Questionnaire, 14.

54 On the complex relationship between female sales personnel and female customers, albeit for an earlier period, see the fascinating *Counter Cultures: Saleswomen, Managers and Customers in American Department Stores, 1890–1940* (Urbana and Chicago 1986).

55 North York respondent 2, Questionnaire, 8; Toronto respondent 2, Questionnaire, 12; personal correspondence, Ottawa respondent 2 to author, 30 April 1991.

56 Toronto respondent 4, Questionnaire, 29.

57 'New Anti-Discrimination Legislation,' *Ontario Housing*, Feb. 1961, 3.

58 Personal correspondence, Lois Strong to author, 29 May 1991.

59 Boneham, Questionnaire, 6.

60 For an elaborate discussion of this point see Ruth Schwartz Cowan, *More Work for Mother: The Ironies of Technology from the Open Hearth to the Microwave* (New York 1983).

61 See also McGahan, *Urban Sociology*, 226.

62  See 'Reeve Lewish Launches "Humbertown,"' *Etobicoke Press*, 11 Nov. 1954, 2.

63  Personal correspondence, Marjory Henly to author, 2 April 1991; Don Mills respondent 1, Questionnaire, 9.

64  Toronto respondent 2, Questionnaire, 12; quotation cited in Rosemary Box, 'A Spring Fashion Bazaar for Suburban Living,' *Chatelaine*, March 1955, 14.

65  Toronto respondent 3, Questionnaire, 2; West Toronto respondent 2, Questionnaire, 12; Baines, Questionnaire, 6; Dorothy Manning, 'I Quit My Job to Save My Marriage,' *Chatelaine*, June 1955, 16–17, 78–80, and Sheila Stringer Coe, 'I Won't Be a Working Wife,' *Weekend Magazine* 7, 7 (1957): 9–11, 36.

66  North York respondent 2, Questionnaire, 15; London respondent 3, Questionnaire, 6.

67  For important discussions of the significance of married women's paid employment in these years see the articles by Franca Iacovetta and Joan Sangster in this volume.

68  Lapp, Questionnaire, 16.

69  Toronto respondent 4, Questionnaire, 24.

70  See Strong-Boag, 'Canada's Wage-earning Wives.'

71  North York respondent 2, Questionnaire, 16; North York respondent 1, Questionnaire, 6.

72  Toronto respondent 4, Questionnaire, 24; Cobban, Questionnaire, 16; Boneham, Questionnaire, 16.

73  Don Mills respondent 2, Questionnaire, 16; Baines, Questionnaire, 16. On female university professors see also Alison Prentice, 'Bluestockings, Feminists or Women Workers? A Preliminary Look at Women's Early Employment at the University of Toronto,' *Journal of the Canadian Historical Association* (1992).

74  Toronto respondent 4, Questionnaire, 5.

75  Baines, Questionnaire, 15; Strong, Questionnaire, 15.

76  Baines, Questionnaire, 15; Lapp, Questionnaire, 15; Baines, Questionnaire, 15.

77  West Toronto respondent 2, Questionnaire, 15; Toronto respondent 2, Questionnaire, 15; Toronto respondent 4, Questionnaire, 23.

78  See Shirley Tillotson, 'Human Rights Law as Prism: Women's Organizations, Unions, and Ontario's Female Employes Fair Remuneration Act, 1951,' *Canadian Historical Review* 72,4 (1991): 532–557, for some examples of contemporary feminism.

79  Strong, Questionnaire, 16; London respondent 3, Questionnaire, 14–15.

80  Personal correspondence, Don Mills respondent 1 to author, 6 April 1991.

JOY PARR

# Shopping for a Good Stove: A Parable about Gender, Design, and the Market

We are accustomed to thinking of women as shoppers and shoppers as women. 'Born to shop' bumper stickers are affixed (whether sardonically, wearily, or proudly) to cars driven by women rather than by men. Described for a decade as something women do by nature, that they are born to, shopping has been proclaimed by talk-show hosts and by writers of mass-market paperbacks as a women's addiction, a disease to which women particularly are prone.

There was, of course, a time in Ontario when no one, either female or male, shopped, when necessities were found or chased or made or traded. There followed a time when the men of Upper Canada turned their family's produce or remittances into cash and then goods on their trips alone to town. Women in modern times have been made shoppers by their circumstances, rather than by their natures. But these circumstances – the changing social setting and the experience of shopping – have not been much studied. Thinking about shopping, at once work and weakness, invisible and obsessional, seems to make women scholars nervous.

Shopping is not always the same experience. This article is about shopping for a stove in Ontario in the years 1950–5, about trying to find a particular product to meet a clearly but variously defined need. Stoves were made in a limited number of forms by a finite number of firms, and they were sold according to studiously defined practices by well-established stores. The goal of the article is to get to know women of that time better by studying their experience as shoppers: the assumptions about womanliness acted out in the shops and built into the goods for which women shopped; the ways in which women were kept ignorant of technical information and how they found out what they needed to know in order to buy; and the latitude they had or lacked to get manufacturers to make for them what they wanted to use. This is, first, an article about women in Ontario in the early 1950s, and, second, an experiment in diagnosing the power politics of shopping. It is, finally, a parable about a stove.

After ten years of depression, six years of war, and five years of disruption in the return to peacetime production, a substantial portion of Ontario households were in need of a stove. In 1950 a stove, in contrast to a refrigerator, was an undisputed household necessity. Unlike the refrigerator, it was rarely touched by men, and was used almost exclusively by women to perform tasks most men had not mastered. Stoves were major purchases, but their principal users were not usually major income earners. They were manufactured in both Canadian firms and American branch plants to drawings made by male designers, and they were sold by male commission salesmen. Thus, stoves provide a particularly good prism for investigating gender politics in the postwar world of goods.

## SELLING AND BUYING

I have found no systematic study of who did the shopping in postwar Ontario, but writers in the trade and business press urged their readers to recognize that most of their customers were women: 'Cultivate the ladies, they do 90 per cent of retail buying'; acknowledge woman as the 'nation's purchasing agent'; and 'slant ... sales and merchandising programs to attract the feminine purchaser.' To impress on their staff that women were important buyers whose 'whims' must be catered to, in 1950 the men in the Merchandise Office at Eaton's in Toronto cited 1948 Illinois shopping data which showed that 41 per cent of all electrical appliances were bought by women alone, and 21 per cent by women and men together. The Illinois study suggested that women did even more of family buying among lower income groups and in larger urban centres. From the appliance retailer's perspective, however, there was at least 'the shadow of a man behind every women who buys,' and, in one in five cases, the presence of 'an impatient husband who wants to see how his money is being spent but is easily bored by his wife's inability to make up her mind in a hurry.'[1] Retailers assumed that women 'purchasing agents' reported to male bosses.

In the early 1950s major appliances were sold by male commission salesmen. Female sales staff might have carried 'a more convincing story to the customer.' Both the home economics director and the general sales manager at Moffats, a leading Ontario stove manufacturer, recommended as much in 1952. But the prevailing view in the trade was that 'Saleswomen in the appliance field have fallen flat on their faces. Men don't like them on the selling floor. Women customers don't like to be sold by another woman. Sales girls often dress up too much. Load themselves with expensive hairdos and jewellery. They set up sparks when they came in contact with a poorly dressed housewife dragging two howling kids with her. Some women have succeeded but very few.' What women of the time really thought about buying from appliance saleswomen, or being appliance saleswomen, we do not know. What is clear is that men dominated the well-paid jobs on appliance sales floors. A shopper stepping on to that floor in search of a stove was entering a place in which masculine assertions and intentions defined womanhood.[2]

The postwar conventions of good salesmanship – 'virile salesmanship' as it was called in a story about Moffats – were defined man to man.[3] Adapting these conventions for men who were selling to women mattered to both manufacturers and retailers, given the volume and intense competition in appliance sales in the early 1950s. But given prevailing gender roles, managers faced a stiff challenge in making work that required men to serve women both palatable and effective. It was easy enough to advise men, most of whom were comfortable thinking of their wares as machines, to adopt women's diction: to speak in terms of cooking speeds and not wattages, and to describe oven size in terms of the number of baking dishes a particular model would hold rather than in square inches.[4] Salesmen, however, also were told: 'Sell yourself, you are part of the package your prospect buys'; 'Establish some common interest with your buyer'; 'Be a good listener'; and 'Arouse your prospect's interest.' Such advise took on a salacious edge when a salesman was making a pitch to a woman. Cecilia Long, a Toronto advertising executive, warned of the dangers out on the sales floor: 'Flattery will get you somewhere but over-familiarity will get you nowhere.'[5]

A woman shopping for a stove was appraising a cooking appliance and trying to estimate future cooking performance. A man trying to sell her a stove had to step outside the prevailing masculine role, to the extent that he must suppress his inclination to explain how the stove was produced, and instead present himself as an authority on what the stove would produce – that is, on cooking. Manufacturers organized cooking schools for salesmen, though these attempts were usually reported as comical failures. In their 'Use Value' campaign of 1950–1, the most Moffats could persuade men to demonstrate was that water poured on top of the range would drain to the spill tray underneath. As one wag noted, the closest the appliance dealer, housewares manager, or salesman 'ever came to basting a chicken was when he spilled champagne on one at the annual company dinner!'[6]

Reckoning that salesmen knew their culinary expertise would not bear scrutiny by an experienced homemaker, manufacturers tried to bolster male

'Life with and without Buy-ology,' *Westinghouse Salesman,* July 1951, 8–9

confidence by conjuring up a female customer who would not be a threat. They urged salesmen to imagine a dewy customer shopping for 'the first range in her young life, or her first Moffat range.' Canadian Westinghouse conjured up a new bride, and in 'An open letter to Westinghouse dealers' had her groom reassure salesmen: 'There is nobody in this town who knows more about electrical appliances than you do – and, strictly between ourselves, there is nobody who knows *less* than my bride-to-be.' The groom went on to dismiss the threat of counterveiling female authorities by asserting that, 'Like most newly weds my wife is going to be too proud or too shy to ask for advice from her friends or family – but if she feels that you, gentlemen, can guide her in the proper use of home appliances and help her avoid humiliating cooking failures, I think she will probably look upon you as her friend, and will probably buy from you again.'

Illustrations in sales guides portrayed difficult customers as older, ugly, and overbearing, and good sales prospects as younger, attractive, and generously obliging. Salesmen thereby transformed their own fear of their most knowledgeable and discerning female customers into a negative commentary on the shoppers' womanliness.[7]

Manufacturers believed they had more to gain by challenging women's traditional cooking knowledge than by making salesmen competent cooks in the estimation of women customers. In a competitive market, each manufacturer wanted to redefine cooking as the satisfactory *operation* of its product, to emphasize recently purchased equipment rather than knowledge of ingredients or skills in preparation as the keys to 'baking and roasting success.' The rhetoric in advertisements depicted cooking as a competitive, capital-intensive process. Manufacturers and retailers thus sought to shift credit for fine cookery from the expertise of the housewife to the engineering of the appliance.[8]

Sales pitches entailed a tactful but firm derogation of what women already knew about cooking by comparison with what they would need to know to get the most out of their new investment. Women cooks must be persuaded to subordinate themselves to their man-made equipment. The salesman's job was to 'impress upon her [the woman customer] that the full benefit of all the wonderful things the range can do, all the work it can save, all the perfect cooking it can achieve are directly influenced by the way the range is handled. This is especially important with housewives who have long-standing cooking habits based on the use of old-fashioned or non-electric ranges. They have to be shown, and given confidence, in how much their Westinghouse Range will do for them – how little they need do themselves.' Most manufacturers included books of recipes from experts in their 'test kitchens,' adaptations said to be specifically for their stove models, and then interleaved the recipes with instructions for operation of their equipment. Women journalists doubted that these tactics would succeed. Abbie Lane, woman's editor of the Halifax *Chronicle and Star*, told Ontario marketers that homemakers would not accept 'the test kitchen and the home economist as the originator of recipes,' that for 'ordinary folks' 'recipes have been in the family for years and that means something.' Other women flatly denied that what they did in the kitchen was manage an investment.[9]

The elaborate accessorizing of early 1950s stoves, like the scientifically tested recipe, had more to do with selling than cooking. The accessories at this stage were a way for manufacturers to differentiate one brand of white metal box from another. Later in the decade they would begin to try to get consumers personally to identify with these distinctions. More important for the salesman, the features provided content for the sales pitch: a stove with twice as many features had 'twice as much for you to talk about – dozens of special sales features which mean added advantage to you [the salesman] in the days ahead.'

Yesterday                    ... and Today

'The Farmer's Wife,' *Westinghouse Salesman*, February 1948, 9

But the elaboration of features could undercut the promise that new equipment was easy to use. American studies from the late 1950s suggested that while retailers thought customers bought for extra gadgets and style, customers actually were looking most for ease of use, service, and warranty. Ottawa businessman D.B. Cruickshank, worried about this contradiction in 1949: 'Evidently the average householders' choice is limited to what the average shop offers ... It appears to be sales managers' standards which are being forced on the consumer because the latter has no power of individual choice.'[10]

The life-size cardboard cutouts of 'attractive models' in strapless evening dresses that were propped up against stoves in the stores, like the couturier fashion shows that manufacturers staged amid their appliance displays at the Toronto CNE, were planned to bring a positive association to stylishness in stoves. Thor's Canadian branch tried historical fashion shows as well, hoping to set women 'reflecting how much better is their lot to be living in a day of simpler and saner fashions – and in a day when manufacturing enterprise removed so much of the household drudgery that plagued their grandmothers.' Westinghouse combined the style and labour-saving messages in a rural before-and-after cartoon: first it showed a harried farm wife feeding pancakes to a grinning foursome of hired men; then a neatly coiffed woman, playing bridge, smoking and gossiping with three women friends, the wooden kitchen chairs superseded by Breuer chrome, the wall display of the family patriarch and lenten bulrushes by a northern landscape, the wood stove by a new Westinghouse electric. But in many ways this pitch would have failed: it turned out grandfather, the church, and the working men of the farm in favour of northern wasteland, female leisure, and a baby crawling unremarked towards the stove.[11]

Women working at home for free were sensitive to criticisms that their days were unproductive and that household tasks required little skill.[12] They were not won over by claims about 'how little they need do themselves' once they had a new range, partly as a woman marketer noted, 'because they resent being told that a product can do their job better and quicker than they can.'[13] An appliance that 'saved' the labour of a woman who did not work for wages cost, but did not save, money. Women whose home work was unmeasured and unpaid were not well positioned to press for purchases on the basis of labour-saving features, even if they could see ways in which the new equipment would improve their work efficiency. General Steel Wares discovered by 'scientific market research' in 1954, as they planned to launch their new McClary ranges, that 'most housewives would like to own a new automatic range but they feel the money could be better spent on other things of interest to the whole family.'[14]

Many factors, then, made the appliance sales floor a bad place to shop for a stove. A cook could not try out the performance of the range, even in the limited way in which a driver, visiting an automobile dealership, could test drive a car. The men selling stoves were not experts in their use, either in their own estimation or in that of their women customers. The manufacturers who provided the sales information about their ranges wrote copy to distinguish their product from that made by rival firms. They sold by looking into a mirror that reflected back other producers, rather than venturing through the looking glass into the distinctive world of the buyers beyond; they concentrated on the men who were their competitors rather than the women who were their customers.[15] Retailers sold the idea that new equipment was better than old, following the manufacturers' scripts that emphasized features and surficial styling rather than functioning. Nowhere in this process were the questions the female shopper formulated as cook satisfactorily addressed. Women protested that they got 'the brush-off' when they went to investigate their prospective purchases – that is, to shop; they complained that marketers slapped 'a great big illustration and just a little reading matter' on their advertisements, whereas for a 'big purchase' they wanted to 'read advertisements packed with information.'[16] In reaction to the irrelevance of the sales floor to the real work of shopping for a stove, women buyers researched their purchases through word of mouth. They asked neighbours and kin how well the equipment they had purchased met their needs – a route that offered information about the performance of the equipment in the home, so long as acquaintances were candid about their mistakes. Retailers, exasperated, claimed that all shoppers cared about was price. More likely, given the authority women customers accorded the experience of their friends and neighbours, the shopping for value and performance had already been done through more reliable, non-retail routes. At the point of sale, the only questions worth posing to a salesman about stoves concerned price.[17]

DESIGNER STOVES

The processes by which stoves were designed were as far removed from the kitchen as was the appliance sales floor; they were equally revealing about the ideology of gender roles in the postwar years. The leading domestic appliance manufacturers had long histories as builders of industrial equipment – turbines for hydroelectric power generation and giant boilers for steam plants. In this work the consumers were sovereign: manufacturers produced goods designed to the buyer's specifications. As Robert Campbell observed in *Canadian Business*, 'the equipment would be built the way the customer wanted it and not the way the manufacturer thought it ought to be.' Large engineering firms setting out to make household equipment departed from this time-honoured convention, however, assuming that their new client, the housewife, would know 'that her humble role is to select from what is offered and not to advance opinions on what she'd like or why.'[18]

Thousands of Ontario women had worked in heavy industry during the war, and some, like aeronautical engineer Elsie Gregory Macgill, had made important design contributions to forward the war effort. But in the urgent national struggle to reconstruct the economy after the war and create new industries through which to recoup depression losses, the masculinity of machine-making was reconstructed as well. Honouring machine-makers on their own terms became a species of patriotism; the unquestioning faith in the possibilities of the new technologies and materials developed for military purposes became a gesture of faith that peacetime prosperity could be recouped from the wreckage of war. Alan Jarvis, an influential figure in both British and Canadian industrial design after the war, used the example of the Mosquito bomber to make this case: 'When we go shopping for those things with which we will fill our post-war homes, we ought, therefore, to remember the back-room boys who are trying to solve in the field of industrial design the same *kind* of problem which faced the designer of the Mosquito: how to make use of modern inventions, modern methods of production and

'That's what comes of having a production man for a husband.'
*Westinghouse News*, 2 June 1948, 9

newly discovered materials, so that we of the twentieth century shall have in our homes objects which are efficient, inexpensive *and* beautiful.'

In consumer goods, government industrial design initiatives after the war emphasized the use of new materials, such as light metal alloys, and 'the immediate possibilities of Canadian production,' rather than the functional efficiency of household equipment in the home. From the point of view of the Department of Finance, of course, this emphasis made perfect sense. The goal was to maximize sales at home and abroad of new materials and of goods made from those materials, gains that counted as growth in the Gross National Product. By contrast, efficiency changes inside the home were definitionally outside the reckoning of the national income accounts. The comical aspects of giving production engineers free rein wherever they might roam did not go unremarked, but both state and industrial strategic priorities focused on 'modern' materials and production methods, as men defined them. As Stuart Ewan has argued, form followed power, in this case the power to specify what gains forwarded the national interest.[19]

Functionalism, the assertion that form must follow function, was one of the rallying cries of postwar industrial design, but functionalism within the modernist's creed did not make the user paramount. Even in a publication titled *Design for Use*, Donald W. Buchanan, head of the National Industrial

Design Council, argued that 'the hall mark of any well designed, industrially produced object' was a 'combination of functional efficiency and due proportion in form and structure.' Materials and production processes had the most direct influence on form and structure. Functional efficiency, which particularly in household equipment would have required attentiveness to the needs of women workers in domestic settings, consistently lost out in the designer's arbitrage among form, structure, and usefulness. Some even argued that a product was functional if it looked 'its part,' if in the contemporary system of signs it was possible 'to recognise actually what it is.' In the criteria for industrial design awards formulated a year after the '*Design for Use*' statement, Buchanan and his colleagues did not demand functional efficiency, but required only that objects be 'suitable' rather than optimal for their functions. Suitable implied 'further that the object be both comfortable and easy to handle,' an amplification that drew attention to form rather than performance, to the object itself rather than the task to be done.[20]

Retailers were perplexed that articles that 'had widely established consumer acceptance and appeared to be excellent value' were ranked low by council design experts 'on account of lack of originality of form.' American industrial designers who valued sales appeal tended to leaven the strict formalism that the British theorists whom Buchanan and his colleagues in the national design bureaucracy so admired. But in this leavening the users' needs did not rise to the top. Henry Dreyfuss, who designed appliances for General Electric in the United States, cheerfully argued before the Canadian Manufacturers Association in Toronto in May 1952 that it was a good thing that industrial design had 'entered the home through the back door,' into the kitchen, where 'wear and tear were faster' and the housewife, 'a gadget-conscious mammal,' could be persuaded to 'have the drab parts of her house brightened-up with handsome bits of machinery.' Dreyfuss found women users too mercurial, disingenuous, or hedged in by their relationships to men to provide reliable information about what they really wanted. An infrequent user of household appliances himself, he dismissed as retrograde instincts the labour patterns women had developed to manage their work in the kitchen. Monte Kwinter, managing editor of a Toronto-based product design journal in the 1950s and later minister of consumer and corporate affairs in Ontario, stated this view even more strongly, arguing that 'it would be advantageous to General Electric and to industry as a whole to educate people to understand what they should want ... in other words, to give them what they need rather than what they want.'[21]

The Canadian Association of Consumers, whose membership at the time was restricted to women and which worked closely with the National Industrial Design Council during the early 1950s, took a contrary view. Under the leadership of women with close links to the governing federal Liberal Party, the assocation pursued two goals: to represent the interest of women consumers through briefs to government and industry, and to urge Canadian women to be discriminating shoppers, making the market system work for them by refusing to buy goods that did not meet their needs.[22]

In 1946 the association's early leadership had laid a bolder plan, hoping to build on its experience with the all-woman Consumers Branch of the Wartime Prices and Trade Board. Drawing together suggestions from a national survey of Local Councils of Women and consumer councils, Mrs W.R. Lang, an Ottawa resident who represented the Women's Missionary Society of the United Church, reported that women across the country wanted a consumer research bureau to 'help consumers ... crystallize out their needs and desires,' which they acknowledged 'are often vague and inarticulate.' This agency, perhaps within the federal Department of Trade and Commerce, would bring 'great benefits not only to the consumer but also to the manufacturers' by conducting basic research into 'the necessary activities of housewives'; it would examine how various kinds of equipment would 'affect the time and energy of those using them' and formulate specifications that would 'express the needs and wishes of the consumer before things are manufactured.' In the same way that the National Research Council had the job of reinterpreting basic science for Canadian industrialists, this body would bridge the gap between women consumers' needs and their ability to formulate authoritative engineering specifications. The British Institute of Planning and Design was currently engaged in such work, and the Swedish Home Research Institute had undertaken a similar role, on the initiative of leading Social Democratic women, since 1942.[23] Organizers hoped that this agency would improve women's place in the world of goods by removing three scarcely acknowledged but almost insurmountable barriers that the contemporary system of gender relations had put in their way: it would create productivity data for household work, subvert the male monopoly over engineering solutions to technical problems women experienced within the home, and present manufacturers with design alternatives that were genuinely functional and saleable.

The plan was never realized. The consumers' association that emerged from the contending models proposed by communist, social democratic, and liberal women in the late 1940s relied on a small and uncertain federal grant to fund its activities. Rather than following the National Research Council precedent, the women of the Canadian Association of Consumers operated in the same way that women worked within the home, using unpaid labour, saving and sharing information as it came to hand, and hoping through astute petitioning and wise purchasing to minimize the irrationality of the choices that the market inattentively put before them.

Work with the National Industrial Design Council put the CAC's optimistic liberal principles to a stern test. The association's concern from the start was with poor performance in household goods. It began by recruiting suggestions from members in the expectation that the Design Council would forward them to 'departments of household science for investigation in report.' Such a process would allow women, 'instead of stewing over an inconvenience and feeling helpless to improve upon it,' to complain constructively to 'a source which will take immediate action' and to create 'findings which it will be worthwile giving to manufacturers.'[24] For its part, the Design Council hoped to convert consumers to modern design principles. Its pamphlet, *It Pays to Buy Articles of Good Design*, mailed out to all CAC members, praised goods that were simple rather than ornamented, revealing rather than hiding their functions, and 'natural' in the materials from which they were made rather than imitative of materials from which they were not.[25]

A member of the Canadian Association of Consumers agreed to served on the jury for the annual design awards, established in 1953, and here the conflicts between consumers' and designers' priorities quickly crystalized. Awards were regularly given to goods that the woman juror and her committee thought faulty, and withheld from wares they favoured. The award insignia created the impression that products had been performance tested when they had not. Aware that their participation in the judging validated this misimpression, Kathleen Harrison, chair of the CAC Design Committee, tried in 1954 and 1955 to persuade the council to separate household equipment from decorator goods, and to withhold awards until the equipment had been tested by an established research group. In the meantime, members of the Ottawa branch began to test goods in their homes, although their work had to be limited to small electricals and housewares, and the volume of the task soon overwhelmed the small group of volunteers. The Design Council declined to make performance testing part of its own ajudication process or to require certification of performance testing from manufacturers. The only response was an extraneous change in the award regulations to require 'evidence of suitability for the Canadian market' – a specification of sales rather than usefulness. Harrison thought she had arranged for a public airing of the dispute through a 'provocative' article in *Canadian Homes and Gardens* entitled 'How Good Is Design Award Merchandise?' but the editorship at the journal changed and the article never appeared. Their experience with the award jury left the female consumers association knowing that designers and industrialists often wanted their validation rather than their contribution. At the Design Council a confidential memo linked the breach to the fact that 'the male of the species is not considered a consumer in the CAC!'[26]

A WOMEN'S STOVE

The women of Ontario had strong views about stoves. When the Design Council and the Canadian Association of Consumers in 1954 jointly requested suggestions for the improvement of household goods, two-thirds of the responses concerned kitchen equipment.[27]

The survey showed that women were disenchanted with the existing merchandising system and wanted better ways to get the product knowledge they needed to choose among the stoves manufacturers offered for sale. This meant, first, that they wanted fewer model changes. When appliance manufacturers, following the example of automobile makers, changed their designs every year, they removed from the market the very models women wanted most to buy – those now proven by performance in the kitchens of family and friends. 'Why,' one woman wrote, don't manufacturers recognize they would be better off adopting 'a wait-and-see attitude rather than permit themselves to be dazzled by the immediate selling power of novelty into scrapping models which may be inherently better, as the consumer will, in time, come to recognize?' Second, worn down by 'the sheer physical effort of shopping' and aware that smaller manufacturers did not have the advertising budgets or the clout with retailers to secure due attention for their products, women suggested that makers 'establish cooperative demonstration rooms' to ensure 'that *everybody's* product could be seen and inspected by prospective purchasers.' Showing a sharp sense of the differences between oligopoly and perfect competition, one woman argued that this change would actually make the market process, which was supposed to allow the best goods to rise to the top of consumer acceptance, work better by ensuring that 'the smaller manufacturer gets every assistance in his struggle to compete.'[28]

The survey also showed that women wanted the form of stoves to be changed in a fundamental way. They wanted ovens raised above 'waist level' – or, in designers' terms, counter level. 'Why, oh why,' wrote Mrs R.F. Legget of Ottawa, 'do manufacturers persist in placing on the market stoves that are beautiful to look at, with the chromium glistening enamel, but back-breaking to use?'[29] This was a long-standing female complaint in Ontario. In 1946 the chrome-plated modern tabletop range included in the Art Gallery of Toronto 'Design in the Household' exhibition drew much criticism. Visitors' questionnaires showed that consumers wanted 'the oven [to] be restored to its old position above the stove. Housewives find that stooping over to attend to baking is an unwelcome form of exercise.'[30] Historically, the most common Canadian solid-fuel-burning ranges had had ovens set beside rather than below the burners. Early gas and electric stoves followed this form. Buchanan, sceptical when he could find only one Canadian electrical range, a McClary, with the oven at what the housewives claimed was the right height, referred the matter to an authority, Dr J.B. Brodie, head of household science at the University of Toronto. She made common cause with the housewives, arguing that plans 'to "streamline" everything and have a working space around the kitchen at one level ... are evolved by those who do not work in a kitchen and we know that they are not efficient.' Her words were well chosen. Buchanan, a proponent of British Good Design principles, regarded steamlining as a heresy hatched by American salesmen. He circulated Brodie's report to makers, hoping 'some enterprising manufacturer will devise a better and more functional type of range, that will appeal to the consumer on the grounds of both *appearance* and *ease of handling*.' Through a colleague, he assigned a group of University of Toronto architecture students to look at the problems of range design 'afresh, without preconceived prejudices as to what is "modern."' But both the students' mockup and an ungainly one-legged English-style cooker, designed to preserve the plane geometry of the countertop, met with lukewarm responses from members of the public who participated in design quizzes at Toronto and Ottawa exhibitions in the late 1940s.[31]

When 75 per cent of CAC members surveyed in 1951 still favoured high-oven ranges, Mrs R.G. Morningstar of Toronto, the CAC representative from the Canadian Dietetic Association, was dispatched to interview manufacturers. The results were not encouraging. Though the high-oven mockups were no wider than the stoves currently in production, manufacturers declared them too massive. They cited the failure of high-oven models in American market tests. Alexander McKenzie at McClary's added that 'he felt that older women were not familiar with modern controls' and that, when using a high-oven, they would 'keep peeking into the oven to see how the product [was] baking.'[32]

One Ontario firm, Findlay Stove Manufacturers of Carleton Place, did agree to take up the project. They exhibited a sample high-oven stove at the Toronto exhibition in 1952. During the next three years they conducted surveys of their own and refined their design, working in close concert with the CAC Design Committee. The Findlay Hy-Oven was launched in 1955 and, that year, won a National Industrial Design award. The CAC publicity chairperson in Toronto wrote letters to 279 newspaper and magazine editors and

*Canadian Homes and Gardens*, October 1955, 56

women's radio commentators under the banner 'From Modernity to Convenience' and garnered 1666 lines of newspaper publicity. Findlay's advertising
copy noted that the Hy-Oven ended stooping and bending and that it took up
only forty-one inches of floor space; illustrated with floor plans, it demonstrated how the new model would fit conveniently into existing kitchens. But
the Hy-Oven did not sell, either in Canadian or export markets.[33]

Part of the problem with the Findlay Hy-Oven may have been Findlay's. A
small if venerable eastern Ontario firm, Findlay's may have lacked the market influence and advertising budget to launch any radically different product
successfully in a sector increasingly dominated by large American firms. But
there was also a problem with the high-oven design, ways in which its usefulness compromised the ability of the form to satisfy other consumer needs.
Mrs G.J. Wherrett, Design Committee chairperson of the CAC, in 1952
reported rumours that women who saw the Hy-Oven at the Toronto CNE
'liked the convenience of the high oven, but wanted the appearance of the
low oven.' In her 1954 NIDC/CAC contest entry, Mrs John M. Dexter of
Burritt's Rapids, Ontario, still held the view that women preferred 'the old

high-oven stove to the most modern, streamlined one.' Attending to 'manufacturers' compliants that the high-oven stove does not lend itself to good
design in a modern kitchen,' however, she offered a compromise sketch of a
range with a retractable oven that could be raised while in use and stowed
below counter level at other times.

Henry Dreyfuss argued that American high-oven revivals had failed in the
market because 'the table-top stove flush with the other cabinets in the
kitchen had become such a style factor that the ladies refused to be budged
away from it.'[34] The CAC pitch for the Hy-Oven – 'From Modernity to Convenience' – posited too stark a transition. Modernity was not irrelevant to
women shopping for convenience. Women were shopping for stoves *and* for
the characteristics the presence of a particular stove would bring to their
kitchen. They were unlikely to see, as they imagined a stove transported
from the sales room to their kitchens, exactly the same transformation as the
designer, the manufacturer, and the advertiser had each envisioned. Not that
any dysfunctional contraption offered for sale would have found acceptance
with women buyers simply because it was perceived as creating the right cultural effect; rather, for the woman shopper, as for all the men who had created
the array of products from which she would choose, a stove was more than
just a stove.[35]

The tabletop range, its work surface level with the surrounding counters,
was a central feature in the portrait of the kitchen as laboratory, an image
that Margaret Hobbs and Ruth Pierson have shown was expounded widely in
Canada in the 1930s.[36] Its enamel, sparkling cleanliness and its clock, timer,
array of knobs promising orderliness and scientific control, the range was the
necessity among 'the electrical tools of her trade' which radio announcers for
Canadian Westinghouse in 1951 proclaimed were 'rapidly changing the
homemaker's kitchen into a convenient, attractive workshop.' In the postwar
years, the laboratory kitchen signaled the worth of domestic work to women
leaving the paid labour force and the feasibility of combining waged and non-
waged work for those who were not.[37] The messages were not unmixed, for
the unyielding regularity of the laboratory aesthetic brought home the imagery of the factory or the office, and the sense of being controlled rather than
being in control which some women returning to the home had hoped to
escape.[38] Later in the decade the once admired laboratory-look in kitchens
was derogated as the 'utility' look, a characterization that in Ontario brought
to mind the austere minimalism of wartime goods.[39] Wealthier householders
then installed conveniently high wall ovens in their custom-designed kitchens and traded in the tabletop ranges which, by the late 1950s seemed 'to
reflect a greater pre-occupation with the romance of science than with the

comforts of home.'[40] But at the time that the men at Findlay's and the women of the CAC were trying to launch their Hy-Oven, they were struggling against not only a machine-makers' practice and a national economic strategy that did not take domestic labour into account, but a generation of consumers seeking the signs of science with which to validate their unpaid work within the home.

This is a story that can only be told of Ontario in the early 1950s. Then the wartime experience of women in the Consumers Branch, and the relatively unformed practices of mass consumption in domestic durable goods, gave some women confidence to plan ways in which they would shape the design and merchandising of the equipment they would use. The persistence of small Canadian foundries, accustomed to manufacturing in short runs for specialized markets, meant there was one local firm ready and able to undertake the experiment. By the end of the decade the small Ontario manufacturers had lost their independence. The Canadian Association of Consumers had abandoned its attempt to specify the form of household equipment before it was manufactured, and had begun rather to prepare buyers' guides to help shoppers sort their way through the goods manufacturers and retailers offered up for sale. The ranks of the appliance salesmen dwindled, their usefulness as intermediaries across the gender gap between makers and consumers disproven in the hectic postwar boom. By the late 1950s Ontario appliance retailing was dominated by suburban discounters, with small staffs who wrote up bills of sale for hopeful if weary women who disembarked from station wagons shopping for a good stove.

NOTES

This article was written while I was a Bunting Fellow at Radcliffe College. I am grateful to Jehan Kuhn, Eve Blau, and Alice Friedman for comments on the early drafts. Audiences at the Hagley Museum and Library (Wilmington, Del.), Northern Lights College (Fort Nelson, BC), and Malaspina College (Duncan, BC), and colleagues in the Toronto Labour Studies Group offered useful critiques of subsequent versions.

1 'Cultivate the Ladies,' *Hardware in Canada (HIC)*, Aug. 1946, 26, 28; Frank Wright, 'The Woman Nation's Purchasing Agent,' *Canadian Business*, Aug. 1946 132; Archives of Ontario (AO), T. Eaton Co, S69 Merchandise Office, vol. 12, 'Business Conditions and Forecasts, 1940–52' B.E. Mercer to W. Park, 9 Feb. 1950, summarizing talk at the Retail Federation by Edythe Fern Melrose, and article in *Hardware Metal and Electrical Dealer*, 4 Feb. 1950. The study from which the data used by Mercer and Park was drawn was Paul Converse and Merle Crawford,

'Family Buying: Who Does It? Who Influences It?' *Current Economic Comment,*
11 Nov. 1949, 38–50. Mirra Komarovsky compared a number of postwar studies
showing similar outcomes in 'Class Differences in Family Decisionmaking on
expenditures,' in Nelson N. Foote, ed., *Household Decisionmaking* (New York:
New York University Press 1961), 255–65. On the male shadow, see Wright,
above; on the impatient husband, see 'Mrs Consumer Speaks Out on Design,'
*Industrial Canada,* Jan. 1955, 78. The literature on women's level of autonomy in
various types of decision-making is well summarized in Rosemary Scott, *The
Female Consumer* (Toronto: John Wiley 1976), 119–25.

2  For positive views of women in appliance sales see McMaster University Special
Collections (McMU), *Moffats' Sales Chef,* Jan.–Feb. 1952, commentaries by C.A.
Winder, general sales manager, and Elaine Collet, 'The Woman's Angle.' The negative view is from a male sales consultant, 'More Selling, Less Crying,' *Marketing,* 18 March 1955, 24. *Marketing* was the leading Canadian trade weekly in its
field. For contending views on why commission appliance sales is a man's job in
the United States, see 'Women's History Goes on Trial: EEOC v. Sears, Roebuck
and Company,' *Signs* 11, 4 (1986) 751–79, and Ruth Milkman, 'Women's History
and the Sears Case,' *Feminist Studies* 12, 2 (1986) 375–400.

3  For example, McMU, Westinghouse Collection, box 7, file 27, *Westinghouse
Salesman,* May 1948, 2, 'Eight Sound Rules for Selling,' and on Moffats, *Market-
ing,* 2 Oct. 1948, 56., 'Virile Salesmanship and Advertising Built World-wide
Canadian Business.'

4  McMU, *Westinghouse Salesman,* Charles Pearce, 'Watch your Language!' and
'Why True-temp Is Better,' July 1947, and G.I. Harrison, 'I Lost the Sale because
...' June 1948; McMU, Moffat *Sales Chef,* 'The Woman's Angle,' March 1951;
'Would-be Purchasers Still Getting Brush-off, This Customer Declares' *Market-
ing,* 13 April 1946, 10.

5  'The Sales Clinic,' *Canadian Business,* Jan. 1948, 92; Harrison,'I Lost the Sale
because ...' 9; 'Life with Buy-ology,' *Westinghouse Salesman,* July 1951, 8–9;
'Selling via Demonstrations,' *Marketing,* 30 July 1949, 8; 'Manufacturer's Retailers' Guide Promotes Many Competing Products,' *Marketing,* 16 Sept. 1950, 18;
'Canadian Women Want Product Facts,' *Marketing,* 12 Dec. 1951, 18.

6  Robert M. Campbell, 'You Can't Wash Dishes with Aesthetics!' *Canadian Business,* June 1951, 41.

7  McMU, Moffat *Sales Chef,* Dec. 1950, 5, Nov. 1948, 'Women's Views of Moffat
News'; McMU, *Westinghouse Salesman,* April 1951, 11; *Moffats' Sales Chef,*
July 1950, 7, March–April 1950, 6; Campbell, 'You Can't Wash Dishes with Aes-
thetics!' 41.

8  On selling an appliance as a redefinition of a task, see Carolyn Shaw Bell, *Consumer Choice in the American Economy* (New York: Random House 1967), 224;

McMU, Moffat *Sales Chef*, Nov. 1948, Feb.–March 1951, 17, July–Aug. 1947. Suzette Worden sees this pattern in interwar Britain, 'Powerful Women: Electricity in the Home, 1919–40,' in Judy Attfield and Pat Kirkham, eds., *A View from the Interior: Feminism, Women and Design* (London: Women's Press 1989), 140. Keith Walden describes a similar campaign by manufacturers to turn attention from local skills towards goods sold in national markets in 'Speaking Modern: Language, Culture, and Hegemony in Grocery Window Displays, 1887–1920,' *Canadian Historical Review* 70, 3 (1989): 296, 308–9.

9  The quote is from McMU, *Westinghouse Salesman*, Sept. 1950, 'Help Yourself to Future Range Sales'; 'Practical Ideas for Advertisers in Cultivating Women Customers,' *Marketing*, 11 Dec. 1948, 14; 'Would-be Purchasers Still Getting Brush-off,' 10.

10  McMU, *Moffats' Sales Chef*, Sept. 46 and Nov. 1948, 'Service Page'; *Marketing*, 30 Nov. 1948, 18; Peter J. McClure and John K. Ryans, 'Differences between Retailers' and Consumers' Perceptions,' *Journal of Marketing Research* 5 (Feb. 1968): 37; National Gallery of Canada (NG), 'Design in Industry,' vol. 7.4, file 2, D.B. Cruickshank, 'Industrial Design, What We Are Doing about It,' speech, c. 7 June 1949. Scott, *Female Consumer*, 67–8; on appliance gadgets and sales in other settings, see Judy Wajcman, *Feminism Confronts Technology* (University Park: Pennsylvania State University Press 1991), 103–4, and T.A.B.Corley, *Domestic Electrical Appliances* (London: Jonathon Cape 1966), 136.

11  McMU, *Moffats' Sales Chef*, March–April 1950, Nov. 1952; *Marketing*, 15 Aug. 1953, 3; 'The Farmer's Wife,' McMU, *Westinghouse Salesman*, Feb. 1948, 9.

12  See, for example, Norton Calder, 'Women Are Lousy Housekeepers,' *Liberty*, Nov. 1954, 15; 'Wasted Effort,' *Saturday Night*, 30 Oct 1954, 3.

13  'Women Best Ad Readers, Shrewder Buyers: Long,' *Marketing*, 29 April 1955, 8.

14  '50 per cent of Ranges 10 Years Old Basis for McClary Campaign,' *Marketing*, 8 Oct. 1954, 6, 8; Dianne Dodd notes that in the interwar period in Canada, advertisers responded to this concern by emphasizing the benefits of labour-saving domestic appliances to the whole family: 'Women in Advertising: The Role of Canadian Women in the Promotion of Domestic Electrical Technology in the Interwar Period,' in Marianne Ainley, ed., *Despite the Odds* (Montreal: Vehicule 1990), 144–5; Corley suggested in the British case that women might fear being thought lazy if they had too many appliances, or would have preferred that money be spent on items more immediately pleasing to their husbands: *Domestic Electrical Appliances*, 133. See, similarly, Vance Packard, *Hidden Persuaders* (New York: David McKay 1957), 62, and Maxine L. Margolis, *Mothers and Such* (Berkeley: University of California Press 1984), 167.

15  On this point, see Harrison White, 'Where Do Markets Come From?' *American Journal of Sociology* 87 (Nov. 1981): 543–4, and Susan Strasser, *Satisfaction*

*Guaranteed: The Making of the American Mass Market* (New York: Pantheon 1989), 289.

16  See 'Would-be Purchasers Still Getting Brush-off,' 10, 'Canadian Women Want Product Facts,' 1 Dec. 1951, 18, and 'Women's Purchasing Viewpoints Explained ...' 19 Jan. 1952, 4, all in *Marketing*.

17  'Charting the Course for Selling ...' ibid., 30 Nov. 1946, 2; 'Selling via Demonstrations ...' ibid., 30 July 1949, 12; *Westinghouse Salesman*, July 1951, 9; 'Mrs Consumer Speaks Out on Design,' *Industrial Canada*, Jan. 1955, 78; AO, T. Eaton Co, S69 Merchandise Office, vol. 12, M. Park to B.E. Mercer, 12 Feb. 1951, A.E. Nurse to B.W. Smith, 15 Feb. 1951, Park to Smith, 20 Feb. 1951. William H. Whyte invokes this dilemma well in 'The Web of Word of Mouth,' *Fortune*, Nov. 1954, reprinted in *Consumer Behaviour*, vol. 2 (New York: New York University Press 1955), 118–20.

18  Campbell, 'You Can't Wash Dishes with Aesthetics!' 40–1; similar patterns are observed from Britain and Australia: see Corley, *Domestic Electrical Appliances*, 52, and Wajcman, *Feminism Confronts Technology*, 100–3.

19  Thomas Fisher Rare Book Room, Robarts Library, University of Toronto, Alan Jarvis Collection, MS 171, box 22, 'What's All This Fuss about Modern design?' *Target*, 9 Oct. 1945, 10; NG, 'Design in Industry,' vol. 7.4, file 1, statement by the Affiliation of Industrial Designers of Canada, 3 July 1947; on the priority of materials and the promise of Canadian production, see NG, 'Design in Industry,' vol. 5.5D speech by C.D. Howe, minister of reconstruction, opening the Design in Industry Exhibition, 1946; John B. Collins, 'Design for Use, Design for the Millions: Proposals and Options for the National Industrial Design Council 1848–1960' (MA thesis, Carleton University 1986), chapter 2; McMU, Westinghouse Collection, *Westinghouse News*, 2 June 1948; Stuart Ewen, *All Consuming Images* (New York: Basic 1988), chapter 9.

20  National Industrial Design Council, *Design for Use* (Ottawa: King's Printer 1947), preface by Donald Buchanan, 5; on acting the part, see NG, vol. 5.5D, 'Design Centre Exhibition 1948,' Dora de Pedery to H. O. McCurry, 23 Sept. 1948. De Pedery, a sculptor who had been instrumental in wartime initiatives to establish a postwar design council, may have been influenced in her view about the representation of function by the American critics Sheldon and Martha May Chandler, who argued in 1936 for 'functional expressiveness' as a central industrial design principle: *Art and the Machine* (New York: McGraw Hill 1936), 14–15; the emphasis on being 'true to materials' and signifying usefulness is strong in *It Pays to Buy Articles of Good Design* published jointly by the National Gallery of Canada and the Canadian Association of Consumers (CAC); *Industrial Canada*, Jan. 1948, 141; D.W. Buchanan, 'Completing the Pattern of Modern Living,' *Canadian Art* 6 (spring 1949): 112; *Foreign Trade*, 25 Nov. 1950, 898.

21  B.W. Smith from Eaton's Merchandising Office, 25 Feb. 1953, AO, T. Eaton Co, S69, box 19, 'Design Index and Awards, 1946–60'; Henry Dreyfuss, 'The Silent Salesman of Industry,' *Industrial Canada*, July 1952, 65; Henry Dreyfuss, *Designing for People* (New York: Simon and Schuster 1955), 65–6, 202; National Archives of Canada (NA), RG 20, A4 1434, file 2, National Industrial Design McGill Conference, 'Design as a Function of Management,' 18 Oct. 1956, commentary on paper by C.H. Linder.

22  On representation, Canadian Association of Consumers, 'Your Questions and Answers,' Ottawa 1947, question 9; on the forces of the market on design, see, for example, Mrs W.R. Walton, president of CAC, before the Toronto Business and Professional Women's Club: 'If we buy badly designed articles we encourage the production of more badly designed ones of the same type and if we buy well designed ones the badly designed articles will fade and die for lack of customers,' NG, Design in Industry, vol. 7.4, file 5, NIDC press release, 22 Dec. 1952; NA, MG 28, I200, vol. 1, CAC 1954 annual meeting, Mrs Rene Vautelet, presidential address: 'The big business of buying is our business and our housekeeping dollars are the steering dollars of the land.'

23  Metropolitan Toronto Reference Library, Baldwin Room, Harriet Parsons Papers, Mrs W.R. Lang, 'Report re Questionnaire, May 3 1946.'

24  NA, RG 20 997, vol. 2, minutes of the National Industrial Design Committee (NIDC) 23 and 24 April 1951; RG 20, vol. 1429, National Design Branch and Consumers Association of Canada, file 1000 240/C27, extracts from the annual meeting of the CAC, 29 Sept. 1954 .

25  NIDC and CAC, *It Pays to Buy Articles of Good Design*; Collins, 'Design for Use,' notes the didactic tone of this work.

26  NA, MG 28, I200, vol. 1, Canadian Association of Consumers, Design Committee Report, mid-year report, April 1955, report to annual meeting, 5, 6 Oct. 1955; NG, 'Design in Industry,' vol. 7.4, file 7, Mrs K.E. Harrison, chairman of the Design Committee, to the Executive of the Canadian Association of Consumers, 26 Feb. 1955; NA, RG 20, vol. 1429, file 1000 240/C27, Mrs C. Breindahl, CAC, Ottawa, to Donald Buchanan, requesting performance testing, 15 April 1955, and reply by Buchanan, 20 April 1955, describing the change in award specifications, and Kathleen Harrison on behalf of the CAC to Donald Buchanan, 23 April 1955, stating that volunteers are overburdened and do not feel they constitute a valid testing unit. This file also includes the home-testing questionnaire formulated by the Ottawa branch and their April 1956 report on their work in 1955. An unsigned confidential memo for the consumer relations council of the NIDC, written around October 1955, summarizes the history and work of the CAC from the persepctive of the Design Council.

27  There were 896 responses in total, 366 of them from Ontario. NAC, RG 20, vol.

1429, file 1000 240/C27, 'Review of the 1954 NIDC–CAC contests for suggestions for the improvement of household goods'.

28 'Mrs Consumer Speaks Out on Design,' *Industrial Canada*, Jan. 1955, 76, 78, and 80.

29 'What the Women Want,' *Canadian Homes and Gardens*, Jan. 1955, 36.

30 Barbara Swann, 'The Design in the Household Exhibition,' *Industrial Canada*, March 1946, 77–8; there are excellent curatorial records describing this exhibition in the Art Gallery of Ontario archives.

31 There are clear illustrations of early Canadian high-oven ranges in a fine article by Hillary Russell, '"Canadian Ways": An Introduction to Comparative Studies of Housework, Stoves and Diet in Great Britain and Canada,' *Material History Bulletin*, no 19 (spring 1984), 1–12; NA, RG 20, A4, vol. 1433, National Design Branch, file 'George Englesmith, architect,' Buchanan to Englesmith, 16 Sept., 14 Nov. and 21 Nov. 1947; Donald Buchanan, 'Take Another Look at Your Kitchen Range,' *Canadian Art* 5 (spring/summer 1948) 182–3; J.B. Craig, F. Dawes, and J.C. Rankin, 'A Cooperative Problem in Industrial Design,' Royal Architectural Institute of Canada, *Journal* 25 (May 1948): 154N5. For Buchanan on streamlining, see 'Design in Industry: The Canadian Picture,' RAIC, *Journal* 24 (July 1947): 234–5, and 'Good Design and "Styling" – The Choice before Us,' *Canadian Art* 9 (Oct. 1951), 32–5. 'These Are the Ones the Experts Picked,' *Canadian Art* 6 (Christmas 1948): 59–60, shows the University of Toronto mockup and a British Maxwell Fry design; NG, 'Design in Industry,' vol. 7.4, file 2, D.B. Cruickshank, 'Industrial Design, What Are Canadians Doing about It?' June 1949.

32 June Callwood, 'Housewives' Crusade,' *Maclean's*, 1 Oct. 1952, 60; NA, MG 28, I200, vol. 1, file 10, Canadian Assocation of Consumers, report of the consumer relations committee, 20–21 Sept. 1951, and Mrs R.G. Morningstar, 'Survey of Time and Motion Studies for Household Equipment,' report 23, 1952; NG, 'Design in Industry,' vol. 7.4D, file 4, minutes of the NIDC meeting, 15 and 16 April 1952.

33 NA, RG 20, vol. 1429, file 1000 240/C27, 'Review of the 1954 NIDC-CAC Contest,' 4; University of Guelph Archives, M.S. McCready Collection, A0021, 'From Modernity to Convenience,' *CAC Bulletin*, Jan. 1955; NA, MG 28, I200, vol. 1, CAC 1952 annual meeting, 'National Industrial Design Report' by Mrs G.J. Wherrett and Design Committee Report by Mrs W F Harrison, April 1955, 13–14 June and 5–6 Oct. 1955; *Furniture and Furnishings*, April 1955, 83; on early export performance, see NA, RG 20, 998 13-2, D.G.W. Douglas to J.P.C. Gauthier, Department of Trade and Commerce report, 15 July 1955, 5.

34 NA, MG 28, I200, vol. 1, CAC, 1952 annual meeting, report by Mrs G.J. Wherrett, Design Committee; 'What the Women Want,' *Canadian Homes and Gardens*, Jan. 1955, 36; Dreyfuss, *Designing for People*, 69.

35  On the 'characteristics' of goods, see Jean-Christophe Agnew, 'The Consuming
    Vision of Henry James,' in Richard Fox and T.J. Jackson Lears, *The Culture of Con-
    sumption* (New York: Pantheon 1983), 67–74; on the assertion of Jean Baudrillard
    that 'the real effect of consumption has been to herald "the passage from use value
    to sign value,"' see Tomlinson, Introduction to Alan Tomlinson, ed., *Consump-
    tion, Identity and Style: Marketing, Meanings and the Packaging of Pleasure*
    (New York: Routledge 1990), 18–21. Bauderillard makes this argument in 'The
    Ecstasy of Communication,' in Hal Foster, ed., *The Anti-Aesthetic: Essays on
    Postmodern Culture* (Port Townsend, Wash.: Bay Press 1983), 126–33; on con-
    sumer reinterpretation of designs, see Cheryl Buckley, 'Made in Patriarchy:
    Toward a Feminist Analysis of Women and Design,' *Design Issues* 3, 2 (1986): 11,
    and Phillipa Goodall, 'Design and Gender,' *Block* 9 (1983): 50–61; on reciprocity
    between the values goods bring to users and users bring to goods, see Penny
    Sparke, *Electrical Appliances* (London: Unwin Hyman 1987), 6, and Susan
    Strasser, *Satisfaction Guaranteed: The Making of the American Mass Market*
    (New York: Pantheon 1989), 15.
36  Margaret Hobbs and Ruth Roach Pierson, '"A kitchen that wastes no steps ..."
    Gender, Class and the Home Improvement Plan, 1936–40,' *Histoire sociale/Social
    History* 21, 41 (May 1988): 9–37.
37  McMU, Westinghouse Collection, box 8, file 21, 'Canadian Westinghouse Pre-
    sents,' broadcast script for 11 Feb. 1951; J.K. Edmonds, 'The Mechanized House-
    hold,' *Marketing*, 5 Nov 1954, 17.
38  On the ambiguous messages carried by factory and laboratory imagery, see Stuart
    Ewen, 'Marketing Dreams: The Political Elements of Style,' in Tomlinson, ed.,
    *Consumption, Identity and Style*, 48–9, and Ewen, *All Consuming Images*, 215–
    16.
39  'Kitchens,' *Canadian Homes and Gardens*, Oct. 1958, 30.
40  'Long-range Planning for Tommorrow's Kitchens,' *Design*, 104 (Aug. 1957): 50.

JOAN SANGSTER

# Doing Two Jobs: The Wage-Earning Mother, 1945–70

In the late 1950s, before I began school, my mother would put me in our car and drive from our suburban house into the city of Toronto. I attended a day nursery while she worked part time in a physics laboratory. On the first day of work one fall, my mother remembers hoping that the neighbours would think she was going shopping, since working women with young children were often judged to be less than ideal mothers. I remember resenting my placement at the nursery; sometimes I concocted inventive plans to prevent our departure – behaviour for which, as a current day-care mom, I now suffer some remorse.

Despite her accurate assessment of the popular perception of working moms, my mother's decision to go out to work was far from unusual in this era. Although women's overall participation in the workforce declined immediately after the war and was not to reach its wartime high again for some years, there were significant changes emerging in the patterns of Canadian women's wage work. In the postwar era, more and more married women and women with children were going out to work; by the 1960s this rapidly escalating trend was reshaping the marital and family profile of women in the labour force in a very profound way. During this period, however, married women's wage work was often discussed in the media as a problem; their needs were inadequately addressed by social policy; and, sadly, their daily struggles, worries, and satisfactions were less than visible in the popular culture of the time. For women in the 1950s June Cleaver remained the dominant popular image of motherhood, despite its incongruity with many women's lives.

This article examines the wage-earning mother in Ontario in the twenty-five years after the war's end by exploring three themes: the popular debate about working moms; the efforts of Ontario policy-makers to address mothers' increasing wage work; and, last but not least, women's own interpretations of their combined mother work and wage work. Connections between the latter two themes are especially important; we need to link our analyses of social policy with women's actual experience, asking how the initiatives promoted by governments addressed, ignored, and possibly shaped the texture of working women's lives across the province. Drawing on oral histories of women who worked in blue- and white-collar work, teaching, and nursing in Peterborough, a small city located in the heart of rural Ontario, I want to relate women's practical coping strategies for combining family and work, their understanding of the social and legal barriers to mothers' participation in the workforce, and their own interpretations of the debate about working mothers.

Though it had a strong manufacturing sector that traditionally employed substantial numbers of women, Peterborough's employment trends also reflected the postwar movement towards more white- and pink-collar work, as well as expanding educational and health-related employment for women. Historically, women had a high participation rate in the local workforce, matching Ontario's average and surpassing the Canadian one. In this respect, the city offers an ideal case study; in fact, its supposed 'averageness' later made it the target of numerous consumer studies testing everything from toothpaste to cars.[1]

At the same time, the city provides a unique view of women's lives in rural and small-town Ontario. Small cities like Peterborough often lacked the social infrastructure and public services, such as day care, offered in Toronto. The city's population remained fairly stable and ethnically homogeneous in this period, less affected by immigration trends than larger centres: the majority were Canadian born and designated their ethnic identity as 'British.'[2] Indeed, the city fathers claimed a strong ethnocentric pride in this homogeneity, and also boasted about the peaceful and closely knit nature of the community.[3] While they certainly exaggerated those claims, a small-town atmosphere characterized by a cultural insularity, strong family ties, and a history of industrial paternalism was still apparent in the postwar period.[4]

THE SILENT REVOLUTION

In the twenty-five years after the end of the Second World War, the number of married women and of women with children in Ontario's labour force increased dramatically. At the beginning of the war only one in twenty married women worked for pay; by 1951 it was one in ten; and by 1961, one in five. By the mid-1960s the census indicated that one-third of Ontario's work-force was female and that more than 50 per cent of these women were mar-ried, a marked contrast to the interwar period.[5] The actual numbers of women working for pay were undoubtedly even higher, for statistics missed women doing seasonal, part-time, or domestic work. Indeed, it is important to remember that these statistics only indicated alterations in the formal wage economy; married working-class women had *always* 'worked' in the household, and many had earned money through the informal economy. Moreover, concern with the expansion of married women's wage work in this period betrayed distinct class and race biases; married women who were recent immigrants, were from some ethnic and racial communities, or were the very poor already had high labour-force participation rates.[6] As more working-class, lower-middle-class, and particularly middle-class women entered the paid labour force, however, new attention was focused on married women's work for pay.

The most significant increase in paid female labour in the 1950s was women in the second phase of their work lives, between thirty-five and forty-five years of age, who had left the workforce while their children were young and were returning to wage work. By the late 1960s the age of women rejoin-ing the workforce after childbearing was declining, and the number of work-ing women with pre-school and especially school-age children was increasing dramatically; the labour-force participation rate of working mothers in Ontario was growing by about 7 per cent a year, far outpacing increases by any other group.[7] These postwar trends were a radical departure with the past, so much so that economic soothsayers misinterpreted or underestimated them.[8]

Both demographic and economic forces shaped the changing labour force. A smaller birth cohort in the 1930s and later age of entry of girls in the work-force in the 1950s created a demand for female labour that was augmented considerably by the economic expansion, especially in the tertiary sector, after the war. At the same time, earlier age of marriage and childbearing through this period left women ready to rejoin the workforce by their late thirties.

Increasing demands for labour in the private and public sectors pulled women into the workforce; at the same time, economic need encouraged women's search for wage work. 'Economic motives' were cited as the reason for their wage work by 75 per cent of those married women surveyed by the federal Women's Bureau in 1958. Most working wives were in lower-income families where their salaries meant the difference between mere subsistence and a more secure, though certainly not affluent, life style.[9] Moreover, definitions of need were changing in the postwar period: the purchase of a car, some appliances, and especially a home increasingly became family goals. Women who started work during the insecurity of the Depression were often anxious to offer their children choices in education and work they never had; younger women who went out to work during and after the war had expectations shaped by economic prosperity and by reconstruction promises of increased income security.

Perhaps some women's images of work and womanhood had also been altered during the war. Despite economic and social policy support for the sexual division of labour and an ideology of domesticity during and after the war,[10] the postwar period did indicate some incremental changes in women's sense of identity: more women were confessing their desire to work after marriage, declaring that childbearing did not spell the end to their work lives.[11] The opportunity to work was also crucial. One of the largest barriers to married women's work in the 1930s was the vigilant enforcement of a marriage bar by employers;[12] in the postwar period, as 'women's productive rather than reproductive labour was increasingly valued' by business and the public sectors,[13] this marriage bar was abandoned.

As many sociologists and historians have already shown, the expanding female workforce was concentrated in 'female ghettos,' with lower wages (on average, one-third lower than men's) and limited means of vertical mobility.[14] Women in the professional category were predominantly teachers and nurses; moreover, as the educational system expanded, women remained at the lowest rungs of its hierarchy. Other than manufacturing, women were primarily employed in the clerical and service sectors: indeed, by 1951 clerical workers formed the largest female occupational grouping in the Canadian workforce. Married women in particular were more likely to be ghettoized in the service sector and to be part-time workers, with fewer benefits than full-time workers.[15]

Ontario led this national trend towards more wage-earning mothers. A highly urbanized province, with a large manufacturing base and service sector, Ontario accounted for 40 per cent of the Canadian female workforce in 1965. The labour participation rate of married women in the workforce was higher here than in any other province, though, admittedly, women's paid work varied considerably across the province, with urbanized areas indicating a higher participation rate of wage-earning wives. Even small cities like Peterborough had significant numbers of wage-earning women; in 1951 and 1961 the city's female labour-force participation rate was 31 per cent, and by 1971, 42 per cent – numbers that surpassed the overall Canadian average.[16] Ontario, perhaps more than any other province, saw the growth of wage-earning moms and participated in the debate about their proper role – in or out of the workforce.

Despite the mounting evidence that women were spending more of their lives in the workforce than out of it, public opinion surveys indicated that women 'were perceived as "until" workers,'[17] with less claim to jobs, pay, or benefits than male workers. Married women were well aware that 'they didn't enjoy unqualified social approval,'[18] and mothers in particular felt they had to 'rationalize their choice'[19] with considerable proof of their need to work. Working wives often claimed that their husbands were the 'real' bread-winners because 'loyalty to their husbands would not permit' them to challenge his claim to this important status.[20] Women's reluctance to claim the true value of their work was probably related directly to the ongoing, popular debate about working wives and mothers, a forum that did not offer strong ideological support to their wage work.

THE POPULAR DEBATE

Many of the popular images and stories in film, television, and mass-circulation magazines during the 1950s and early 1960s presented the wife and mother who worked in the home as the archetypal, normal, and superior model for North American women. While the single Girl Friday had become a standard icon of popular culture, June Cleaver – the middle-class, suburban homemaker – was considered her married successor. As Ellen Tyler May has argued for the United States, the era of the Cold War was accompanied by, and indeed helped to sustain, a domestic ideology of nuclear family 'containment' that extolled home and family centredness, pronatalism, and hetero-sexuality, one that celebrated the security of traditional gender roles for men and women.

In the Canadian media, too, full-time motherhood was continually lauded as women's natural choice; *Chatelaine* articles of the 1950s portrayed women who spurned heterosexual marriage or rejected childbearing as abnormal or 'selfish.'[21] Women who concentrated on their careers were portrayed ambiguously or with suggestions of personal unhappiness.[22] When the National Film Board produced a series of fictionalized films to discuss mental health in 1951, it featured Clare, 'the successful career girl,' as the centrepiece for the theme of 'Hostility.' Clare, 'starved for affection in her early years,' turns her energies to 'intellectual pursuits, school and work' and to achievement. Although she has a 'socially acceptable outlet for her hostile feelings,' she has 'no friends, warmth or affection in her life.'[23]

Canada's national television also reinforced traditional gender roles. In advertisements, women pursued either 'beauty or the cult of domesticity'; other CBC programming let women play only 'supplementary' and 'decorative' roles, while men were 'the masters of argument and fact.'[24] Employed wives and mothers – as current, interesting, and important characters – were simply neglected. Popular images of womanhood in the movies and TV were not without subtexts and contradictions;[25] nonetheless, it is not surprising to find that many working women do not remember looking to the popular media for role models. As one single working mother put it in her interview, magazines and television could 'annoy me, because they weren't in touch with reality.'[26]

At the same time, married women's commitment to domesticity was not completely taken for granted; in the print media, in particular, a debate was emerging over the meaning, value, and appropriateness of married women's work for pay.[27] As Veronica Strong-Boag has argued, the overall contours of this debate distorted the reality of married women's work: by emphasizing women's choice about whether or not to work it ignored the economic need that compelled women with families to work outside the home, erroneously portraying Canadians as entirely middle class.[28] Furthermore, magazines, especially in the 1950s, seldom examined the lives of single working mothers and offered typical portraits of married women that were highly ethnocentric: the women were inevitably white, Anglo, and often suburban, a misleading image that negated the strong presence of minority and immigrant women in the labour force.

The popular debate over working wives and mothers changed its focus over the postwar period; immediately after the war, many commentators were primarily concerned with whether women would willingly give up their good wartime jobs and pay-cheques.[29] By the early 1950s, the gradual movement of married women into paid work was becoming the focus of concern. Though there was some grudging acceptance of working wives by the late 1960s, working mothers were still a contentious issue. As the 1970s dawned, *Chatelaine* under its feminist editor Doris Anderson became a trailblazer, exploring day-care issues, discrimination in the workplace, and the difficulties of balancing two jobs;[30] many remaining opponents, however, still claimed the negative effects of mothers' wage work on children.

Both those supporting and those opposing working mothers often assessed the issue primarily from the perspective of family integrity and children's welfare. Would women's wage work hurt marriages 'or cause children to suffer?'[31] Women's ability to do two jobs – homemaking/mothering and wage work – was explored, as was women's competence in certain professions, the effects of female earning on the economy, and the consequences for a woman's life. The focus, in other words, was, first, on family welfare; second, on women's needs; and, least often, on women's rights.[32]

Opponents of working mothers based their arguments on the disastrous effect this wage work would have on marital and family relations. In a typical 'I Quit My Job to Save My Marriage' article, one author claimed that divorces were often the result of a wife's work outside the home.[33] Medical and psychiatric experts were often cited to prove that men's psychological needs for masculine fulfilment were better served when wives provided comfort and support, not competition in the workforce.[34] The most emotional opponents of mothers' outside work were sometimes women themselves: one argued that women's education was a waste unless it focused on homemaking;[35] another worried that undermining the anchors of traditional masculinity and femininity – breadwinning and domesticity – would 'unman'[36] the husband and denigrate women's homemaking role. As Strong-Boag argues, such claims were often based in a healthy dose of reality: homemakers were the butt of masculine ridicule and denigration, so much so that many women in the home anxiously attempted to justify the importance of their work.[37]

Opponents, drawing on popular Freudian psychology, also pointed to the harmful effects of women's work on their children. Canada's social-work journal, Canadian Welfare, featured the respected voice of Benjamin Spock urging his professional audience to solve the problem of women who, 'resentful' of their wife-and-mother role, sought outside work.[38] Working mothers, the most vociferous opponents wrote, were more likely to have neglected children. Look at my neighbour, fumed one opponent sarcastically in Chatelaine, 'a Child Psychologist ... she spends long hours in the office while a maid brings up her kids ... and they are the worst brats in the neighbourhood!'[39] While such extreme articles were infrequent, the cumulative effect of this debate engendered negative and guilty feelings in working women. As a nurse remembers of the 1950s: 'The magazines then, even Chatelaine, [said] if you were a working mother, your kids were going to be convicts in time to come ... we were urged to come back to work [by the hospitals] but when we did, we felt shunned by our peer group ... [for] neglecting our home duty.'[40] Some of the condemnations of working mothers undoubtedly drew on a broader current of mother-blaming, which even working mothers had trouble shaking.[41] As a teacher, herself a working mother, remembers: 'In the staff room I remember hearing men talk, and if anything was wrong with kids, it was because mothers were working.' Yet she too was critical of maternal care: 'Sure, there are a few bad apples whose mothers were working ... but there were other [problem] mothers who were out on the golf course, then having a few drinks before dinner.'[42]

Finally, some of the opponents, though recognizing the necessity of work for a very few (such as widows or the truly impoverished), portrayed working mothers as evidence of an increasingly materialistic society on an unnecessary consumer binge – 'on a treadmill, to buy frills'[43] – which could only lead to disaster. This latter view was also emphasized by religious leaders, indicating how lectures against working mothers extended into the pulpits of the nation. The Peterborough newspaper relayed various local sermons criticizing working mothers: 'Being a mother was a full-time job,' declared one Protestant minister, while a Catholic priest insinuated that working mothers were the cause of increasing delinquency.[44] Similarly, the widely circulated *United Church Observer* bemoaned the fact that some 'hard-boiled' women were compelled by the values of competition and status-seeking in work outside the home, rather than by the ethical and nurturing values of true motherhood.[45]

Faced with such harsh, emotional attacks, supporters of working mothers were frequently on the defensive, so much so that they reassured rather than challenged these fears; one such *Chatelaine* author reassured her readers that 'if home life suffered at all ... [a woman] will not, of course, work.' Given the experts' stress on the natural superiority of maternal care, well evidenced in advice literature of the time, it was difficult to find the grounds to defend mothers leaving the home. Supporters did, however, maintain that work outside the home would be good for marriages and families because it allowed women fulfilment and intellectual stimulation that would reflect well in their roles as wives and mothers. In retrospect, some women expressed their satisfaction with work in precisely this vein. One professional woman noted that she felt her work added positively to her role as mother, because she 'could talk to [her] children about more than the house.'[46] Other mothers pointed to their children's independence and desire to pursue an education and careers as legacies of their own example.

Positive images of working wives also stressed the beneficial economic consequences of their work to family security. That reassured readers that women were not taking traditional male jobs, but were being induced into the workforce by labour-hungry employers. An overarching acceptance of the prevailing sexual division of labour outside and inside the home was noteworthy: even sympathetic writers assumed that women 'would still be doing two jobs,' as a *Chatelaine* columnist put it.[47]

Thus, even writers supportive of working mothers framed their arguments within a dominant discourse of family containment, pronatalism, and family welfare. Women's individual needs and/or rights were never as central to this debate as were family concerns. Moreover, the definition of family welfare employed was constructed primarily on reigning psychological assumptions, *not* on the edifice of economic needs and concerns. This popular debate over working wives was, admittedly, quite different from that of the 1930s, when many people worried primarily about women taking jobs away from men. A growing level of acceptance of work after marriage (though before children), and possibly of part-time work in women's later life, had emerged, distinct from the earlier, more blanket condemnation of working wives. Now, however, concern was focused on the 'new' middle-class woman worker, and antagonism was focused primarily on working mothers with younger children.

Even those sympathetic to working mothers often assumed an apologetic tone. In its pamphlets of the late 1950s and 1960s, the federal Women's Bureau reassured the public that the majority of married women workers were childless or widowed, not mothers of young children;[48] even the latter, it said, were not necessarily willing wage earners, for 'women with heavy [family] responsibilities are not likely to be working unless they are under great financial pressure.'[49] Similarly, the government-produced *Labour Gazette* claimed many working women 'would prefer to be at home.'[50] The implication was clear: good/better-off mothers stayed home with young children; poor mothers might not be able to.

Still, this emphasis on the necessity of women's wages to their own and their families' survival was desperately needed. In the labour movement's press, the economic necessity and class dimensions (though the word *class* was never used) of mothers' wage work were far more apparent, particularly in progressive unions with a substantial female membership such as CUPE. Their union publications, as well as their briefs to government, continually provided evidence that married women's wage labour was necessary for family survival. It was conceded that new goals, such as home ownership, shaped family needs, but these small promises of prosperity were also defended as workers' fair due.

Unfortunately, though, the large majority of working women, who were unorganized, remained isolated from the supportive arguments of the labour press. Moreover, it was no secret that some unions, especially those without a substantial female membership, were unsympathetic to issues such as maternity leave, as were their rank and file to the concept of working mothers. These problems were privately recognized and lamented by by female trade unionists, though they were less often the subject of public debate within the labour movement.

While the mainstream press was more likely to pose the so-called problem of working mothers as a moral issue, the business press was predominantly concerned with how more married women workers would affect business efficiency, wage rates, and economic expansion. Though paying lip service to issues of family welfare, business writers also analysed the expanding female workforce as a demographic and economic phenomenon, and, significantly, as an economic possibility, with potentially positive consequences for consumer spending and labour recruitment. The fact that women had pay-cheques to spend; that women were supporting households in the 1957–8 recession that hurt male workers differently; and that women provided a flexible pool of available part-time labour for sectors like retail were all noted positively.[51] While some employers highlighted the negative side of hiring a married woman, claiming, for example, that she would become pregnant and be absent to tend to children, they nonetheless argued for the economic possibilities of married female workers. The attraction of using an available, cheap pool of labour to expand one's enterprise was clearly the bottom line. As one Bell Telephone spokesperson put it, employing married women was simply a matter of 'recruiting every available source [of labour] believed to be productive.'[52] Indeed, the need for an expanded pool of female labour became one motive behind changing government policy.

ONTARIO'S SOCIAL POLICY: THE ESTABLISHMENT OF A
WOMEN'S BUREAU

The increased demand for women's labour power by business and government was a central reason for the establishment, in 1963, of the Ontario Women's Bureau. The feminist professionals on staff clearly hoped to use the bureau also to ease the difficult burdens faced by employed mothers and to widen their limited job and child-care opportunities. By examining social policy relating to the maternity leave, child-care, and anti-discrimination legislation suggested by the bureau, the attitude of business and government towards working mothers, as well as women's own understanding of the possibilities and limitations of social and legal reform, can be highlighted.

Established in 1963 by a Conservative provincial government as a research and information conduit between the public and the government, the Women's Bureau was in part a political initiative designed to win support from a growing female workforce and from the vocal middle-class/professional feminists – groups such as the Professional and Business Women and the Federation of University Women – who lobbied the government on women's issues.[53] Even more crucial, the bureau was an economic initiative devised to monitor the changing labour needs of business and government and to 'facilitate the integration of women into the labour force.'[54] A former director, Lita-Rose Betcherman, remembers her superior using the government's own quest for female labour as an example: 'He pointed out that he might be able to replace someone like me, in a director's role, but he could not find women to replace our secretaries.'[55] From the very beginning, the Bureau was centrally concerned with the employment of women with families, who were returning to wage work after childbearing.

Both politicians and Women's Bureau employees often publicly framed their goals in a language of productivity, efficiency, and maximum usage of the labour power. 'One of the worst brain drains is women who do not use their education,' Betcherman argued. 'Women are going back to work after they have a family, but they are underemployed, their education wasted.'[56] To support its claim that women's labour was underutilized, the bureau provided its own research that showed that more than 90 per cent of the Ontario women they interviewed expected to work during their marriage, with the majority interested in returning to work after they had children; almost 61 per cent of these women wanted full-time, not part-time work. In order to ease the re-entry of mothers into the workforce, the bureau set up counselling programs to offer advice on retraining and to provide information on the legal rights of working women to individuals and the community.

Deferring to accepted notions of proper female work, the bureau assumed that most women wanted to enter fields such as clerical work and teaching. Indeed, one of the bureau's surveys of women's occupational goals revealed how resilient the ideological constructions of gendered work were: in all age groups, women's two top choices were always teaching and secretarial work, with some other feminized occupations such as nursing and social work thrown in for variety.[57] With its mandate shaped within these limits – aiding the integration of women into the jobs where they were 'needed' by government and business – the bureau did not challenge the prevailing gendered division of labour. Moreover, in its early years, the bureau focused primarily on better-educated, Canadian-born women, and less on immigrant and minority women. Later on in its mandate, the bureau began to recommend more non-traditional work for women and to address the needs of immigrant women.[58]

Despite its less-than-revolutionary goals, the bureau found itself continually dealing with persisting myths about women workers which reflected and helped to sustain the social and economic barriers to women's employment. As Betcherman noted, it was wrongly assumed that women were 'passing through the workforce on their way to the alter,' that they 'worked for frills, while men are breadwinners.'[59] Individual women who encountered many varieties of prejudice brought their problems to the bureau; although often sympathetic listeners, bureau employees had no means of providing redress to women fired for reasons of marriage or pregnancy, passed over for promotions, or limited by the sex-typing of jobs. In one such case, a writer asked why nothing could be done about a situation at a Peterborough clock factory, Westclox, when *only* female production workers had been asked to take a wage cut in 1969, probably 'because of the old breadwinner idea.'[60] While the bureau staff were sympathetic, they could actually do nothing. Moreover, it is significant that the complaint was raised by a social worker who did not work at the plant; the workers themselves were more likely to see hope in pressuring their union to support them than in finding redress through the bureau.

MATERNITY LEAVE AND THE WORKING WOMAN

One of the repeated problems relayed to the bureau by women workers was their vulnerability to management's prerogative to fire married or pregnant employees. The latter was especially significant: women could be routinely fired when they became visibly pregnant, and they had few guarantees of returning to their job after childbirth. Although larger employers in particular were instituting maternity-leave plans, many were opposed to legislation infringing on their right to decide the employment status of pregnant women or to close off jobs by sex and marital status. In the 1950s and 1960s the legal right of employers to fire married and pregnant women, as well as the prevailing social disapproval of pregnant working women, sustained the powerful message that mothers did not belong in the workforce.

Prejudice against married women and against women with children varied considerably across occupations. In some professions, married women encountered unstated marriage bars: in Peterborough, for example, one married women claimed she 'didn't even bother applying to the School Board'[61] in the 1950s because it was known to favour single women. Ultimately, though, she did find employment in one of the less popular rural schools. When a university was established in Peterborough in 1964, its first president dismissed any claims of persisting sex discrimination in Ontario universities as 'behind the times.'[62] Yet, for a number of years, married women with academic qualifications were discouraged from teaching there if they had husbands working at the university.[63] Where tradition was less elitist and labour shortages were more severe, such as in white- and blue-collar work, women usually found that their marriage was accepted, but maternity was not.

For those who opposed legislated maternity leave, pregnancy suggested the intrusion of women who didn't 'belong' in the workforce; it violated their notions of appropriate gender and family roles. 'If a woman is strong enough and greedy enough to work during pregnancy,' wrote one long-time female worker to the federal government, 'then she should be treated as any other worker. I do not sympathize with work-till-last-minute woman. I have worked with them and most are prima donnas and use pregnancy to get privileges. When I first started to work it was considered unnatural to work during pregnancy and women were asked to leave at three months, then the husband assumed his duty of looking after her. This was good, sensible and healthy.'[64]

Many working women were clearly thinking very differently. An Ontario study done in the 1960s, based on a carefully chosen sample of twenty-one representative employers, indicated that up to 70 per cent of women were interested in returning to work after a pregnancy. Yet only a minority of women, usually under collective agreements, were assured maternity leave, and only a minority of those women suffered no loss of seniority. Even the unions surveyed by the bureau were reluctant to champion the issue of maternity leave in actual contract negotiations.[65] Only one union leader, from the more radical United Electrical Workers, argued, at least on paper, that maternity provisions 'should be in every contract.'[66]

Management, however, was clearly unsympathetic to legislated maternity leave. Businesses declared that women's right to re-employment after childbirth was a 'privilege' more than a 'right.'[67] A researcher at the Ontario Women's Bureau noted that one large company operating in Peterborough dismissed the issue in a 'smart aleck' way; another massive Toronto life insurance company with many women workers said it had given maternity leave 'no concrete thought'; and a major retail store lectured that it generally gave such leave only to 'girls with five years service.'[68] Some school boards even suggested that teachers should plan their pregnancies to produce summer babies, so as not to disrupt the school year! Finally, any suggestion that women be given cash benefits was decidedly unpopular: this would be seen as a 'reward for pregnancy,' admonished male employers, overtaken with visions of female employees becoming pregnant to 'cash in.'[69]

Women's recounting of their actual experiences of pregnancy, of course, were far different from the picture imagined by these employers. Most women's decision to resign on pregnancy was influenced, first, by the knowledge that management would probably fire them, and, second, by the existing social disapproval of visibly pregnant women at work. Moreover, very few women considered working straight through a pregnancy and returning to work soon afterwards as an attractive choice; it was more likely to be an economic necessity. One war bride who settled in Peterborough remembers lying in the hospital, having just given birth to her third child, when her husband was admitted with a medical emergency. 'His sick benefits had a six-week waiting period, so I had to go to work' to support the family, she recalls.[70] In ten days she had a job waitressing; nonetheless, it was not an experience she would have chosen.

Women who began wage work before the Second World War tended to see leaving when you became pregnant as close to a legislated imperative. More than one woman remembers the shared expectation that the plant nurse would keep an eye on women workers in order to detect pregnancies. In small workplaces, and in a small city like Peterborough, one's marital status was well known; once married, the company was on the lookout for pregnant employees. Women expected to be routinely asked if they were married, or planned to have children. 'Why did you go and get married?' an interviewer at a large electrical factory 'joked' with one woman; he then refused to hire her.[71] If a woman didn't resign on pregnancy, she knew dismissal could follow. There were few cases where women's physical condition interfered with their job, though, in one case, a new immigrant from Britain remembers that her 'combined morning sickness and whooping cough' made winding motors at General Electric 'so unbearable' that, when the foreman asked her to leave, she was secretly relieved.[72]

At the same time, younger mothers who began their working life in the 1950s, after the marriage bar had been broken, saw the pregnancy bar as the next frontier. One nurse recalled the first time she and her fellow workers witnessed a woman disregarding the informal rules of resigning when pregnant and their distinct feeling of amazement and secret admiration: 'I remember we always quit at the hospital when we were pregnant ... finally, in the early 1960s, someone just kept working when she was pregnant ... and word spread like a forest fire about this woman ... we all thought: how *brash*.'[73]

Indeed, in the postwar period women increasingly questioned, and occasionally resisted, dismissal on pregnancy. 'I wanted to keep the independence of my own pay-cheque,' remembers one woman who worked in a cereal factory. 'If I had gotten seventeen weeks leave [in 1951], I would have been happy. [But] they wouldn't even let you come *back* [after having a baby]. That was to keep the married woman home, barefoot and pregnant!'[74] Occasionally, women used subterfuge to keep their jobs: a Quaker Oats worker simply wore large clothes and a girdle and kept her mouth shut. As a result, she joked, 'she just about had her baby on the Muffets line.'[75] If women did stay at work, it might be the result of 'a favour' from management. In the local clock factory, a woman reluctantly gave her notice; her foreman asked her if pregnancy was the cause and then offered her an easier, sitting job for a number of months, since she was the sole family breadwinner at the time. This informal paternalism or 'kindness,' as she interpreted it, was not the same as a legal right to a job.[76]

If a woman actually protested her dismissal, she would likely find management an impossible adversary. In 1960 a separated, pregnant woman in the Peterborough Quaker Oats plant was fired when her pregnancy was detected. She courageously took it through the grievance procedure as wrongful dismissal. The union, the United Packing House Workers, supported her and brought in Mary Eady as their Board of Arbitration nominee, but they ultimately lost the grievance. The majority of the board agreed that the company had the right to decide on the marital, family, and financial status of its workers. Noting that the company had a firm policy of hiring only single women, management added that, once married, a worker could only continue until her sixth month of pregnancy and she should not be re-employed unless 'she is the sole supporter of a family due to the husband being disabled or dead.' This was unwritten but 'well-known' company policy, moral and justified because it was the same as that of other companies. The company also used specific information from the personal record of the employee to justify her dismissal. As Eady noted, all this was irrelevant to the issue of unwritten, informal, and unfair management rights: 'If a worker could do the job,' her minority report protested, 'she should not be discriminated against because of pregnancy or marital status.'[77]

Such protests were few and far between; most women did not have a union to appeal to and simply complied with the pressure to leave work, usually at the point when their pregnancy became visible. One teacher remembers that in the 1950s she felt compelled to hide the physical signs of her growing stomach from the children. Apparently, thought of a pregnant woman in front of impressionable children was too much for parents and principals to bear: it might encourage little ones to ask difficult questions about reproduction.

Health and safety concerns about women working while pregnant certainly existed, especially in some blue-collar jobs, but they were not the only or major reasons that women were fired. When maternity leave was first discussed in the 1960s, male medical experts were often called upon to offer opinions on where, when, and how long pregnant women could work. Their replies often acknowledged that most women could work during pregnancy without 'the threat of physical damage,' but their recommendations commented extensively on whether these women should ultimately leave work and offer 'consistent maternal care' to their children.[78] For some of these experts, maternity leave was still a *moral*, not a health issue. Too many women, pontificated one doctor, were working for unnecessary consumer purchases. Once a child is born 'the child must come first and the family should live on the husband's salary alone.'[79]

Until women's legal right to maternity leave was established through collective agreements or through legislated reform, such moral judgments and social inhibitions acted as the arbitrary, informal law of the land. The Women's Bureau's survey of the issue indicated the lack of consistency in women's options; it also showed how peripheral the issue of women's right to maternity leave was seen to be in the immediate postwar period.

THE WOMEN'S EQUAL EMPLOYMENT OPPORTUNITY ACT

As a means of countering discrimination against married and pregnant workers, the Women's Bureau began to urge the passage of anti-discrimination legislation. When business was sounded out on the prospect of such legislation, it was not enthusiastic. Some of this opposition flowed directly from misogynist views of women's intellectual capabilities. A Canadian Manufacturers Association employee claimed that women didn't want advancement, and that many stenos 'couldn't think ... they need to acquire men's mentality.' More often, company personnel representatives pointed to women's family responsibilities as a rationale for their opposition. Women workers did not need an extension of rights, they claimed, since they were not good training or management risks; they were hard to work with and they put family and children before work, causing 'atrocious absenteeism' – though charges like these were seldom accompanied by solid evidence.[80] These views were voiced by male and female personnel specialists alike. The latter had already been socialized to the dominant prejudices of the business world; moreover, they sometimes indicated that their opposition to legislation promoting equity was related to fears about their own status in the workforce. Any legislation designed to remove discriminatory barriers, one worried, might mean that 'employers just wouldn't hire women anymore.'[81]

Women from the union movement, on the contrary, expressed positive support for legislation barring discrimination, though they sometimes shared their private discouragement over the prevailing views of married women's wage work within their own movements. 'The idea of man as the provider is still a problem ... even women accept it,' commented a prominent female unionist in a male-dominated union. Nonetheless, these women unionists argued strongly for anti-discrimination legislation. In unions like the United

Auto Workers, the Women's Committee mobilized its members to put pressure on the government to pass the bill. Their vocal political lobbying not only bolstered the bureau's case for such a bill, but was extremely important in pushing the government to proceed with such legislation.[82]

In 1970, under Betcherman's direction, the bureau produced what was popularly called the Women's Equal Employment Opportunity (WEEO) Act. It set out women's right to an (unpaid) maternity leave, and prohibited advertising jobs by sex and dismissal because of marriage or pregnancy.[83] Ironically, labour and its allies in the NDP were ultimately disappointed in the bill because of its exclusion of women in smaller workplaces, the loose provision for exemptions, and the failure to give sex discrimination the importance it deserved by placing responsibility for enforcement with the Human Rights Commission.[84] The truth, according to Betcherman, was that the commission was not enthusiastic about assuming this responsibility, since it worried that, with few resources, its anti-racist work would be placed second to increasing numbers of sex-discrimination complaints. Betcherman and others decided that, politically, for the time being, the Women's Bureau had the ideological commitment to enforce the act and so should maintain its administration.[85]

To women struggling within the Bureau to secure anti-discrimination legislation, the act still seemed to be a breakthrough: by confronting questions of equity, and by stressing the rights of pregnant women and women with children to wage work, it established new legal rights and challenged the existing social thinking about working mothers. The WEEO Act was never able to deal systemic discrimination a lethal blow, but by employing a language of equal rights, yet with some attention to the social value of women's childbearing, it set out new parameters for the debate on working mothers.

The Conservative government's support for the WEEO Act, argued Betcherman, emerged from its own 'Red Tory' proclivities,[86] as well as its confidence – shaped by good economic times – that this act would facilitate better use of female labour power. The government was undoubtedly also aware of the growing impact of the federal Royal Commission on the Status of Women, and the political advantage of leading with anti-discrimination and maternity-leave legislation before being forced by political pressure to implement it.

At the time, the radical possibilities of the legislation were downplayed by the provincial minister of labour, who reassured opponents that women would never want access to male jobs such as construction work – indeed, that they should be protected from these jobs.[87] The government carefully justified the act with the existing language of productivity as well as equity. Sex discrimination, commented the bureau, reflected an 'unproductive' way of using the workforce, while the WEEO Act would simply 'create an environment in which female labour could achieve [its] optimum performance.'[88]

WEEOA marked a new departure for the bureau; it also represented a symbolic shift in feminist and labour politics. Individual women responded to its anti-discrimination clauses immediately, unleashing their long-bent-up grievances and asking for redress.[89] Collectively, women in and out of the union movement were also becoming more organized and articulate about working women's issues. Three years later, when Betcherman and others produced a green paper for the government outlining future policy relating to women's equality, they found that many women's groups now criticized the government recommendations as 'too little too late.' Even if the climate was still less than welcoming for many working mothers, a stronger sense of rebellion and entitlement was clearly developing.

CHILDREN: THE LAST STRAW

Ultimately, employers and businesses reluctantly accepted the bare bones of the WEEO Act and found it less expensive and unwieldily to implement than they had claimed. Employers remained completely unsympathetic, however, to one of the bureau's other concerns: publicly funded child care.

If visibly pregnant workers were something of an anathema to employers and even some fellow workers, then working mothers whose children were not visible were even more of a problem. The topic of working mothers, commented one survey for the federal Department of Labour, inevitably takes on the negative 'connotation of fearful neglect, latch keys and cold suppers.'[90] Many employers told the Ontario Women's Bureau that working mothers would incur more absenteeism and be less productive, and that they would be uneconomical to train since they would inevitably leave under pressure of family duties. Yet the thought of providing day care was unacceptable to them, even though the wartime experiment with day nurseries was just over a decade old. Day care was not seen as a necessary cost to be paid in return for the female labour they needed; rather, the private family was expected to absorb the duty for child care.

In the 1960s, women interviewed by the Women's Bureau who expressed an interest in returning to work often added that it was impossible because they had young children.[91] Their statements combined a realistic assessment of the limited child-care offerings with an ideological image of parenthood as women's special vocation and duty. Indeed, the feeling that women actually *should* be home with their children was so strong that some working mothers repeated it. One 1958 study quoted a typical comment of a single working mother who felt that 'every woman with three children should be at home all the time for her children's sake. I think my kids lost something along the way.'[92] Similarly, some women I interviewed who had to work when their children were young expressed regret, either individually or with the general trend: 'I would have preferred to be at home with the children.'[93] Women's regrets were also related to the exhausting double day of family and wage work they endured; in fact, this double burden was a major reason why many women tried *not* to return to work after having children. As one woman who resigned from her factory job explained, she dreaded doing two jobs: 'even now ... I look at the woman coming home and having to prepare dinner [for her kids and] I think, I just *couldn't* have done all that.'[94]

The pressure to leave employment once you had a child was true of professional, white-collar, and blue-collar women, though surveys indicated that the last group were more likely to reject this advice and return to work when children were young. This may have been related partly to income level and partly to protection of these jobs through union contract seniority provisions. Social approval for working mothers was also related to class and economic position. Middle-class mothers, remembers Betcherman, 'didn't work' in the 1950s; working-class women 'had to,' and they surveyed their decision to return to work with less guilt.[95]

Women who worked as teachers and social workers had the added burden of having been educated within the dominant social science paradigms of the time. This model endorsed the father/breadwinner, mother/caregiver family as the most 'normal,' well-adjusted one and accepted the view that a child should have consistent maternal care during its 'tender' years.[96] When a Peterborough social worker went back to work shortly after having a child in the 1950s, her decision was looked at 'critically' by colleagues; 'many people did not think very much of that,' commented her spouse in retrospect.[97]

For some women, however, there was little sense of choice involved; they had to return to work. 'What was I to do?' asks one immigrant woman who worked for a bank in the 1950s; she remembers the feeling of desperation when she found herself pregnant, but the family had need of her pay-cheque. 'I knew I *had* to return to work but there were no such things as nurseries here (which she had seen more of in Britain); we couldn't afford our apartment without my pay-cheque so my mother came over [from Britain] and lived with us to look after the baby.'[98]

This woman's solution was the most prevalent one in the 1950s and 1960s. In one Canadian study done in 1967, the majority of working women with pre-school children were using relatives and friends to care for their offspring free, though sometimes there were some reciprocal services given. The next most popular choice was a babysitter, while only an estimated 1 per cent were using day-nursery or day-care programs.

Many working mothers in Peterborough relied on immediate family to care for young children; they were left with grandmothers, or the parents shared child-care by working shifts. Married women who worked at the textile mill took the afternoon shift, from five to eleven, after caring for children during the day, and nurses laboured at night while their husbands were at home with sleeping children. As one nurse remembers, this meant working nights and doing housework during the day – an exhausting schedule.

Far more working mothers in the 1950s and 1960s had school-age children; these women relied on family aid, short-term babysitters, and latch keys as their child-care solutions. Nieces were asked to babysit, or older children helped; as one single mother remembered: 'My eldest daughter was literally my right hand.'[99] In Peterborough, women also found older women, often widows, who would look after children after school. Those who relied on unknown babysitters still recall the worry of calling home constantly to check on the homefront. One single mother came home to find 'her sons outside in the rain.' Her six-year-old informed her that the babysitter had been entertaining a male visitor in the bedroom.[100] The babysitter was promptly fired, but the dilemma of finding someone else became the new problem.

Despite women's own experiences with worry and exhaustion, publicly funded child care remains one of the most unacceptable ideas to women of this generation. This may be related to a misunderstanding of the financial costs of day care and a sense of pride in their own individual survival. As a union activist who began factory work in Peterborough in the 1960s remembers: 'Many women were unsympathetic to day care when we raised it ... they had coped, so why couldn't we?'[101]

Many women also associated public day care with welfare status. If women already sensed they were criticized because of their wage work, they felt vindicated when a close family member provided care for their children; this solution offered the respectability of keeping children within the privacy of the family. 'We coped entirely on own,' remembered one woman proudly; we didn't have to go 'outside [the family].'[102] Moreover, in a society in which organized pre-school care had weak cultural traditions, women felt hesitant and worried about placing their children with strangers, even qualified ones.

In fact, in rural areas and small cities like Peterborough, there were *no* full-time day-care centres for women to use. In Toronto, day nurseries had been established during the war, and some survived the postwar cuts, particularly because politicized parents organized to save them; the result was at least a minimal consciousness of such facilities as public services. In other areas of the province, the story was different: 'outside Toronto,' commented one relieved politician in 1949, there is 'no pressure for the establishment of day-care centres.'[103] Even by the 1960s, as middle-class women's lobby groups concerned with the economic inequality of women workers became more vocal, they could not rouse their members on the issue of child care.[104]

Part of the problem was the intractable understanding of day care as a welfare service of last resort. After the Second World War, Ontario's child-care policy was firmly based on the view that a mothers's role in the workforce was marginal and/or undesirable. This understanding became entrenched in social policy of the 1940s and 1950s, which was designed to limit child-care expenditures drastically by adopting 'careful screening and social investigation'[105] of those requesting subsidized day care.[106] This policy clearly penalized working mothers, for it articulated a hierarchy of need in which only physically disadvantaged children, or the most impoverished of households, were justified in using child care. Government bureaucrats unequivocally dismissed the need for mothers to work in order to purchase cars, furniture, or even homes: apparently beds, shelter, and transportation were 'frivolous' in their eyes.[107] Working to improve one's standard of living or to save for children's education would also have been unacceptable reasons for mothers' wage work; any thought of mothers, like any other citizens, having a right to work would have been considered the most unacceptable of all.[108] Although Jane Ursel argues that a postwar sense of 'entitlement'[109] characterized the public attitude towards social policy, it did not in any way extend to care for pre-school children.

The predominant language of welfare surrounding child care was perpetuated in the 1960s with the provision of federal aid under the welfare provisions of the Canadian Assistance Plan. Although this funding ultimately expanded public day care, the political discourse of day care as welfare provision put ideological limitations on its development as an educational or social 'right' – and indeed on its use by working mothers.

Since local initiative was crucial to day-care provision, municipal parsimony was also part of the problem. The reluctance to spend money had a strong ideological component: daycare violated a concept of the nuclear patriarchal family which many local politicians felt must be defended, particularly because more married women *were* working. When the issue of a municipally funded centre was first broached in Peterborough in 1966, the city's welfare committee and administrator said the city was uninterested. Two vocal aldermen on the welfare committee voiced their opposition in no uncertain terms. One raised the financial issue, saying taxpayers' money should not be used to look after children whose mothers were working. Another made clear his ideological opposition: 'I am a firm believer,' said Alderman Curtin, 'that all children need proper, and if possible a mother's care.'[110] Even the local newspaper found their opposition questionable in a time of women's increasing need to work for wages.

A year later, the city's first day-care centre was established on the initiative of the local Children's Aid Society and the Community Chest, with aid from the local Health Unit and Family Counselling. The centre was not intended to provide care to all working parents, but rather was seen as a measure to aid single mothers and children at risk. The CAS, remembers a former social worker, believed that the centre might help to reduce their protection budget; it was to help 'prevent disintegration of family life and to offer security and attention to children ... where there was a need for assistance.'[111]

By the next decade, social experts were finally beginning to dispute prevailing myths that day care 'led' women to work and that it was a 'cold,' unnatural environment or even a 'communist plot.'[112] Still, a current within the social-work profession continued to link day-care need only to low-income families, and to the prevention of delinquency and other social ills.[113] By the early 1970s community organizations in Peterborough began to advocate more strongly for child care; one social worker told the Ontario Welfare Council that it was 'tragic' that such services were lacking in Peterborough, and asked if 'industries employing mothers' could not assume more responsibilities for providing day care.[114]

Despite the increasing support for day care in social service circles, local politicians remain wedded to a welfare interpretation of child care – right up to the present day.[115] Day care was neither validated as an educational aid for all children, nor seen as a right, let alone a need of all working parents. The discourse of day care as a last resort for the disadvantaged ultimately cast a negative pall on the very concept of wage-earning mothers: in the same breath that Alderman Curtain rejected day care, he reinforced an image of the 'proper' mother, at home with her child, rather than out working. It is no wonder that so many working mothers felt a strong pressure to make do within the extended family; their solutions were directly related to a social policy that offered few practical aids and little ideological support for their work outside the home.

Perhaps day care remains an unpopular issue precisely because it is so potentially subversive to reigning notions of women and work. Socialized and accessible day care not only challenges a traditional sexual division of labour, and images of innate sex differences and abilities to care for others, but also questions the dominant story that women's wage labour is a 'choice,' or a luxury, not a necessity or a basic social right.

## MOTHERS INTERPRET THEIR WORK

How then did women justify their wage work in an era that offered them little positive ideological reinforcement or practical help in terms of social policy? Interviews of working mothers who returned to work after having children in the 1940s and of mothers joining the workforce for the first time in the postwar era, offer women's own interpretations of their need to work of their experience of pregnancy and mothering, and of the difficulties they encountered as working moms. Their memories offer us a means of understanding the reality *they* saw, the economic and ideological premises on which they based their choices, and the way in which they negotiated the contradictions, even in their own minds, between their two jobs.

Mothers who went out to work had to balance the knowledge of their own and their families' needs with a public perception that mothers were working outside the home for unnecessary or selfish reasons. In retrospect, the vast majority of women were at pains to stress the economic necessity that compelled them to go out to work. One woman whose spouse was seasonally employed, and who worked all her life as a domestic, beginning in the 1930s, made it clear that her earnings kept her family eating: 'My husband really didn't want me to work, but it was our main source of income.'[116] At the same time, women acknowledged the changing definitions of economic need and were forthright about their dreams for economic advancement, especially for their children. One woman who started a factory job after the war and took four maternity leaves, each time returning to work, indicated that her earnings were the only means of giving her children something she was denied: 'If they were to have an education, then I had to work.'[117]

Women often felt that they needed to justify any family money not spent directly on food and shelter; one war bride referred at first to her wage work as 'purely selfish' because she used her earnings to take her children home to Britain to see their grandparents.[118] On one level she recognized the importance of sustaining these ties; but on the other she found it difficult to challenge prevalent stereotypes about women working for 'extras.' And even in working-class households with very tight budgets, women sometimes had a hard time convincing their husbands that their wage work was appropriate: one woman remembers her blue-collar husband's profound uneasiness when she resumed work as a typist, even though her children were in school. 'My husband didn't want me to work ... but without my job we couldn't have afforded new [appliances] ... nor this house.'[119]

In some cases, husbands feared that their status would be diminished by their wives' work: 'It was sort of a feather in his cap then, you know, if the wife didn't work,' remembered one woman.[120] One means of accommodating these fears was for women to turn to the informal economy, taking in children, or doing sewing to make money. In other working-class households, the necessity for more than one income led to a readier acceptance of women's full-time wage work; as one war bride who worked in an office indicated, '[my husband] was supportive because it was simply a financial matter ... mind you, he never changed a diaper.'[121]

Nonetheless, cutting across all classes and occupations, women recall husbands' worries that a wife's wage work would detract from her domestic and child-related duties. Husbands who performed a substantial amount of domestic work (particularly chores traditionally done by women) were in a distinct minority; the majority of women worked a double day, and then some. The long-established practice of women's unpaid work in the home left women 'ironing until one or two in the morning.'[122] Women developed coping strategies, from 'a regimented household,' to purchasing some services, to lowering some of their expectations: 'eventually,' the mother above realized, 'my kids had to wear some wrinkled clothes.'[123]

While working mothers made their decisions based, first, on economic need; second, on their desire to contribute in a meaningful way to their families; and, third, on their own needs, they were often well aware that the wider society viewed their motives suspiciously. If your husband was alive, remembered a Bell operator, you were 'just working for extra money ... you were seen as sort of selfish.'[124] Some working mothers, such as widows, were deemed more worthy earners than others. As one widow explained, employers 'understood' her need to support her children and have specific hours of work.[125] Such women's determination to work rather than go on mothers' allowance was often lauded by employers and fellow workers. Single mothers who were separated or divorced were caught somewhere in this hierarchy of need. As one divorced woman explained, people 'felt sorry' for her because she was divorced, but they also understood her need to work outside the home.[126] Yet another woman with an alcoholic husband who did not support the family recalls that the perception of her predicament was less than sympathetic: when she looked to her priest for advice, he said, 'Well, Jean ... you made your bed ...'[127]

Although women remember their wage work primarily in a context of economic need, they also note the consequences of personal satisfaction, independence, and camaraderie they experienced in the work world. Women in white-collar work, and most particularly in professional jobs like teaching, also drew on professional pride to explain their persistence with work outside the home. 'I taught for the fulfilment, not the money,' joked one woman who worked in a number of rural schools.[128] Women who worked extremely hard to secure a post-secondary education were reluctant to 'waste' it, to abandon work and intellectual stimulation they enjoyed. As one nurse remembers, she 'wanted to keep up with the times; things were changing in the profession, and I didn't want to get left behind.'[129] For teachers, the satisfaction of helping problem students, developing new curriculum, or receiving praise from colleagues all offered antidotes to the ambiguous public perception of working mothers. Indeed, in the 1950s and 1960s, when teachers were needed, they were often approached by principals or boards and urged to take jobs – a part of their work history they emphasize strongly.

The 'independence' of one's own pay-cheque, even if it was not enough to raise a family on, and the community of the workplace also contributed to women's sense of positive identity as workers. As one woman who worked at Bell put it, 'I left work a number of times, but always came back. I loved the girls ... and I loved my independence.'[130] Because she had seen her mother work as a child, she knew the freedom and satisfaction it could potentially bring, despite the double day.

In contrast to the satisfaction gained, the hardest thing about working, women said again and again, 'was concern for your kids.'[131] Many working mothers coped with combined mother and wage work by accepting part-time or seasonal work that allowed them to shape their work around children's schedules; this led them to jobs at department stores like Sears, domestic work, or waitressing employment that was low paying and less secure.

Full-time workers who had to rely on family, friends, or babysitters to look after children found that the practical difficulties of providing child care could always be overcome - somehow. Even in families where there were two working spouses, women invariably looked after child care arrangements as well as many extra child-care duties. 'It was just understood that I would stay home if a child was sick ... of course, I was the one to stay up at night with the children,' explained women in diverse occupations.[132] If the husband was unenthusiastic about her work, a woman felt even more pressured to assume the burden of child care.

The practicalities of finding child care, however, were almost secondary to the worries of leaving the children. Uneasy feelings about leaving children while the mother worked depended on the children's age, the mother's sense of her own need to work, and also on her occupation. Women working in white- and blue-collar jobs were certainly aware of the image of the 'bad' working mother, too; indeed, many working-class women I interviewed did not return to wage work after children precisely because they and their husbands believed it was preferable to have a home-centred mother when children were growing up.[133] But as Betcherman noted earlier, there was a class distinction in how women coped ideologically; women whose families were in most need – that is, deserted, widowed, divorced, or lower-income families – had less trouble justifying their wage work. To them, it was just something you had to do: their definition of family welfare was more likely to incorporate a materialist sensitivity to the family economy, in contrast to the definition of family welfare promoted in the mass media which concentrated more on a psychological definition of well-being removed from material necessity.

One way that women coped with anxiety about appearing to be a bad mother was to work hard at dispelling the image. One white-collar worker remembers joining the PTA particularly for this reason. Another professional woman who lived in the suburbs, which she identified as a particularly unwelcome environment for working moms, joked about her attempt to become a supermom: 'I had to be super mom, nurse, wife. Because I worked, I drove. Because I drove, I was the chauffeur for all the kids in the neighbourhood. I took kids to dancing, swimming. I'd work all night, then jump in the car in the day. It took me five years to realize I was running my head off.'[134] The self-realization that no amount of extra motherwork would solve the public's misperception was often reached by many women; a sense of collective anger about this false view, however, was rarely articulated.

Though a large number of women claimed not to take great stock in advice literature in magazines, the prevailing social suspicions of working mothers obviously affected their outlook. Many felt worry, uncertainty, or, at worst, guilt about working outside the home at some time during their working lives. The fact that women can recall the exact incidents that triggered their guilt is itself revealing. 'Once my son broke his ankle and had to stay home alone and I had to go in,' remembered one white-collar worker. 'I felt so terrible ... If I needed to work on weekends to make ends meet, I felt bad about leaving the kids, but you know, I just *had* to.'[135] Some women dealt with the lack of ideological support for their work by lamenting their financial need to work; others justified *their* personal need, but were critical of other women, such as those with pre-school children or working spouses, who they felt should not be working for wages. The reality that women spent much of their time raising the family, combined with the pervasive popular image of women's 'natural' nurturing role, meant that balancing mother work and wage work could produce many contradictory feelings for women. 'I was a mother first, a teacher only second,' stated one woman emphatically, only moments after explaining the great satisfaction she derived from her job.[136]

Although women could easily mix feelings of guilt with the knowledge that they had to or wanted to work, it is revealing that one woman who was actively involved in union politics and who attended many conferences on women and work during the 1960s was better able to concentrate on women's economic needs and rights. She had little patience for those who focused on the morality of mothers' work; her intellectual metamorphosis as a union activist helped her to see the negative side of the motherhood myth and to acknowledge the sheer economic necessity of married women's wage work.

When analysing their past, women are well aware of the barriers they faced in the work world in terms of job choice, lack of upward mobility, and outright opposition to pregnant women or mothers working. The extreme occupational segregation of the workforce by gender; the lack of vertical mobility for women, especially if they had families; and the pressures of the double day were all acknowledged by women, with various levels of acceptance and criticism. Though most would reject the label 'feminist,' some describe being streamed though education and social pressure into sex-typed jobs. In the 1940s, remembers one woman, 'no one [at school] talked about careers for women ... if you made it to high school, you could be a secretary or teacher, period.'[137] Similarly, women recognize that the paternalistic rules employers enforced for working mothers, such as bringing a note to say they had a babysitter or refusing promotions, seemed unchallengeable then, though they would be seen as discriminatory now.

At the same time, these women, whether they really felt wage work was a choice or not, rightly claim respect and pride for their important contribution to the family economy. Often they are anxious that we see their strong commitment to mothering, and even their decision to follow female occupations, as positive choices that reaffirmed an important part of their identity. One nurse, for example, pointed out that few women were encouraged to think of medicine as possible in the 1950s; her nursing education – at the time, often a considerable cost to working-class families – must be interpreted as a step towards self-reliance and as an intellectual endeavour to explore medical issues, as well as a the product of her socialized feeling that, as a woman, she could and should nurture others.

Perhaps most personally evocative for me is the testimony of a woman who was employed when she was first married at General Electric, one of the best-paying factories in the city. She was later reluctant to return to this kind of work, even though, widowed at a young age, she had to find a way to support her children. Instead, she extended her part-time work as a cook to full-time work: to her, this offered more job flexibility and satisfaction. Fifteen years ago she came to work at my childrens' day care, where the pay was decidedly lower than GE. 'You could have made more money at GE.' I asked. 'Oh, of course,' she replied. 'I haven't made a lot of money in my work, and they weren't what people would say are "exciting" jobs, but ... I love the children and I feel that I have made a difference for them too.' Her self-effacing words in fact underestimate the extent to which her care and devoted attention *has* made a tremendous difference to the children in the day care. It is not her decision to pursue wage work in a female 'ghetto' that we must critique, but rather our society's shameful financial and social undervaluing of her work.

CONCLUSION

Contrary to earlier images of the postwar period as a time of full-time domesticity for women, by the 1950s and 1960s there were an increasing number of women with families going out to work. Though the dominant image of married women in the popular media may have focused on their domestic roles, and assumed a middle-class life style and a male breadwinner, many women faced a very different reality.

Wage-earning mothers faced a spirited public debate over the meaning, value, and consequences of their work outside the home. The debate in the popular media betrayed persisting economic and ethnic biases, as commentators neglected the historically high labour-force participation rate of low-income and immigrant women and concentrated instead on what they perceived to be a 'new' influx of 'better-off' women into the workforce.[138] Furthermore, this debate, waged largely in the print media, did not take as starting points the economic needs of families, nor the right of women to wage work. Rather, the perennial question, *'Why* do married women work,' was asked again and again; even those sympathetic to women workers felt they had to study this question exhaustively to assure the public that women were working to survive, not for frivolous reasons. As one *Saturday Night* author pointed out, it would be unthinkable to ask, 'Should married men work?' yet women with families were constantly subjected to precisely this question.[139]

The issue of mothers' wage work was often measured in relation to its effect on family welfare. Although working-class women might measure that welfare by material need, the media debate tended to stress a social and psychological definition of family welfare that became the yardstick for those supporting and those defending mothers outside work. Given the stress at that time on family togetherness, and the psychological emphasis on devoted mothering as the cornerstone for well-adjusted children and communities, it was difficult to make an airtight case that mothers' increasing wage work was a positive feature of social life. Opponents' strongest card was always the portrait of latch-key children, smoking on street corners, fast on the way to becoming juvenile delinquents because maternal supervision was lacking.

Whatever the supposed moral consequences of working mothers, business and government recognized the important economic role of married women's increased labour-force participation. For this reason, the Ontario government's social policy initiatives included the establishment of a Women's Bureau to offer advice on labour policy and to aid the integration of women, especially those returning to work after children, into designated female occupations. Feminist bureaucrats within the bureau were always interested in achieving more than this goal; with other political allies they were able to persuade the government to initiate the WEEOA to alleviate discrimination against women on the basis of gender and marital and family status.

Women's ability to become economically independent, however, was circumscribed by the persistence of a firmly entrenched gendered division of labour in the workplace as well as in the home. At the same time, work traditionally done by women was undervalued. Other important social policies still assumed that women with families should preferably work only in the home. Nowhere was this assumption more clearly apparent than in the province's day-care policy: child-care initiatives were obstructed by a discourse of day care as welfare for the disadvantaged, rather than as aid for working parents or educational care for children. While both employers and government were anxious to make use of mothers' labour power, they were not ready to assume the social cost of caring for their children, particularly because such work was already absorbed as unpaid or low-paid labour within the home.

Working mothers in this era did not enjoy the full ideological blessing of the media and the social experts, and they had few practical social supports or legal protections to fall back on. This isolation was particularly so in rural areas or in small cities, which lacked even limited social services like day care. Furthermore, the knowledge that women could be arbitrarily dismissed on pregnancy or because of their family status – policies clearly defended by management, as in the Quaker arbitration – offered a clear message that mothers simply did not enjoy the right to wage work.

Given this inhospitable atmosphere, women's own contradictory feelings about their work lives become understandable. The ideological and physical wear and tear of combining motherwork and wage work took its toll. Women felt uncertain about the effects of their work on their children, and they worried that the negative consequences of working mothers, continually highlighted in popular debate, might contain an element of truth.

It was primarily the knowledge that their wages were needed by the family, or that their work was socially productive, which gave working mothers the fortitude and pride to persist. In hindsight, many women stress the importance of their outside work to family security and advancement, and the positive consequences of their work for their children's development. Indeed, given the larger influx of mothers into the workforce which took place in the decades after 1970, some women take a certain pride in their place as pioneers of a radically altered workforce.

The radical potential of those alterations, however, has yet to be fully realized. Mothers' paid work should potentially raise questions about economic power and hierarchy within the family, about women's responsibility for unpaid domestic work and their 'natural' role caring for young children, about women's rights to equal economic citizenship and respect, and about the social responsibility for child care. These issues remain unsolved challenges for many of today's working mothers.

NOTES

1 *Financial Post Magazine*, 15 Nov. 1981.
2 For example, the 1951 *Census of Canada*, vol. 2, table 48, shows that 87 per cent of the city were Canadian born, and another 10 per cent were born in the British Isles. In 1961, 87 per cent were still Canadian born, and 9 per cent were British born (1961 Census, vol. 1, table 52). In the 1961 *Census of Canada*, vol. 1.2, table 38, 87 per cent of the city described themselves as ethnically 'British.' The largest ethnic minorities were the French (5 per cent) and German (3 per cent).
3 Promotional material for the city celebrated the 'pioneer race' of British descent which dominated the city. Peterborough Museum and Archives, clipping file, 'A Pioneer Race,' nd. The city remained predominantly Anglo/Celtic in background. The few immigrants in the immediate postwar period were primarily from Britain or from northern European countries.
4 On paternalism see Joan Sangster, 'The Softball Solution: Women Workers and Male Managers at Westclox, 1923–60,' *Labour/Le Travail* 32, 1993.
5 National Archives of Canada (NA), Department of Labour, RG 27, Women's Bureau Papers (hereafter Bureau), vol. 4171, Submission of the OFL to Royal Commission on the Status of Women (RCSW). By the time the OFL gave its brief to the commission in 1966, 60 per cent of women workers were married.

6 Some female immigrants had a very high labour-force participation rate. See, for example, Franca Iacovetta, 'From Contadina to Worker: Southern Italian Immigrant Working Women in Toronto, 1947–62,' in Jean Burnet, ed., *Looking into My Sister's Eyes: An Exploration in Women's History* (Toronto 1986). On Black working women in this era see Dionne Brand, ed., *No Burden to Carry: Narratives of Black Women in Ontario, 1920–1950s* (Toronto 1991).

7 Michael Krashinsky, *Day Care and Public Policy in Ontario* (Toronto 1977), table 1, 'Growth of Labour Force Participation of Mothers in Ontario and Canada.

8 In the late 1950s the Gordon Commission on the future of the economy predicted confidently that, by 1980, women would not be more than 26 per cent of the workforce – a substantial miscalculation. *Canadian Business*, Feb. 1958.

9 Canada, Department of Labour, Women's Bureau, *Survey of Married Women Working for Pay in Eight Canadian Cities* (Ottawa 1958). The majority of women earned between $1000 and $2000. Sixty per cent of their husbands earned less than $2000. By the 1970s the National Council of Welfare estimated that '51 per cent of two spouse families would fall below the poverty line if wives did not work.' National Council of Welfare, *Women and Poverty* (Ottawa 1979), 20.

10 Ruth Roach Pierson, *They're Still Women After All: The Second World War and Canadian Womanhood* (Toronto 1986).

11 Archives of Ontario (AO), Department of Labour, RG 7, Women's Bureau (WB), 7-1-0, file 1371, Employment survey, 'What Women Think about Working.'

12 Canada, Department of Labour, Women's Bureau, *Occupational Histories of Married Women Working for Pay in Eight Canadian Cities* (Ottawa 1959).

13 Jane Ursel, *Private Lives, Public Policy: 100 Years of State Intervention in the Family* (Toronto 1992), 230.

14 Pat and Hugh Armstrong, *The Double Ghetto: Canadian Women and Their Segregated Work* (Toronto 1986).

15 Canada, Department of Labour, *Woman at Work* (Ottawa 1964), 23–5. See also Julie White, *Women and Part-time Work* (Ottawa 1983). Ann Duffy and Norene Pupo, *Part-time Paradox: Connecting Gender, Work and Family* (Toronto 1992), 44.

16 The 1951 Census, vol. 5, table 3; 1961 Census, vol. 3, table 4; 1971 *Census Tract*, Peterborough, table 2. The 1951 rates were based on those over the age of fourteen who were working; after 1951, those fifteen and over were included. The Canadian average for 1951, 1961, and 1971 were 24 per cent, 29 per cent, and 39 per cent.

17 NA, RG 27, WB, vol. 4171, Briefs to the Royal Commission on the Status of Women. Study done by Hickling-Johnston on status of women in Canada.

18 *Survey of Married Women Working for Pay in Eight Canadian Cities*, 59.

19 Ibid.

20 Ibid.
21 'Why Some Women Never Marry,' *Chatelaine*, Nov. 1954; 'A Minister's Frank
   Words for Brides and Grooms,' *Chatelaine*, May 1954. Articles such as these support the contention that it was not simply pressure to assume a domestic role, but
   also compulsory heterosexuality and pronatalism that made this era oppressive
   for many women.
22 This is even true of some articles written by feminists. See June Callwood's article, 'The Incredible Women of Madison Avenue,' *Maclean's*, 5 Nov. 1960.
23 *Canadian Welfare*, 15 April 1951.
24 Paul Rutherford, *When Television Was Young: Primetime Canada, 1952–67*
   (Toronto 1990), 332, 200.
25 As historians of Hollywood have contended, smouldering gender tensions lay
   beneath the surface of many movies. See Molly Haskell, *From Reverence to Rape*
   (New York 1974), and Brandon French, *On the Verge of Revolt: Women in
   American Films of the 1950's* (New York 1978).
26 Interview with JF, 9 July 1991.
27 Ursel, *Private Lives, Public Policy*, suggests that the turn to women's productive
   labour occurred with relatively little 'notice and controversy,' 234. The debate,
   however, was ongoing and fairly extensive.
28 Veronica Strong-Boag, 'Women with a Choice: Canada's Wage-earning Wives
   and the Construction of a Middle Class, 1945–60,' paper presented at the Canadian Historical Association, Charlottetown, 1992. This fixation with middle-class
   women was apparent in discussions of gender discrimination as well; one female
   writer critical of the Royal Commission on the Status of Women maintained that
   Canadian 'women had little to complain about'; the examples she used were
   invariably those of more privileged, middle-class, and professional women. See
   'Do Women's Rights Have Wrongs?' *Globe and Mail*, 26 Jan. 1967.
29 'What War Women Will Do When It's All Over,' *Saturday Night*, 24 June 1944;
   'Should Women Return Home?' *National Home Monthly*, 46, May 1958.
30 Doris Anderson, 'Women's Magazines in the 1970s,' *Canadian Women's Studies*
   11, 2 (1980), points out that *Chatelaine* combined traditional articles (recipes,
   beauty, and how to have a happy marriage) with more substantive reporting on
   women's issues.
31 *Chatelaine*, Aug. 1952.
32 There were exceptions. See 'Will Married Women Go to War Again?' *Saturday
   Night*, 30 Jan. 1951; 'How Canada Wastes Its Woman Power,' *Saturday Night*, 2
   April 1960; 'How I Do My Two Jobs,' *Chatelaine*, May 1954.
33 'I Quit My Job to Save My Marriage,' *Chatelaine*, June 1955. The author, of
   course, had no concrete proof other than the perceptions of some court workers
   she talked to.

34  'The Role of Sex in Happy Marriage,' *Chatelaine*, March 1959. For a classic 'mother-blaming' approach, suggesting that bad mothering produces aggressiveness in males and thus war, see 'Do Women Make Wars?' *Chatelaine*, July 1948.

35  'Don't Educate Your Daughter,' *Chatelaine*, Sept. 1954. The letters to the editor in reply also indicate that some readers rejected her indictment of women's education.

36  'A Minister's Frank Words,' *Chatelaine*, May 1954.

37  Strong-Boag, 'Women with a Choice.' See also Barbara Ehrenreich, *The Hearts of Men* (New York 1983), for contemporary, derogatory view of homemakers.

38  Benjamin Spock, 'What We Know about the Development of Healthy Personalities in Children,' *Canadian Welfare*, 15 April 1951. The emphasis is mine, though it is clear in the article that women's outside work is constructed as a problem.

39  'Don't Educate Your Daughter,' *Chatelaine*, Sept. 1954.

40  Interview with FM,19 June 1991.

41  See Wini Breines, 'The 1950's: Gender and Some Social Science,' *Sociological Inquiry* 56,1, 1986, on theories of 'maternal overinvolvement.'

42  Interview with SI, June 1991.

43  'I Quit My Job to Save My Marriage,' *Chatelaine*, June 1955.

44  *Peterborough Examiner*, 6 and 15 March 1950.

45  'The Real World of Women,' *Observer*, 15 Oct. 1967.

46  Interview with LB, 11 July 1991.

47  'Back to Work,' *Chatelaine*, Aug. 1969.

48  *Women at Work*, 22.

49  *Survey of Married Women Working for Pay in Eight Canadian Cities*, 39.

50  *Labour Gazette*, March 1954.

51  'Working Women Ease Burden of Unemployment Problem,' *Financial Post*, 11 June 1960; 'Working Women Spur Spending,' ibid., 19 April 1958; 'Lament for Wasted Resource: Home-Stuck Mothers,' ibid., 15 Oct. 1966; 'Wives with Paychecks,' *Canadian Business*, Feb. 1954.

52  'Wives with Paychecks.'

53  The *Globe and Mail* implied that this was a 'play for the women's vote in the upcoming election,' 12 Sept. 1963.

54  'The Role of the Women's Bureau: Ontario,' *Labour Gazette* 67, Jan. 1987.

55  Interview with Lita Rose Betcherman, 1991.

56  AO, RG 7, WB (7-1-0-1629). Betcherman, who had a PhD in history, knew only too well how this worked; when she graduated in the late 1960s, a career in academe was considered almost impossible for a married woman. As a result, she turned her impressive talents to the fields of human rights, women's, and labour issues.

57  AO, RG 7, WB, F 207-5-5-9, 'Women's Bureau Job Selector: A Report of the Employment Preferences of Women and Girls.'

58  Betcherman remembers talking in her speeches about widening occupational choices for women. Similarly, the federal Women's Bureau did discuss the need for better vocational training for young women in the 1960s.

59  AO, RG 7, WB, vol. 2, WEEA file, Notes for *Topical*, 30 Sept. 1970.

60  AO, RG 7, WB, series 8, box 1, 'Correspondence.'

61  Interview with PP, June 1991.

62  *Peterborough Examiner*, 14 Jan. 1966.

63  This occurred under the first two administrations, as indicated by some of my female colleagues who managed to remain despite active discouragement. Others, of course, did not. This is described in Trent's official history as discouragement of spousal hiring, but, in fact, it was directed against women. See A.O.C. Cole, *Trent: The Making of a University* (Peterborough 1992).

64  NA, RG 27, Bureau, vol. 1904, 38-11-3-4, file on Maternity Leave.

65  Some union reps replying to the provincial Women's Bureau even opposed it, since it would lead to 'discrimination against women.' AO, RG 7, WB, vol. 1, Maternity Leave file, Miss Whitton of Office Employees International. On trade-union attitudes, see also Maureen Baker and Mary-Anne Robeson, 'Trade Union Reactions to Women Workers and Their Concerns,' *Canadian Journal of Sociology* 6, 1, 1981.

66  AO, RG 7, WB, vol. 1, Maternity Leave file.

67  Ibid.

68  Ibid.

69  Ibid.

70  Interview with CL, July 1991.

71  Interview with DC, 24 July 1991.

72  Interview with CL, July 1991.

73  Interview with FM, 19 June 1991.

74  Interview with TE, Jan. 1990.

75  Ibid.

76  Interview with DC, July 1991.

77  Report of a Board of Arbitration: In the Matter of a Dispute between Local 293, United Packinghouse, Food and Allied Workers, and the Quaker Oats Company of Canada, June 22, 1960. Mary Eady was the head of the CLC's Women's Bureau. My thanks to Bill Hickey for giving me a copy of this arbitration from his files.

78  NA, RG 27, Bureau, 'Maternity Protection for Women Worker,' 1967. The doctors consulted did offer varying opinions: some admitted that women could return to work six weeks after the birth, especially since breast feeding was less prevalent; others urged women to remain home.

79 Ibid.

80 AO, RG 7, WB, vol. 1, Sex Discrimination Legislation file.

81 Ibid.

82 Pamela Sugiman, '"That wall's comin' down": Gendered Strategies of Worker Resistance in the UAW Canadian Region (1963–70),' *Canadian Journal of Sociology* 17,1, 1992.

83 In the legislature, the bill was actually officially called 'An Act to Prevent Discrimination in Employment because of Sex or Marital Status.'

84 AO, RG 7, WB, vol. 1, Sex Discrimination file. As well as omitting small workplaces, there were also some loopholes in the act that allowed certain jobs to be designated by sex; maternity leave was a mere twelve weeks.

85 Two years later the enforcement of the sex discrimination clause did go to the Human Rights Commission.

86 Interview with Betcherman, 1991.

87 AO, RG 7, WB, 9-0-128. The government was of two minds about following the advice of the bureau to reject the 'protection' approach to legislation; it sometimes revealed a preference for this approach.

88 AO, RG 7, WB, vol. 1, Sex Discrimination file, Betcherman's notes on CAALL Conference.

89 In the two years following the legislation, the government received 4400 inquiries, 433 complaints, and 126 advice calls. AO, RG 7, WB, vol. 7, WEEA file. These numbers are certainly higher than complaints under the earlier Equal Pay Bill. See Shirley Tillotson, 'Human Rights Law as a Prism: Women's Organizations, Unions, and Ontario's Female Employees Fair Remuneration Act, 1951,' *Canadian Historical Review* 72,4 (1991): 544.

90 Canada, Department of Labour, Women's Bureau (Sheila Woodsworth), *Maternity Protection for Women Workers in Canada* (Ottawa 1967), 5390.

91 AO, RG 7, WB, 7-1-0-1371, 'What Women Think About Working.'

92 *Survey of Married Women Working for Pay in Eight Canadian Cities*, 59.

93 Interview with BM, 8 Aug. 1991.

94 Interview with BD, Nov. 1990.

95 Interview with Betcherman.

96 Carol Ehrlich, 'The Male Sociologists Burden: The Place of Women in Marriage and Family Texts,' *Journal of Marriage and the Family* 33, 3 (August 1971), and Wini Breines, 'The 1950's: Gender and Some Social Science,' *Sociological Inquiry* 56,1, 1986.

97 Interview with SJ, July 1991.

98 Interview with FH, July 1991.

99 Interview with BM, 8 Aug. 1991.

100 Interview with BG, 25 June 1991.

101 Interview with JJ, 25 Aug. 1990.

102 Interview with MV, 26 June 1991.

103 AO, RG 29, Department of Public Welfare, box 21, file 878 (717-12-6-2), draft of memo from minister of public welfare to minister of education, 27 June 1949.

104 For example, the Ontario Business and Professional Women couldn't get members to implement a questionnaire on child care owing to the 'apathy' of club members, and the committee on child care was left to die a 'stagnant' death. AO, Ontario Business and Professional Women's Clubs Association, D. Milligan to J. Wilson, 19 Feb. 1966.

105 AO, RG 29, box 20, file 841 (717-12-6-1), conference with Mr Heise on admission policy for nursery and day-care Centres, 8 Feb. 1951.

106 In 1950–1 only $264,671 was spent in the entire province, and some years over the next decade actually saw cutbacks in the level of funding. Table 14, 'Provincial Expenditures in Ontario on Day Care,' in Krashinsky, *Day Care and Public Policy in Ontario*, 35.

107 AO, RG 29, box 20, memo from director of welfare services re social investigations: St Stephens Day Care Centre, 8 Jan. 1951.

108 On day care policy, see Susan Prentice, 'Workers, Mothers, Reds: Toronto's Postwar Daycare Fight,' *Studies in Political Economy* 30, autumn 1989.

109 Ursel, *Private Lives, Public Policy*, 252.

110 *Peterborough Examiner*, 20 July 1966.

111 Interview with former CAS official in T. Muller, 'Daycare in Peterborough,' honours paper, Trent University, 1990.

112 'Debunking the Day Care Mythology,' *Canadian Welfare*, Sept./Oct. 1971.

113 These two perspectives were not necessarily mutually exclusive and could be voiced within the same speech. For an article that stresses the economic need and the right of mothers to work, but also tends to see these families as potential 'problems,' see 'Run Mother Run, See Mother Run,' *Canadian Welfare*, May/June, 1967.

114 AO, Ontario Welfare Council Papers, box 48, Vincent Castellano to OWC, 'Responses on Daycare Services,' 28 Aug. 1969.

115 In 1993 City Council cut back on its subsidies to middle-income families, claiming only those in need should be aided. Despite opposition from child-care users, council pushed the changes through.

116 Interview with DA, July 1991.

117 Interview with AH, July 1991.

118 Interview with CL, July 1991.

119 Interview with RH, Nov. 1989.

120 Interview with BL, 11 July 1991.

121 Interview with FH, July 1991.

122 Interview with FM, 19 June 1991.

123 Interview with BM, 8 Aug. 1991; with FM, 19 June 1991.

124 Interview with BG, 25 June 1991.

125 Interview with PM, 24 June 1991.

126 Interview with PM, 20 June 1991.

127 Interview with JF, 9 July 1991.

128 Interview with BM, 8 Aug. 1991.

129 Interview with FM, 19 June 1991.

130 Interview with DB, 25 June 1991.

131 Interview with BG, 25 June 1991.

132 Interview with LB 11 July 1991.

133 This information is taken from interviews for my book with working-class women who began work in the late 1930s and the 1940s, but who did not return to work after they married and had children.

134 Interview with FM, 19 June 1991.

135 Interview with BG, 25 June 1991.

136 Interview with BM, 8 Aug. 1991.

137 Interview with DB, 25 June 1991.

138 It is important to note that, before the Second World War, many working-class women did not work outside the home unless they absolutely had to. In the 1950s and 1960s both working-class and middle-class married women increased their work outside the home.

139 'Will Married Women Go to War Again?' *Saturday Night*, Jan. 1951.

FRANCA IACOVETTA

# Remaking Their Lives: Women Immigrants, Survivors, and Refugees

On a bitterly cold day in the fall of 1952, Katie Werner, a young German woman who had married a Polish soldier billeted in her home during the final Allied assault on Hitler, arrived at the train station at Port Arthur in northwestern Ontario. Forewarned about the region's climate and keen to make a good impression, Werner dressed in a combination of her finest and warmest – a lined trenchcoat, a wolf-fur collar, and high-heeled shoes. As she stepped off the train into a ferocious wind, she knew the outfit was a mistake. 'I thought I had come to the subarctic,' she recalled years later. While walking from the station to the hotel where she would stay until her husband's return from a logging camp, her silk-stockinged legs grew so numb that she was sure they had fallen off. The only warm part of her body, she added, was her fur-collared neck![1]

Whereas Werner's arrival had met with little fanfare, crowds of people welcomed Elaine Dewar and Angela Bianchi to their respective new homes in Ontario. A war bride from Glasgow, Scotland, Dewar and her child arrived in Sault Ste Marie in December 1946 to rejoin the Canadian soldier she had married. She was part of a contingent of war brides who received an official welcome from town dignitaries and were treated to a gala Christmas luncheon organized by the Ladies Auxiliary of the local branch of the Canadian Legion. The festivities were replete with a decorated tree, presents for the children, and entertainment supplied by the town's talented youth. A large group of well-wishers met Angela Bianchi and her husband as their train rolled into Toronto's Union Station in November 1953 carrying thousands of newcomers completing the inland voyage from Halifax. Bianchi's two sisters, several brothers-in-law, and some cousins from her village in central Italy had arrived to escort home yet another set of kin who had come to join them in the city.

A Jewish survivor of Nazi slave-labour camps, Sarah Ginsberg also arrived in Toronto with her husband, a co-survivor she had married in a refugee camp. As most of their relatives had perished in the Holocaust, no one was waiting for them at Union Station. Equipped with the address of a Jewish family in Brantford who had offered them work, they secured some funds from a Toronto immigration office before heading for the promised jobs and a temporary home with their Canadian sponsors.

Elena Krotz also came to Canada from a displaced persons' camp. In 1949 she was recruited by Canadian officials to work on contract as a domestic servant. A single, eighteen-year-old Czech woman, Krotz had escaped arrest by the Communist authorities in Prague, where she had participated in student protest activities. With the help of some well-placed church people, she had made her way to a British-controlled refugee camp in Germany. Once in Canada, she spent several frustrating weeks in a government hostel before being posted with a farm couple near the southwestern Ontario town of Wroxeter. When her new employers met Krotz at the local train station, they were 'shocked' to find that she had only two briefcases for luggage and that the battered bags carried all her worldly possessions – one change of clothes and a blanket.[2]

Who were these immigrant and refugee women who entered Ontario in the years immediately after the Second World War? How did they remake their lives in the villages, towns, and cities of the province? If we are to understand more fully the character of post-1945 Ontario society, especially its gendered, class, and multi-ethnic dimensions, we need to explore the predicaments and experiences of tens of thousands of foreign-born women – volunteer immigrants, Holocaust survivors, and refugees – who came in these years. This article, a preliminary look at a complex subject, considers the diversity of the British and European women who entered early postwar Ontario as well as the responses of middle-class Ontarians keen to influence the women's lives. Above all, it investigates how such women remade their lives in the new society. In the process of doing so, they also affected the lives of kin and neighbours and contributed to the vitality of their respective ethnic colonies. To varying degrees and in a variety of ways, the arrival of numerous 'foreign' women also affected the character of many of the province's postwar workplaces, markets, social institutions, and wider communities.

Since a comprehensive treatment of Ontario's new foreign women is not possible here, this article offers selective examples drawn from a cross-section of women who came from different national, racial/ethnic, religious, class, marital, and political backgrounds and who settled in different localities in the province.

For thousands of female newcomers, resettlement in Canada meant being relegated to the lowest-paid sectors of the female job 'ghetto' – domestic service and low-skilled factory positions and thus taking on the 'dirty' jobs that Canadian women shunned. In addition, most of the recollections of immigrant women contain painful stories of prejudice. The fierce taunts of intolerant neighbours and passersby, or the harsh, even cruel, criticisms of an angry employer, harried doctor, or frustrated government worker surface in many such recollections. It would nevertheless be misleading to think of immigrant women exclusively as passive victims, to assume that they led completely isolated lives or that their presence never made any difference to the people they encountered or the places they inhabited. The experiences of newcomers frequently involved multiple encounters with 'others' such as neighbours, public health officials, welfare workers, or welcome delegations of the Local Council of Women. Invariably, such encounters were inegalitarian: even the assistance of sympathetic volunteers keen to help financially strapped immigrants find housing and land a job was offered in the hope that they might eventually 'Canadianize' the newcomers. Yet, when immigrant women accepted such services or actively sought them out, they did not necessarily fall completely victim to the ideological pressures to conform entirely to Canadian ways. Wherever they settled, immigrant women faced prejudice, constraints, and limited work opportunities, but many of them also found ways to confront, adapt to, and, on occasion, challenge those obstacles.

FROM WAR-TORN EUROPE TO PEACETIME ONTARIO

Ontario has long been the most popular provincial destination for newcomers entering Canada, and, certainly, the pattern continued during the post-1945 era. Between 1946 and 1965 more than half of Canada's two million immigrant arrivals chose Ontario. Among the adults, probably close to half of the Ontario-bound newcomers were women. Most entered the country in what for women was the usual way, through the family classification scheme – that is, they were sponsored by fathers or husbands. Others came as contract workers destined for placements in domestic service, the needle trades, and other industries where Canadian employers and officials had deemed there were acute labour shortages. Only a minority came as independent immigrants approved for admission on the grounds that they possessed skills or a professional expertise highly desired by Canada. Some women came to Ontario from Europe's displaced persons' camps or other temporary shelters, while many others arrived directly from their home towns.

Most immigrants in early postwar Ontario were white Britons and Europeans – not surprisingly given that before 1965 Canada's doors were very nearly closed to immigrants of colour. While postwar government schemes to recruit West Indians as domestic servants began in the 1950s, such women remained a tiny minority of immigrants before 1965. Only modestly larger was the contingent of Chinese women who came in the years after the repeal in 1947 of the infamous Chinese Immigration Act that since 1923 had denied them entry. White Europeans, however, came to Ontario in the tens of thousands and, in the case of the British, Italians, and Germans, in the hundreds of thousands. Had Canadian officials not restricted admissions of Jewish refugees, Ontario likely would have been home to a still larger group of European Jews (see table 1). Approximately 38 per cent of Ontario's million newcomers came from the British Isles, and another 25 per cent from Northern and Western Europe. The so-called 'exotic continentals,' East and South Europeans, made up about 35 per cent of the province's newcomers. By contrast, Asians topped the list of immigrants of colour, but represented merely 1 per cent of the postwar arrivals (calculations derived from Table 1).

Within Ontario, the heaviest concentration of immigrants developed in the southwestern 'industrial corridor' of Toronto-Hamilton-Guelph and the surrounding districts, though rural areas also witnessed a significant influx. Northern cities that had long attracted immigrants, places such as Port Arthur and Fort William (Thunder Bay), Sudbury, and Sault Ste Marie, also received comparatively large numbers of newcomers.[3]

Women, many of them in their twenties and thirties, figured prominently in the migration flow to Ontario. The provincial statistics do not permit a gender breakdown for Ontario immigrants, but the national figures, which do record sex and age, suggest general patterns. For most groups, women made up a significant proportion of the adults (age eighteen and over) in their respective group, usually registering between one-quarter and one-half of the total adult volume. Among the Britons and Europeans, the proportions hovered between 47 and 56 per cent (see table 1). While not all women emigrated for reasons of marriage and family, for many the immigrant experience included marriage and childbirth. By 1961 a larger proportion of Canada's foreign-born women were married (71.5 per cent) than was the case for Canadian-born women (65.6 per cent). Certain groups, including Italians and Ukrainians, were especially youthful immigrant populations composed of many young parents and small children.[4]

Although most of Ontario's female immigrants shared either a British or a European background, the women nevertheless arrived with different life experiences, perspectives, and resources. They were a large and diverse collection of women – a diversity hardly captured by the popular label of the era,

'New Canadian.' While its widespread adoption was meant to improve on earlier labels such as 'foreigner,' the category sidestepped the question of difference among the immigrants by implying that distinctions were less important than their common process of becoming something else – Canadians. Indeed, many social experts involved in immigrant reception work advocated a policy of downplaying national differences among newcomers, of discouraging ethnic identification, and of encouraging plenty of 'mingling' between newcomers and Canadians so as to foster Canadianization. Such intentions were evident, for instance, in the activities mounted at St Andrew's Memorial House, a Toronto friendship house that in the late 1940s ran a community program designed particularly for professional (East European) refugees. It consisted of a lecture series on Canadian affairs, English-language instruction, a library of Canadian materials, and regularly scheduled bridge clubs, chess games, and musical and social evenings. While board members and volunteers were genuinely concerned to promote racial harmony by encouraging Anglo-Celtic Torontonians to join the programs and befriend the new immigrants, they deliberately discouraged the immigrants who joined their programs from using their first languages and from clustering in 'nationality groups.' That such actions offended at least some newcomers and provoked tensions between staff and immigrants is evident in a report issued on St Andrew's House by the Toronto Welfare Council. It noted: 'There is a vocal group who wants to feel free to speak their own language but the House feels that too much leeway in regard to the language spoken at the House would be harmful to House purposes and objectives.'[5]

The extraordinary circumstances of the Holocaust, the Second World War, and the refugee crisis greatly affected the character of European female migration. For example, while most of Canada's female newcomers gained entry through the familiar channel of family sponsorship, more of them were recruited as workers for placement in Canadian jobs than had been the case in earlier eras. Most numerous among such recruits were East Europeans brought from the displaced persons' camps. The newcomers differed by national, ethnic, and religious backgrounds and with respect to class, education, and occupation. Particularly among the DP women from Soviet-occupied Eastern Europe and among Jewish survivors, there was a significant minority of educated, professional women who hoped to resume interrupted careers. Their success or failure in this regard influenced their perceptions of their adopted homes. Many would end up competing for low-skilled industrial and service-sector jobs with women from peasant and working-class backgrounds. Others found alternative careers – for example, as social workers with language skills that enabled them to serve an immigrant clientele.

The newcomers also held divergent political views. The majority of post-war immigrants generally were unsympathetic to Communism. Nevertheless, there were real differences between intense anti-Soviets among the Baltic, Polish, and, later, Hungarian women and, say, Italians or social democratic Finns. Those coming from nations with a popular Communist Party might not possess the same intensity of anti-Soviet feeling as those whose homelands had come under Soviet control. Ontario's workplaces, markets, and English classes drew together women who recently had been enemies. Sometimes, relations were strained. In other cases, women had the opportunity to get to know others whom they had once been taught to treat as enemies.[6]

The wartime experiences of a Holocaust survivor like Gerda Frieberg, transported by Nazi soldiers from her Polish home town to a concentration camp in Czechoslovakia, contrasted sharply with those of peasant and fisherwomen from rural Italy and Portugal who had passed the war years in family households. For Frieberg, who had spent the war in a women's slave-labour camp, these years had meant long hours at factory work and the daily horrors of witnessing Nazi soldiers beat Jews. As a woman, she lived too with the constant fear of rape, a fear that did not end when the Soviet Red Army liberated her camp in 1945. Warned that the soldiers might sexually assault them, she and other female inmates hid for weeks until the situation stabilized. Frieberg survived the war along with her mother and sister. At war's end she went home with her mother and sister, only to discover that no one else in the family had survived. They then made their way to a displaced persons' camp in Germany. By 1953 she had settled in Toronto, where she worked as a seamstress and, later, designer. She also immersed herself in humanitarian work. But, as she recalls, the sexual vulnerability she had experienced as a female survivor stayed with her. 'My fear of men,' she said, 'has never left me.'

How different Frieberg's story is from that of Nina Laurenza, an Italian from Calabria who spent the war years raising a child and running the family farm while residing in a house located next to her parents' home. Like much of the Italian south, Laurenza's village was bombed periodically during the war, but she never believed herself to be in real physical danger. Her husband returned safely from the war. By 1954 the couple had settled in Toronto, though that migration had occurred in stages, with Laurenza joining her husband after a two-year separation. For women like Laurenza, the war, though frightening, had not been horrific. Although the fighting took its toll in men's lives and made plenty of young widows, Italians and other South Europeans had not had to face a genocide.

The same was true of the Catholic and Protestant women living in the East and Central European nations that had fallen to Hitler. Many of them, however, were affected directly by the war. Moved to German-controlled factories and labour camps, some spent the war years in strange countries in the employ of the Nazis and their collaborators. They included women like Rita Girse, a Latvian Catholic who was twenty years old when war broke out. When the Germans invaded, Girse's family had tried to flee, but the family was stopped by German soldiers. Girse and her sister were placed in a Nazi-run hospital in the Latvian capital of Riga, where they tended injured German soldiers. Several months later the sisters, along with dozens of other women, were moved to Germany. They feared being recruited into a German women's army corp. By coincidence, they encountered a Latvian man from home who had been put in charge of overseeing new recruits for Nazi factories. (Evidently, he was collaborating with the Germans.) For the sisters, the chance meeting was fortuitous; they were picked for factory work in a small German town. There, they narrowly escaped death when, one day in 1944, they skipped work because Allied bombing in the area had increased significantly. That day a section of the factory was bombed out and all the workers were killed.

At war's end the sisters travelled miles to reach a refugee camp in the American-controlled zone of Germany, where they had heard 'there were many Latvians ... and a high school.' With a resentment still evident many years later, Girse recalled that, for weeks after her arrival in the DP camp, the American authorities tried to determine whether she had been a Nazi sympathizer. When, finally, she was able to convince them that she had been in Germany under a Nazi forced-labour scheme, she was permitted to register at the University of Heidelberg. At the time she had wanted to be a dentist. A few years later she was in Canada on a domestic-service placement. After completing her posting, she worked as a hospital lab technician in Toronto and married a Lithuanian man she had known in the camp. A year later, in 1954, the couple bought a farm near the southwestern town of Delhi. Girse farmed and raised two children. The interruption in her education caused by the war, and the labour contract she had filled during her first year in Canada, had changed permanently the course of her life. Apparently no longer convinced she could pursue her ambition to be a dentist, she had returned to her rural roots. That decision likely pleased Ontario officials keen to see immigrants filling the depleting ranks of farm families.[7]

ENCOUNTERING ENTHUSIASTIC ONTARIANS

Soon after the war, patriotic and socially conscious middle-class Ontarians were propelled into action by the anticipation and then arrival of the European and British immigrants. Journalists, professional social workers, charitable volunteers, women's groups, and ethnic Canadians debated questions of citizenship, democracy, and family; they mobilized resources for receiving the newcomers and exerting a 'Canadianizing' influence on them. Predictably, large cities like Toronto and Hamilton were the places of concentrated immigrant reception work, but they were not the only sites of feverish activity. In towns and small cities across the province, local citizenship and women's groups, welfare agencies, service clubs, religious bodies, and political groups of various stripes joined the reception campaigns. Immigrant women figured prominently as targets for Ontarians keen to encourage wives and mothers of young children to adopt Canadian ways.

The views of enthusiastic Ontarians towards the postwar immigrants were, not surprisingly, influenced by the main ideological currents of the day. The Cold War had begun. There was strongly felt anxiety that after the long upheavals in economic and social relations occasioned by the Great Depression and the Second World War, Canadians did not know what 'normal' family life was. Since the family and home were thought by many, especially social experts, to be the best places for developing sound moral character and citizenship, this supposed situation was viewed with enormous concern. Moreover, the fear was compounded by the belief that Canada, especially Ontario, was about to receive an influx of even more 'dysfunctional' foreigners – the casualties of war, refugee camps, and Soviet aggression – who might require expensive support on their arrival in the province but might never turn into useful Canadians. The severe housing shortage of these years, a shortage that forced many married couples and families to 'double up,' and the increase of married women in the paid workforce, added to this collective angst. It also led some to blame mothers for the period's social ills, real and perceived, be they 'latch-key' children, juvenile delinquents, or purveyors of obscene literature.

The post-1945 era, of course, was not the only time that the family was said to be in a state of crisis, but the moral panic of the late 1940s and 1950s was largely shaped by the particular circumstances of the day. It is also worth noting that Ontario reformers were operating with a particular configuration of the family, one based on an unrealistic middle-class model that many working-class families had never managed to attain. It assumed that everybody ought to live within the confines of a private, single-family household and that men and women performed gender-specific roles. As the male head of the household, the man was expected to be a successful breadwinner earning sufficient wages to support his wife and children. The woman 'paid' for her keep by providing a well-stocked, well-managed, and nurturing home for husband

and children. That this model had never fit countless working-class and immigrant families did not stop enthusiastic postwar reformers from romanticizing the past and from encouraging Canadians, New and Old alike, to embrace 'traditional' family life. The Cold War added a new urgency to this call by equating the predominance of respectable, middle-class, family values with the superiority of Western democracies such as Canada.[8]

While these were not the sole themes in postwar discussions of immigrants, the twin metaphors of family and democracy did inform the views of numerous commentators and activists who favoured immigration. They hoped to recruit the immigrants into their larger social and ideological project of ensuring postwar economic security and aiding the West in its moral campaign against the Soviet Union. Immigrants who were staunch opponents of Communism, women and men who became Canadian citizens, stories about the successful recruitment of entrepreneurs – all were celebrated as examples of the opportunities available in the West. Staff workers with the International Institute of Metropolitan Toronto, an immigrant aid agency serving non-British immigrants in the city, warned in 1959 that lonely, isolated immigrants stumbling along by themselves would be especially vulnerable to Communist propaganda. 'Our duty,' explained one worker, is 'to guide them against loose thinking and against judgement based on labels rather than realities. Negligence on our part to associate with them will bring the eager communist to their rescue.'[9] Such notions also affected advocacy work. For instance, the Canadian Association of Social Workers lobbied strenuously in favour of admitting displaced persons, insisting they were desirable immigrants who would become useful New Canadians as long as careful screening of Communists was undertaken. It also advised that these people, now accustomed to living in chaotic 'mass' groupings of 'little Europes,' be settled in Canada in separate 'family groups' of nuclear households so as to facilitate their resumption of normal family life.[10]

Family ideologies similarly informed the views of those who became active in providing immigrant services. A whole range of family and child agencies were devoted to the task of 'guiding' the adjustment of immigrants and were prepared to intervene in the lives of families they considered dysfunctional. Also active was a variety of other groups, including feminist organizations such as the Provincial Council of Women of Ontario (PCWO). A consideration of its programs offers a good illustration of how enthusiastic Ontarians responded to the new foreign women in their midst. An umbrella organization representing local councils of women in towns, districts, and cities across Ontario, the council endorsed immigrant and citizenship work as part of its overall platform to promote wholesome family values, heterosexuality, and democracy in the postwar world. A 1956 report of the Mental Hygiene Committee drew a clear link between individual 'mental hygiene' – a term that combined an older moral rhetoric of healthy living with an emerging interest in psychiatric well-being – and the moral state of the nation. A 'wholesome family life,' it insisted, had been proven to be critical to individual and national health; recent evidence showed that children began their 'training in citizenship' in the home and that 'healthy' living in the home and community prevented such deviations as alcoholism, sexual perversions, and divorce.[11]

The council pledged itself to promoting moral and democratic values through its support of social and recreational programs designed to build sound moral, democratic, and patriotic character among Canada's youth. It also endorsed a program of immigration services, lobbying for more liberal admission laws and committing resources for reception and citizenship work. As a feminist organization devoted to enhancing women's status and improving women's participation in electoral politics, council members wanted immigrant women (and not just their husbands) to become naturalized citizens.[12] Such ambitions could fit with their class perspective. For example, a combination of patriotic voluntarism and class and racial bias was evident in a 1947 council resolution advocating the selective recruitment of DP women for domestic work in Canada. Among reasons for support were fears that the failure to acquire 'home help' might discourage Anglo-Celtic Canadian mothers 'from enlarging their families, thus decreasing the birth rate and limiting families,' and that the current low supply of maids was having a deleterious effect on voluntarism in the country. This situation, the resolution declared, was 'depriving the nation of the leadership of capable women.'[13]

A voluntarist ethos combined with an assimilationist impulse informed a whole range of immigration activities undertaken by the various local councils and affiliates of the PCWO. Committees organized reception ceremonies for new arrivals, including women, and invited the newcomers to mingle with members of their newly adopted community – both as a way of encouraging friendly feelings between Old and New Canadians and of teaching newcomers how to talk and act like 'Canadians.' They held information evenings where movies and lectures on Canadian life were mounted and the superiority of Canadian freedoms and customs celebrated. They hosted public health lectures on Canadian child-rearing techniques, held cooking lessons using Canadian recipes, and provided English classes. Some council women visited the homes of immigrant women, welcoming them to the neighbourhood, but also encouraging them to attend English and citizenship classes. Others led informal tours through their own homes, introducing the newcomers to middle-class Canadian households and (implicitly or explicitly) encouraging them to aspire to such standards. In big cities like Toronto, they 'screened' homes, checking the condition of rental apartments and trying to ensure that newcomers were not being bilked by unscrupulous landlords.[14]

Cold-war politics also shaped this voluntarist impulse, as was evident when the PCWO targeted professionally educated refugees considered to have special needs. Drawing a connection between refugee work and anti-Communist work, the Canadian Federation of University Women, a council affiliate, offered 'aid' to university-educated European refugee women 'without regard to race, creed or politics.' In 1957 it 'adopted' twenty-two university women living in Germany who were refugees (likely Hungarians) from Soviet-occupied territories. They were supplied with food, clothing, and books. Federation representative Mrs Graeme McLean revealed the politics informing their humanitarian actions. The refugee women, she noted, were subject to an intensive Communist propaganda campaign encouraging them to return to their homelands. Should they return, she added, we Western democracies will have lost 'a battle in moral supremacy.'[15]

The PCWO also attracted ethnic Canadian women's organizations. Some, including the Ukrainian Women's Association of Canada (UWAC), were composed of the Canadian daughters and granddaughters of pre-1945 immigrants and generally shared a middle-class, pro-Canadianization perspective. The UWAC combined a strong anti-Communist stance with a pro-Canadian position. By the late 1940s it had established some branches outside its prairie stronghold, including in Ontario, had run food and clothing drives to help refugees overseas, had created student scholarships in Ukrainian institutions, and had undertaken reception work in Canada, meeting new arrivals at train stations, finding newcomers accommodation, and offering them 'counselling.' The UWAC hoped to make new recruits among their recently arrived DP female compatriots; while the newcomers' anti-Soviet views doubtless helped in this regard, they did not prevent friction between 'old' and 'new' women from surfacing, and the UWAC was less successful than other Ukrainian women's groups in attracting numerous recruits. The reports of the Ontario branch nevertheless make clear the UWAC's conservative agenda: it sought to encourage its new recruits to subscribe to its long-standing maternalist ideology that equated womanhood with the roles of wife and mother, and to play out these roles in a Canadianized fashion. As the Ontario president, Mrs Evanetz, declared in her 1957 report to the provincial council, the organization's 'function' was 'to help the Ukrainian women to become ideal home-makers and encourage them to take an active interest in [Canadian] community affairs.'[16]

The responsibilities of Canadian citizenship that immigrant women were expected to fulfil were many, but they included duties associated with conventional, middle-class ideas about the well-organized and contented stay-at-home mom. More specifically, immigrant women, whatever their Old World background, were expected to aspire to a middle-class Canadian model of family life. The records of the International Institute of Metropolitan Toronto suggest that the emphasis of social workers was on encouraging immigrant women, especially East and South European women who were seen to be stuck in the most backward 'traditional' families, to adopt Canadian techniques in everything from cooking and shopping to marital relations and parenting. In their confidential counselling sessions with men, IIMT caseworkers encouraged European men to adopt what they believed was a more modern, companionate model of the family. In part, that meant eliminating what they saw as the totally domineering position of husbands over wives in the 'traditional' European family. As the 'Cookbook project' adopted by institute staff in the late 1960s indicates, when experts advised immigrant wives and mothers to follow the guidelines established by the Canada Food Guide they were not only providing currently accepted nutritional advice. They were also trying to affect the behaviour of newcomers by encouraging, for instance, a budget-conscious mentality generally touted at this time and deemed essential to successful resettlement in Canada. The Italians were enouraged to buy 'cheaper' cuts of meat (than, presumably, lean veal), while the Portuguese were encouraged to replace fresh fish with the frozen variety. Various immigrant groups were encouraged to use canned fruits and vegetables as an economy measure.[17]

If immigrant women who adopted Canadian ways in domestic life were applauded, the converse was also true. Those who did not appear to appreciate Canadian opportunities invited criticism. One example involved the British war brides who settled in small Ontario towns. As British women, the war brides were considered highly desirable newcomers who most closely resembled Canadians in cultural and political traditions. It was assumed they would acculturate most easily to Canadian ways, especially as they had Canadian husbands and relatives to guide them. In some circles, gossip could be heard concerning the moral character of the war brides: Were these 'good times girls' who had trapped Canadian soldiers into marriage? Generally, however, their arrival was met with much fanfare. This was particularly true of smaller towns where daily the local press reported on happy reunions.[18] The news that some of them were disillusioned and returning home engendered resentment and embarrassment on the part of immigration advocates who had expected these British women to make a smooth transition to Canadian family life. By December 1946, less than a year after the women began arriving in Canada, some fifty 'disgruntled brides,' as a Sault Ste Marie *Star* reporter dubbed them, had returned home 'fed up' with Canada's high prices, clothing shortages, and the continuing housing crisis that forced them to reside with in-laws. Some commentators were defensive, saying that the 'disillusioned' brides were a tiny minority. But others, including a welfare expert, suggested that the 'abnormal' context in which these marriages had been made and the new demands of Canadian life, had contributed to the 'broken marriages' by exacerbating the 'normal differences found in the early years of any marriage.'[19]

MAKING THEIR WAY

The debates, activities, and campaigns of middle-class Ontarians were not sufficient in themselves to determine absolutely the adjustments of newly arrived women immigrants, survivors, and refugees. We must also consider the resources and options available to them within their new communities – however limited they might be – as well as their particular family circumstances, class, age, language backgrounds, and marital status. So, too, must we take into account the women's dreams and demands, and whether these were fulfilled or quashed. We need also to see the process of immigrant women's adjustments to postwar Ontario as relational, as involving numerous encounters between newcomers and oldtimers, among immigrants of various types, and among kin, friends, and neighbours.

More often than not, immigrant women acted in ways that frustrated the social experts and enthusiasts keen to exert an influence over them. Even when they acted in ways that pleased the experts, as when they enrolled in English and industrial sewing classes, the immigrants' motives for doing so were their own. The women also differed with respect to their desire to 'fit in' with Canadians. Some, including Caterina Allen, a Dutch war bride from an urban, middle-class background who settled in London, Ontario, welcomed the chance to mingle with her mostly Canadian neighbours, many of them university students. A young woman whose own education had been disrupted by the war, Allen found the young Canadians more interesting than her Dutch co-nationals, whom she dismissed as dour, church people. Other women, either by disinclination or lack of opportunity, developed fleeting or sporadic relationships with those outside their circles. Still others were more cut off from the world beyond their doorstep than they would have liked.[20] Some selective illustrations suggest the various arenas in which women newcomers remade their lives.

The first examples involve immigrant housewives and their own households. Because of the gender bias that historically has characterized Canadian immigration policy, most women, as noted earlier, have gained entry into Canada as the dependants of men. Even more than that, their legal status as dependants has profoundly influenced the ways in which Canadians and others have viewed them. Considerable slippage occurs between our understanding of their official admission and legal status as immigrant dependants and our understanding of them as victimized souls. We tend to assume that because immigration laws seriously limited their means of entry and officials tagged them 'dependants,' the women themselves were necessarily passive and subservient wives unable to hold independent opinions and lacking any influence over husbands and other family members. As a result, we underestimate and undervalue the actual efforts of immigrant women to get families re-established or even to fill labour shortages in the new society. This is particularly the case with immigrant housewives. Their work as housewives and stay-at-home mothers is not fully appreciated, even though they played a decisive role in easing the transition of their family and kin members into the new society and in replenishing working husbands and children. It is also assumed that, somehow, their entire being was consumed by domestic work – as though immigrant women did not have dreams and desires, as though they were completely cut off from the other women of their neighbourhoods and communities. Indeed, concern about the isolation of ethnic housewives has led many of us to conclude that even with all its attendant problems, paid work offered them better opportunities for adjustment.[21]

The reality, of course, was far more complex. For one thing, the decision to emigrate involved much greater input from women than the official admission laws denote. To be sure, some women were cajoled into emigrating. This was the predicament that German-born Helena Anders faced when her husband, who had been receiving positive reports of Canada from a brother who had emigrated a few years earlier, insisted they follow suit. The poor quality of flats they rented in Toronto during the early 1950s confirmed her pessimism, though she enjoyed eating white sliced bread – 'it tasted like expensive cake' – and fresh apples and oranges. It took several years of coping with unfriendly stares, struggling with English, and juggling a variety of housekeeping and other jobs before she finally felt settled. Although the decision to emigrate had not been her's, she was determined to make the move work and her efforts to find jobs, participate in German clubs and associations, and attend English classes helped ensure the couple's positive adjustment to life in Toronto. Alongside examples like the Anders were thousands of East European women refugees and survivors who eagerly sought emigration to North America and were more than prepared to go alone. They exploited the limited avenues before them, applying for admission as landed immigrants or passing themselves off as seamstresses in order to be recruited into Canadian government labour schemes. Significantly, sympathetic welfare workers in the camps, such as Canadian YWCA volunteers, tried to help them improve their chances by offering them quick lessons in button sewing and hemming so they could pass the Canadian trade tests administered by selection agents.

Even among the family-based migration chains emanating from Southern Europe, where most women gained entry as dependants, numerous examples emerge of women actually initiating the migration process. Margherita Caravelle was so anxious to get out of her war-torn village in Italy and join a sister in Toronto that her new husband's initial protest to the contrary did not dissuade her. Through persistent argument she eventually wore him down. By the fall of 1949 the couple, with the earnings made from the sale of personal belongings and from the tiny parcel of land given to Caravelle as a bridal dowry, was living in Toronto's west end. The usual pattern of sponsoring-husband and sponsored-wife was neatly reversed in the case of Carla Alexis, a skilled furrier from Greece who temporarily left behind a husband and four children in 1951 when she gained admission to Canada as an independent immigrant. When, a few years later, Alexis had earned sufficient money to re-establish the family in Toronto, she sponsored their arrival. As Alexis's husband earned low wages at dishwashing, she continued to fulfil the role of chief family breadwinner, a situation that, according to their eldest daughter, ensured they were 'much better off than in Greece.' The daughter remained silent, however, on how her mother's breadwinning role affected her father and the relations between her parents.[22]

An immigrant woman's perception of the value of her role in the family household was contingent upon a number of factors relating to pre-migration experiences and postwar realities in Ontario. Immigrant housewives who explained why they had preferred to stay home and raise a family, for instance, expressed the view that a new home in a peaceful world offered them the promise of real security. That the idealized search for family and security was expressed in conventional terms did not make the desire any less compelling. For women who had witnessed the horrors of war and experienced its impact directly, that desire was deep seated. While their notions of child-rearing and family might well differ from Canadian middle-class ideals, they shared with many Canadian women the dream of a better life. Such sentiments pervade the recollections of Holocaust survivors who associated getting married, having children, and becoming economically rooted in a new land as a sign not of putting the past behind them (which was impossible), but of being alive.

Eva Kogler, a Polish-born Ukrainian who settled in Port Arthur with her husband in 1948, also articulated this desire to erect a stable home life in peacetime Ontario. For her, becoming a housewife and mother in what she called a 'nice, quiet city' was synonymous with acquiring security after years of uncertainty. Kogler had been a young, single woman when war broke out in Europe, thus disrupting her education, separating her from family, and obliging her to work for strangers. Transported by the invading Germans from Poland to Vienna, she was employed as a housekeeper to a well-placed German family. After the war, she had returned home to find her village reduced to ashes. She then made her way to Czechoslovakia, where she befriended a Czech man she later married in a DP camp in Germany. When her husband landed a contract job with a northern Ontario logging company, she found it difficult being separated from him, even temporarily. Such insecurity had been bred in wartime. Even after she joined him in Port Arthur a year later, she had to get accustomed to his long winter absences in the bush, where he continued to work for years. Significantly, Kogler adjusted well: she spent the winters on her own, raising children, making daily decisions, and running a household. Staying at home, she explained, was the right decision for her, and, despite an obvious modesty, she expressed pride in having raised four children and limited her expenses so she could save to buy a house. The pressures of child-rearing and her husband's recurring absences were tempered by the presence of 'lots of Ukrainians,' especially Ukrainian mothers with whom she forged valued friendships.[23]

Many immigrant housewives, far from simply acquiescing to domineering husbands, played vital roles in their households, acting as the family's financial manager, allocating funds for groceries, clothing, and house bills. While it is impossible to say for certain how common such activity was, we know from several sources that it was fairly widespread. My study of Italian immigrants in early postwar Toronto, for instance, indicated that many housewives acted as family budget managers and generally influenced decision-making in the family. A 1970 survey of sixty Polish immigrant families in Toronto similarly showed that husbands and wives negotiated matters. In conducting the survey, the sociologist involved had wondered whether 'traditional' patriarchal authority within Polish families, as measured by men's role as family-decision maker, had eroded as a result of immigration. He concluded that it had. Although his analysis is flawed by a tendency to posit ideal types – he assumed rather than proved that the model of the domineering husband and submissive wife accurately described gender relations in pre-migration Polish society – the findings are still revealing. All the men interviewed said they consulted with their wives. Close to three-quarters of them said they shared 'final decision-making' with their wives in matters concerning 'larger purchases,' while one-quarter said they shared all decisions with their wife. In changing jobs, all men said they consulted with their wives. Finally, the family budget was 'controlled by the father alone' in only 18.3 per cent of the cases. The study remains inconclusive on whether gender relations were truly changed because of immigration, but it does indicate that immigrant women had a say in how their households were furnished, what food their family ate, and what their husbands chose to do in work and leisure.[24]

Another important feature of immigrant women's stories was their participation in the churches, clubs, and other associations of their local ethnic community. Kolger recalled her participation in Thunder Bay's Catholic Ukrainian church, Our Lady of Protection, helping out with dances and attending meetings. Volunteer work in postwar Canada was not simply the domain of middle-class, Canadian women, for many immigrant women played an active role in bolstering the ethnic organizations of the postwar era. At times, this involved joining already existing organizations; at other times, it involved helping to build altogether new ones. For immigrant women like Latvian-born Rita Girse of Delhi who settled in rural Ontario, getting involved in ethnic organizing was more than a social event or charitable act; it was a tool for ensuring that her children, whom she enrolled in heritage classes and folk dancing, did not lose their culture. While some women participated in immigrant community life through ladies' auxiliaries and making meals for ethnic events in their community, others, including Holocaust survivor Gerda Frieberg, assumed leadership roles. Frieberg became an important human rights activist in the Toronto Jewish community.

There were other ways in which immigrant women, whether married or single, working or attending school, were active participants in their ethnic communities. As a teenager, Tina Lindstrom was drawn into her parent's volunteer activities. Many immigrant children, newly conversant in English, found themselves interpreting for parents and other adults. It placed them in awkward predicaments as prepubescent girls and boys explained the intricacies of a mother's pregnancy symptoms to a doctor or a family's finances to a welfare worker. Lindstrom enjoyed volunteer work. The daughter of a Finnish journalist, she had come to northern Ontario with her parents in the early 1950s. In Port Arthur her parents opened up a Finnish book store and, while her father continued to write for newspapers back home, her mother ran the shop. As enterprising and comparatively well-educated Finns, Lindstrom's parents soon began providing translation services to later arriving compatriots. Lindstrom began helping to translate documents, finding accommodation for new arrivals, and accompanying them on job interviews. She was often taken out of school to assist. When a gas line was being built in the area, for weeks she rose at 5:00 a.m. each morning to accompany various men to the 'pick-up' spot where contractors were recruiting work gangs. The many trips made to doctors' offices to act as interpreter to pregnant and ailing Finnish women was, she recalled, a real 'learning experience' for a teenaged girl. All this activity had a lasting effect on Lindstrom, who immersed herself in Finnish associational life, participating in theatrical productions, gymnastics, folkdance clubs, and credit unions. Years later she became the first woman president of the largest Finnish organization in Thunder Bay.

Still other women, including Polish-born Lina Barowsky, sought activist roles both within and outside their own ethnic circles. A journalist who had joined the Polish resistance and participated in the Warsaw ghetto uprising of 1944, Barowsky had paid a heavy price for her anti-Nazi activities – her husband's death at Auschwitz and her own detention in a prisoner-of-war camp. By the late 1940s Barowski was in Toronto hoping to apply the social work and interpretation skills she had developed after the war as an UNRRA (United Nations Relief and Rehabilitation Administration) worker in the refugee camps. The first few years were disappointing, but after enduring several low-paying jobs and getting remarried, she took some social work courses and landed a job with a child protection agency handling immigrant cases. At the same time, she remained active in local and national Polish-Canadian associations. Barowsky's work experience and professional and language skills significantly improved her chances of professional success in Canada and enabled her to move fairly easily from a world of Polish associations to one inhabited by middle-class Ontarians. Still, her ethnicity created barriers. According to Barowsky, she was refused a job as a social worker with the IODE (Imperial Order Daughters of the Empire), a middle-class woman's organization with a strong patriotic bent, because she was a foreigner.[25]

WORKING FOR PAY

Immigrant women contributed significantly to the rising numbers of women, especially married women, who entered Ontario's, and Canada's, post-1945 labour force. Above all, their presence reflected economic need, but many of them also enjoyed the greater independence and bargaining power that earning money gave them in their dealings with husbands. For women like my mother, a former Italian peasant who worked for years as a sorter and seamstress in a Toronto laundry while she also raised six children, bringing home a pay cheque meant having a say in how it would get spent.

Still, immigrant women's role as the family's secondary wage earner was a graphic illustration of the gap that existed between the prevailing ideology of the family breadwinner and the fact that many immigrant men, like many Canadian working men, could not earn enough to support their families. In the early postwar era, when many immigrant children in Ontario were too young to work or were prevented from doing so because of stringent schooling laws, wives and mothers were the most likely family member to take up the slack. In some cases, a wife's wages prevented the family's income from falling below the poverty line; at other times, it enabled the couple to pursue strategies, such as home ownership, intended to improve their economic security. Like the Czech-born Elena Krotz, who for years bolstered the insecure earnings of her nursery-worker husband, such women made a very tangible difference to their family. Krotz remained for years in Hamilton's labour force, moving from one job to another as the opportunity arose. Her work ranged from seasonal jobs in the produce industry, where she picked apples, to factory jobs, and a short stint as a saleswoman in a shoe store. Her earnings eventually enabled them to begin a small orchard business. For several more years she kept family finances afloat with her factory earnings until the family business got off the ground, whereupon she assumed office and bookkeeping duties.[26]

That large numbers of immigrant women from non-British and non-Canadian backgrounds entered Ontario's paid workforce is evident from the 1961 unpublished census tracts for the province. These data, which provide the ethnic origins for Ontario's working women, unfortunately do not distinguish between prewar and postwar immigrants. But the figures do show that while the British and Canadian group made up the majority of Ontario's working women (692,448), 'ethnic' women made up a significant proportion of the total – almost 40 per cent. The vast majority of them (244,349 or 97 per cent) were Europeans. Many of them, perhaps as high as one-half, were postwar immigrants.[27]

In contrast to the high concentration of British and Canadian women who found clerical and other white-collar jobs, European women dominated the less appealing and lower-paid jobs located in the manufacturing and service sectors. Employed as machine operatives, seamstresses, assembly-line workers, and 'cleaning ladies,' they worked long hours at either monotonous or hazardous jobs that were physically demanding. Women assembling items in plastic novelty or leather tanning factories, for example, endured dust and foul-smelling fumes, while laundry workers, be they sorters of dirty laundry, steampressers, or folders, tolerated the humid summer months of southern Ontario, when the climate combined with the steampresses and dryers to produce sauna-like conditions. Cleaning ladies employed in private homes worked in total isolation from other women, while many office cleaners had to juggle night-time jobs with day-time domestic responsibilities. From the perspective of the Ontario economy, the presence of large numbers of immigrant women in the post-1945 Ontario workforce helped to ensure a smooth transition from a wartime to a peacetime economy. To the delight of Ontario employers, by filling critical labour shortages and jobs shunned by Canadian-born women, their presence also probably helped to keep female wages lower than they might otherwise have been.

More difficult to track is the relative impact that European women had on the workforces of specific locales throughout the province. Certainly that impact was uneven, in absolute and relative terms. Cities in the heavily industrialized southern corridor, especially Toronto but also Hamilton, Guelph, and neighbouring places, saw larger proportions of immigrant women, both British and non-British, in paid work than did rural and northern locales.[28] While a woman's entry into paid work depended on many factors – including a husband's or father's attitude and the availability of babysitters or day-care services for children – this unevenness reflected in large part the presence or relative scarcity of job opportunities for women within the local economy.

A comparison between Toronto and Thunder Bay illustrates this pattern nicely. Jobs for women were simply more numerous in Toronto, a city whose economy included plentiful 'female' jobs in 'light' industry (the garment trade or food processing) and service (office and house cleaning). Here, by 1961, European-born adult women exhibited very high rates of labour-force participation (40–48 per cent) within their respective ethnic groups. Thousands of them joined the armies of female workers employed in garment and textile shops, laundries, plastic novelties factories, and leather-goods shops. Their presence in some cases dramatically changed the ethnic composition of a workplace. Huge numbers of Italian women, for example, flooded the once predominantly Jewish workplaces in the city's needle trades. Laundries, soft-drink factories, leather-goods shops, and bakeries once staffed largely by English-speaking women of Canadian and British backgrounds were transformed into multi-ethnic workplaces where women from Romania, Poland, Italy, and elsewhere clustered.[29] They became sites of multiple encounters between foreign and Canadian-born women and immigrant women from diverse backgrounds.

The politics of the anti-Soviet newcomers, unfamiliarity or inexperience with unions, or the burdens of the double-day that so many married working women endured also affected the shop. In Toronto's needle trades, for instance, where earlier generations of immigrant Jews and other workers had struggled for workplace rights and established unions, the arrival of so many newcomers with little interest in or experience with unions, and burdened by the need to get established, justifiably worried the old Jewish union leaders. Throughout the 1950s the International Ladies Garment Workers Union was frustrated in its efforts to organize the cloak and sportswear sectors of the industry (where in particular many Italian women, including working mothers, had found jobs), even though these shops developed a notorious reputation for undercutting workers' wages and subjecting them to speedups.[30]

As working immigrant women travelled to and from work, the riders on Toronto's subway trains, streetcars, and buses also visibly changed. The complaints that postwar Torontonians voiced about the great babbling of foreign languages in the city's public places would have been applied to the unprecedented number of 'foreign' women in the city's main thoroughfares. As a young Greek woman travelling the subway with her factory-worker mother recalled, some Torontonians did not merely offer the newcomers cold stares; they also confronted them directly, admonishing them for talking in foreign tongues and insisting they speak English.[31]

By contrast, Thunder Bay offered comparatively fewer job opportunities for women. Here the biggest employers were employers of men – pulp and paper mills, railways, and a shipping industry hiring freight handlers and dock workers. Men also had access to jobs in logging, and, indeed, many of the city's immigrant men began life in the region as bushworkers. Few immigrant women could follow the course taken by Leda Oja, an Estonian DP who, following the completion of her domestic contract in southern Ontario, spent a decade working as a cook in northern logging camps. Like other camp 'cookees,' as they were known, she was married to a bushworker. Years later she opened a craft shop.[32]

The relative lack of jobs does not mean, of course, that Thunder Bay's immigrant women did not earn money. Like women in other resource towns, some found ways of earning an income in the 'informal' economy, taking in laundry and babysitting. And they gobbled up the relatively few jobs that were available. These included some garment-factory jobs (in particular, a Port Arthur men's pants factory) and various service jobs in restaurants, ethnic halls, churches, and private homes. Maria Curtola took on a job that very directly affected her household. For fifteen years she acted as a foster mother for the Children's Aid Society. The daughter of a chronically underemployed shoemaker in Italy, Curtola had come to Port Arthur in 1953 after being sponsored by her sister, a war bride who had married an Italo-Canadian soldier. Maria later married her brother-in-law's friend, a factory worker. Unable to land a job but determined to earn an income, she became a CAS foster parent. Despite poor English, she communicated easily with the white and Native Canadian children and teenagers who were placed in her home for periods ranging from a few months to two years. She and her husband grew attached to some of the children, and in 1955 they permanently adopted one boy, an Irish-Canadian orphan. They tried, in vain, to adopt one of the girls, too. It was the emotional trauma produced by their loss of the girl that led her to cease foster parenting altogether. Thereafter, she babysat for mostly Canadian mothers in her neighbourhood.

Katie Werner ran a boarding house in town, another way in which immigrant women bolstered husbands' wages. Her decision to buy a large, nine-bedroom house on borrowed money stemmed from a desire to earn money and her frustration with the quality of flats in town. After insisting that she and her husband move several times within a matter of a few years, she hit upon the idea of running a boarding home when a large house came up for sale. With few savings, she borrowed most of the $1000 downpayment, from friends, neighbours, and a local grocer. Throughout the decade that Werner ran the boarding house, most of her tenants were Canadians, not immigrants. Her role as landlady involved her in the lives of some of her boarders. One such case concerned a young Canadian tenant who lived there with her husband and a young child. As the husband, an alcoholic, could not be counted on to pay the rent, on each pay day Werner would accompany her tenant to her husband's payroll office in time to snatch the rent and grocery money from him before he drank it away.

In operating small businesses, many immigrant women contributed directly to household finances and helped change the ethnic face of Ontario's streets. They ran grocery stores, dry-goods stores, dry cleaners, hair salons, and fish and butcher shops that dotted the streetscape of many Ontario towns and cities. Although small family businesses are normally associated with men, women in fact played a critical role in the establishment and success of countless businesses. In many cases, it was the woman who was actually based in the shop, ordering supplies and serving customers. When describing the electronics repair shop that she and her husband ran in Thunder Bay, Anna Strimz, a Croatian woman who had married a Yugoslavian man she had met in a DP camp, admitted that, unlike her husband, she had had no background in electronics. But she actually learned a lot about repairs and, much to her delight, serving customers had made her learn English 'fast.' A Viennese Jew who survived the Nazi death camps, and later married a co-survivor she had met in Czechoslovakia after liberation, recalled how the couple had opened up a dry-cleaning shop in Toronto in 1950 without any prior experience and on borrowed cash. When he died a few years later, she continued running the business for decades.[33]

Women who ran grocery and dry goods stores also adapted. This was the case with Rosa Lalli, an Italian woman who, along with her construction-worker husband, ran a corner store in Toronto's west end. As she recalled with obvious pride, she developed a whole range of skills, including ordering appropriate amounts of deli meat and fresh bread and keeping the books. Katie Werner, the German boarding-house keeper who, by 1960, had turned her efforts to running a grocery store, similarly declared: 'It was a real proposition. I tiled the hallway ... the stairs, I put a new toilet cover in the bathroom, put a new floor down. I did this in between [running] the store and the kids.' The major difference between the stores was the clientele: Lalli's store served a largely (though not exclusively) Italian immigrant clientele, whereas Werner's served a mixed one. But both played a role in supplying 'ethnic' foods to their local communities.[34]

BEYOND HOME AND WORKPLACE

Far from simply shunning social arenas where their language was not spoken or their kin did not dwell, Ontario's new foreign women could also be found in social arenas beyond their homes and workplaces. The arrival of such large numbers of them put pressure on existing social services, for instance. Neighbourhoods and communities struggled to accommodate the demands of immigrant women (and others) for such services as English classes, libraries, medical care, job placement, and welfare. The success of such programs depended on the willingness of immigrant women to participate. Moreover, the nature of their participation helped determine the outcome of those programs and shaped the relations between the newcomers and their 'hosts.'

The enrolment of immigrant women in English classes offers a case in point. As with so many other services, Ontarians who advocated and helped to staff English classes for immigrants saw them as part of a broader social program of encouraging the newcomers' adoption of a Canadian way of life. The assimilationist thrust of such programs was evident in the words of one advocate, who used the metaphor of 'missionary' work to describe teaching English night classes to Toronto's immigrants.[35] Nevertheless, such activists were not simply myopic assimilationists; they understood well that learning English might improve job opportunities and that the success of such programs depended on the immigrants' willingness to attend them. There were numerous successful experiments in teaching English to immigrant women, and instances where teacher and pupils appear to have been on friendly terms. In 1959, for example, the Salvation Army reported that their classes for New Canadians had been an ongoing success. The teacher, a Salvationist, was herself an immigrant from Yugoslavia, and the sixty students in the class had received among the highest marks in the province. Several years later the Belleville Social Planning Council issued a positive report on the weekly

English classes for immigrant women held at a local church. The women, who included Greeks, Italians, Finns, Hungarians, and Chinese, placed their children in the on-site nursery while they attended two-hour classes. As the report reveals, the women came to class precisely because it helped them meet needs as they arose – in this case, seeking paid work. 'We find,' it read, 'that as these women become proficient in English, they are able to get jobs. Their places are quickly filled by other ladies brought by interested friends and relatives and by a diligent search by our recruiting and public relations officer.'[36]

The pressure that some immigrants, including better educated and professional women from Europe, put on the province's local libraries is another indication that at least some non-English-speaking women willingly entered 'foreign' arenas in order to fulfil their needs and desires. To the apparently pleasant surprise of librarians, women figured prominently among the New Canadians who became avid users of Ontario libraries. They included women like Mary Papas, a Hungarian refugee who arrived in Toronto shortly after the Hungarian revolution of 1956 and who spent hours each day poring over books she yet could barely read. She eventually landed a library staff job. Book-hungry immigrants prompted public libraries to increase their acquisitions and their 'foreign' offerings. While unwilling to assimilate completely to Canadian ways, many immigrants were nevertheless understandably interested in learning something about their adopted country. In Windsor, the Willistead Library responded to demands from newly arrived immigrants for materials about Canada by ordering more books and introducing evening programs featuring guest lectures, movies, and English classes. A Toronto librarian commented on the many Italians and other immigrants in the area who were daily using the local library. The evening programs, moreover, were overcrowded – forcing staff to increase offerings.[37]

Immigrant women also came into contact with other women at the baby clinics and other public-health facilities set up for immigrant mothers and their children. Again, it was the women's willingness to use these resources, and the way in which they used them, that affected not only the programs' success but also the relations between host and newcomers. One illustration of the tensions that could develop between immigrant women and public-health experts involved a Toronto baby clinic that catered to Italian women. The public health nurses who ran the clinic were continually frustrated by the fact that while the clients made use of the practical forms of assistance the clinic offered, such as vaccination shots and free milk supplies, most did not stick around long enough to attend the prescriptive lectures on Canadian child-rearing practices. Clearly, the women were exercising choice over how they would raise their children. And yet, the very fact that the Italian women saw the clinic as serving certain important needs explains why, the ire of the nurses notwithstanding, the clinic remained a going concern. While Italian mothers might not have attended lectures, they came in large numbers to register their children, to have them vaccinated and checked.[38]

Other examples of the relations between female newcomers and host could be explored, such as department stores and the efforts of manufacturers and major retailers to attract an ethnic female clientele. It was not until the 1950s, for example, that Eaton's College Street, Toronto's upscale department store, began to consider immigrant women as potential buyers in their store and to conduct consumer surveys to determine how to tap that market. Ontario manufacturers pondered the same thing as they calculated the huge potential sales to be made from thousands of new households getting established. Trade journals offered local manufacturers hints on how to appeal to the 'ethnic' shopper.[39]

CONCLUSION

The enormous diversity in the national origins, class backgrounds, and pre-migration experiences of the British and European women who entered early postwar Ontario, coupled with their different age, marital status, family background, and work and settlement careers, suggests the folly of attempts to lump them together and explain away their experiences as the predictable hardships of female newcomers. We make such generalizations at the risk of rendering immigrant women faceless and entirely passive and of ignoring the complexity of their lives. In considering some of the ways that immigrant women, survivors, and refugees remade their lives in Ontario, this article asks readers to move beyond stereotypes of immigrant women as exclusively passive victims, whether of sexist immigration policies, segmented labour markets, or domineering husbands. It asks that we view them as historical actors who, with varying degrees of success, pursued adjustment strategies amid serious material and other constraints. They did so, too, in the face of external pressures from social experts and other enthusiastic Ontarians determined to transform them into Canadians – all the while meeting daily obligations to husbands, children, compatriots, and employers.

Table 1
Immigration into Canada and Ontario by Ethnicity, Age, and Gender, 1946–65

| | Females under 18 | Males under 18 | Females over 18 | Males over 18 | Canada | Ontario | Women as % of total | Ontario as % of total | Ethnicity as % of Ontario |
|---|---|---|---|---|---|---|---|---|---|
| Albanian | 12 | 14 | 56 | 246 | 374 | 270 | 18 | 72 | 0.02 |
| Algerian | 0 | 0 | 61 | 74 | 135 | 9 | 45 | 7 | 0.00 |
| Arabian (Saudi Arabian) | 46 | 50 | 237 | 329 | 732 | 327 | 39 | 45 | 0.03 |
| Argentinian | 0 | 0 | 620 | 706 | 1,326 | 764 | 47 | 58 | 0.06 |
| Armenian | 69 | 79 | 652 | 697 | 1,696 | 701 | 43 | 41 | 0.06 |
| Australian | 0 | 0 | 3,607 | 2,837 | 6,444 | 2,688 | 56 | 42 | 0.21 |
| Austrian | 621 | 609 | 7,396 | 8,358 | 22,604 | 11,443 | 35 | 51 | 0.91 |
| Belgian | 1,740 | 1,892 | 8,394 | 9,125 | 23,467 | 9,546 | 43 | 41 | 0.76 |
| Bermudian | 0 | 0 | 152 | 212 | 364 | 226 | 42 | 62 | 0.02 |
| Bohemian | 4 | 14 | 22 | 29 | 69 | 59 | 38 | 86 | 0.00 |
| Brazilian | 0 | 0 | 619 | 781 | 1,400 | 775 | 44 | 55 | 0.06 |
| English | 36,132 | 38,591 | 197,182 | 168,922 | 487,097 | 291,760 | 48 | 60 | 23.15 |
| Irish | 4,973 | 5,009 | 28,838 | 34,630 | 83,553 | 69,989 | 40 | 84 | 5.55 |
| Scottish | 11,757 | 15,889 | 65,257 | 55,040 | 164,633 | 105,703 | 47 | 64 | 8.39 |
| Welsh | 869 | 884 | 6,049 | 5,343 | 14,825 | 8,482 | 47 | 57 | 0.67 |
| Bulgarian | 38 | 63 | 244 | 677 | 1,109 | 633 | 25 | 57 | 0.05 |
| Ceylonese | 0 | 0 | 116 | 127 | 243 | 150 | 48 | 62 | 0.01 |
| Chinese | 771 | 3,547 | 10,388 | 7,343 | 26,574 | 7,725 | 42 | 29 | 0.61 |
| Corsican | 0 | 0 | 0 | 1 | 1 | 1 | 0 | 100 | 0.00 |
| Croation | 38 | 37 | 189 | 326 | 590 | 295 | 38 | 50 | 0.02 |
| Czech-Slovakian | 774 | 808 | 3,471 | 5,718 | 11,157 | 6,966 | 38 | 62 | 0.55 |
| Dalmation | 1 | 0 | 0 | 8 | 9 | 4 | 11 | 44 | 0.00 |
| Danish | 17,722 | 20,214 | 26,689 | 30,206 | 97,623 | 53,331 | 45 | 55 | 0.23 |
| East Indian | 88 | 162 | 3,105 | 4,642 | 8,417 | 2,727 | 38 | 32 | 0.22 |

Table 1 (*continued*)

| | Females under 18 | Males under 18 | Females over 18 | Males over 18 | Canada | Ontario | Women as % of total | Ontario as % of total | Ethnicity as % of Ontario |
|---|---|---|---|---|---|---|---|---|---|
| Egyptian | 12 | 9 | 2,913 | 3,213 | 6,164 | 1,229 | 47 | 20 | 0.10 |
| Estonian | 1,471 | 1,482 | 5,635 | 5,313 | 14,377 | 9,284 | 49 | 65 | 0.74 |
| Finnish | 1,719 | 1,786 | 6,698 | 7,446 | 18,978 | 12,972 | 44 | 68 | 1.03 |
| French | 3,805 | 3,887 | 20,100 | 26,313 | 59,143 | 9,763 | 40 | 17 | 0.77 |
| German | 12,803 | 13,985 | 83,984 | 96,358 | 289,573 | 132,636 | 33 | 46 | 10.53 |
| Greek | 1,664 | 2,115 | 26,649 | 28,361 | 64,695 | 29,791 | 44 | 46 | 2.36 |
| Hebrew/Jewish/Israel | 4,488 | 4,821 | 21,138 | 24,238 | 57,103 | 21,478 | 45 | 38 | 1.70 |
| Hong Kong | 0 | 0 | 5,008 | 3,071 | 8,079 | 2,554 | 62 | 32 | 0.20 |
| Hungarian | 3,305 | 4,747 | 13,067 | 20,570 | 42,618 | 13,167 | 38 | 31 | 1.04 |
| Italian | 14,610 | 17,821 | 129,303 | 159,263 | 365,839 | 229,644 | 39 | 63 | 18.22 |
| Japanese | 36 | 29 | 1,119 | 516 | 1,868 | 667 | 62 | 36 | 0.05 |
| Jugo-Slavian\Yugosla | 979 | 1,089 | 15,097 | 20,109 | 40,190 | 21,975 | 40 | 55 | 1.74 |
| Latvian | 56 | 55 | 578 | 623 | 2,108 | 1,541 | 30 | 73 | 0.12 |
| Lebanese | 66 | 93 | 1,465 | 1,788 | 3,618 | 1,776 | 42 | 49 | 0.14 |
| Lettish | 1,189 | 1,195 | 4,983 | 5,641 | 13,008 | 7,299 | 47 | 56 | 0.58 |
| Lithuanian | 1,028 | 1,042 | 4,199 | 5,755 | 12,428 | 7,441 | 42 | 60 | 0.59 |
| Luxembuger | 15 | 13 | 158 | 280 | 498 | 154 | 34 | 31 | 0.01 |
| Magyar | 930 | 948 | 3,750 | 5,745 | 11,373 | 5,708 | 41 | 50 | 0.45 |
| Maltese | 756 | 875 | 3,333 | 6,150 | 12,398 | 10,669 | 33 | 86 | 0.85 |
| Mexican | 7 | 8 | 479 | 227 | 731 | 252 | 66 | 34 | 0.02 |
| Moravian | 0 | 3 | 9 | 8 | 20 | 15 | 45 | 75 | 0.00 |
| Moroccan | 0 | 0 | 1,191 | 1,188 | 2,379 | 516 | 50 | 22 | 0.04 |
| Negro | 144 | 124 | 3,777 | 1,935 | 6,457 | 2,365 | 61 | 37 | 0.19 |
| Dutch/Netherlander | 2,193 | 2,669 | 21,161 | 22,681 | 71,973 | 38,449 | 32 | 53 | 3.05 |
| New Zealander | 0 | 0 | 878 | 768 | 1,646 | 568 | 53 | 35 | 0.05 |

Table 1 (*concluded*)

| | Females under 18 | Males under 18 | Females over 18 | Males over 18 | Canada | Ontario | Women as % of total | Ontario as % of total | Ethnicity as % of Ontario |
|---|---|---|---|---|---|---|---|---|---|
| North American Indian | 26 | 30 | 29 | 16 | 101 | 15 | 54 | 15 | 0.00 |
| Pakistan | 0 | 0 | 362 | 519 | 881 | 380 | 41 | 43 | 0.03 |
| Persian/Iranian | 12 | 8 | 231 | 257 | 531 | 143 | 46 | 27 | 0.01 |
| Polish | 6,630 | 6,720 | 30,233 | 39,464 | 87,207 | 47,037 | 42 | 54 | 3.73 |
| Portuguese | 470 | 476 | 18,356 | 21,445 | 43,498 | 21,718 | 43 | 50 | 1.72 |
| Rhodesian | 0 | 0 | 267 | 289 | 556 | 234 | 48 | 42 | 0.02 |
| Roumanian | 303 | 305 | 1,671 | 2,052 | 4,638 | 2,265 | 43 | 49 | 0.18 |
| Russian-USSR | 892 | 892 | 3,740 | 3,267 | 9,387 | 3,733 | 49 | 40 | 0.30 |
| Ruthenian | 1,071 | 1,117 | 4,305 | 7,561 | 14,054 | 6,419 | 38 | 46 | 0.51 |
| Danish | 1,220 | 1,315 | 11,002 | 16,705 | 33,034 | 13,454 | 37 | 41 | 1.07 |
| Icelandic | 33 | 27 | 176 | 165 | 459 | 95 | 46 | 21 | 0.01 |
| Norwegian | 537 | 624 | 3,361 | 4,756 | 10,980 | 2,584 | 36 | 24 | 0.21 |
| Swedish | 325 | 340 | 2,226 | 2,837 | 6,305 | 2,438 | 40 | 39 | 0.19 |
| Serbian | 37 | 40 | 197 | 753 | 1,027 | 558 | 23 | 54 | 0.04 |
| Slovakian | 44 | 44 | 363 | 150 | 601 | 383 | 68 | 64 | 0.03 |
| South African | 0 | 0 | 823 | 775 | 1,598 | 824 | 52 | 52 | 0.07 |
| Spanish | 155 | 156 | 3,896 | 4,024 | 8,727 | 2,485 | 46 | 28 | 0.20 |
| Spanish-American | 8 | 9 | 49 | 19 | 85 | 33 | 67 | 39 | 0.00 |
| Swiss | 345 | 394 | 5,550 | 8,716 | 16,563 | 6,118 | 36 | 37 | 0.49 |
| Syrian | 104 | 116 | 501 | 621 | 1,670 | 687 | 36 | 41 | 0.05 |
| Tunisian | 0 | 0 | 37 | 37 | 74 | 23 | 50 | 31 | 0.00 |
| Turkish | 10 | 11 | 811 | 926 | 1,801 | 606 | 46 | 34 | 0.05 |
| Ukranian | 2,041 | 2,398 | 6,371 | 10,426 | 22,444 | 11,346 | 37 | 51 | 0.90 |
| Total | 141,194 | 161,680 | 834,568 | 909,717 | 2,327,927 | 1,260,065 | 42 | 54 | 100.00 |

NOTES

My thanks to other contributors in this volume, especially Joy Parr; my women's history study group, particularly Cynthia Wright; and Ian Radforth for their valuable comments on earlier drafts. I am indebted to Andrew Boyd and Martha Ophir for their expert research skills; to Paula Draper, director of the Holocaust in History Oral History Project, for several interviews and a recording of Gerda Frieberg's wartime recollections; and to Sandy Bair and Bruce Muirhead for making my stay in Thunder Bay both productive and fun. I would like to acknowledge the financial support of the Ontario Ministry of Culture, Tourism and Recreation and to extend my sincerest gratitude to the woman who have graciously permitted me and other researchers to interview them.

1  Interview by author. In regard to personal interviews, I have used fictitious names and occasionally modified tiny details to ensure privacy. The interviews (36) were culled from the following sources: Oral History Project, Multicultural History Society of Ontario (hereafter MHSO interview); Holocaust in History Oral History Project (hereafter Holocaust project interview); and interviews by author. The ethnic composition of the sample (which treats Jews separately) is Czechoslovakian (2); Croatian (1); Dutch (4); English (2); Estonian (1); Finn (2); German (3); Greek (1); Hungarian (2); Italians (5); Jews (4); Latvian (2); Lithuanians (2); Polish (2); Portuguese (1); Ukrainian (2). In addition, Gerda Frieberg permitted me access to a taped recording of her presentation to the Ontario Women's History Network, annual conference, Toronto 1992 (hereafter Frieberg recollection).

2  Sault Ste Marie *Star*, 21 Dec 1946 (Mrs E. Dewar changed to Elaine); interview by author; Holocaust project interview; MHSO interview.

3  Unless otherwise specified, the calculations are based on annual data gathered from the Immigration Branch *Annual Reports*, 1946–65 (see table 1). On residential and other patterns see Warren Kalbach, *The Impact of Immigration on Canada's Population* (Ottawa 1970); Anthony Richmond, *Postwar Immigrants in Canada* (Toronto 1967); Warren Kalbach and Anthony Richmond, *Factors in the Adjustment of Immigrants and Their Descendants* (Ottawa 1980).

4  The median age of immigrants was 24.9; most groups registered a median age of between 23 and 25. On age, marital status, and family size see Kalbach, *Impact of Immigration*; Canada *Census* 1961, Percentage Distribution of Ethnic Groups by Marital Status and Age.

5  Archives of Ontario (AO), International Institute of Metropolitan Toronto (IIMT), MU6381, file: St Andrew's House Study, 'Toronto Welfare Council Report'; ibid., file: Memos, notices, promotions etc., 'Statement of Purpose, Programme, and Needs for Expansion,' cited in Martha Ophir's excellent 'Defining Ethnicity in Postwar Canada: The International Institute of Metropolitan Toronto, 1953–1974'

(MA major research paper, History, University of Toronto 1993). St Andrew's joined efforts with others in 1956 to establish the IIMT. On contemporary views of immigrant adjustments see, for example, J.E. Parsons, 'Notes from My New Canadians,' *Saturday Night*, 23 Dec. 1961; J. Kage, 'From Bohunk to New Canadian,' *Social Worker* 29, 4 (1962); Benjamin Schlesinger, 'Socio-Cultural Elements in Casework: The Canadian Scene,' *Social Worker* 29, 4 (1962).

6  Holocaust project and MHSO interviews. On the displaced persons see, for example, Milda Danys, *DP: Lithuanian Immigration to Canada after the Second World War* (Toronto 1986); Karl Aun, *The Political Refugees in Canada: Estonians in Canada* (Toronto 1983); N.F. Dreisziger et al., *Struggle and Hope: The Hungarian-Canadian Experience* (Toronto 1982); Henry Radecki with Benedykt Heydenkorn, *A Member of a Distinguished Family: The Polish Group in Canada* (Toronto 1976); Ian Radforth, *Bushworkers and Bosses: Logging in Northern Ontario* (Toronto 1987); Irving Abella and Harold Troper, *None Is Too Many: Canada and the Jews of Europe* (Toronto 1983); Paula Draper, *Holocaust Education and Memorial Centre* (New York nd); Eta Fuchs Berk (as told to Gilbert Allardyee), *Chosen: A Holocaust Memoir* (Fredericton 1992); Frances Swyripa, *Wedded to the Cause: Ukrainian-Canadian Women and Ethnic Identity 1891–1991* (Toronto 1993). Studies of other groups include Joyce Hibbert, ed., *The War Brides* (Toronto 1978); Grace Anderson and David Higgs, *A Future to Inherit: The Portuguese Communities of Canada* (Toronto 1976); Franca Iacovetta, *Such Hardworking People: Italian Immigrants in Postwar Toronto* (Montreal/Kingston 1992). See also Peter Li, *The Chinese in Canada* (Toronto 1988); Agnes Calliste, 'Canada's Immigration Policy and Domestics from the Caribbean: The Second Domestic Scheme,' in Jesse Vorst et al., ed., *Race, Class, Gender: Bonds and Barriers*, 2nd ed. (Toronto 1991); Vic Satzewich, *Racism and the Importation of Foreign Labour into Postwar Canada* (London 1991).

7  Frieberg recollection; interview by author; MHSO interview

8  Franca Iacovetta, 'Making "New Canadians": Social Workers, Women, and the Reshaping of Immigrant Families,' in Franca Iacovetta and Mariana Valverde, eds., *Gender Conflicts: New Essays in Women's History* (Toronto 1992); Ruth Roach Pierson, 'They're Still Women After All': The Second World War and Canadian Womanhood* (Toronto 1986); Alison Prentice et al., *Canadian Women: A History* (Toronto 1988); Beth Light and Ruth Pierson, *No Easy Road: Women in Canada, 1920s to 1960s* (Toronto 1990); Veronica Strong-Boag, 'Home Dreams: Women and the Suburban Experiment in Canada,' *Canadian Historical Review* 72, 4 (1991); her 'Women with a Choice: Canada's Wage-earning Wives and the Construction of the Middle Class: 1945–60,' paper presented to the Canadian Historical Association, May 1992; the other contributions in this volume; Susan Prentice, 'Reds, Mothers, Militants: A History of the Postwar Daycare Campaigns in Toronto' (PhD thesis, York University 1993). For the United States see especially Elaine Tyler May, *Homeward Bound: American Families in the Cold War Era* (New York 1988).

9  AO, IIMT, MU6415, file:  Ethnic Press 1959-60, Press release, untitled, by Anne Davison, cited in Ophir, 'Defining Ethnicity in Postwar Canada.' A useful sampling of contemporary opinions includes P.C. Shapiro, 'Better Sort of Emigrants and Refugees,' *Saturday Night*, 17 May 1945; C.W. Woodside, 'Problem in Integration: The New Canadians,' *Saturday Night*, 8 Jan 1955; C.J. Devetten, '6 Ways Canadians Can Help Immigrants to Citizenship,' *Financial Post* 10 Jan 1953; Peter C. Newman, 'Are We Doing Enough to Help Our Immigrants?' *Financial Post*, 8 Feb. 1952; R. Williams, 'How to Keep Red Hands Off Our New Canadians,' *Financial Post*, 12 Mar 1949; M. Ross, 'How the Immigrant Becomes Canadian,' *Saturday Night*, 23 Dec. 1957; B. Cahill, 'Do Immigrants Bring a Mental Health Problem to Canada,' *Saturday Night*, 22 June 1957; S.M. Katz, 'How Mental Illness Is Attacking Our Immigrants,' *Maclean's*, 4 Jan. 1958; J. Kage, 'Immigration and Social Service,' *Canadian Welfare*, 1 March 1949; Ruth Hamilton, 'In a Strange Land,' *Canadian Welfare*, 15 Jan. 1948.

10 National Archives of Canada, Proceedings of the Senate Standing Committee on Immigration and Labour, No. 13, 25 June 1947. My thanks to Susan Armstrong Reid for this reference.

11 AO, Provincial Council of Women of Ontario (PCWO), MU2348, Minutes of Meetings 1955–9, Report of Mental Hygiene Committee, 15–17 May 1956 annual meeting.

12 See, for example, ibid., MU2343, Minutes of Meetings, 29–31 May 1947, Mrs James Roberts's president's address; MU2348 (1955–9), file 1958, reports of local councils; MU2351, file 1957–8, reports of committees and affiliates; resolutions for 10 June 1949.

13 Ibid., MU2343, Minutes of Meeting, 12 Feb. 1947, final form of immigration resolution.

14 Ibid., MU2343, Annual Meeting, 29–30 May 1945, condensed reports of local councils (including Brantford, West Algoma, Windsor); MU2348, Annual Meetings, 1955–9, file: 1958, Reports of local councils (including Chatham, Hamilton, Kingston, Ottawa, Weston); file: 1959, Reports of local councils (including Hamilton, Toronto).

15 Ibid., MU2351, President's Papers 1958–60, file: 1957, Report of Mrs Graeme McLean, June 1957. See also Halifax Local Council report on Hungarian refugees in this file; MU2343, Minutes of Meeting, 27–30 May 1948, Brantford Council resolution; MU2351, President's papers, 1958–60, Valerie Kasurak, Report of Chairman of Citizenship and Migration (Valerie Kasurak) to Mrs John C. Duff, president, Kingston, 28 Sept. 1957; MU2348, Meetings 1955–9, file: 1958, Kasurack, Report of Chairman of Citizenship and Immigration, 1958–9; MU2343, IODE report on citizenship tests and programs.

16 Ibid., MU2351, Minutes of Meetings, file: 1957–8, 14–16 May 1957, Report of Mrs Evanetz; Swyripa, *Wedded to the Cause*; my thanks to Frances Swyripa

for additional information on the fortunes of this group during the postwar years.

17 Iacovetta, 'Making New Canadians'; AO, IIMT, MU6410, file: Cookbook Project, 1968–71, 'Food Customs of New Canadians,' Toronto Nutrition Centre, 1967.

18 For example, Port Arthur *News-Chronical*, 12 Jan. 1946, 4 and 7 March, 25 May, 3 and 18 July, 10 and 11 Sept., 2 Nov. 1946; Hibbert, *War Brides*.

19 Port Arthur *News-Chronicle* ,12, 13, 21, 22, 30 Nov. 1946; Kay Rex, 'Disgruntled Brides Greatly in Minority,' ibid., 14 Dec. 1946; editorial, 23 Dec. 1946.

20 MHSO interview; Iacovetta, 'Making New Canadians'; Roxanna Ng and Judith Ramirez, *Immigrant Housewives in Canada: A Report* (Toronto 1981).

21 Ibid. See also Monica Boyd, 'The Status of Immigrant Women in Canada,' *Canadian Review of Sociology and Anthropology* 12, 4 (1975); E. Ferguson, *Immigrant Women in Canada* (Ottawa 1970); Laura Johnson, *The Seam Allowance: Industrial Home Sewing in Canada* (Toronto 1982); Roxanna Ng and Tania Das Gutpa, 'Nation-builders? The Captive Labour Force of Non-English-Speaking Immigrant Women,' *Canadian Woman Studies* 3 (1981); Alejandre Cumsille et al., 'Triple Oppression: Immigrant Women in the Canadian Labour Force,' in Linda Briskin and Lynda Yanz, eds., *Union Sisters: Women in the Labour Movement* (Toronto 1983); *Canadian Woman Studies* 8 (1987), 10 (1989); *Resources for Feminist Research* 16 (1987).

22 MHSO interview; Holocaust project interview; interview by author; MHSO interview.

23 Interview by author.

24 Iacovetta, *Such Hardworking People*, chapter 4; Radecki with Heydenkorn, *Distinguished Family*, 133–7.

25 MHSO interview; Holocaust project interview; interview by author; MHSO interview.

26 MHSO interview. School-leaving age was sixteen. See also Iacovetta, 'Making New Canadians' and *Such Hardworking People*; Nancy Forestell, 'All That Glitters Is Not Gold: The Gender Dimensions of Work, Family and Community Life in the Northern Ontario Goldmining Town of Timmins, 1909–1950,' (PhD dissertation, Ontario Institute for Studies in Education 1993).

27 Calculations based on Statistics Canada, unpublished census data, 1961, Experienced labour force, female, by (ethnic) origin for Ontario. Significantly, census-takers excluded Native women from the Canadian data. I thank the Ottawa researchers for their persistence in locating the material.

28 For example, the Hamilton-based Canadian Cottons Ltd factory described in F.S. Gilbertson, 'Operation DP: A Gamble That Paid Off,' *Industrial Canada* 50, 1 April 1950.

29 Calculations based on Statistics Canada, unpublished census date, 1961, Experienced labour force, female, by (ethnic) origin for Toronto; Canada *Census*, 1961, population for Metropolitan Toronto. For each selected ethnic group the calcula-

tion was arrived at by dividing the total number of working women into the total number of women (aged 15–64) within that ethnic group in Metropolitan Toronto. The percentages were as follows: all groups, 45; British, 45; German, 51; Dutch, 19; Polish, 42; Ukrainian, 49.

30  MHSO, International Ladies Garment Workers' Union Collection (microfilm), Sam Kraisman (Toronto) to Bernard Shane (Montreal), 27 March 1956; Edith Wallace to Sam Kraisman, 25 Nov. 1965. My thanks to Ruth Frager for making these references available to me. See also Frank Drea, 'Garment Jungle Hit by Unionist,' Toronto *Telegram*, 5 and 16 May 1960; Drea, 'Immigrants Thrive in Fur Industry,' *Telegram*, 12 April 1960; Toronto *Star*, 5 and 10 May 1960. For the earlier period see Ruth A. Frager, *Sweatshop Strife: Class, Ethnicity, and Gender in the Jewish Labour Movement of Toronto, 1900–1939* (Toronto 1992).

31  MHSO interview.

32  Sheryn Seibert, 'Oja's Home: A Showplace of Estonian Handicrafts,' *Northern Mosaic* (Thunder Bay Multicultural Centre), Dec. 1975; Tom Dunk, *A Working Man's Town* (Montreal 1992).

33  Interview by author (three); Holocaust project interview.

34  Interview by author (two). See also Boyd, 'Status of Immigrant Women' and 'How Do the Immigrants Fare' in Department of Labour, *Survey of Married Women Working for Pay in Eight Canadian Cities* (Ottawa 1958).

35  Josephine Phelan, 'The Library and the New Canadian,' *Ontario Library Review* 41, 1 May 1957. See also files on sewing and English classes contained in AO, International Institute of Metropolitan Toronto (IIMT) Collection, MU6474; Edith Ferguson, *Newcomers and New Learning* (A project of the IIMT, Toronto, 1964–6).

36  AO, PCWO, MU2348, Minutes of Meetings, 1955–9, Report of the Salvation Army, May 1959; ibid., Social Planning Council of Ontario, box 30, Local councils, file: Voluntarism and volunteer bureaus, Report of the bureau of Belleville and District.

37  MHSO interview; Joan Magee, 'Work with New Canadian,' *Ontario Library Review*, May 1, 1951; J. Phelan, 'Programme for the Italian Community,' *Ontario Library Review* 1 Nov. 1963.

38  City of Toronto Archives, A. Cecilia Pope to Doris Clark, 15 April 1958, with enclosed report 'Civic Action in a Well Baby Centre,' 16 April 1958.

39  Cynthia Wright, '"The Most Prominent Rendezvous of the Feminine Toronto": Eaton's College and the Organization of Shopping, 1920-1950' (PhD dissertation, Ontario Institute for Studies in Education 1992); Ernest Waengler, 'The New Canadian Market Deserves Your Attention,' *Industrial Canada*, 1 Nov. 1958. For a discussion of some of these themes in an earlier period see, for example, Susan Porter Benson, *Counter Cultures: Saleswomen, Managers and Customers in American Department Stores 1890–1940* (Urbana 1986); Elizabeth Ewen, *Immigrant Women in the Land of Dollars: Life and Culture on the Lower East Side, 1890–1925* (New York 1985).

ESTER REITER

# First-Class Workers Don't Want Second-Class Wages: The Lanark Strike in Dunnville

On 31 August 1964 the union representing the women workers at the Lanark Manufacturing Company Ltd had been making little headway in its first contract negotiations. Lanark was a wire-harness plant in Dunnville in the Niagara Peninsula which produced automobile wiring for companies such as Ford and Chrysler.[1] When operating at full capacity, it employed about 500 people, 80 per cent of them women, including many French-Canadian teenagers.[2] The bargaining committee of Local 543 of the United Electrical Radio and Machine Workers of America (UE) had been meeting with Lanark management since May 1964.[3] One month earlier, in April, the UE had won a majority of the votes necessary to become the legally recognized bargaining agent for the Lanark workers.

By the end of August, tensions on both sides had mounted. The union was demanding substantial pay raises. Lanark workers in Dunnville were earning much less than workers elsewhere in Ontario received for doing similar work, but the company refused to consider their demands. Lanark Manufacturing Co began to resemble a war zone. A corps of Barnes security guards hired by the company circulated throughout the building. Management ordered a seven-foot-high barbed-wire fence to be constructed around the plant, and huge searchlights were installed. Finally, on 31 August, while the afternoon shift was in the plant, negotiations broke down after yet another fruitless meeting. By then, eight days had passed since the report of the Conciliation Board, and the union was in a position to call a legal strike. It was the beginning of a long and a very bitter battle.

Yvette Ward, a Quebec-born francophone, had been active in organizing the plant and was a member of the negotiating team. She recalled the first day of the strike well, since it was her fortieth birthday and she was well dressed for the meeting with management. While the union officials went to the UE office in Welland (about forty minutes from Dunnville) to collect the strike signs and material, she and the remaining members of the negotiating team hoped to keep everything quiet inside the plant until the union staffers returned and announced the failure to settle. It wasn't possible. One look at the faces of the negotiating team told the workers the outcome. The Lanark workers walked out of the plant, many with parts still in their pockets.

Anticipating a strike, the plant managers had ensured that the local authorities were ready. The Dunnville police quickly descended from every direction, with much pushing and shoving. One policeman, Yvette noticed, was reaching for the young women's breasts while he was pushing them. Becoming angry, she walked across the road, warning the policeman, 'Leave them alone or else!' The policeman grabbed at her – to his regret. Mrs Ward, mother of twelve children at that time, was neither small nor weak, and she was furious. In addition, she was armed. Her clothing that day included dress shoes, which in the 1960s had very high, narrow, and pointy heels. 'I couldn't stand it. Wow, it was just like ... I went loony on him. I kicked and kicked and smacked him and everything else. He was going to arrest me. He had me and was holding me, and as he was holding my hands, I was kicking him. He went down ... All I could see was that face and I wanted to destroy it. I was so insulted.'[4] The policeman was on the ground and Yvette remembers that, as she was about to put her foot in his face, an old man she didn't know pleaded with her to stop. 'No, no, lady, that's okay. You got him. You got him!' Even without the finishing blow, the policeman ended up in the hospital.

The other officers hustled Yvette off to the police station while she was still yelling 'I want to charge this guy! I'm going to lay a charge!' The union staff men, returned from Welland, found out about the ruckus and hastened over to the police station, but even they couldn't quiet her down. 'I'm not listening to any of you guys! He's going to get charged,' Yvette insisted. Finally, after an hour of wheeling and dealing, they came to an agreement. The police released three young boys who had been arrested at Lanark at the time of the walkout, and Yvette promised not to lay charges against the policeman.[5]

The militancy and high level of hostility that marked the first day of the strike characterized much of the dealings between the Lanark officials, the workers, and the union both before and during the strike. Company officials had the power to call on the organized power of the state for their own ends. By 2 September, one hundred Ontario provincial police arrived to help the company deal with the strikers. Management applied for an injunction, which was quickly granted, to limit the number of picketers to four.

This article tells the story of that strike, exploring both the sources of power behind management's intransigence and the militancy of the women workers. It argues that this strike challenges generalizations about male-dominated industrial unions and their lack of support for women workers. It contributes to a growing literature on women's involvement as militant workers in labour struggles. However, as Yvette Ward's actions demonstrated, it also testifies to the strength of the women workers who were not constrained by normative ideals of passive, 'ladylike' behaviour prevailing in the early 1960s.

## UNIONS AND WORKING WOMEN IN THE YEARS AFTER THE SECOND WORLD WAR

There's more to this story, but why is it significant? A new generation of Canadian women scholars is beginning to examine the complex relationships among women workers and their gender, class, and ethnic alliances.[6] Ruth Frager's work on two Eaton's strikes is revealing: in 1912, for example, common ethnic bonds fostered male workers' support of the women's concerns; in 1934, however, women strikers were able to mobilize support on the basis of gender solidarity, but help from the male leaders of their own union was not forthcoming.

Women's understanding of their rights at a time when there was no organized women's movement to insist on gender equity in paid work is just beginning to be explored. The ways in which industrial unions functioned as protectors of male privilege have been well documented, but generalities invoking the power of patriarchy do not explain the gender politics of the labour movement.[7] This study of the Lanark strike finds strong union support for the women workers, even though the union knew that the company was obstinate and that its chances of winning were slight.

Workplace justice in the 1960s, as Pam Sugiman argues in her thoughtful study of women in the United Auto Workers, was defined by a male discourse and a predominantly masculine agenda.[8] Neither working women nor their trade-union representatives challenged the gender ideologies and segregated work arrangements that led to separate seniority lists and large pay differentials between the earnings of men and of women. However, the democratic principles of industrial unionism meant that women workers, in certain situations, did look to their union to defend their interests.[9] Women, although few in number in industrial unions, did not always quietly accept being underpaid and overworked; and, at times, they had the support of male-dominated trade unions in their struggles.

Ruth Milkman describes situations where working men's class interests led them to support the struggles of women.[10] She notes that unions such as the

United Electrical Workers, in an industry with a sizeable number of women workers, developed formal policies far more supportive of women workers than other unions, where it was easier to protect the male workforce by attempting to maintain a male monopoly over most jobs.[11] For those who believe that gender segregation and low-wage jobs reflected women's passivity, the story of the strike waged by the 'Lanark girls'[12] suggests a different interpretation. I hope this analysis of the struggle at Lanark will contribute to a growing history of Canadian women and Canadian unions that includes working women's collective action, along with a critical examination of male support for those actions.

To understand this particular strike and its implications, we need to locate it in the context of political and legal developments within the general labour movement. It is useful to look at women's employment, especially in unionized manufacturing jobs during this period, and to examine the particular labour relations at Essex Wire Inc., which owned the Lanark plant. Finally, the United Electrical Workers' efforts in supporting the organzing drive and the resulting strike need to be explored. Since the early 1960s feminists have a critiqued the lack of representation of women in the labour movement and have worked for adequate recognition of women's concerns and for a place for women trade unionists at all levels of the union hierarchy. This recovery of trade-union women's militancy challenges us to appreciate the complexities of gender and class politics in labour solidarity.

UNIONS IN CANADA

After the founding convention of the United Electrical Workers in Buffalo, New York, in 1936, a five-year steady advance in organizing, striking, and winning recognition was paralleled by comparable developments in other mass-production industries in the United States.[13] Initially, industrial organizing in Canada was difficult, but after 1940 union membership soared.[14] By the early 1940s the United Electrical Workers had entered Canada. Welland, Ontario, had a history of labour activity dating from the building of the canals in the early nineteenth century. Although bitter battles were waged during the depression years, the big organizing successes came in the 1940s. Welland workers signed up with the United Electrical Workers by the thousands in 1943, so that, by the war's end, UE locals 523 and 514 were the bargaining agents for virtually all the industries in Welland.[15]

Wartime needs during the early 1940s, profitable companies, and a relative labour shortage contributed to union militancy in Canada and resulted in a wave of strikes, primarily for union recognition. In an attempt to stem widespread worker militancy and to keep workers at their jobs, Order-in-Council PC 1003 in 1944 legalized compulsory collective bargaining. The model, based on the Wagner Act in the United States, was adopted by all jurisdictions in Canada after the war. Appropriate bargaining units were determined by an administrative board with little instruction from the legislation, resulting in a system of collective bargaining by enterprise and a fragmented bargaining structure. This meant that large discrepancies could exist within an industry, depending on the power had by workers in an individal plant. Thus, the size of the bargaining unit and the kind of employer determined the contract settlements that workers were able to acheive. While unions no longer had to resort to strikes for recognition, the struggle over a first contract could still make or break a union at a workplace. The prevailing Canadian practice of compulsory conciliation and a cooling-out period before strikes was still mandatory.

One battle that ended in compromise was whether unions were to be open or closed shops. The dues checkoff or Rand formula (for Justice Ivan Rand, who used it in an arbitration in 1945) which became standard in many collective agreements did not require all employees in a unionized workplace to join a union but did require them to pay union dues, since they benefited from the results of collective bargaining. This formula was later put into the legislation. Managers reserved rights over decisions in production, investment, and technology, as a result of collective bargaining and the interpretation of collective agreements by arbitrators. Thus, unions were expected to limit their concerns to wages and benefits negotiated at the end of a contract, and not to question managerial authority over numerous shop-floor issues such as staffing, technology, and work organization. This division of authority set the legal context for the Lanark strike.

The labour movement was fraught with tensions. Organizationally, it was divided between the craft unionists affiliated with the Trades and Labour Congress and the industrial unionists attached to the Canadian Congress of Labour. The two groups finally merged in 1956 to form the Canadian Labour Congress, just one year after the AFL-CIO merger in the United States, but considerable competition among the unions persisted.

While collective bargaining legislation strengthened labour, the power of employers was also growing. The overall prosperity in Canada in the 1950s and 1960s was based on increases in productivity and expanding markets owned and controlled by large transnational, mostly United States-based, corporations. In the years after the Second World War, foreign ownership of the Canadian economy grew, particularly in the manufacturing and resource sectors. By the end of the 1960s American-controlled capital in manufacturing reached a high of 47 per cent. To some extent, these productivity gains were produced by unprecedented, rapid speedups in certain industries, such as auto production. Available jobs were in the factories, so many Canadians abandoned farming and moved to where the jobs were. Farm employment went from 15.6 per cent of the workforce in 1951 to only 5.6 per cent by 1971. The industrial boom, however, was uneven and unstable. In periodic slumps at the end of the 1950s and early 1960s, unemployment rates rose while the cost of living accelerated.

Thus, the American ownership of Lanark Manufacturing Company, was part of a more general trend in manufacturing. As well, many of the Lanark workers came from families who had migrated to southern Ontario in search of factory jobs. The unsteady nature of male employment and the rising cost of living contributed to the desirability of waged work for women.

After the rapid growth of unions in the 1940s, the union movement was weakened by schisms resulting from the 'red scare.' Some unionists, in particular the social democratic leadership of the CCF, proposed measures to cleanse the labour movement of so-called subversives, while others opposed what they called 'red baiting.' Even without the existence of legislation such as the anti-Communist Taft-Hartley Act passed in the United States in 1947 to undermine union strength, many unions purged themselves of some of their most militant members on the grounds that they were Communists or Communist sympathizers. Despite their allegiance to the Soviet Union in international policy, Communists as trade unionists in Canada had supported rank-and-file democracy to a greater extent than their more bureaucratic rivals and had played an important role in the organization of many of the major unions[16]. The Cold War deluge did not silence committed Communists, who had always been a small minority, but it had a disastrous impact on the influence of many left-wing organizations, including the Social Democrats. A number of unions – the United Electrical Workers, the Mine, Mill and Smelter Workers, the International Leather and Fur Workers, and the largest union in British Columbia, the International Woodworkers of America were expelled from the Canadian Congress of Labour in the late 1940s, as was the Canadian Seaman's Union and the coastal fisherman's union in the early 1950s. The expelled unions then had to deal with raiding by other unions, some of which were set up to replace them.[17]

The United Electrical Workers struggled with raiding attempts in both the United States and Canada in the early 1960s, suffering particularly heavy losses in the United States. In 1964, during the UE organizing drive at the Lanark plant in Dunnville, the union was defending its plant in Toronto, Sola Basic, from raiding by the International Association of Machinists.

WOMEN IN PAID WORK

Beginning in the mid-1950s, there was a steady increase in the participation rate of women in the labour force. By 1964, the year of the Lanark strike, 30.5 per cent of women in Canada were in the labour force, making up 28.9 per cent of all employed workers. In Ontario, 34 per cent of all women were in the labour force.[18] The 1950s marked a large increase in the employment of married women. In 1951, only 30 per cent of employed women were married, but by 1961 this number had increased to almost half (49.8 per cent).[19]

Few of these women were in unionized jobs. By the early 1960s women's representation in organized labour was increasing, but in 1963 only 16.3 per cent of all union members in Canada were women. The majority of women belonged to international unions rather than national or government-employee organizations.[20] They were woefully underrepresented in leadership positions. In 1970 only 2.8 per cent of executive board members in international unions were women.

Little has been published in Canada on the role of women in unions for the period of most rapid growth during the 1940s. Although women continued to enter the labour force, unionized women were few in number and little is known about their activities in Canada during the 1950s and 1960s.[21] It is not until the 1970s, when public service unions were formed and female union membership expanded, that Canadian labour histories give more attention to the impact of women.[22]

There are indications, however, that women, where they could, participated in the labour militancy of the time. A long and ultimately unsuccessful attempt was made to organize retail workers in Toronto in Eaton's department store. One of the union organizers, Elaine Sufrin, described the organizing drive supported by the Canadian Congress of Labour from 1948 to 1952.[23]

Textiles was one of the few sectors in manufacturing where women were in the majority. In two major strikes in the textile industry in Quebec in the late 1940s, in the Dominion Textile's cotton mills in Montreal and in Valleyfield, more than one-third of the 6000 striking workers were women. The same union, the United Textile Workers of America, AFL, organized the women who worked in the Empire Cotton Mill in Welland in 1946. The walkout, which led to union recognition, was initiated by the young French-Canadian women workers in the spinning room.[24]

There were few women members in the two largest unions in Canada, steel and automobile unions. In 1964 the Steelworkers of America (USWA) had 116,409 Canadian members, of whom only 3.5 per cent were women; the United Automobile, Aerospace and Agricultural Implement Workers of

America (UAW) had 5379 Canadian women members, 6.8 per cent of the total membership. The number of women in the electrical unions was somewhat higher. In the United Electrical Radio and Machine Workers of America (UE), for example, 18 per cent of the workers were women (approximately 3700); approximately the same number of women were in the smaller rival union, the International Union of Electrical, Radio and Machine Workers (IUE), where they were about one-third of the total membership.[25]

Women's low rate of union participation relates to the absence of women in most industries, rather than to their reluctance to join unions.[26] Motor-vehicle manufacture, for example, was an overwhelmingly male industry. Out of a workforce of more than 32,000 workers in Canada in 1961, fewer than 7 per cent were women – and three-quarters of these women were clerical workers.[27] In some automobile plants, women were employed in sections such as upholstery and wire harnesses, where the wires and terminals were produced that make up the electrical system behind the dashboard and under the hood.

Some car manufacturers, such as Ford, contracted out the production of the wire harnesses to independent factories. Wages in these secondary industries were lower than those in the rest of motor-vehicle production. They also tended to locate their plants in low-wage areas. Average earnings in motor vehicle parts and accessories for 1961 were between $2000 and $4000 for the women who worked in this industry. In motor-vehicle production itself, the majority of men earned between $4000 and $6000, and women between $3000 and $50000 annually.[28] The Lanark plant in Dunnville, Ontario, which produced auto parts for the large Ford plants was an example of such contracting out to a secondary manufacturer.[29]

Although women worked in the large manufacturing plants in Welland during the Second World War, these opportunities disappeared with the war's end.[30] Options were limited for women in the Niagara region, in small cities and towns such as Welland, Wainfleet, Dunnville, and Port Colborne, so the women travelled by car pool to whatever town offered them a job. Women could get seasonal work in the canneries, and in a few textile plants in Dunnville and Welland. Women were also hired in Plymouth Cordage, the rope plant in Welland, and one of the two shoe factories in Port Colborne. Some found work in General Tire or in Switson's, a manufacturer of small appliances.[31] When the Lanark plant opened, half the workforce came from Welland, about one-fourth commuted from Port Colborne and the rest came from Dunnville, Wainfleet, and other small places in the area.

Average wages for women in the region near the Lanark plant were considerably below the average for Ontario, and both male and female workers experienced frequent layoffs. Where women in Ontario, on average, received $1.61 hour for work in motor-vehicle parts and accessories in 1964, few of the factories in the vicinity of Dunnville offered women more than $0.75 an hour in starting wages.[32] Outside these industrial workplaces, women found work in restaurants or as caregivers.[33] Indeed, in 1961, almost 60 per cent of the women who worked for pay in Welland found jobs in either retail trade (which included restaurants at the time) or in community, business, or personal service.[34]

THE LANARK PLANT

The Lanark plant in Dunnville was owned by a large United States corporation called Essex Wire. The company had incorporated in the United States in 1930 and had obtained the patent for ignitions for Ford cars in 1938. Essex Wire manufactured a variety of wire and cable products for automobiles and electrical equipment. A United States publication, *Labor Today*, reported that Essex was among the top fifty most profitable corporations in 1963.[35]

Similar to many smaller plants operating on the periphery of the industry, the company paid low wages by locating in low-wage areas. It also engaged in a variety of union-busting activities. Essex International, by all accounts, was a company with a particularly notorious anti-union record. For example, in February 1964, just prior to the strike in Dunnville, it recruited strikebreakers from the southern United States and hired private, armed, uniformed police brandishing shotguns, pistols, and clubs in an attempt to break a strike by the International Union of Electrical Workers (IUE) in its Hillsdale, Michigan, plant. Governor Romney of Michigan finally intervened by shutting the plant down to force the company to negotiate.[36]

Another strategy employed by the company in the United States was to set up three plants doing identical work in a triangle and to try to arrange for representation by a different union in each plant, thereby preventing unified bargaining and keeping wages low. A similar tactic was tried in Canada, where Essex established a plant in Windsor, Ontario, organized by the United Auto Workers in 1952. In 1961 the company opened another plant in Dunnville, Ontario, under the Lanark name and began to phase out its operation in Windsor. This move only angered the local branch of the United Automobile Workers.

Soon after the first thirty workers were hired for the new plant in Dunnville, the company signed a five-year contract with another union, the International Association of Machinists (IAM), for the Lanark plant. The union contract was signed when only 6 per cent of the workforce had been hired, although the plant was expected to number more than 500 workers when it was fully operational.[37] Women workers were hired at $0.75 an hour and remained at that rate for forty-five days. Regular hourly rates of pay were $0.93 for women workers and $1.38 to $1.98 for male workers.

Less than one year after opening the Dunnville plant, the company delivered an ultimatum to the UAW workers at the Essex Wire plant in Windsor, asking the women workers to accept a 25 per cent pay cut in the first year of a five-year contract and a wage freeze for the following four years. The company wanted to reduce wages for women in the Windsor plant from $1.42 an hour to a minimum of $1.05 an hour. Denying common ownership, the company claimed it was worried about the 'competition' from Lanark in Dunnville. Most of the four hundred workers in Windsor were laid off. The remaining thirty-eight workers decided to strike in February 1962, since they had nothing to lose. The plant was closed.

Both the United Auto Workers and the United Electrical Workers charged collusion between the International Association of Machinists (IAM) and the Lanark management. UAW Local 444 in Windsor was furious. It maintained that 'the former Windsor plant was stolen from the UAW by the International Association of Machinists CLC when it sneaked into Dunnville with the aid of the company.'[38] Because of this history, the Windsor UAW local readily offered support to the Lanark workers after they went out on strike for a first contract.

WORKING AT LANARK

The Lanark plant was a big, low, cement-block building covering approximately one large city block on Highway 3, with 'nowhere for the air to go.' During the summer, even the foreman, whose job was to see that the assembly lines didn't shut down – not physically demanding work – would be soaking wet with sweat. In the centre, above the washrooms, managers' air-conditioned offices with large windows overlooked the plant. The managers could and did monitor most activities, including those who used the washroom and how much time they took.

The plant consisted of a variety of stationary machines for cutting the wires, braiding them, making the terminals, and welding, and three or four long assembly lines – some extending the entire length of the plant – as well as a warehouse area.[39] In some areas of the plant, for example in the moulding department where the punch presses for making the terminals were located, the smell was terrible. In this section a compound was heated to form a rubber plug, and the hot rubber had a sickening odour.

The sexual division of labour at Lanark clearly favoured the men. Their jobs involved classifications such as male leader, machine repair, and wire-cutter setup – work that was much better paid than the women's tasks, and that enabled them to move around the plant. Only the women who were utility workers had some mobility, since they trained new workers on the machines, repaired faulty harnesses, and moved the heavy harnesses around. The rest of the women had the repetitive jobs, the stationary jobs, and the menial jobs.[40]

Some women worked on the braiders – machines placed a cotton weaving around the wire, which was then cut to the lengths needed for a particular harness. Others worked on the moulding machines or punch presses, where the terminal would be put around the wires, or in electrical welding, where the wires were spliced together. Each machine had its dangers; safety guards were either not available or not used in the rush to keep up a rapid pace, and so accidents happened. The inhumanly fast pace contributed to frequent accidents. Some women lost the tips of their fingers on the punch press or were burned while welding. One worker recalled an accident on the punch press: 'One woman, she screamed and screamed. It was hot, that thing, and it was caught on her finger. Her finger wasn't cut but it was crippled and all burned ... poor woman. The machine had fallen on her finger and the men were trying to lift the machine. I couldn't take it. I went to the washroom.'[41]

By all accounts, work on the big line called the rotary or assembly was the hardest of all. Workers on the rotary stood in one spot on a cement floor for their entire shift, keeping up a certain speed. As the line moved by, a worker arranged the wires on a board or jig marked with pins to tell her where to put them, twisting her arms to push the wires into the appropriate fuse box. Each worker put about five wires on the board; one did the front and one did the back of the harness. A completed harness could have about forty or fifty wires in all. The last three or four women on the line were called tapers, and they had a particularly difficult job. They walked along with the moving line taping groups of wires together. Then they pulled the unit off the assembly and put it on racks. The racks filled with electric harnesses were heavy and would occasionally fall over.

Muscle strain on the assembly line was common because of the twisting that was necessary to push the wires in. It was not unusual to have young women pass out on the rotary – from the heat, from motion sickness, from overwork. The speed was kept as fast as possible. Calloused fingers and, for some of the tapers in particular, crippled hands are a lasting reminder of Lanark days. One worker, Rosemary Couisineau (Akey), described the job as 'just total exhaustion and stress. Sometimes you'd come home and the tightness in your back felt like you were all in knots ... It's difficult to understand the physical part of it. You had to work so hard and so fast. If you made a mistake, the verbal abuse you'd get ... When the 3:30 bell rang, everybody just hustled to get out of there. I remember Orville Hébert, the foreman, saying, 'a bunch of animals, slow down, bunch of animals.' He was sitting in a nice, cool, cushy office.' Predominantly young women were put on the rotary because, as one worker described it, 'you had to hurry up. That's why we had more energy than the older girls, because we were young.'[42]

Given these conditions, it is remarkable that some of the women recall their years at Lanark with fondness. Those who worked there as teenagers managed to enjoy themselves despite the terrible conditions. One woman who was just seventeen recalls that everyone got along really well. 'It was like a big family but we just couldn't get a raise.' Rita Todd, who was only fifteen when she began work on the rotary explained why she has good memories: 'We worked hard – people worked hard at Lanark – but for me it was fun. For me and Yolande and Diane. When we see each other, we talk about Lanark. We used to sing on the rotary. I remember this one guy said to me (and I was so shy but singing was all right), he said, "you girls keep this singing up, we're gonna put you on the Ed Sullivan Show."'

Friendships made the workplace tolerable for the older workers as well – the sociability, the conversations, the exchange of stories.[43] Some of the workers worked overtime and as many as seven days a week. Even this difficult schedule was not without its moments, since going to work gave the young women freedom from the constraints of home. One woman recalled how she and the other 'girls' would pile into a car to go to a hotel on their Saturday night break. 'We'd hurry up and eat and rush back to work. And then sometimes we'd go for a couple of drinks after. Oh, if my mom only knew!'[44]

THE UE LANARK 'GIRLS'

Factory work was only one of the work duties, for the women. Even the young, unmarried women often had heavy family responsibilities, while the older workers had to arrange that their families were looked after while they away from home. Some, like Rosemary Cousineau, were single parents; they worried about making ends meet on the abysmally low wages as well as about meeting the emotional demands of a child. An introduction to a few of the striking workers from Lanark provides a glimpse of the lives of these women.

Velma Kucy, who helped organize the plant, was one of the older workers. She left school at fourteen, although she had been a good student, and worked for pay througout her life, except for a few years when her children were very small. She worked wherever jobs were available: at the canning factory in Fonthill, as live-in babysitter, at General Tire, in Harry's Barbecue restaurant, and as a server at banquets. Velma was in her twenties and had three children when she took a job at Lanark. Her husband was laid off from his job at Stelco tubes in Welland. She explains, 'I just got ticked off although it was a no-no for me to work.' The children stayed at her mother's house from Monday to Friday while she went off to work.

Marie Lamontagne was born in Cochrane, in northern Ontario, where her family had moved from Quebec. She came to Welland with her fiancé's family and worked in Plymouth Cordage. After she married, Marie stayed home. Her husband, Nelson, worked in Union Carbide in Welland and was the president of UE Local 523 for many years. When the children were small, she took in boarders. She cooked, cleaned, and packed lunches for six men who worked different shifts; some worked days, some afternoons, and others at nights. Her husband would help when he could. She recalls how he would return home from his shift in the factory at midnight. The baby would wake and cry, and Nelson would rock her. 'I was working and I was tired ... The minute we went to bed, that kid started crying, I don't know why.' When her oldest daughter was about sixteen and able to help at home, she went to work at Lanark, on the day shift, from 7 a.m. to 3:30 p.m., and returned home to face the demands of tired, hungry children wanting their supper. Getting the groceries was her relaxation. 'I used to shop on Friday night. I used to go to the mall and walk around and relax. It relaxed me, you know.'

Yolande Deschamps came from a large French-Canadian family in Sherbrooke, Quebec. When she was nine, her parents piled the seven children and the furniture into a pickup truck for the move to Ontario, where her father hoped to find work. She recalls the disaster of a flat tire, and how her cousins counted them all in disbelief as they piled out of the truck when the family finally arrived at her aunt's house in Port Colborne. As the oldest daughter of ten children, even as a child she had heavy household responsibilities. 'When I was nine years old, I was cleaning house like a twenty-year old.' Yolande was working at Lanark when the tenth baby arrived. She loved the baby, but another baby meant more work. 'I was so happy. But then I have to take charge of nine kids, go to work, do the cleaning, the laundry – do everything. When my mom came home a week later, I couldn't look at her. She came in with the baby and I was washing the sink in the bathroom and I couldn't come out ... It was all worth it, though.'[45]

Rita Todd went to work on the rotary at Lanark when she was fifteen years old. With thirteen people in the house (she had ten brothers and sisters), the extra money helped her parents meet expenses. She needed to work for wages, but was also happy to go to work. Rita remembers when she applied for the job that she put her hair up and wore high heels and a dress in order to look older. 'I loved it because I was so young ... Here I am working in a plant with other young people. I'd rather go to work than be at home where there was lots to do.'[46]

Ethel Kekich, another prominent leader and strong union supporter, had three children at home and a husband in and out of hospital with a weak heart when she took a job at Lanark. Born on a farm in Yugoslavia, she worked hard all her life and did all kinds of work both before and after the Lanark factory: waitress, cook, nursing assistant, and in the canning factory. When her husband was in the hospital, she would make up a list of chores for the children to do as they stayed alone in the house until she returned from work. She cooked the next day's supper each evening for the children to put in the oven at dinner time.

The Lanark women were hardworking, spirited people. They wanted to organize for better pay and for more humane working conditions. They saw the International Association of Machinists as a company union that would not protect them or struggle against management abuses, and they were angered by the union's acquiescence to the low wages. They joined the United Electrical Workers in the hope that this union would be behind them.

THE ORGANIZING DRIVE

For its part, members of the Welland Local 523 of the United Electrical Workers union had several reasons for wanting to organize the plant. Many of the workers came from Welland, and the union was well informed about the appalling conditions in the plant. Some of the women had brothers, husbands, or fathers who were in the union and who considered the poor treatment of the workers as an affront to their family and friends. The women from Welland who worked at Lanark came from union families, and they understood and respected the need to act collectively.

The organizing drive had the support of head office in Toronto. Angered by the move by the International Association of Machinists to take over the Sola Basic plant in Toronto, the United Electrical Workers leadership wanted to teach the IAM a lesson. These reasons were not mutually exclusive; as a pamphlet appealing for support explained: 'These workers have been sold out by the IAM to the company and need a good strong Union to help them get decent wages and conditions.'[47]

Most of the women active in organizing Lanark for the United Electrical Workers were workers with more job experience, those who had the better women's jobs in the plant. Despite the hardship and hard work in their own lives, they saw their union activities as helping others less advantaged than themselves. They described their involvement as a desire to help 'the little guy,' or as a reaction to the unfair treatment of the young 'girls.'

Yvette Ward recalled a foreman whom they called 'Barry the Pig' because of the way he leered at the young women and frightened them. She described Lanark as a sweatshop, exploiting children as young as fifteen with threats that if they didn't work harder they would be out of a job the next day. 'It was a real nightmare on the assembly line. I had never seen anything like that. Everyday I kept thinking, my daughter's fifteen, she could be one of them.'[48]

Ethel Kekich, a utility person on the rotary, had a job that involved moving around the assembly line. Like Yvette Ward, she objected to the way management threatened the young women. They pushed them to do more and more harnesses and would rap on their backs if they weren't done in time. 'They were speeding up the rotary and the girls would have to run like wildcats or something. It was hard for me too, but I wasn't just fighting for myself, I was fighting for the girl that was lower than I was. You hire somebody, you give them a chance. You know what I mean. They're human. We're not a machine for them.'[49]

For Velma Kucy, a relief worker on the moulding machines, the poor pay and her anger at management strategies were the biggest factors in her decision to help organize. 'They paid far better wages in Windsor, moved out and came down here, and signed – with almost no employees – a five-year contract. That was the whole sticker. Apparently it was a company that's moved all the way around just for that reason.'

The women who played a prominent role in organizing for the United Electrical Workers had clear ideas about why they wanted to replace the International Association of Machinists with another union that would protect the workers' interests better. Some of the younger workers, however, did not even recall that there had been another union before the United Electrical Workers. Others, like Rosemary Cousineau (Akey), remember how high the stakes were for her and how she had to think over her decision very carefully.

Yvette said to me, 'I know you're scared. I think I would be too if I were a single mother.' And she told the younger gung-ho girls, 'you leave her alone, don't pressure the single moms. They have to decide for themselves.' I think it was her quiet way of doing it that convinced me. That and the younger girls who said, 'we don't know what you're going through, but hey, that's okay.' And I thought to myself, well gee whiz, it can't be any worse, the way we're treated now. Maybe if we had a union we'd have more protection.'

Signing people up took place both inside and outside the plant. For example, the workers who lived in other towns travelled to Dunnville in car pools, since there was no public transportation. Ethel Kekich asked the five young passengers who rode with her from Port Colborne, 'Do you want to make it better for yourself or worse for yourself?' Mrs Côté of Dunnville did the same, as did Velma Kucy who drove in from Fonthill.

Inside the plant, people would distribute the union cards in the course of their work, which was why the workers with the better jobs were so important to the organizing drive. Velma Kucy, whose job was relief person, carried union cards in her cigarettes as she went from machine to machine. When somebody went to the washroom she would take her cigarettes along, sign the card, and bring it back. Yvette Ward worked on repairs to faulty harnesses and so had a view of what was going on in the entire plant. She knew how people felt, who were the union supporters, and how reliable they were. Ethel Kekich carried cards around in her apron. She would slip cards under the wires and people would take them home and sign them.

The organizing drive took place in February–March 1964. Even in a situation where there was a great deal of discontent, union records show that the drive was not easy work. Yvette Ward and the United Electrical Workers' staff organizers, John Trufal, Bruce Smith, and Nelson Lamontagne, visited workers in their homes and held weekly meetings in Welland and Dunnville for both the afternoon and the evening shifts. It was far easier to sign people up from Welland or Port Colborne, which were union towns, than from Dunnville, which was a more conservative place. Not all the people who signed cards actually voted for the UE during the election. There were a few workers who felt that it would have been better to wait until the International Association of Machinists contract with Lanark had expired.[50]

As the company became aware of the organizing drive, it used both the carrot and the stick in its strategies to ward off the threat from the United Electrical Workers. It reopened the contract with the IAM, improved benefits, and offered a 4 per cent across-the-board wage increase amounting to about eleven cents an hour. The IAM charged that the UE has 'caused the harmonious relationship between our members to be disrupted,' and pledged to 'restore the happy relationship which existed between members.'[51]

The company also tried to intimidate the workers, firing one young women, Jacqueline Clark. They charged her with signing up workers on company time and produced a sheet with a list of names, which they claimed were UE supporters. Although Jacqueline was pro union, the list turned out to be contributors to a gift for one of the foremen! She was later reinstated after the UE filed a grievance with the Labour Board.

The UE leafleted regularly, keeping workers informed of what was happening. After two to three weeks of intensive effort, the union had a majority of the workers signed up. By 15 March 342 cards had been signed, and the UE applied to the Ontario Labour Board for certification. After some delays requested by the IAM and the company, the vote finally took place on 12 April. The UE won the secret vote and a negotiating committee of six was elected, three from the day shift and three from the afternoon shift.[52]

Negotiations began in early May and proved very difficult. By early June the national leadership was called in and Ross Russell, the UE national director of organization, joined the negotiating committee. Wages were the biggest stumbling block. The union asked for a minimum of $1.40 an hour for the women, still 40 cents below the starting rate of women doing the same work in the General Electric factories in Toronto or Peterborough. Plant-wide seniority was another major issue.[53] As negotiations stalled, the UE applied for conciliation, beginning the steps necessary to launch a legal strike.

The company's response was to argue that they had to compete with the harness plant in St Thomas (also owned by Essex) and to threaten to close the Lanark factory. When the conciliation officer met with both sides in late June, management was so unyielding that, in disgust, the day shift walked off the job on 26 June in a one-day wildcat strike. In July the plant manager, J.R. Jupp, was replaced by Ken Holt, reputed to be a 'heavy' from the company's United States offices. At the same time, layoffs of more than two hundred workers had the union concerned about the plant's future. On 13 August the Conciliation Board met and the union planned a strike vote for the following week, cautioning workers not to quit because they 'couldn't take it any more' or to walk out illegally, since that would 'hurt our cause.' Of the 424 workers voting, 90 per cent authorized a strike, and the company set up a meeting on 31 August at 1:30 p.m., the first day a strike was legal. At the final meeting, the company sent a Mr Cuff from the Central Ontario Industrial Relations Institute in Toronto, who reiterated the position they had given four months previously – the same conditions as the old IAM contract. However, the company had new contracts to produce harnesses for 1965 cars, so workers had been rehired and the company was busy with production. This was an opportune moment to strike.

For some of the young women, the initial walkout was fun:

The walk-out. That was wild – okay everybody walk out. You're young and you go – it's a party. To tell you the truth, I think we just followed. Did you think when you were sixteen? ... After that I can remember that they had put up a big tent across the street there at the store and we'd go there. It was fun. Isn't that awful? When you're more mature, you think, well geez, you're on strike; this is serious business ... They had food over there and we'd go picket and there was always action on the picket line.

Another woman who was seventeen at the time recalled how excited everybody was:

Hey, we're on strike. Hey, we're going for more money. We're gonna have this, we're gonna have that. We never did ... Oh, there was no way I was staying in. And then my boyfriend - that's when I met my husband - he was working for GM and he was very supportive of me. He was a union man ... Most of the people that worked down there, their husbands were union men, so it wasn't too hard for us to say, well, what's a union? Cause we knew a little bit.

Within twenty-four hours of the start of the strike, the company successfully applied for an *ex parte* injunction limiting the number of pickets to four. Lanark management applied for the injunction under the name of its legal owner, Essex Wire Inc., although it had earlier maintained that Essex Wire and Lanark were 'competitors.' Fifty Barnes uniformed private police had been hired and the Ontario Provincial Police were called to Dunnville to help the local police who had been there from the start. The former president of the International Association of Machinists led a group of thirty former members (primarily men) back into the plant.

The company advertised for scabs and the strike turned violent. Paul Sutton was a lead hand with a wife and two small babies in 1964. He remembers the strike as exciting, sometimes tedious, and sometimes scary. He was one of the men who stayed out. Like the older women with families, it was serious business for him.

This was their [the strikers] livelihood and it was being taken away from them ... Maybe in Toronto or someplace up there, but in our area it really was unheard of – bringing people to work when you're out on strike. Where did these people come from? That was their thing – to break the unions, to break the morale of the people ... They wouldn't give you a five cent raise, but they'd spend thousands of dollars on these guards from Hamilton, Barnes, the security company. They had Doberman Pinchers out there guarding the police. And then they go and bring in all these people that they wouldn't hire before. They're bringing them in by the busload to keep the plant running. That was the kind of mentality that we were up against.

Given the limited options women in the area had, they did not take kindly to watching their jobs taken by strikebreakers. The lines were drawn very clearly between those who stayed in and those who stayed out. There were some people, mostly from Dunnville, which was not a union town, who had no idea of what the strike was about and who continued to go to work.[54] As one young woman described it:

It broke our hearts when we saw people still going in ... and they did everything they could to stop the scabs from working. The police used to protect the scabs going in and out. But ... We couldn't do anything. You couldn't hold them up on the line. The dammed cops were sitting across the street and down across from out picket line. So we'd just fight back – even with the police. We'd do anything to get back at 'em. They're supposed to be protection for the public, right? They're not supposed to be biased. But they sure were ... It was all one-sided ... I was in court every week for something or other.

Management was able to enlist ample support from the various agencies of the law. Indeed, at one point, the strikers counted no fewer than one hundred Ontario Provincial Police marshalled against the picketers. The combination of vicious management tactics, support from the state, and high stakes for the workers made this a particularly volatile situation. The resulting violence and the workers' militancy contradict conventional notions of 1960s femininity. However, newspaper coverage in the *Hamilton Spectator*, for example, gives some glimpse of how these gender rules were used to trivialize the issues and the militancy of the strikers. In the following account the physical characteristics of the women are described in detail, while the women's demands are noted only elliptically as disputes over wages, working conditions, and seniority.

Trim Strikers Eyed by Police
DUNNVILLE They're probably the prettiest strikers the policemen have seen. The girls – more than 200 of them – spend their time picketing and the policemen spend their time watching the girls.

Occasionally the girl pickets do a jig, more often they burst into union songs, and most of the time they flash winning smiles at the young constables and occasionally ask them to light their cigarettes for them.

But it isn't like this all the time and that's the trouble.

... Since the strike began police have charged 33 pickets with offenses which included assault, intimidation, wilful damage, creating a disturbance and blocking the highway. One non-striker has been convicted of assault.[55]

In contrast, the union charged that the penalties meted out to strikers were 'extreme and vengeful in relation to the alleged offenses.'[56] Court records document what the strikers maintained – that the legal system treated them unfairly when they were charged with union-related activities. Offenses by strikers against the scabs – such as throwing a tomato at a car, kicking the side of a car, throwing eggs, impeding a car, writing on a windshield with lipstick – were subject to fines of over $125. One striker ended up in jail for forty-five days on a charge of damaging the windows at Lanark with a slingshot. In contrast, two men charged with shooting up a store with a sawed-off shotgun were sent home after paying a fine of $64.50.

One woman, Bella Levinski, was picketing at the plant when a car sped by, almost hitting her and another picketer. The driver, James Gilbert Reid, a strikebreaker, then parked his car, walked back towards the gate, and physically assaulted Bella, yelling 'dirty Communist.' She fought back. Extricating herself from the large plywood picket around her neck, she hit him with it while he pummelled her with his fists. This fight was finally broken up by four OPP officers. Reid, who according to one provincial police witness was drunk at the time, was fined $75 plus $34 in costs in magistrate's court.[57] Levinski received a heavier penalty for a much less serious charge. A few weeks later, while on picket duty, she was charged with damaging a $6.90 car aerial and was fined $150 or fifteen days in jail by the same magistrate.

The courts also acted callously when it came to respecting language differences and ignored some basic prerequisites for fair representation – for example, that a witness should understand what is going on in the courtroom. Mrs Côté, a francophone who did not speak much English, was struck in the forehead by a rock thrown at her while she was walking the picket line. A piece of paper, with 'f--- you' written on it, was wrapped around the rock. Yolande Deschamps (Kranyk) had witnessed the incident and went to court with Mrs Côté when the case was heard. Mrs Côté asked Yolande to accompany her to the front of the courtroom so she could help translate. The judge ordered her to sit down and demanded that Mrs Côté manage on her own. Yolande still remembers the feeling, 'Me, I'm not used to that – going to court at seventeen ... I felt this small [when he ordered her back] ... They never charged the guy. They thought it was a big joke.'

Bruce Smith, the UE business agent for Welland, described some of the tactics the company used which fell outside the legal system. Twenty-five to thirty shady-looking leather-jacketed men with large dogs would patrol along the fence of the plant, past the open gate. He described one particularly terrifying trip home from the picket line with two young women in the back and his wife in the front seat of his car. It was midnight when he left for Welland, and he noticed two cars full of these tough-looking 'hoods' following him as he left for home. It got worse:

Halfway to Welland, on the sideroad, we saw another car; it started to pull out and by the time I passed the sideroad, I was going at least a hundred miles an hour. If not for my speed, I presumed they were going to stop us, beat the hell out of the girls and leave me pretty well in bad shape. And that's the kind of a strike it was. Apparently they did the same thing in the United States, with the strike down there.'[58]

Rather than intimidate the strikers, these tactics made them angry and, in response, they were fearless. The older women, in particular, were furious, and for them notions of fairness precluded any constraints about what was or wasn't appropriate feminine behaviour. 'They [the company] had no right to do half the things they did, and when they started playing dirty, then hey, it's just like in baseball. I can hit the ball just as far as you can, if I get the right pitch.'[59]

Ethel Kekich recalled how she and Velma Kucy let the air out of a car's tires one night while four policemen were sitting in it. They then banged on the back of the trunk. The policemen started the car, realized it was going 'thump, thump,' figured out why, and ran around trying to find the perpetrators. By this time, Ethel and Velma had got away. One of the famous stories among the strikers was how Ethel and Velma took two scabs for a ride. Almost thirty years later the accounts vary somewhat with the teller, but the main point remains. These women would not put up with scabs and they dealt with them in their own way, fearlessly and with a sense of humour.

We saw these two kids coming out – they were good-sized kids – and they saw us coming out of the tent and getting into the car. We drove right out of the parking lot where the tent was and we stopped and we said 'Would you like a ride?' They said 'Sure, we'll have a ride.' We drove for quite a while and we got to a sideroad. I said, 'Boys, take your shoes off, you've got a long walk ahead of you.' We never really threatened them or anything. I just said, 'This is as far as we're taking you.' So they just kind of looked at us and said, 'Do you really mean it?' I said, 'Uh-huh, we mean it.' They said 'we're not getting out. You can take us home.' I said, 'we're not going home, we're going back to the picket line.' And I just got out of the car, opened the door, and said, 'You've got two feet and your're gonna walk ... Don't forget, the next time you get picked up by a bunch of strikers they're not scabs.'[60]

The strikers had a good laugh about the two guys who 'got lost last night on their way home from work ... That really boosted our morale.'[61]

The company advertised for strikebreakers on a regular basis in the Dunnville paper, calling for young women willing to come to work for $1.00 an hour. The union responded with advertisements entitled 'Don't let *This* Happen to *YOUR DAUGHTER*,' describing the company and asking people to protest and not go to work for Lanark. One of the more shameful company moves company was its recruitment of young Native workers from the Cayuga area to the east of Dunnville whom the company had previously refused to hire. Yvette Ward and Ross Russell spoke to the chief of the reserve, who had worked in a unionized cement plant in the area and thus, was quite sympathetic. He joined the strikers on the picket line the following day and encouraged his people not to scab.

As the strike went on, there was a veritable war between those who were out and those who continued to work. Some of strikers had their tires slashed, dye poured over their cars, windshields broken, and sugar put in their gas tanks. They retaliated in kind with paint bombs, made by putting paint inside a lightbulb and throwing it, and by hurling foul-smelling, rotten eggs and tomatoes. After the injunction limiting the number of pickets to four, other ways were found to obstruct the strikebreakers. So many nails would 'fall' out of the pockets of the few allowed to picket just before a shift ended that management purchased a huge magnet on a roller that they ran along the plant gates before the cars drove out. The male staff of the UE did not encourage these doings, but they could not and did not try to control what the women did.

Velma Kucy and Yvette Ward recalled the time the strikers blockaded Highway 3 to prevent the scabs from entering the plant, tying up traffic for hours. They rented two moving trucks and, at 6 a.m. the next morning, two male strikers put the trucks right in front of the gates and 'abandoned' thirty or forty cars on both sides of the building behind the trucks, 'just mish-mashed, sort of like a crossword puzzle.' On Highway 3, for a block on either side of the plant, there was nothing but cars. They put the cars in gear, locked the doors, and left them. Velma recalls: 'Nobody could get in the plant. I was one of the later ones coming up and when I got my car up there, the police was right on my car and I just barrelled out the door – One cop was right behind me and I can remember Jean – standing there and screaming, 'Run!!!!!' They called the towtrucks and towed all our cars away and impounded them all.' The union picked up the cost of the truck rentals and the towing charges.

Ross Russell, the UE national director of organization, was one man fondly remembered by the strike leaders. He was credited with dreaming up some of the more dramatic tactics to draw attention to the strike, the details of which he left to the local staff. The Lanark workers' forty-three-mile march from Hamilton to Queen's Park to ask for government intervention in the strike was one of Ross's ideas.

In early October fifty women, including Yvette Ward, Velma Kucy, three sixteen-year-olds, and fifty-one-year-old Elsie walked from Hamilton to the provincial courthouse in Toronto to protest the use of an injunction in the Lanark strike. They walked along Highway 2, picketing Ford plants in Hamilton and Oakville as well as Ford and Goodyear dealers to dramatize the strike issues. They remember the tired feet and the fun they had; the UE staffers remember the aggravation. One of the sixteen-year-olds had never been out of the Niagara Peninsula before. For her 'it was fun. Because we walked and we delivered little pamphlets, papers and whatever on the strike – we slept in a union hall one night and then we slept in a motel and we were on TV. This was all exciting.'

The strikers made sure that the UE staff, John Trufal, Bruce Smith, and Nelson Lamontagne (who was released from his regular job at Union Carbide to help organize at Lanark), were teased as much as possible. The men – young, married men and very serious about their union work – were determined to behave like 'gentlemen' with the women, and the women used these ideas of gendered 'proper' behaviour to make their lives difficult. Yvette Ward always had some helpful suggestions along these lines. On the night they spent in a motel in Port Credit during the march to Toronto, the UE staff men took a room across the road from where the women were staying so there could be no rumours of any 'fooling around.' Trufal asked Yvette to see that the young women stayed in and behaved themselves. She listened to the first half of his instructions, but made sure that everyone had fun in the motel playing tricks on John, who was a perfect target. Yvette Ward recounts:

We sent three of the girls to knock on their room door and say, 'Yvette won't let us go to the bar,' and they walked right into their room. And John kept saying, 'Get out of here! Get out!' Ethel [Kekich] and I were killing ourselves laughing. The next morning, we said to John, 'I fell asleep last night and I heard some girls went to your room.' 'Don't you talk to me about that! You weren't doing your job!' He was blaming me. He was so much fun to play tricks on because he'd get all upset.

'That Russell,' he would say, 'if he ever shows his face in Welland again, I'm going to kill him!'

At Queen's Park the Lanark strikers, along with the printers who were also on strike, had a meeting with the Minister of Labour Rowntree, Attorney General Wishart, and Provincial Treasurer J.N. Allen, the MPP from Dunnville. They were asking for government intervention (as had happened with Essex in Michigan) to force the company to negotiate. They also protested the stiff fines strikers had been receiving in court.[62] Their appeal fell on deaf ears.

All the strikers remember the strike headquarters, a tent pitched on the lawn rented from a store located across from the factory. One of the hallmarks of this women's strike was the quality of the food; by all accounts it was delicious and plentiful, the borscht in particular. One of the strikers who has few memories of Lanark or the details of the strike clearly recalls the tent. 'Oh, I can remember when we picketed, all the nice hot coffee and hot chocolate, the food that would come. People were very very generous – I remember that. I don't even know where it all came from, but we always ate well.'

The strikers reaped the benefits of the Welland United Electrical Workers Women's Auxiliary. This auxiliary had been in operation since 1960, to 'promote educationals, community involvement and offer cheer and help in times of misfortune and industrial troubles.' The women, who were wives of UE staff men and activists, understood the importance of involving all the members of the family in support of a strike. They themselves, many with small children to look after, saw little of their husbands for almost a year, from the time of the organizing drive until the strike ended. The prolonged tensions of the Lanark strike took a heavy toll on their husbands, whose dedication was a family affair. John and Millie Trufal, for example, put their house up as collateral for bail money for arrested strikers a number of times. These women kept their families going, supported their men, and identified with what their husbands were doing. They picketed, they spoke to the families of strikers, they washed the tablecloths used in the strikers' tent. Along with the strikers, they prepared food to bring to the picket line and provided other practical supports for the strike. Throughout the six months of the strike, the contribution of the women's auxiliary to keeping up morale was enormous.

With a few exceptions, most of the strikers had the support of their families.[63] Facing the hardship of living on $14 a week strike pay required the collective effort and the collective resources of a household/family to manage. Yet the Lanark women did more than survive – they faced the challenge of the strike with humour, zest, and great bravery. The support of households, families, and the community made a significant difference.

LANARK AND THE LABOUR MOVEMENT

Although the United Electrical Workers Union in 1964 was still outside the House of Labour, the Canadian Labour Congress, many unions supported the strikers in every way possible. UAW Ford and Chrysler workers from Hamilton, Windsor, and Peterborough in particular responded generously. Throughout September and October, considerable energy was put into mobilizing the community and other workers and in keeping up morale. Strikers leafleted plants in Welland, Hamilton, and Peterborough and organized rallies, meetings, and a dance for support of the strike. Members of the teamsters and other unions from the Welland area joined the Lanark workers on the picket line. Financial and moral support for the strike came from unions as far away as Calgary. The bulk of the support came from the United Auto Workers and the United Electrical Workers in southern Ontario and from virtually the entire unionized workforce of Welland.[64]

On 20 October, less than two weeks after the march to Toronto, more than 2000 unionists rallied in Dunnville in support of the strikers. The cross-section of trade-union leaders sitting on the platform as honoured guests featured twenty-one men and one woman.[65] The speeches at this rally tell a great deal about class and gender politics in this period. Speakers calling for support of the Lanark women used two distinct arguments. The first was labour solidarity for ungendered, undifferentiated workers. It was important for unionists to protect and defend each other. The second approach considered gender, not to acknowledge women as a particularly exploited group of workers, but rather to call on strong men to defend their weaker sisters or daughters.[66]

Charles Brooks of the UAW, Windsor, was the featured speaker. He told the rally that companies were seeking to smash small local unions, but 'the big brothers in the labor movement are not going to stand by and let them do this.' In conclusion, he said, 'We can either surrender or fight our way out. God save the Queen and all the little queens (women on strike from the Lanark plant). The union will help see you through.'[67]

The strike dragged on, the company refused to negotiate, and some of the workers looked for other jobs. Difficult as the work was in Lanark, at least it was recognized as 'women's work.' In a sympathetic view of the hardship the strike was causing, a picture in the *Hamilton Spectator* in late October showed three Lanark strikers looking somber because they were employed in non-traditional jobs. They were working on a demolition crew, tearing down an old bridge in Dunnville. So desperate were they for a job, they would even do men's work.[68]

In late November the UE prepared a brief to Attorney General Wishart maintaining that the courts were biased against strikers in the Lanark and Globelite plants (Globelite was another UE plant on strike in Scarborough, Ontario). They criticized the use of the injunction, which created 'the environment for companies to launch large-scale strikebreaking.'[69] The UE was joined by the UAW and the International Typographical Union in a meeting with Wishart to demand that injunctions be revoked. The meeting was fruitless, and Wishart refused to do anything.

The UE staffers did what they could to keep up morale, but by Christmas time the strikers' hopes were dimming. Welland UE workers donated enough money for each picketer to receive a turkey and a $10 bonus, and they organized a huge party for all UE workers' children. On 10 January the workers finally decided to end the strike and on 11 January, after nineteen weeks on the picket line, they returned to work.

Yvette Ward, who led the strikers back into the plant, described the return as one of the most difficult things she has had to do in her life. Bruce Smith recalls: 'I was there that day. The Sunday we had the meeting and we told the strikers and the strikers knew that it was all over. They [the company] were back to almost normal in production. So we put it on the table and said, look, it's a lost cause now – we're not fooling anybody about that.' Eighty people returned to work. As predicted, the Native people were the first of the strikebreakers to get laid off, followed by a few others that had also crossed the picket line.

CONCLUSION

In October 1991 some of the Lanark strikers gathered together for a reunion at the UE hall in Welland. There were stories and anecdotes about the march to Toronto, about the strike, and about the years working at Lanark. The spirited accounts were a reminder that laughter, jokes, and fun are not separate from the serious matters of meetings, strikes, and union work. They are the heart and soul of struggle. The women located events that happened long ago by referencing dates with family histories – birthdays or the year the youngest started school. One of the strikers, Gisele Rozon, brought a shirt to the reunion that said 'Take this job and shove it.' She had it made to wear for her last day at Lanark before she retired.

Although the strike was lost, Lanark was the first real fight against the injunction, which was used much more sparingly later. Locally, the UE managed to demonstrate labour solidarity in very tangible ways, and the Lanark strike succeeded in letting companies in the Niagara Peninsula know that taking on the UE meant a fight.

The Lanark strike was a wonderful example of what women could do – many of them young, non-English-speaking women in an anglophone province – when they had a commitment to making things better through collective action. Their energies in this strike were directed against their unfair treatment as workers, rather than the particular injustices they suffered as women workers. The gender scripts accepted by both the strikers and the male unionists were profoundly uneven in duties and responsibilities: the women had to worry about two jobs, the men only their paid one. There was no gender equality in the Lanark situation. The union staff were all men. The male workers from Lanark had easier, more interesting, and better-paid jobs than the women. The men involved in the strike, particularly the UE union staff, were supported by the work of their wives who made it possible for them to dedicate themselves so wholeheartedly to this strike. Many of their wives, in addition to coping as 'union widows,' contributed directly to the strike through the women's auxiliary.

Now, thirty years later, the mutual respect between the union men and the women strikers remains. The strikers viewed their United Electrical Workers staff – John Trufal, Bruce Smith, and Nelson Lamontagne – as decent, dedicated, hardworking men who did everything they could to support the women and to win the strike. The men, in turn, admired and respected the courage and the perseverance of these young women. We can look backward and be critical of the failure to acknowledge formally the gendered nature of the exploitation of the Lanark women as workers, but the Lanark strike was a strike by and for women and about how they were treated at work. It is also an instance where women's problems - inadequate pay; difficult, demanding, and low-status jobs; and harassment – were treated as workers' issues, not exclusively women's concerns. Yvette Ward summed it up:

A lot of times I sit and think about it. Lanark, to me, was a landmark in the history of labour because these kids weren't afraid. They went ahead and did it, even though they knew they might lose their jobs forever. It is an example for others to look at and say, 'We don't have to put up with all this. We can do something about it and let be whatever happens.'

I can't help but remember the unity and the courage and the knowledge that all of the girls from that time had – and the few men that were working there. We were bound together so tight. These girls were working for peanuts, and didn't have much to fight for, but they did. They fought for six months steady without a stop and never gave up for one minute ... It was the experience of a lifetime.[70]

NOTES

I would like to thank Millie Trufal, John Trufal, and Yvette Ward for making this research possible. John Trufal, United Electrical Workers national representative, retrieved the strike documents stored in the UE hall in Welland. Millie Trufal, president of the Welland UE Women's Auxiliary, introduced me to Yvette Ward, co-chair of the strike committee. Together we were able to locate a number of the strikers, and a reunion was held in October 1991. Individual interviews for this article were conducted in July 1992. Karen Hadley did background research, Canan Rosnuk assisted in interviewing, and Julianna Nedeljkovic transcribed the tapes. Meg Luxton's comments were particularly useful, as were the thoughtful suggestions of Joy Parr. Bruce Smith carefully checked the text for accuracy.

1  The Niagara Peninsula consists of the area in southern Ontario between the two great Lakes, Lake Ontario to the north and Lake Erie to the south. The Lanark plant in Dunnville drew workers from cities and towns within approximately a 50-kilometer radius. The town of Wainfleet is located approximately 25 kilometers east of Dunnville. Port Colborne is about 40 kilometers east of Dunnville, while Welland is 10 kilometers north of Port Colborne, or 50 kilometers from the plant. There is no public transportation between these cities and towns to help employees get to work.

2  These figures came from a seniority list dated 15 October 1963, just before the organizing drive, which tabulated male and female workers. For the estimates of workers' ages, I have relied on interview material. Some corroboration of interviewers' judgments about the ethnicity of the women workers is available from the seniority lists. It seems safe to assume that people with names like Agatha Lacroix or Audrey Paquet are French Canadian.

3  The United Electrical Radio and Machine Workers of America is often referred to in its shortened form, as the United Electrical Workers, or by the initials UE.

4  The UE staff consisted of John Trufal, national representative, and Bruce Smith, business agent for the Welland area, who had their union office in Welland. Nelson Lamontagne was president of the Welland local and worked at Page Hersey. He was seconded to the union to help with the strike. His wife, Marie, worked in the Lanark plant.

5  Personal interview, Yvette Ward, Jan. 1992.

6  Joy Parr, *The Gender of Breadwinners: Women, Men, and Change in Two Industrial Towns, 1880–1950* (Toronto: University of Toronto Press 1990); Ruth Frager, *Sweatshop Strife: Class, Ethnicity and Gender in the Jewish Labour Movement of Toronto, 1900–1930* (Toronto: University of Toronto Press 1992);

Pamela Sugiman, *Labour's Dilemma: The Gender Politics of Auto Workers in Canada, 1937–1979* (Toronto: University of Toronto Press 1994).

7 The most forceful presentation of this position is by Heidi Hartmann, 'Capitalism, Patriarchy and Job Segregation by Sex,' *Signs* 1 (spring 1976): 137–69.

8 Sugiman, *Labour's Dilemma*.

9 Nancy F. Gabin, in *Feminism and the Labor Movement: Women and the United Auto Workers, 1935–75* (Ithaca: Cornell University Press 1990), provides an illuminating history of women workers' experience in automobile manufacturing in the United States.

10 Ruth Milkman, *Gender at Work: The Dynamics of Job Segregation by Sex during World War II* (Chicago: University of Illinois Press 1987).

11 In the United States since 1910, more than one-third of the workers in electrical manufacturing have been women. Ibid., 13.

12 The women who worked at Lanark called each other 'girls' and that is how they were referred to. Since many of them were very young women, this designation was almost literally true.

13 Philip S. Foner, *Women and the American Labor Movement* (New York: Free Press 1982), 333–7.

14 Craig Heron, *The Canadian Labour Movement* (Toronto: Lorimer 1989), 65–93.

15 Canada Foundries and Forges in Welland was organized by the United Electrical Workers, Local 275, in 1943.

16 See Heron, *The Canadian Labour Movement*, 65–93.

17 When Hal Banks, a convicted gangster, was imported to Canada by the CCL with the approval of the Canadian government in order to destroy the Seaman's Union by means of intimidation and other criminal tactics, Welland was one of the few places where the besieged Seamen had strong support from the community because of presence of the United Electrical Workers.

18 *Facts and Figures: Women in the Labour Force, l969* (Women's Bureau, Canada Department of Labour).

19 Julie White, *Women and Unions* (Canadian Advisory Council on the Status of Women; Ottawa: Minister of Supply and Services 1980).

20 The internationals claimed 47.8 per cent of union women. The remainder were divided between national and government unions. Corporations and Labour Unions Return Act (CALURA) report for 1964.

21 Pam Sugiman's book is an important exception. Labour historians Bryan Palmer (*Working Class Experience*, Toronto: Butterworths 1983), and Craig Heron in their comprehensive accounts of the Canadian labour movement have no mention of women during these years. What available material there is comes from the general histories of Canadian women, in particular Alison Prentice et al., eds., *Canadian Women: A History* (Toronto: Harcourt Brace Jovanovich 1988),

and Collectif Clio, *L'Histoire des femmes au Québec depuis quatre siècles* (Montreal: Le Jour 1992).

22 See Palmer, *Working Class Experience,* and Heron, *The Canadian Labour Movement.* Unionized women first claim our attention in the 1970s, when feminists became active. In the United States, see Gabin, *Feminism in the Labor Movement,* and Milkman, *Gender at Work.* In Canada, see *Labour's Dilemma* by Pam Sugiman.

23 For more about these strikes, see Rick Salutin, *Kent Rowley, the Organizer: A Canadian Union Life* (Toronto: Lorimer 1980), and Eileen Sufrin, *The Eaton Drive: The Campaign to Organize Canada's Largest Department Store, 1948 to l952* (Toronto: Fitzhenry and Whiteside 1982).

24 One of the organizers, Val Bjarnason, was a member of the UE executive in the 1980s. Fern A. Sayles, *Welland Workers Make History* (Welland: Winnifred Sayles 1963), 168. AFL refers to the American Federation of Labor.

25 Figures are from the CALURA report for 1964 (Ottawa: Dominion Bureau of Statistics 1967).

26 The limited evidence from this period supports this argument. White, *Women and Unions,* demonstrates this same situation for a later period.

27 *Census of Canada,* 1961, vol. 3, part 2, Labour Force Industries.

28 Ibid., part 3, 28–62.

29 UE strike bulletin, Local 543, 2 Sept. 1964.

30 John Trufal, when he got a job at Page Hersey in Welland, ended up working the same machine that his mother had operated during the war. A mischievous foreman like to point out that his mother had been much faster than he was. John's response was that she knew she was going to be there for only a short time and was determined to make as much money as possible while she could. She wouldn't even take the time to go to the washroom, he complained.

31 Almost all these plants have since closed, and the area faces serious economic crisis.

32 The factory listings are compiled from interviews. Wage rates for the area were also gathered from interview material, while the averages for Ontario are found in Statistics Canada, *Employment in Manufacturing, l964.* Women in Ontario averaged $1.41 an hour for all manufactturing jobs, while men earneed, on average, $2.33 an hour.

33 The 1961 census indicates that average annual wages for men in Ontario were $4371, and for women, $2726. Men in Dunnville earned on average $3461, and women, $1744, while in Welland the averages were $3925 for men and $1932 for women.

34 *Census of Canada,* 1961, vol. 3, part 2.

35 Al Millstein, 'Essex Wire Strike,' *Labor Today,* 1964, 15–18.

36 Governor Romney was quoted in the *New York Times* calling the company

action 'reprehensible, immoral and a disgrace to Hillsdale, the state and the nation'. Lanark Strike Committee leaflet.

37 Twenty of these workers had been members of the International Association of Machinists in an Essex plant in Simcoe, Ontario, which had recently closed.

38 Local 44 news, 13 Nov. 1964.

39 Interview with Rosemary Akey, April 1992.

40 Job classifications are from a seniority list dated 15 Oct. 1963.

41 Interview with Marie Lamontagne, April 1992.

42 Interview with Rita Todd, April 1992.

43 Interview with Marie Lamontagne.

44 Anonymous interview (her mother is still alive!).

45 Interview with Yolande Deschamps, April 1992.

46 Interview with Rita Todd.

47 Pamphlet issued by UE Local 523, 24 March 1964.

48 Interview with Yvette Ward, Feb. 1992.

49 Interview with Ethel Kekich, April 1992.

50 Interview done by Canan Rosnuk with a non-striking Lanark worker, August 1992.

51 IAM pamphlet.

52 UE pamphlet, 13 April 1964.

53 Local 548, UE pamphlet, 9 June 1964.

54 This observation was made by a number of the strikers interviewed – Paul Sutton, Yvette Ward, as well as the Welland UE organzing staff.

55 *Hamilton Spectator*, 10 Oct. 1964.

56 Brief to Attorney General A.A. Wishart, 1964.

57 Welland *Evening Tribune*, 9 Oct. 1964.

58 Interview with Bruce Smith, April 1992.

59 Interview with Ethel Kekich.

60 Interviews with Velma Kucy, April 1992, and Ethel Kekich.

61 Interview with Rosemary Akey.

62 'Historic March Demands Government Action in Dunnville strike.' *UE News*, 18 Oct. 1964.

63 I was told of one case where the daughter was a militant UE member who strongly supported the strike, while her mother scabbed. Unfortunately, I was unable to contact this person.

64 Some of the unions were the Hamilton Can Workers Union, the Calgary Labour Council, UAW Locals 707 and 28 in Toronto, 199 in St Catherines, and 200 and 444 from Windsor. The Calgary District Council and the Oil, Chemical and Atomic Workers International Union Local 9 in British Columbia wrote to the Ontario Supreme Court protesting the *ex parte* injunction. CUPE gave its full

moral support, as did CUPE Local 37 in Calgary. Women's auxiliary 50 of the UAW also donated money. The Teamster Joint Council supported the Lanark workers, as did the Oakville and District Labour Council.

65  *UE News*, Oct. 1964.

66  As we have seen in the remarks of Ethel Kekich and Yvette Ward, these understandings were shared by the women as well.

67  The men on the platform were Ken Girard, chairman of the Chrysler steward body of the UAW, Windsor; Stan Bulloch, publicity director of the ITU; Bob McCormack, president of ITU, Toronto; Ross Russell, director of organization for the UE; Harold Stire, president of the Mine Mill local in Dunnville; Ray Peters, president of GE Local 524, Peterborough; Bob Reilly, a chief steward of Local 1005, UAW Stelco, in Hamilton; John Ball, president of Westinghouse Local 504, Hamilton; Bill Slomecky, vice presdient of the Mailers Union Local 5, Toronto; Bill Longridge, secretary treasurer of Mine Mill of Canada; P. Claude Bolt, president of the Can Workers Union, Hamilton; George Steplock, UAW, Ford Oakville; George Harris, UE national executive; Jim Connell, president of the 6300 member UAW Local 199 at McKinnon's in St Catharines; Jim Salvi, president of UE Local 536 at Cyanamid; Nelson Lamontagne, president of UE Local 523; Syd Silver, president of UE Local 527 in Peterborough; Len Shulta, representative of the Teamsters Union, Hamilton; and Terry Fraser, trustee of IBEW, Local 105, Hamilton. The woman in the picture was most likely a Lanark worker.

68  *Hamilton Spectator*, 20 Oct. 1964.

69  Statement to Attorney General Wishart, 30 Nov. 1964.

70  Interview with Yvette Ward.

E.A. (NORA) CEBOTAREV

# From Domesticity to the Public Sphere:
# Farm Women, 1945–86

The period 1945 to 1985 witnessed a profound transformation of rural Ontario, a reflection, in many ways, of the larger socioeconomic developments in the province. Most of the changes in farming as an industry have been amply researched and documented. In the past, however, they were studied from an economic or production perspective. Seldom have the human consequences of socioeconomic changes on farm families and particularly on women been examined, nor has much attention been paid to women's contributions to the survival of farming as we know it in North America. Yet these changes have meant severe transformations in gender relations on farms, just as they have modified farm women's roles and increased the saliency of farm women's contributions to the survival of what is known as the family farm. Most existing farm studies give the strong impression that men farm single-handedly and that women are confined to household duties or to occasional 'help' on the farm. It was not until the end of the 1960s, with a few exceptions, that references to women farmers appeared in the farm literature in Canada. One could easily conclude that men were the sole farmers and that farming was exclusively a male occupation. The first serious studies of women in agriculture have appeared only in the last twenty years.[1] Previously, women were depicted, if at all, as farm helpmates or gofers, even if they worked on the farm fifteen or thiry-five hours a week in addition to a full-time job providing personal services to the farmer, the children, and the farm workers. Women's work on the farm and in the household was invisible, and for policy-makers and economists it was inconsequential. While farm women always worked in the home and on the farm, and at times off the farm to earn extra money, they accepted the undervaluation of their work and their definition as farm wives, rather than as farmers and as economically active persons. The very narrow concept of farming, centring strictly on the production process, denied the significance of women's reproductive work and ignored their contribution to farming and to overall life.[2] For farmers it was a different matter. Without the personal services at home and the 'help' on the farm, few farmers could have persisted in their enterprise. Farmers, however, were not eager to change the existing arrangements and to share the control over farm, finance, and home to a greater extent with women. Yet conditions, perhaps external to their wishes, transformed agriculture and the farm family in Ontario.

The object of this article is to shed light on the effects of the rural transformation on farm women's lives. The first hypothesis of this study is that, because farm women's lives are embedded in their families, farms, and rural communities, they will be affected by the socioeconomic and political changes in these contexts. Therefore, the emphasis will be on examining selected changes that occurred between 1945 to 1985 in the Ontario farming community and the overall society and on evaluating how these changes modified farm women's lives. The second hypothesis is that farm women are not passive bystanders, accepting changes to their families, farms, or rural communities, but that they actively engage in a struggle to protect farming as an enterprise and a way of life. However, the forms of this struggle change over time. Women's contributions on many family farms in Ontario have changed radically in the last forty years. In the 1980s, while still working on farms and being responsible for home-making, family care, and personal services, a majority of farm women worked off the farm, at higher rates proportionally than urban women, to earn much-needed cash to maintain their family and farm.[3] Furthermore, no longer satisfied with being excluded from 'modern farming,' many of today's farm women are eagerly learning all that is involved in financial and agricultural management of a farm business and are getting involved in public activity. The third hypothesis is that some farm women are developing a new self-concept or identity that allows them to become autonomous persons and to expand their roles legitimately into the public sphere.

The geographic location of this study is southwestern Ontario, the area where most Ontario farms are concentrated. It is the most intensely settled and cultivated region of the province, containing almost all types of Ontario farming. The focus is on farm women living on small and medium-size farms, because they represent the majority in rural Ontario. The approach is mainly documentary, consisting of a review of existing studies on farms and farm women, official statistics, and archival material. As well, farm newspapers were reviewed, some going back over twenty years, to detect any changes in the reported stories and images of farm women.[4] In addition, a small number of farm women of Euro-Canadian (British and Dutch) background in three different age groups were interviewed, to learn of their personal experience and to include their voice in this article.[5]

The results of this study should be treated as indicative of general trends that took place only in Ontario, because it is difficult and risky to generalize about farm women. Their living and working conditions in farming and in rural community life can vary greatly. Not only do the types of farms (both commodity and scale) place different demands on women's work and responsibilities, but women's family and occupational status influence women's opportunities, options, and position within the community.[6] Furthermore, women's life conditions, gender, and power relations are modified by the various cultural patterns, interpretations, and ethnic traditions of Ontario's rural population. Property rights have also changed, and the number of women farmers is increasing in southwestern Ontario.[7] Thus, any statement about farm women in Ontario has to be made cautiously, keeping this variability in mind.

In the following sections I describe some of the changes that have occurred in southwestern Ontario; they have transformed farming as well as the lives of farm women and families. In the first section I discuss the major changes that, between 1945 and 1970, affected farming in southwestern Ontario and farm women's lives. In the second I present some of the actions farm women undertook individually and in groups, when faced with the changes that threatened the loss of many farms in the last fifteen to twenty years of the period under study. In the final section I discuss the changes in farm women's self-concept which permitted them to engage in new activities with greater freedom and less apprehension, and to come more fully into their own as autonomous persons and women.

Farming in Ontario was and is very diverse. The decline in farm units over the forty years between 1945 and 1985 was not uniform for all farm types. Some types dwindled and disappeared as distinct and formally recognizable units, others multiplied and became increasingly important in the Ontario farm economy. The changes in the structure of agriculture in Ontario from 1961 to 1986 were dramatic. The overall decline of farm numbers continued, from 121,333 to 72,213 (about 40 per cent), but not all farm types were affected in the same way. Some farms passed from male into female hands and, although small in numbers, they show that different ways of farming are possible and viable.

During the first two decades after the Second World War rural Ontario,

TABLE 1
Rural-Urban Domestic Amenities

| | 1941 | | 1951 | | 1961 | |
|---|---|---|---|---|---|---|
| | Canada | Ontario | Canada | Ontario | Canada | Ontario |
| Cars | 47.0 | 69.6 | 52.0 | 72.2 | 77.5 | 87.6 |
| Inside running water | 12.2 | 14.8 | 32.9 | 40.8 | 60.6 | 75.5 |
| Shower | 6.5 | 10.7 | 15.5 | 25.2 | 40.4 | 58.2 |
| Flush toilet | 8.1 | 9.5 | 19.9 | 25.1 | 43.8 | 56.4 |
| Fridge | 3.6 | 9.3 | 21.9 | 42.5 | 80.0 | 92.0 |
| Radio/TV | 60.6 | 66.2 | 88.6 | 88.4 | 67.3 | 80.3 |

Compiled from D. White, 'Rural Canada in Transition,' in Tremblay and Anderson, *Rural Canada in Transition* (1966).

compared with other parts of Canada, produced the largest share of agricultural products. During the war, the province was enjoying a period of relative prosperity linked to industrial expansion, farm contracts with the United Kingdom, and farm subsidies, all of which stabilized, to certain extent, the fluctuating prices of farm products and incomes. At the urging of farmers and the public, and to insure continuity and stability of farm incomes, the Agricultural Price Support Act was passed in 1944 as a temporary wartime measure, and then continued as a transitional measure in 1950. Agricultural production and incomes peaked during the Second World War and the Korean War. The war industry enhanced the expansion of urban employment. Many new projects were undertaken by the provincial governments of Drew and Frost, not all directly related to farming, but some with strong influences on changes in rural areas. Developments such as municipal planning, flood control, conservation of forests, and road building offered new job opportunities and shaped rural Ontario in ways that strongly affected farm family living.[8] Rural homes in Ontario were gradually modernized and were consistently rated higher in various amenities than the national averages for Canada (table 1). While these amenities were a welcome innovation making work easier for rural home-makers, they hardly decreased the amount of domestic labour performed by rural women. 'With all the new household labour saving devices, I still had no time for myself. I could not do any reading or writing ... with the increasing work pace on the farm, this was just not possible,' said a retired farm woman in her late sixties living on a mixed grain-livestock farm. She taught school before marrying a farmer.[9]

In the postwar years the government encouraged farmers to become better organized. The 1944 Act Respecting Agricultural Committees was intended to make farmers more actively involved in the planning of farm production and the regulation of processing. By the 1960s the Farm Product Marketing Board was established as the administrative agent for the twenty-seven major Ontario cooperatives, and it marketed most of Ontario's field crops. Similar boards were also established for livestock and dairy products. In the 1945–70 period, 70 per cent of Ontario farmers had membership in marketing and processing cooperatives. However, there was no place for farm women in these organizations. Membership was for household heads, one per family farm.

Wartime industrialization drew much labour from rural areas, and farm labour became scarce and dear. In the ten years following the end of the war, farm labour costs almost quadrupled. The rapid turnover of farm labour and the burden of providing for live-in help exacerbated these difficulties. One older farm woman recalls: 'I just carry food out to the men, when they are working. Last year it was not that simple as it sounds, sometimes they would be 6 or 7 miles away from the house. Preparing hot meals and getting them to the men was practically a full-time job. I must say I got tired of it, and I keep saying 'I am not going to do it another year,' but I find myself doing it again, when the time comes around.'

The scarcity and the cost of farm labour also contributed to a fast mechanization of agriculture. By 1958 there were as many tractors as farms, and more tractors than horses in the province. Mechanization, however, was a domain of men. 'I have never had a chance to drive a tractor. This was men's work, I could not do it,' reminisced an eighty-six-year-old retired farm woman. Another retired farm woman said: 'Men always did the "tractor thing," we [women and children] had to do the other work.' This trend forced women to work on farms even more intensely, expanding their overall work hours. Almost all farm women (98 per cent) were actively involved in one or more productive activities on farms, replacing between two and five-and-a-half months of hired labour per year. Three out of five women on dairy farms regularly fed and milked cows and cleaned barns. One-half of all women on poultry farms were responsible for taking care of birds on a regular basis. Two in five did the accounting work, and one in four replaced hired labour in field work.[10]

The electrification of rural Ontario made possible the acquisition of more powered equipment on dairy and other livestock farms as well as electrical appliances for the homes. One study of farm expenditures shows that only 13 per cent of family outlays were spent for household appliances, whereas 87 per cent were allocated to the purchase of farm equipment. More often than not the home had to wait to get the appliances and equipment it needed. As one retired farm woman recalled: 'The farm always came first. No matter how badly you needed an appliance or how sick you felt, the farm always had the priority. We got hydro in 1947 and I had to wait over ten years before getting my electric fridge.' A younger farm woman said: 'We were overjoyed in 1957 when my aunt got her first washer/wringer. It was fantastic! Before that we used to do laundry by hand, this was hard work!' By the beginning of the 1960s, 56 per cent of all farm women in Ontario had freezers, 95 per cent had fridges, and 50 per cent used food lockers in freezer plants. This refrigeration revolutionized farm women's way of providing for family food needs.[11] 'The best thing I ever got was my freezer. I was so pleased ... it made my life much easier. I almost quit canning. I put everything into my freezer, corn, vegetables, meats and baked goods ... It saved me a lot of time,' said another retired farm woman who was married in 1933 and lived through the war on a mixed farm.

Mechanization required the capitalization, specialization, and enlargement of farms to justify the cost of machinery. The investment in land and buildings more than doubled during this period, and the investment in implements, machinery, and livestock more than trebled. The new production technologies that accompanied the mechanization of agriculture required new buildings, labour-saving equipment, increasing use of fertilizers and insecticides, as well as bought feed and vitamins for livestock and poultry. Although farm input prices kept rising, they rose more slowly than prices for farm products. Not only were many Ontario regions now geared towards growing crops and raising livestock more suited to their regional ecology, but individual farms began to reduce the variety of crops and animal products they produced. The emphasis on fewer major commodities made farms more productive, but also more vulnerable to price fluctuations. This trend undermined farm women's traditional domain of economic activity and their source of independent income and control. The production of eggs, butter, cheese, and other home-produced goods was gradually reduced. 'Every Saturday evening I took 4 gallons of cream and 10 dozens of eggs to town. Stores used to be open in the evenings then. I got $3.50 for it, enough to buy the dry goods I needed for the home. This was the only money I ever had ... I could keep what was left over,' recalled an older retired farm woman. Farm income 'in kind,' which is a partial indicator of domestic production, declined from 23.5 per cent in 1935 to 13.5 per cent in 1955 as a percentage of the total gross farm income. A younger retired farm woman said: 'I never had any money. When I needed a better dress I would order it from the [Eaton's] catalogue. He [her husband] had to pick it up and pay for it ... [laughs].' These changes seem to have deprived some women of their personal incomes.[12]

In the 1950s farms were still not specialized; some 40 per cent derived their income from up to four products, and about one-half from up to seven. Diversification of production was still used as an insurance strategy by many farmers. 'We produced most of our necessities, almost everything ... eggs, milk, butter, cheese, meats, potatoes, fruits and vegetables, and I used to can and preserve a lot of food for the family, for the whole year,' said an older farm woman. Through farm specialization, farming was gradually losing its relative self-sufficiency and beginning to depend on purchased, industrially produced inputs, in the field, for livestock operation, and for daily household necessities such as food and clothing. All this required more cash. Moreover, by the 1950's some signs of concentration of production could be discerned: 70.4 per cent of the farms produced 96 per cent of the total farm sales. Farm families with smaller incomes were on an increase, placing more economic pressure on farm women. At that time, almost one in five agricultural workers (19.2 per cent) represented non-paid family labour, mainly women, almost twice as many as hired farm hands (12 per cent). There was much prejudice against women farmers, and they could not obtain paid employment on farms. Women, even if they were trained as farmers, had difficulties in getting hired for this work. An older farm woman, born in England, recalled: 'I was trained in an agricultural school. When I came to Canada I tried to get a job as a farmer, but people would not take me seriously. I never could get work for pay, yet all women work on farms for free, and this seems normal.' Indeed, the largest proportion of non-waged farm workers were farm women and children. Children as young as seven were known to drive tractors. Daughters worked alongside sons on the farm. 'I was the third girl in our family. My older sisters helped mother around the house, but I was always outside, on the farm, working with the boys, my brothers,' said a retired farm woman in Grey County. She was married in the 1940s and has run a farm since her husband fell ill, had surgery, and retired from farming. This woman felt quite confident in managing her farm, and only wished she had more help.[13]

Ontario farming traditionally has relied on mortgages to advance its economic competitiveness. One eight-county study showed that since 1910 about half of all farms in the sample held mortgages over ten years and that fully 50 per cent of these were obtained from private individuals. Only one-fourth of the farms had always been mortgage free. While in the past most loans were obtained from individuals, in later years formal institutions provided loans and credit. Farm women in all age groups felt it was easier to deal with individuals than with institutions 'if the lender was fair,' although they did not recall women getting any loans. Moreover, when loans came from relatives or friends, they might have been interest free. 'At one time my father-in-law owned almost the entire township. He was a farmer and a shrewd businessmen, but he also was very fair, and he was well liked and always open to discussion,' said a younger farm woman. Even in the 1970s some farm women reported holding private mortgages in their farm land. A younger farm women, who bought her land in the mid-1970s, explained: 'We have a private mortgage from the farmer who owned the land we bought. The farmer retired and we got the land.' However, at the end of the 1960s the majority (69 per cent) of farmers obtained their loans from chartered banks. At that time farmers, and particularly the farm women, did not always have a full understanding of the implications of borrowing cash from formal institutions.[14]

Electrical power and the new road network were reaching into many isolated areas; together, they made possible closer contact with the urban society and industrial goods. Road construction also provided temporary off-farm employment to farmers in remote areas. Education was also changing. A women in her late seventies remembered, 'Sometimes I did not go to school for two or three months because I did not have shoes. School was quite a ways ... I stayed home and helped mam around the house and the barn.' With primary and secondary school consolidation, rural education was changing, from the 'little red one-room schoolhouse' to larger, central district schools with better teachers and programs. However, the farm population still had a lower educational level than urban dwellers. The first yellow school buses began travelling the country roads, taking children from farm and home to schools, where they received a more formal education and spent more time away, out of the influence of the family sphere. This deprived farm women of much-needed children's help around the house, yard, barn, and farm. In 1951 only 29.6 per cent of this population had nine years of education, compared with 55 per cent in urban areas, but farm women tended to have more schooling than farm men.

After the Second World War the population of the province increased greatly. A strong immigration flow from Europe and the United States, which peaked in the mid-1950s, brought more than 2.6 million people into Canada. The provincial government of Premier Frost favoured immigration, and Ontario became the home to 57 per cent of those new immigrants. Not all immigrants stayed in Canada and most settled in cities, but many also made their home on farms, adding to the diversity of Ontario's rural population. Since there were fewer women than men in rural areas, many farmers married women of urban backgrounds who brought small-town culture into Ontario farming. All these changes, along with the great farm turnover, added to rural cultural diversity; in the decade 1967–76 more than half of Ontario farms changed hands, and many of the new farmers had urban backgrounds. As a result, it difficult to speak of an Ontario-based, unified, rural-farm culture.[15]

Still, life on the farm was very male centred. Male heads were the legal property owners, and their dominance in the family can be gathered from the way major decisions were made. In the majority of cases (80 per cent) the farmer alone made the decision to acquire farm machinery; in the case of home appliances, the decision was made jointly by husband and wife. An older farm woman said, 'I never got involved in farm business decisions, this was something the men [husband and sons] discussed among themselves.' Women's area of decision-making was limited: it applied to meal planning and, to a lesser extent, clothing.

Joint decision-making on domestic issues was also reported. Sometimes this family decision-making is seen as an indication of greater farm family democratization. However, since shared decisions mainly applied to the household or to the domain of women, joint decision-making also could be interpreted as another way for the farmer to retain control over the family budget. In general, few women were able to decide on their own on purchases for the home or for themselves, and even fewer had a say in important farm decisions. A generation later, younger farm women reported more sharing of farm decision-making than their older sisters did. However, even this decision-making pattern tended to shift with the family life cycle. Before children were born, there was more sharing of both farm work and farm decisions. When families had pre-school children, women seemed to retreat into the home and their participation in farm decisions to decrease. When children went to school, women had a greater possibility to engage in farm work and they also became more involved in discussing farm decisions with their spouses. However, when teenage or young adult sons began to work with their fathers on the farm, women once again became marginalized from farm decision-making. As one older farm woman stated: 'When the kids were younger and in school, we [she and her husband] used to work together on the farm, as real partners. We used to discuss everything, what had to be done with regards to farming. Now that Billy is working with his father, they talk everything over among themselves. I feel sort of left out. Sometimes I try to get my 5 cent worth in ... but they don't always listen.'[16]

Decision-making in the community was also out of reach for most farm women. 'We never had a say in church or on the school-board ... It's not that we did not have ideas ... It just was not done,' said a retired farm woman. 'My husband was on the school-board many for years ... but I never took part,' confirmed another in the same age group. Participation in social activities was limited, too. 'We always went to church on Sundays, and always contributed to bake sales ... pies, cookies ... for fund-raising. Sometimes we went to fairs, that was fun. There was also the Farm Forum, almost the only thing at that time, but quite often we were so tired that we went straight to bed, to sleep,' said another retired farm woman in her late eighties.[17]

A generation later a few lone and dissenting women's voices argued that women's participation in farm, home, and community matters should be enlarged. For example, Agnes Johnson, in an interview about her weekly radio program, said: 'Women should receive more recognition in marital equality and expect equal opportunity in employment.' The Ontario Farmer's Union began to recruit farm women 'not as auxiliaries, but as legitimate members' and elected its first local woman president; she maintained that women have 'something, a special quality' they can bring to family and community affairs. Newspapers carried titles like 'General Farm Organization needs woman's interests, points of view.'[18].

If it was difficult for women to start life on a farm, it was even harder for women to become farmers. Marriage to a farmer was the easiest way to reach this goal. Farms were seldom passed on to daughters. 'My father-in-law worked very hard to leave the boys land. Each son got land for his farm. The girls [daughters] got money, $20,000 each, that was a lot of money. That was the way things were done,' said a younger farm woman. Most farm daughters migrated to cities and towns, following the earlier tradition, to become gainfully employed in professional, clerical, or service jobs before marriage. Between 1900 and 1950 the proportion of local farm daughters marrying farmers decreased from 92 per cent to 77 per cent, and the number of immigrant farm women grew from 3 per cent to 10 per cent. In the 1960s this trend continued further, and more small-town women ended up on farms. In spite of the farm transfer pattern to sons, only 40 per cent of farm sons stayed to continue the family farm business, and even fewer (20 per cent) farm daughters remained on farms. 'In this township, all farm women, except two, are from small towns,' said a younger farm wife in Bruce County. 'We had to learn all about living and working on farms, but we love it. The best part is that we can work together, as a family, most of the time.' This seems to indicate that becoming a committed farm woman is not dependent on whether a woman grew up on a farm, but on what way of life she valued and was willing to work for.[19]

Although Ontario had the highest farm-income average in Canada, except for British Columbia, in the early 1970s none of the farm families derived their entire income from agriculture. Wages and salaries ranged from 34 per cent to 70 per cent, while farm incomes represented only 24 per cent of the total. The distribution of income among family farm households was more unequal than among non-farm and urban households. The importance of off-farm income was increasing for the farm family, from 14 per cent in 1941 to 60–70 per cent of the total family income in 1971, and the economic inequality among family farms continued to grow.[20]

During the early 1970s Ontario farms entered a relatively more prosperous era. Farm prices for crops and livestock were consistently above the cost of farm inputs.[21] Farm women recalled these years as 'good times.' 'I guess it was in the early seventies when we were doing good. We thought there is a future in farming, for ourselves and for our children,' said a younger farm woman on a mixed-crops farm. Another younger farm woman, from a beef farm, said: 'In the seventies there was this "window." That was the only time, four, five years, when our farm was clear, I did not have to go to work, I was a teacher ... I could stay home with the kids. Our kids were small then, and I enjoyed spending time with them, doing chores around the house, the barn or in the vegetable garden and having them around.'

With increasing capitalization of the farms, accounting and financial management became a more important and complicated activity. Almost nine out of ten farm women became involved in this type of work, as the words of this younger farm woman illustrate: 'It is certainly different from the time that my mother lived on the farm. That was the era when farm management was easier, but many women knew nothing about the business end of it and have never written a cheque. On our farm, I do all the banking and have a fairly comprehensive idea of where we stand financially. I think it's far better this way.' Another woman in her early forties recalled: 'The older generation, like my husband's older sister, 16 to 18 years older than we, are not interested in the farm business. They did not do the tax returns, nor they did know anything about accounting, financial statements, farm management or credit. They are unaware of the business side of farming. They did a lot of sewing, canning, knitting and other things to save money, but they did not want to be bothered with farm management problems. In 1967, when I got married, no women knew how to do accounts around here.' During this time many farms continued to modernize and enlarge their enterprises. There was considerable institutional pressure to do so. Prosperity seemed to be within the farm family's reach, and professional advice was favourably received. 'We followed the advice of experts at the college [Ontario Agricultural College], and what the government told us. We took out loans from banks and bought new equipment. We thought we had it made. We did everything we were told to do,' said a younger farm woman who later became intensely involved in women's organizations and in managing both the farm and an off-farm family business.

However, the good times for farms did not last long. In the later 1970s uncertainties about farm incomes were voiced again. 'Wages for almost all occupations have increased between eight to ten-fold in the last 30 years, but only a few large scale farmers have seen their income increase 3 times during the same time period,' noted a farm journalist, who regretted 'the declining proportion of farm product price in the retail cost of food, from 42 per cent in 1961 to 36 per cent in 1971.'[22] Thus, farmers were earning increasingly smaller portions of the food dollars spent by consumers. Fluctuating interest rates rose more than over 20 per cent, affecting farmers who had borrowed and expanded the most. The farm crisis at the close of the 1970s to the early 1980s was different from others. While previously small and middle-size farms were most affected, now modern farms with large capital investment also tended to go out of business. No longer could it be argued that farmers who lost their farms were traditional or poor managers. This situation created considerable scepticism and distrust of expert advice and institutional motivation. 'We did everything we were told to do, to modernize, to expand, to overcome our traditional attitudes [the farmers' fear to go into debt] ... We did not listen to our father, but to experts, and we lost everything,' said a younger farm wife. Another farm woman in her forties on a beef farm explained:

We thought: What do these old folks [parents] know? We know better! Government and the college [OAC] advised us to expand, to buy larger machinery and to take out loans. We had bankers coming to our front steps. We would ask for a loan of $10,000 and they would say: Why not $20,000? That is why we expanded and modernized, until the crunch in the early 1980s. We got into this cycle of expansion-credit-debts-bankruptcy ... The expansion was wrong ... we lost the farm. We went to Alberta, but farming was too complicated there: too many rules and regulations we did not know ... My husband said: 'If I should go bankrupt again, I like to be among friends, let's go back to Ontario.' So, we came back and started this farm with Farm Credit. My husband was the youngest son in the family ... he did not learn from his dad ... not to borrow money. Wanda, his oldest sister did, she hardly ever borrowed money and she and her husband still have their old farm. Now we got rid of banks and experts. We have scaled down our farm business and we don't have any large machinery any more. We have a cow-calf operation. We get a calf, we get profit. We sell them. If we want, we always can start a feeder-lot. But we also have a non-farm business on the side. We went through four businesses since 1982. We don't know how long we are going to last with this one.

A younger woman from a mixed farm remarked:

Its easy for them [the experts and government employees] to give us advice. They get their salaries, no matter what ... It is us, the farmers, who take the risks ... And it's us, the women that have to face the crunch. They [husband and son] plan our farm business, and I often fear when time comes to write a cheque: where will the money come from?

Another farm woman said:

The 1980 crisis was the biggest learning experience in our lives. We learnt how to deal with the banks, with losses, and how to start again from scratch. There is no way that any one can make a go with interests rates of 24 per cent. The bank got us working for them ... all we could do is to try to pay the interests and nothing on the principal! We women, have also learnt all about finances, taxes and business management and our own legal rights! Now we know what it means to co-sign a note with our husbands. We read all the fine print!

A young woman from a farm worth more than $1 million that was lost in the early 1980s talked about recovering their farm family life:

We like to live on a farm. We bought a small dairy farm [with Farm Credit], and our milk quota. We had to learn how to run a dairy farm, we had no experience with dairy. We got an old farm house, we hope to remodel in a few years. Right now, looking after the dairy business is our priority. I have a new baby, the third, so I cannot do much work on the farm, but I am looking forward to working with my husband, as soon as the kids are older.

Farm women responded to the economic stress and the farm crisis created by the fall of crop and livestock prices in the late 1970s and early 1980 with individual and group action. They begun to organize and mobilize forces to struggle for the family farm, as a business and as a way of life, and for the survival of the larger rural community. Many New Farm Women's Organizations (NFWO) sprang up during this decade, on local, provincial, and national levels. Of these, the only explicitly feminist one was Women Today in Huron County.[23] Few farm women wished to be associated with the feminist label. Feminists had a 'bad press' among rural people. They were seen as 'not respectable, not hard working, irresponsible ... trouble-makers, bra-burners,' as a couple of farm women remarked. However, many feminist issues were brought into the open by farm women at this time. In the late 1970s to mid-

1980s the harmonious image of the farm family began to wane and new women's needs were acknowledged in rural areas: women's shelters begun to spring up, and articles about battered women and family violence in rural areas appeared in the farm press.[24] As well, the new educational desire of farm women had to be responded to. Farm women voiced their demands for training in farm management, financing, agricultural production, and marketing, and other economic and policy issues were also high on their list.[25]

The older farm women's organizations, such as the Women's Institutes (WI), no longer seemed to be serving all the emerging needs and were rejected by many younger women. Home-making and social and civic activities, although useful and still valued, did not exhaust younger women's enlarged roles and interests. Some farm women wanted strong organizations active in the fields of agriculture, the economy, and politics. Although the WIs 'have done some good,' it was felt they no longer responded to the needs of these younger women. 'I was never interested in what was going on in the WI' and 'It was just a waste of time for me, I was more interested in farm business and economics' were comments similar to those of many younger farm women. This uneasiness with Women's Institutes emerged as early as the 1960s, illustrating the misgivings that some farm women had with a narrow definition of women's roles.[26] Older women, however, saw the WI meetings as important learning and social occasions, circumscribed by the 'traditional' sexual division of labour. One older woman said: 'We don't approve of the new women's organizations nor of their influence on the WI: they went political ... Can you believe it, they talk about workshops on lobbying!' Older women also recognized the social support roles that the WI played for rural women at earlier times, when communities were more closely knit and contacts with the larger society more limited. A younger woman recalled:

In the late forties, when I was about 8 or 10 years old, I used to spend the summers with my aunt, working on the farm. [This was when grandpa sold part of the farm and mam moved with us into a community near Hamilton and took a job in a factory.] On days before the WI meeting, my aunt and I worked very hard to get everything done, so that we could go to the meeting. Beside going to church, the WI was my aunt's only social outing. We did all kinds of things at the WI: songs, spelling games, reading, and recipes. It was much excitement and great fun. When my aunt retired and moved to a small town, she became very lonesome because there was no network or group similar to the WI, where she could turn for social interaction and support.

Another woman who is in charge of the historical records of a group remarked that social and recreational activities had greater prominence in the organization's records than business and educational aspects. As times changed, however, so did the organizational needs of farm women. Most of the New Farm Women's Organizations emerged in the mid-1970s to the mid-1980s, perhaps as expansions of the 'ethics of care' attributed to women, from concerns for family and farm to the entire surrounding rural community.[27] In that decade some ten to twelve farm women's organizations emerged in southwestern Ontario.[28] Their creation was triggered by the economic crises of North American agriculture, by the diffusion of the women's movement and activism into rural areas,[29] by the lack of participation of farm women in major farm organizations, and by farm women's strong desire to do something effective in support of the family farm and the rural community. The successful example of similar farm women's organizations in the United States was also influential.

One of the first of these groups, Women for the Survival of Agriculture (WSA), was founded by Diane Harkin in Winchester County in 1975.[30] The NFWO's distinguished themselves from the older groups by challenging the rigid sexual division of labour. They dealt with issues concerning the continuation of farming in Ontario and with publicizing women's concerns. The more courageous organizations also had political agendas: to lobby for better farm prices, easier credits, and a greater recognition of the contributions of farming to the well-being of the urban population. Initially, not all women's group agreed with the political activism proposed by some of these NFWOs. For example, Concerned Farm Women (CFW), an independent group in Bruce County, and the WSA of Winchester County were called 'radical.'[31] A CFW woman explained: 'We were labelled as radicals because we went after the bankers and the politicians ... We were ignored by other farm women's organizations and not allowed to speak at some of the WSA meetings ... As I see it now, we were ahead of our times. I say a "radical" is a person ahead of his time.' The fear of being seen as radical induced some southwestern Ontario farm women's organizations to substitute 'support' for 'survival' in the WSA name.[32] Their actions were limited to the promotion of educational activities, such as sponsoring the teaching of agriculture in public schools or informing the public about farming issues. However, towards the mid-1980s many of the goals and strategies of these organizations seemed to converge.

The NFWO addressed women's domestic and farm concerns and also focused on larger issues affecting the entire farming community in Ontario. They provided opportunities for the advancement of women's individual and group strategies in their struggles to support farming and to attain recognition and a voice in the traditional, male-dominated farm organizations. In the public sphere, they attempted to transcend the subtle discrimination that denied women participation. Many NFWO, worked mainly on strengthening women's ability to contribute to the family farm, on making women's work on the farm and in the home more visible, and on giving farm women a chance to improve their agricultural and management knowledge and skills. In others, women attempted through organized group pressure to bring about structural changes to lower interest rates on farm loans, to prevent farm loss through bankruptcies, to assure 'fair' farm incomes, and to recognize women's work and the primacy of farming in food production.[33] The NFWOs brought about new educational programs to improve farm women's ability to deal with economic, management, social, and political issues. They also set the stage for farm women to discuss their experiences and concerns and to articulate the connections between their private lives and the socioeconomic changes affecting farming – for example, through discussions of free trade and the effects of GATT on Ontario farming and farm policies.[34] At the same time, local issues such as rural daycare, stress in family relations, farm accidents, and women's health and battering joined farm bankruptcies and farmers' suicides as issues for discussion and action. The CFW set up bankruptcy counselling and a 'hot line' to provide suicide-prone farmers with advice and support, and a rural day-care program was organized in collaboration with another farm women's organization.[35] One younger farm women said: 'We have to share our experience with other rural people. If nothing else, this crisis ought to teach us [farmers] something ... We cannot allow it to happen in Canada, what has happened in some "developing countries," to turn us from a food producing and exporting country into one dependent almost exclusively on food imports in order to feed our population. We cannot let our farms go out of business.'

There were also new ways in which these farm-women's organizations attempted to reach their goals. Besides 'kitchen meetings,' workshops, public meetings, and the publication of newsletters, farm women also undertook or sponsored research to document their case. This presented briefs and reports to provincial and federal governments which publicized the 'realities of farm life' as they experienced it. The research topics in these studies were defined by farm women and focused on the family stress and mental-health problems produced by economic farm problems, the value of farm women's work, farm safety, and farm loss. Farm women in the new groups also produced legal guides for farm women, explaining the new property and family laws. They created video tapes designed to document farm life from women's perspectives and to educate urban women about the similarity and the differences between rural women and urban women and about the importance of farming for the well-being of urban people.[36]

The NFWOs played significant roles in the decade 1975–85. They brought farm women's concerns to the fore and called public attention to the social consequences of the farm crisis for farm families in Ontario. They also provided a means for legitimizing farm women's issues and for strengthening farm women's voices. To a great extent, the efforts of the NFWOs led to the first National Farm Women's Conference, held in Ottawa in 1980, and to the foundation of the Farm Women's Network (provincial and later national). The NFWOs also assisted women in redefining their roles in the home, the farm, and the rural community and in sponsoring training in non-conventional fields. Farm women, through their organizations, acquired formal access to and a voice in the existing farm organizations in Ontario, and farm women's counsel was sought by both the provincial and the federal governments. In all, the NFWOs facilitated, for some farm women, their own transformation.

Not all farm women worked on family farms run by their spouses. Women also contributed to agriculture and rural life by farming in their own right. Women farmers have always existed in Ontario. In the past, the most certain way of getting to live on a farm was through marriage to a farmer, and the most common path to becoming a farmer was through widowhood. Neither inheritance laws nor cultural traditions assisted women in this aspiration. In spite of that tradition, women farmers existed and remained in the 1980s a permanent and more visible feature of Ontario's farm landscape. While the number of male farm operators was continuously dwindling, a decrease of about 30 per cent between 1971 and 1985, the number of women farmers was holding almost steady if not increasing in parts of southwestern Ontario.[37] There was also a significant shift in the marital status of female farmers: the number of married and divorced women farmers has increased, respectively, from 33 per cent and 5 per cent in 1971 to 50 per cent and 8 per cent in 1985, while the number of widows and single women farmers has decreased from 51 per cent and 11 per cent to 33 per cent and 7 per cent. These numbers illustrate what was perhaps the greatest change in farm women's roles in the last twenty years: their entrance into the formal economy and into public life in their own right. They also indicate a change in women's social position and a shift in their self-concept: no longer did all farm women see themselves primarily in their domestic roles and as help-mates of their farmer husbands, but as individuals capable of formally assuming full responsibility for the running of a farm or business enterprise or for taking on unconventional off-farm jobs and acting in the 'public sphere.'

However, farming in Ontario in the 1970s and 1980s was a highly capital-intensive enterprise and it was not easy to enter farming without the needed capital or land. 'The only way you can start a modern farm today is to inherit the land,' said one younger farm woman. Another woman farm operator told me: 'Today, with the cost of starting to farm, there is no way one can aspire to create one of those large, modern farms from scratch ... today, those of us who want to farm have to find new combinations of crops and livestock and possibly also get into some farming-related business, like "Farm Vacation." I have tried several new ideas, we grow herbs and flowers, along with the live-stock enterprise. I also go to craft fairs and sell my products there.' 'To sur-vive on the farm one has to diversify and remain flexible,' said another younger woman farmer.

In the 1980s the majority of women farm operators owned their farm indi-vidually; fewer women than men rented additional land.[38] Although, on the whole, their enterprises were smaller than those of male farmers, they also carried smaller debts, and about 60 per cent of the farms were debt free. Female operators were cautious in their enterprises and tended to take smaller risks than males. They were found, proportionately, on almost as many cattle and small-grain farms as male farmers, and on about one-half as many dairy, pig, and 'other field grain' farms. Women appeared to prefer to operate miscellaneous specialty, mixed, fruit and vegetable, and poultry farms, and they liked to explore new types of enterprises better suited to small-scale production, such as sheep, goats, horses, and rabbits.[39]

Women farm operators, on the whole, were older, better educated, and had smaller households than male farmers. Most became farmers by choice, but some by default: family conditions placed them in charge of the farm enterprise, sometimes without sufficient experience for the job. Even those women who grew up on farms acknowledge that they have not received the same farming training as men. 'Whenever my brothers were not in school, dad would take them, from age eleven or twelve, to work with him on the farm. He would say 'Hey guys, lets go, I'll teach you how to do men's work.' They would go off to the field while my younger sister and I would be left home with mum,' said a younger woman farmer. The access to sources of farming knowledge also remained limited for women, since they were not part of male farmers' communication networks.[40] Women farmers also experienced difficulties in accessing credit and other resources needed for farming, because of the nature of their farm enterprises and the gener-ally held beliefs about the gendered division of farm labour. One farm woman said, 'The style of diversified farming we have is not acceptable for mortgage, and my income [as a supply teacher] does not count either.

When we need money to finance our farm enterprise, we have to look for private lenders.'[41]

The belief in women's inability to perform 'men's jobs' was challenged by women who farmed alone or with other women. They demonstrated with their own farming practices that this scepticism was a myth.[42] The income women derive from their farms reflected the general trend of farm incomes in Ontario. They represented smaller portions of overall household income of most farm families. Many women farmers, just like men, had to rely on non-farm income earned by themselves or other household members to make ends meet. While most women worked in traditional 'feminine' fields of health, education, and clerical occupations or as 'field help' on other farms in times of harvest, some ventured into off-farm businesses and unconventional fields.[43]

In their farming practices, some women farmers tried to emulate male farming and prided themselves that, with a bit of ingenuity and mechanization, they could do any job as well as a man. Some were just as tough and competitive as any male farmer. 'I can manage the farm-work and chores just like any farmer,' said one younger farm woman. Other women farmers, instead of hiding their 'feminine' inclinations, tried to use them to greater advantage in their enterprise. For example, women treated animals more gently than men, which made animal handling easier and more efficient.

Several new farming patterns have emerged among women farmers in the last two decades. One was of women farmers, married to men with full-time, off-farm employment. The women's incomes from the farm, while smaller than men's, were nevertheless a significant contribution to the family economy and well-being.[44] As one young farm bride stated: 'I am really not truly from a farm. We lived in the country, but my father had always an urban job. Mum, however, loved farming. She kept a few pigs, about one hundred. This was enough to put me and my sister through university.' Another farm bride remarked: 'Mum's farming was important for the family. It paid for our education, some home renovations and occasional holidays.'

A second pattern was that of women farmers (single, divorced, widowed) who were heads of households, where the farm was the major source of family support. On these farms, women, like men in similar work conditions, often had to take on additional work or employment to supplement the farm income and to insure that the farm would not be lost. 'Our goal is not to lose the land and [to] pay it off. This is essential if we want to keep on farming. I work 30 hours a week as an accountant, for a commercial company, from my home [equipped with a computer]. The kids help a great deal with chores, but they have to go to school. Education is another priority for us,' said one farm women, a single mother of three teenagers. 'To stay in farming one must diversify and stay flexible. We went through several businesses in the last few years. The one we have now is running well. I am waiting for my other son to graduate from university next year and see what he chooses to do. We may have to change again, in order to keep the farm. But we are ready to do it, we have learnt our lesson in the late 1970s,' related another farm woman who farms with one of her sons.

Yet a third pattern was one in which both partners – husband and wife – lived together, but had separate farm enterprises. Bonnie, in Wellington County, a mother of three pre-school and school-age children, was an example of this arrangement. Bill, her husband, had his own farm where he grew corn and hay and cared for a few pigs. Bonnie had a small Holstein herd of some thirty milch cows. She was very proud of their high yields and took good care of the cows. She did her own accounting and her separate tax returns. She also hired part-time help, because of her part-time job as a nurse in a nearby hospital. Her life was very hectic, but she enjoyed being her own boss and thought that she needed to work at this pace until the children grew up and had their education.

In spite of the long work hours, risks, and uncertainties of farming, women, whether they were farmers or farm women, seemed to be committed more than ever to life in rural Ontario and to the management and work on their farms or rural enterprises. Women seemed to value farming as an occu-pation and as a way of life. As an occupation, farming gave them a sense of achievement and feelings of independence and self-reliance. They said it met their varied interests and was challenging. Moreover, it seemed to provide enjoyment and pride.[45] As a way of life, they thought, farming allowed them to be and to work closer with spouse and family and to 'teach kids a solid value system: hard work, respect for nature, humility, self-reliance and inge-nuity,' said a woman who had moved back to a farm in the mid-1970s. Another younger farm woman commented: 'I would not want [to live] any other way.' It would appear that it is this value system that motivated many women to move back into a rural community and into farming.

Farming as a way of life might have been more dream than reality, however, since most farm women were busier than ever. Not only did they attempt to do their share of the house- and farm work, but many were also heavily involved in off-farm work and in community activities. On the farm, women had added to their traditional work most of the book-keeping and business management, and they were gradually entering more into farm decision-making and production. Personal computers entered the farm household dur-ing this decade and made many of women's newer activities possible and eas-ier. The incursions of farm women into the public sphere were quite remarkable. In the 1970s and 1980s many farm women held such off-farm occupations as adult-education trainer (for various government programs), life-insurance sales person, fund-raiser for health-related foundations, columnist, book editor, and manager of an off-farm family business, in addition to the more traditional occupations of teaching, nursing, and clerical work.

Women also played active and pivotal roles in local and provincial farm organizations dealing with socioeconomic and political issues of concern to the rural and farm population. Farm women seemed to have taken on these additional responsibilities, not so much in terms of self-serving goals of public recognition, influence, or personal prestige, but as an extension of a feeling of care and responsibility for what was happening to their way of life, to the farm family, the farm, and the community. 'I was nine years on the School Board here. I was elected,' said a younger farm woman, 'but I resigned, as many of us [officers of the CFW] did, to be able to work with people directly. We thought it important to share with other farmers and rural people our experience and learning from the farm crisis.'

With women's busy schedules, some of the traditional household concerns tended to fade into the background. 'Housekeeping is a very low priority for me now. The children are grown and married ... have their own homes ... Newsletter writing, organizing meetings and community work take all the time I have left [after farm work and chores are done],' said an older farm woman in Kent County, a member of a local network and a community leader and activist.

Some of the younger farm women in their thirties and forties still found time for themselves, to pursue their own personal development needs and feel good about it. These women strove to improve their education by taking a variety of credit and non-credit courses offered by community colleges and universities. Besides degree programs and courses on practical subjects, women also took courses on self-development, assertiveness training, and self-confidence building. 'Guess what?' said a farm woman in her early forties, 'I am getting a degree in sociology from Western, through distance education; I love it and I am doing well. I can apply what I am learning [demography] to this [Bruce-Grey] area.' Another farm woman a few years younger discussed her plans of getting a BA in English from the University of Waterloo. A third farm woman, a mother of four adolescent and young adult children, is pursuing a degree in animal science at the University of Guelph. The younger farm women seemed to be thriving on the newly found educational possibilities and were engaged in them enthusiastically. A new generation of farm women may also be in the making: since the mid-1970s the enrolment of women in agriculture-related degree programs in the Ontario Agricultural College (University of Guelph) has been on a steady increase.[46] Many of these graduates may end up living on farms or working in farming-related businesses, although their employment opportunities may differ from men's.[47]

Some of the older farm women in their fifties and sixties, like their younger sisters, have shed the centrality of the home-making role and have accepted the legitimacy and indispensability of their farm and off-farm work. However, they have not yet found the freedom to care for themselves or to insist on their own rights and interests without a feeling of guilt. Such things as setting time aside for personal needs was almost unknown to this generation. Personal fulfilment was attained vicariously, through the achievements of others, and by caring for, meeting the needs of, and providing service to family members. One thoughtful woman said:

There is quite a difference between my generation and that of my daughter or daughter-in-law. The other day we went to visit Nellie. I took her a basket of apples from our farm. Nellie was glad to see us, but in the evening she went to a drawing class ... We stayed and I peeled the apples for apple-butter. She would not do it ... I think it is good that she went to her class, but, why did I have to stay and peel apples? Why do I care? Why cannot I take time off for myself, and feel good about it? For me ... now ... home-making is no longer so important, but I still cannot sit idle and see things go to waste.

In the homes of these older women the traditional sexual division of labour and social relations still prevailed. Women were carrying the heavy burden of the full household responsibility, in addition to what else they may have been involved in. A comment of a farm woman in her early sixties was not atypical: 'When we come home from [farm] work in the evening, after a full day of work, he [the husband] sits down to read the farm magazines, while I have to fix dinner, clean up and maybe do the laundry. I don't have a drier, so I have to hang it up in the bathroom downstairs. I never get time to read things about the farm or anything else.'

A younger farm woman related a conversation with her mother, who is in her seventies: 'Mum has mixed feelings about my getting a college education. On the one hand, she is proud that I am getting it. On the other, she feels that maybe, just maybe, she has missed something in life [by devoting her entire life to work and care of the family].' When I asked this farm woman whether she ever felt guilty of taking so much time for herself, away from family and farm work, by pursuing a higher education, she answered with a resounding 'No!' But, she added, 'you have to have family support to do it. My husband and my children are very supportive of my getting this degree. They say, 'You have worked hard enough already, it's time you take some time for yourself."' 'My sons can take care of themselves. They make lunches and cook dinner and do some housework when I am at work or studying. The whole family has to pitch in, if we want to make it,' said a younger farm women who is away from home a great deal because of teaching adult-education classes and study. 'As I remember, mother was too devoted to us [children and spouse] to do things for herself or to insist on her rights, even if she wanted to. She would feel this was not right, it was selfish,' recalled a younger farm woman.

The group of oldest, retired women had few doubts about their domestic roles and family roles. They accepted them as normal and natural, and saw the expansion of the roles of younger women with disapproval and suspicion. 'It is natural for women to take care of the family and the home. It's women's work and responsibility. I don't know why women now are trying to become like men. We even have a woman minister! She only brought us trouble ... she does not have the same authority as a man. Women should not get involved in men's things,' explained one of these women. 'Women should know their place. It is unbecoming for them to behave like men,' said another very proper, elderly retired farm woman. However, while committed to their domestic roles, many of these women had also worked off the farm in the past and contributed to the family economically. This work was seen as needed, but secondary to women's more central roles of home-making, family, and farm help.

Farm women in southwestern Ontario shared with other women the burden of our androcentric culture, in which institutions and the predominant ideology valued and privileged men over women. Under these conditions, women tended to be subordinated to men and imbedded in the 'family,' and were seldom treated as persons in their own, individual right. This was reflected in the acceptance of the 'traditional' sexual division of labour and it was perpetuated by structures, processes, and ideology in the main institutions, including the family farm.[48] When women were exposed to these circumstances for a great part of their lives, as the retired group of farm women were, they tended to develop a self-concept based mainly on their biological function and on a set of values and behaviours that limited them to subordinated, supportive, and at times dependent relations and roles. Research by feminists shows that women's self-concept formation develops through social interaction and according to the sociocultural conditions to which they are exposed in the family, school, and community. Thus, depending on opportunities open to them, some women can hardly transcend a self-concept in which femininity is solely and primarily defined and rooted in their biological and familial roles of self-effacing support, caring, and devotion to the family. Without possessing an autonomous identity, these women tend to accept as 'natural' the existing sexual division of labour, of power and property, and the consequent social relations in family and community. They tend to defend the socioeconomic and cultural arrangements they know, seeing change as a threat to their very 'nature,' leading to an erosion of the only domain in which they may have at least a semblance of decision-making power and control. Work in the male sphere is done more out of necessity than choice.

When androcentrism in the family and in society was eased at least rhetorically, and male dominance was undermined by economic reality and challenges to the existing order, the possibility opened for women to expand their concept of self and the range of their legitimate actions. At this stage, the incursions into 'male domains' (agriculture, economics, wage work, public involvements in politics, etc.) as equal partners and decision-makers, and not as a subordinated assistants, became legitimate. Having been exposed to more traditional values for a good part of their lives, older women in this level of self-development may be caught in the contradictions between old self-definitions and the new demands on self from which some women find it hard to extricate themselves. While the new demands are often the result of necessity and are accepted as legitimate, their requirements can be experienced as betrayal of commitments to more basic values of family and care, because the traditional division of labour still persists in the home. This accounts for the ambivalence that some women in the older group felt about the recent changes in their roles. In their attempt to meet the conflicting demands, these women tended to deny themselves their own individual needs and potential.

Having experienced change in family and society at an earlier age, younger farm women engaged in new activities, and a different self-concept emerged. At these difficult times many farm women were able to break out of the old patterns. With the greater currency of women's issues in the broader society, the younger farm women were able create new identities for themselves, rethinking their roles and creating new self-concepts and meaning for their lives as women.[49] The difference in the ways that the younger and the older farm women to define themselves lies in the ability of the younger to include concerns for self, without seeing this as giving up the older values. Younger women are still fully committed to the family farm and to preserving farming in Ontario. However, they no longer accept the 'traditional' division of labour in the home and their relegation to secondary places on the farm and in the rural community. In fact, they see that, as they develop as autonomous individuals and redefine farm women's 'sphere of action,' they can be more helpful in the aim of preserving farming in Ontario.

CONCLUSION

Life for Ontario farm women has changed in the forty years from 1945 to 1985, but there have also been continuities. Some of the traditional bases of farm women's power, such as control over domestic production, were eroded by the modernization of agriculture, and some women have espoused domesticity as their main role. However, changes have been coming and forcing farm women to expand their action by incursion into the sphere of men on more equal bases. Thus, farm women are coming into their own, defining new roles for themselves in home, farm, and community life. They are becoming more visible and they speak with clearer voices. Socioeconomic changes on the farm and in the larger society have played crucial roles in this transformation and in bringing issues of importance to farm women into the open. But farm women still cherish rural life and are willing to make sacrifices for the sake of the family farm and the farming community.

Not all women have experienced the farm crises at the same time in their lives or at the same period. Some farms were hit in the late 1970s, others in the early to mid-1980s. Some farms went out of business and others were able to weather the crisis. Thus, there is a great variability in farm women's role and self-definition. Wherever the farm crisis occurred and existing socioeconomic patterns became disrupted, new awareness among farm women has emerged. The latest farm crises and the women's movement in the larger society assisted farm women to transcend their traditional family and homebound self-conception, and helped them to think of themselves in personal, economic, and, at times, in political terms. No longer were younger farm women satisfied with leaving farm business and community decision-making solely in the hands of men. In this process farm women, individually and in groups, challenged such institutions as banks and provincial and federal governments (ministries of agriculture), presented briefs, did research, wrote books and produced video tapes – all to promote their cause.

The three distinct self-conceptions that emerged from conversations with farm women could easily be interpreted as generational phenomena, but there is more here than age.[50] It seems that the stage in life at which a woman is exposed to of social transformation and the opportunity to interact with other women in non-conventional activities are crucial conditions for the development of a new self. Most but not all older farm women are quite satisfied with the traditional division of labour and accept their subordinate position without much questioning or uneasiness. They feel good about their lives and their work, and that they have done their wifely and motherly duties well. They may have entered into the male sphere of action, but they did not see their involvement as desirable or appropriate. In contrast the younger group of women had an instrumental attitude towards home-making. They saw their main role as contributing managerially and economically to the survival of the farm enterprise, whether in on- or off-farm work. These women are very busy, they complain of time shortage and stress, but they are able to take out time for themselves without feeling guilty about it. They love living on a farm and they are committed to pursuing this way of life. They admit quite openly that to keep the farm they have to have an off-farm income or a business on the side. They are open to change and to the search for new opportunities, in order to keep their way of life.

Some farm women have changed, but for many the underlying relationships on the farm and in the rural community persist. These farm women contribute to Ontario farming in their own way. But each group also has its own specific needs. To meet these needs, different approaches have to be taken; they should be defined specifically by farm women on the basis of their own knowledge of farming and the wider society of which they and their farms are a part. What becomes obvious is the crucial and indispensable roles that farm women have played in the continuation of farming in Ontario over the last forty years.

NOTES

Many thanks to Eloise Calhoun and Louise Scott for helping me to contact other farm women. To them this study is dedicated. Thanks also to Joy Saikia, my assistant, and to the University of Guelph archives for letting me use the Helen C. Abell Collection.

1 One of the earliest studies of farm women was done in Alberta by Helen C. Abell, '"The Women's" Touch in Canadian Farm Work,' *Economic Annalist*, 26, April 1954, 37–8; in Quebec, Gerald Fortin examined farm women's contribution to the development of agriculture in the 1960s. See M.A. Tremblay and W.J. Anderson, *Rural Canada in Transition* (Ottawa: AERC 1966). Government-sponsored farm research also included women, not as farmers but as family members; see, for example, N.H. High and M.B. Blackwood, *Population in Process, Dundas County, Ontario, 1918–1949* (nd), or H. Noble, *Farm Title Transfer Survey, 1900–1950* (Toronto, Ontario Department of Agriculture and Food (ODAF), 1955). The essays in the Vanier Institute for the Family publication *The Family in the Evolution of Agriculture* (Ottawa 1968), or Helen C. Abell's study *Rural Families and Their Homes, Ontario, 1959–1968* (Waterloo 1971) begin to discuss this topic. The National Farmer's Union, always more sympathetic to women's issues than the Federation of Agriculture, sponsored studies -

on farm women in *Farm Women in Our Society* (1979). Jane Abrahmson carried out a national study in *Rural Women: Their Work, Their Needs and Their Role in Rural Development*, published in Ottawa in 1979 by the Canadian Council for Rural Development (CCRD). In the United States, Eugene Wilkening pioneered studies of farm families in Wisconsin, with explicit focus on farm women. Prior to this, most farm women were studied only by home economists focusing on women's 'traditional' contribution to home-making. (I place 'traditional' in quotation marks, in recognition of the relatively recent invention of the housewife and home-making as a socially recognized status and activity.) A different view was offered by Helen C. Abell in 'The Role of Modern Women in Farm Organizations' (Mimeo, 1963). She called the attention to women's roles on the farm, as wife, mother, labourer, and decision-maker; and in the community, in social, economic, political, and cultural terms, acting locally, nationally, and abroad. However, it was 1975 before articles on women's activities, with such titles as 'The Liberated Farm-Women' and 'I Can Run a Ranch as well as Any Man,' began to appear in the Canadian rural press in other than family sections. See, for example, *Canadian Farming* (winter 1975, 4–8). At the end of the 1970s the first theses on farm women appeared; see, for example, Linda L. Graff, 'The Changing Nature of Farm Women: Work Roles under the Industrialization of Agricultural Production' (MA, thesis, McMaster University 1979). Internationally, the first influential work was Esther Boserup's *Women's Role in Economic Development* (New York: St Martin's Press 1970). It highlighted relations between the growth of male-based industries and changes in agriculture that affected women's economic status, welfare, and family responsibilities in various parts of the world. For an Ontario farm women's perspective, see Giselle Ireland, *The Farmer Takes a Wife* (Chesley, Ont.: Concerned Farm Women 1983).

2   Reproductive work refers to home-making, childbirth and childcare, the personal services provided by farm women on a daily basis to enable farmers to engage in 'productive' work on the farm. It includes preparing and serving meals, storing food, caring for clothing, cleaning house, all type of care, companionship, and love; it also refers to the birth, care, and bringing up of children. As well, it involves the teaching of values, norms, and accepted behaviour of one's rural society and all kinds of farm support work and services related to farming: doing chores, running errands, stepping in when help is needed, getting ready for planting, harvesting, storing produce, answering the phone, making business calls, and farm bookkeeping. See Frances M. Shaver, 'Social Science Research on Farm Women: The State of the Art,' *Resources for Feminist Documentation sur la Recherche Feministe (RFR/DRF)* 11 (1983): 12–14; Carolyn Sachs, *The Invisible Farmer: Women in Agricultural Production* (Totowa, NJ: Rowan and Allanheld 1983, CCRD, For a good discussion of reproduction, see A.F. Robertson,

*Beyond the Family: The Social Organization of Human Reproduction* (Berkeley: University of California Press 1991).

3  For farm women's off-farm work rates, see M. Dion and S. Welsh, 'Participation de la population active: Une comparaison entre des populations agricole et totale,' paper presented to the Association Canadiénne 'Etudes Rurales, Vancouver, 1991.

4  *Farm and Country,* 1964–92, *Western Ontario Farmer (WOF),* 1966–90, *Canadian Farming,* 1975–90, *The Rural Voice, (RV)* 1980–5, *Union Farmer,* 1980–5, *Today's Country Women* 1984–6, and others.

5  Out of respect to farm women and because I am a feminist, my interviews were conducted as conversation in which experiences were mutually shared. Farm women are not treated as 'objects' in this research.

6  Family positions such as farmer's wife, daughter, sister, mother-in-law, grandmother, and the occupational status of single or married farm operator or labourer, employed off the farm or working exclusively in home-making, have different implications for farm women's gender relations and overall statuses. The stages in the family's life cycle also have implications for farm women's options: because housework and child-care are still defined almost exclusively as women's responsibilities they tend to structure a woman's daily work. Some writers argue that patriarchal relations on the family farm, not life-cycle stages, limit women's options.

7  On women farmers, see Gloria J. Leckie, 'Female Farm Operators: Gender Relations and the Restructuring of the Canadian Agricultural System' (Ph.D. dissertation, University of Western Ontario 1991). Also Sonia Salamon and A. Mackey-Keim, 'Land Ownership and Women's Power in a Midwestern Farming Community,' *Journal of Marriage and the Family,* 41 (Feb. 1979): 109–19, and S. Salamon, 'Incorporation and the Farm Family,' *Journal of Marriage and the Family* 46 (Feb. 1984): 167–77.

8  For socioeconomic changes in rural Ontario, see chapter on Ontario in W.I. Gordon, ed., *Progress and Prospects in Canadian Agriculture,* (Ottawa: Royal Commission on Canadian Economic Prospects 1957), and Joseph Schull, *Ontario since 1867* (Toronto: McClelland and Stewart 1978).

9  Unless noted differently, all quotations are from interviews carried out by the author during the summer and fall of 1992 and the spring and summer of 1993. In all, sixteen farm women were interviewed in Bruce, Grey, Kent, Waterloo, and Wellington counties. Two young farm brides, who were originally on the interview list, were included in the section on women farmers because they talked about their mothers. Both of these women had university degrees and considered themselves 'professionals,' expecting to work off the farm. All the names that appear in this article are fictitious, because some women did not

wish to be identified. The interviews were carried out with farm women in three age brackets: farm women beyond retirement, who are noted in the chapter as 'retired'; women between the age of fifty and retirement, who are referred to as 'older'; and women in their late thirties to early fifties, who are referred to as 'younger' farm women. Some of the interviews were tape recorded, but not all women agreed to it. Thus, some interviews were recorded by hand and later reconstructed.

10 Helen C. Abell, *Farm Families Today* (Toronto: ODAF 1966). Diana Ferris and Helen C. Abell, 'The Farm Family in Canada,' *Economic Annalist* 29, 3 (1959).

11 See Abell, *Rural Families and Their Homes* and *Families*; also her 'Longitudinal Study of Ontario Farm Families, 1959–68 (1970), 'Farm Decision-Making' (1961), and 'The Rural Women's Perception of Rural and Urban Life' (1970), all from ODAF, Toronto. Compare Seena Kohl, *Working Together: Women and Families in South-Western Saskatchewan* (Toronto: Holt, Rinehart and Winson 1976).

12 Marjorie Cohen, 'The Decline of Women in Canadian Dairy,' *Social History* 17, 34 (1984): 307–34; D. Fink, 'Farming in Open Country Iowa: Women and the Changing Farm Economy,' in M. Chibnik, *Farm Work and Field Work* (Ithaca, NY: Cornell University Press 1986); for the decline of domestic production, see Gordon, *Progress*, 305–6.

13 *WOF* 30, 1 (1969): 12; Helen C. Abell, 'Rural Families in the 1970,' ODAF, Toronto 1968), and *Families*; Pamela Smith, 'What Lies behind Statistics,' in D. Morisette, *Growing Strong: Women in Agriculture* (Ottawa: Canadian Council on the Status of Women 1986).

14 See Noble, *Farm Title Transfer Survey*; Abell, *Families*, 'Rural Families, 1959–64' (1966), and 'The Agricultural Ladder,' *Economic Annalist* 31, 3 (1961).

15 See A.H. Richmond, 'Immigration and Pluralism in Canada,' in W.E. Mann, ed., *Social and Cultural Change in Canada* (Toronto: Copp Clark 1970), 81–96; Schull, *Ontario*, 332–4; for farm turnover, see Allan D. Steeves, 'Mobility into and out of Canadian Agriculture,' *Rural Sociology* 44, 3 (1979): 566–83.

16 For decision-making, see Abell's 'Farm Decision-Making' and *Families*; Abell also reports that two-thirds of the women in her Ontario farm family study said that the acquisition of farm equipment and machinery had priority over any purchase of household appliances and equipment (1959). Gertrude Moul, 'Power Relations of Spouses Farming in South-Western Ontario' (MA thesis, University of Waterloo 1992).

17 Helen C. Abell, 'Farm Families and Formal Organizations' (University of Guelph, nd [late 1960s], Helen C. Abell Collection).

18 *WOF* 13, 7 (1968): 13; *Farm and Country* 34,5 (1970): 5, and 27, 5 (1969): 7. Most newspaper articles in the 1950 to mid-1970s reviewed for this study

depicted women solely as home-makers, and cited home science or home economics as the main educational choice of farm women and daughters. Until the mid-1970s, articles about farm women appeared only in the Family Section of the farm press.

19 See Noble, Farm Title and Changes in Acreage: Occupied Farm Land: 1940-66 (Toronto: ODAF 1968); Abell, 'The Agricultural Ladder'; Alan Brookes and C.A. Wilson, '"Working Away" from the Farm: Young Women of North Huron, 1910–30,' Ontario History 27, 4 (1985): 281–99.

20 B.H. Davey, Z.S. Hassan, and W.F. Lu, Farm and Off-Farm Incomes in Canada: An Analysis of the 1971 Consumer Finance Survey (Ottawa: Agriculture Canada, Economic Branch, Publication 74/71 (1974); WOF 29, 6 (1976): 14.

21 Paul Shaw, Canadian Farm Population (Ottawa: Statistics Canada 1979), 202–8; Farming Facts 1989 (Ottawa: Statistics Canada 1989); WOF 13, 1 (1967): 11.

22 WOF 27, 4 (1984): 17.

23 Kathleen Gregg, personal communication; see also her 'Ideological Developments in Farm Self-Help Groups in South-Western Ontario: A Resource for Rural Human Workers' (MSc. thesis, University of Guelph 1990).

24 See M. DeBrabandere, 'Trouble on Family Farms,' Farm Gate 3 (1983): 17.

25 Molly McGhee, Women in Rural Life (Toronto: Ontario Ministry of Agriculture and Food 1984).

26 See Terry Crowley, 'The Origins of Continuing Education for Women: The Ontario Women's Institutes,' Canadian Women's Studies 7, 3 (1985): 78–81; also Women for the Survival of Agriculture Newsletter (1982–4), and Concerned Farm Women's Newsletter (1983–5).

27 Feminist social psychologists suggest that women, because of the social relations in which their lives are embedded, develop a different conception of self, sense of morality, and ethics from those of men. Carol Gilligan, 'Women's Conception of Self and Morality,' Harvard Educational Review 47 (1977): 481–517, 'Woman's Place in Man's Life Cycle,' ibid., 49 (1979): 431–46, and In a Different Voice: Psychological Theory and Women's Development (Cambridge: Harvard University Press 1982).

28 Diane Harkin, 'A Summary History of the New Farm Women's Movement: Canadian Farm Women's Organization,' (Ottawa: Canadian Farm Women's Bureau 1991). See also Farm Women's Bureau, Fact Sheets (Ottawa: Agriculture Canada 1990–2).

29 Linda Z. Schulz, 'Feminism, Down on the Farm,' Branching Out 6, 1 (1979): 38–9; D. Bruners, 'The Influence of the Women's Liberation Movement on the Lives of Canadian Farm Women,' Resources for Feminist Research 14, 1/2 (1985): 18–19.

30 Diane Harkin, personal communication, Aug. 1985.

31  The southwestern regional Women for the Support of Agriculture unites WSA
    organizations from Elgin, Middlesex, Oxford, and Perth counties. All these individ-
    ual organizations were founded in the early 1980s and were inspired by the WSA
    of Winchester County. There are also WSA groups in Norfolk and Simcoe counties.
    See Farm Women's Bureau, *Fact Sheet* (Ottawa: Agriculture Canada 1991).
32  E.A. Cebotarev and K. Beatty, 'Women Strengthening the Farming Community:
    The Case of the "Concerned Farm Women,"' in A.M. Fuller, *Farming and the
    Rural Community: An Introduction* (Toronto: Foundation for Rural Living
    1985), 256–68.
33  See Harkin, 'A Summary History,' and WSA *Newsletter* (1982–5).
34  See Farm Women's Bureau, *Fact Sheet* (Ottawa: Agriculture Canada 1982–5),
    and the CFW's *Newsletter* (1983–5).
35  Sally Shortall, 'Canadian and Irish Farm Women: Some Similarities, Differences
    and Comments,' *Canadian Review of Sociology and Anthropology* 30, 2
    (1993): 172–90.
36  In the early 1980s the WSA Winchester County sponsored, with assistance of
    the Farm Woman's Bureau, a number of studies that were published as short
    research reports. Among them were *What Is Your Worth?* by Susan Watkins,
    and 'Credit, Where Credit Is Due,' 'Going, Going, Gone ...' 'Old MacDonald
    Had a Farm, but Will His Son or Daughter?' 'The Invisible Pitchfork,' and
    'Equal Partners or Just a Wife?' all of which can be obtained from the Farm
    Women's Bureau. The CFW, with independent funds, carried out a survey study
    in 1982 in Grey and Bruce counties. The results were published in Ireland, *The
    Farmer Takes a Wife*. Later, a guide for the new family and property law, *To
    Have and to Hold: A Guide to Property and Credit Law for Farm Families in
    Ontario*, was prepared by Susan Glover and others. The CFW also produced two
    video tapes: the 'CFW,' described the group's history and the causes they were
    struggling for; 'Rural Roots, Urban Connections' communicated to urban
    women the similarities and differences that exist between the two groups, in the
    hope of leading to better understanding.
37          Change in Numbers of Women Farmers, Ontario, 1971–85

|  | 1986 | | 1981 | | 1971 | |
|---|---|---|---|---|---|---|
|  | No. | % | No. | % | No. | % |
| Number of women farmers | 3910 | (5.8) | 3525 | (4.5) | 3952 | (4.3) |
| Female farmers* |  | 29.3 |  | 32.3 |  | 27.3 |
| Male farmers* |  | 24.6 |  | 25.7 |  | 25.8 |

*Proportion of the Canadian total. The figure in parentheses represents the national per-
centage. Source: Leckie, 'Female Farm Operators,' table 3.3.

38  The material in this chapter, if not noted otherwise, is based on Leckie's excellent study, 'Female Farm Operators.'

39  Ibid., 379.

40  Ibid., 315–55; Ann Leffler, R.S. Krannich, and D.L. Gillespie, 'Contact, Support and Friction: Three Faces of Community Life,' *Sociological Perspectives* 29, 3 (1986): 337–55; Martine Berlan Darque, 'The Division of Labour and Decision Making in Farming Couples: Power and Negotiation,' *Sociologia Ruralis* 28, 4 (1988): 271–91.

41  Mary J. Lipkin, 'Brawn, Not Brain: Women and Farm Credit in Canada,' *Canadian Women's Studies* 3, 4 (1982): 53–6. For the difficulties farm women face when they are forced to take over the family farm because of a spouse's death, see A. Gibb in Rural Voice, Dec. 1984, 8–10; D. Ballantine in *WOF*, (1972).

42  In 'Farming Solo,' S. Hamilton describes how a women, with ingenuity and machinery, can manage to survive alone on a farm. *Today Country Women* (spring 1985).

43  Younger farm women were actively searching for income-producing activities (new crops, enterprises, employment) in innovative ways that would be compatible with both a farm business and life on a farm.

44  C.F. Gringstaff and F. Trovato, 'Junior Partners: Women's Contributions to Family Income in Canada,' *Social Indicators Research* 22 (1990): 229–53.

45  Leckie, 'Female Farm Operators,' 360–72.

46  'In some colleges almost all of the total enrollment increase during the decade [1972–82] was in female students and, in some instances, the number of males actually declined from 1970 to 1980.' G.M. Jenkinson, 'Student Enrollment in Faculties in Canada of Agriculture,' [sic] *NACTA Journal* (Dec. 1982): 4.

47  Jo-Ann Willman, 'Women in Agriculture,' *Agrologist* 4, 5 (autumn 1976): 9–10; L. Williamson, 'Farm Women,' *Canada Agriculture* 26, 3 (1981): 21–2.

48  Max J. Hedley, 'Normal Expectations.' *RFR/DRF* 1, 2 (1982); see also his 'Rural Social Structure and the Ideology of the Family Farms,' *Canadian Review of Sociology and Anthropology* 2, 1 (1981): 85–9, and 'Independent Commodity Production and the Dynamics of Tradition,' *Canadian Review of Sociology and Anthropology* 13, 4 (1976).

49  R. Kegan, *The Evolving Self: Problems and Process in Human Development* (Cambridge: Harvard University Press 1982); J.B. Miller, 'Development of Women's Sense of Self,' in *Work in Progress* (Wellesley, Mass.:Stone Center Working Papers Series 1984); *Toward a New Psychology of Women* (Boston: Beacon 1976); J. Surrey, 'The Self in Relation: A Theory of Women's Development' (Wellesley, Mass.: Stone Center Working Papers Series 1985).

MARLENE BRANT CASTELLANO and
JANICE HILL

# First Nations Women: Reclaiming Our Responsibilities

In the past twenty years, First Nations in Ontario – the Cree, Anishinabek, Mohawk, and Algonquin – singly or grouped in confederacies of ancient origin, have been asserting a new identity. This identity is new at least to the popular imagination, which has been conditioned by media images to see the stereotypical Indians as a single category of people on the margins of Canadian society. The affirmation that 'we are a Nation,' voiced resoundingly by the Dene of the Northwest Territories in 1970, has been echoed across the land, at first ministers' conferences and at barricades constructed of overturned vehicles, in classroom presentations by students poised between two worlds, and around ceremonial fires where stories of creation are recounted. Within the oral traditions of the various and distinct peoples called Aboriginal, the understanding of nationhood is rooted in a spiritual world view that recognizes a unique bond between the land as the source of sustenance and the people whose responsibility it is to take care of the land. Sustenance and responsibility are complementary elements of a covenant between Aboriginal peoples and the Creator, a sacred covenant that cannot be denied or abrogated without denying life itself.[1]

This world view and the ethical responsibilities that flow from it have been under serious assault throughout the centuries of Aboriginal-colonial contact. Missionary activity sought to alienate Aboriginal people from beliefs that were labelled 'pagan.' Treaties were applied by the dominion government so as to limit Aboriginal land use and to clear the way for immigrant settlement. Education, mediated through the harshly assimilationist residential schools, sought to separate children from their heritage and to erase Aboriginal identity.

Until the middle of the twentieth century, the remoteness of many reserves and territories made them a refuge of sorts, providing a buffer between Aboriginal people and the most aggressive intrusions of settler society. Since the 1950s that isolation has been shattered and, with the impact of change, the stability and cultural cohesion of communities has been severely stressed.[2] Radio and television have reached into the remotest communities, drawing them into contact with the global village; enforcement of school attendance policies has resulted in relocation of generations of students to towns and cities; the extension of social services, including universal benefits such as family allowances and unemployment insurance, have created ties to the Canadian state which are seen, at least in part, as beneficial; and the worldwide consciousness of human rights which emerged in the 1960s has fuelled the aspirations of Aboriginal peoples for recognition and justice.

Historically, Aboriginal women have been for the most part a shadowy lot,[3] seldom the orators or leaders of resistance in the more distant past, often eclipsed in later years by the men who led the political movement to decolonize institutions of government and local community life.[4] The events that thrust First Nations women into the glare of public attention centred around challenges to the membership sections of the Indian Act, which for generations discriminated against women who married outside the status Indian population.[5] In recent years as well, Aboriginal women have been in the forefront of action to unveil the personal and community effects of the residential school experience and the gross errors of child-welfare interventions in the lives of Aboriginal families.[6]

The leadership provided by women to heal the wounds inflicted by an oppressive colonial past is most often seen at the local level, as they adapt the content and methods of education to include Aboriginal cultural perspectives and languages[7] and as they assume responsibility for local delivery of health and child-welfare services. In urban settings, women are more likely to take up formal leadership roles on boards and committees of service organizations or as executive members in political organizations.[8]

This article provides a perspective on social change in the past forty years through the experience of four Aboriginal women who have done more than live through events; rather, these women have taken an active role in shaping those events.[9] Two of the women are Anishinabe, a nation often referred to as Ojibway, which practised hunting and gathering in the area north and southwest of the Great Lakes; one is Cree, a nation that spans an area from northern Quebec to central Alberta; and one is Mohawk, part of the semiagricultural Six Nations Confederacy that played a pivotal role in the settlement of northeastern North America. Members of the Six Nations now occupy reserves in southern Ontario and in American states bordering the Great Lakes.

The social history of Ontario Aboriginal people since 1950 remains to be written. What we have attempted here is to provide four women's perspectives on how Aboriginal people have adapted to sweeping social change. Their reflections illuminate not only their times, but also their individual choices to hold fast to their heritage as they address the complexities of life in contemporary Ontario.

FOUR WOMEN

Edna Manitowabi is a member of the Anishinabek people – specifically, the Odawa Nation that traditionally occupied territory north of Georgian Bay. She was born in 1940 and spent her early childhood with her family at Wikwemikong on Manitoulin Island, until she was sent away to residential school in Spanish, Ontario, at the age of seven. Edna has written about the loss and confusion which that separation from her family provoked;[10] although she spent only three years in residential school, the disruption to family relationships and to the course of her personal maturation persisted for a much longer time. She recalls, in fragmentary form, disruptive family relationships especially after her father's return from service in the Second World War, and she still experiences anguish over the experience of sexual assault as a child. She was anxious to leave Wikwemikong, seeking escape rather than pursuing a particular dream for herself.

Edna moved to Toronto in 1956, at the age of sixteen. She worked as a domestic, experiencing exploitative relationships and falling further into alienation and self-destructive behaviour. The turning point in her life came during a period of hospitalization, when Edna had a near-death experience. In a dreamlike state she entered a region of incredibly beautiful light and indescribable tranquility. She wanted to move further into that light, but she heard a woman crying pitifully, calling her to come back. When she returned to ordinary consciousness, she found that it was she herself who was crying. This was the beginning of conviction that her life had meaning and that she must search for meaning within her culture.

Edna worked in projects connected with the Native Canadian Centre in Toronto and helped to create the Nishnawbe Institute, which collected oral teachings and looked for ways to preserve and distribute them. She met and married Jim Dumont, a man also of Ojibway heritage, with whom she would share for twenty years her life journey and her quest for knowledge and understanding of their shared cultural roots.

In the years since Edna made a choice to live, she has become a teacher and a ceremonialist. She helps adults and children to search out and experience the wisdom of Anishinabe culture, particularly the special women's gifts that are honoured in the ceremonies of the Midewiwin medicine tradition. She taught the Ojibway language and oral traditions at Laurentian University, and in 1992 she was appointed to the faculty of the Native Studies Department at Trent University, where she teaches a course in Aboriginal women. She is widely sought after as a speaker and workshop leader on Aboriginal women's spirituality.

Jeannette Corbière Lavell became a national figure in 1971 when she challenged the discrimination of the Indian Act in section 12.1.b. Under this section, women who married men not registered as Indians within the meaning of the act lost their right to be registered. Men in the same situation not only retained their status following marriage but their non-Indian spouses gained status as a result. Indian women who rallied to support Jeannette's action spoke poignantly of what the Indian Act provision meant to them: cut off from claiming Indian status, they were unable to reside on the reserves close to the families from which they originated; they and their children were denied social benefits such as education and housing assistance; when they were widowed or divorced or frail with age, they could not even look forward to being buried with their grandmothers.

Jeannette is Anishinabe, also from Wikwemikong, born in 1942. Her mother attended teacher's college in Pembroke, Ontario, and taught school prior to opening a family business. Jeannette's father never attended school. Together the parents operated a store in the village, which is the hub of Wikwemikong Unceded Territory. Jeannette found herself even as a child at the centre of social activity, helping out in the store, talking both English and Ojibway. When she finished high school in the mid-1960s she moved to Toronto and quickly became involved in the emerging Aboriginal organizations. The National Native Youth Council opened her eyes to what Aboriginal youth in many centres across Canada were experiencing; employment as a court worker with the newly established Native Canadian Centre brought her face to face with discrimination and injustice. She was recruited after a few years to the Company of Young Canadians, a corps of community development workers established in the 1960s by the Canadian government to harness the idealism of youth in efforts to mobilize disadvantaged communities across Canada. Here Jeannette's horizons were widened even further, to include an awareness of civil rights and the assertiveness of peoples around the globe who believed they should be free to exercise fundamental human rights.

By the time she married David Lavell, a non-Indian, in 1970, her experiences had prepared her to question why discrimination on the basis of gender should exist, and why she should be formally cut off from the family and community that still formed the basis of her identity. With the help of Clayton Ruby, then a young lawyer, she filed an application to have section 12.1.b ruled inoperable because it violated the Bill of Rights, enacted in 1968, giving protection from discrimination on the basis of sex.

Jeannette's challenge to the Indian Act failed in lower court and, subsequently, on appeal to the Supreme Court of Canada, it was again rejected. What she originally expected to be an action affecting her and her community turned into a national cause that would continue for a decade. The efforts of Indian women to achieve equal treatment under the Indian Act were seen by the mostly male leadership of the major Indian political organizations to be in conflict with other, more pressing objectives. The federal government joined with Indian political organizations to oppose Jeannette's suit and Jeannette found herself variously hailed as a heroine of Indian women's rights and denounced even by persons in her own community as a betrayer of the goals of the larger Indian community.[11]

Jeannette's long struggle, reinforced by actions of other Indian women who demonstrated in public and protested in international forums, bore fruit in 1982, when the newly patriated Canadian Constitution included a clause making discrimination on the basis of gender unconstitutional. In 1985 Bill C31, a bill amending the Indian Act, provided for reinstatement of Indian status, on request, of women like Jeannette who had been previously removed from the Indian register. Bill C31 further established that, in future, neither male nor female would lose or gain Indian status on marriage, but elements of the new law continue to enforce discrimination against descendants of reinstated women in comparison with those who enjoy status through male descent.

After years in the glare of publicity, Jeannette returned with her husband and children to Manitoulin Island to teach school at Wikwemikong. When it became evident that one of her children required special education services that were unavailable on the Indian reserve, the family moved to London, Ontario, where Jeannette continued to teach, gaining promotion to the position of principal of a school on a reserve in the region. In 1990 she accepted an appointment with the Ontario Ministry of Citizenship as a race relations consultant, working at first with groups in the general community and later focusing on design of a strategy for Aboriginal anti-racism education. As of 1994, she is continuing her work as a consultant with the Ontario government and with Aboriginal communities, developing an advocacy strategy for vulnerable Aboriginal people – those with physical or learning disabilities whose needs have largely been neglected in policy formation and service provision. She has also re-entered the Aboriginal political scene, with her election in 1994 as Speaker, or national leader, of the Native Women's Association of Canada.

Sylvia Maracle is a Mohawk from the Bay of Quinte Band whose territory lies forty miles west of Kingston, Ontario, on the main thoroughfare between Toronto and Montreal. Sylvia was born in 1955, the oldest of five children. She was not quite six years old when her mother died in childbirth, as a result of complications from diabetes. Sylvia and her brothers and sisters were split up, going into Children's Aid care for a time. Later Sylvia stayed with aunts and uncles in the village adjacent to the reserve or in the nearby city of Belleville. She had regular contact with her paternal grandparents, who were too old to be able to cope with the daily care and schooling of young children, but who profoundly influenced Sylvia's understanding of life, family, and responsibility.

Perhaps because of her exposure to life outside the Mohawk community, perhaps because of innate curiosity, Sylvia took note of things which were taken for granted in her grandparents' household but which were different from customs in the surrounding white environment ... the bag of tobacco that hung on the wall over the woodstove, the modelling of gender-specific skills by male and female members of the family, teaching that might or might not be accompanied by talk, grandmother's leading role in defining how children should be instructed, and grandfather's gentleness and patience in trying to instil understanding of those instructions.

By the time she enrolled in journalism at Ryerson Polytechnical Institute, Sylvia was consciously trying to bridge the two worlds in which she lived.[12] It was her grandparents again who provided direction, giving her tobacco so she could introduce herself to an elder woman on the Six Nations Reserve near Brantford, the first of many elders who would carry on the education her grandparents had begun.

While still at Ryerson, Sylvia began working with the Ontario Federation of Indian Friendship Centres, a body that coordinates the communications, program development, and funding agreements with government agencies on behalf of twenty-six Friendship Centres across Ontario. For the past dozen years Sylvia has served as executive director of the federation.

Since the 1960s, Aboriginal people have been moving out of their rural communities to urban centres in substantial numbers, to seek education, adventure, employment, or shelter from harsh conditions in their communities of origin. The Friendship Centres, the first of which was started in 1959 to assist the adjustment of migrating Aboriginal people, have become fixtures on the urban scene. They are centres now for activism on the part of Aboriginal peoples who are asserting their determination to retain and express their Aboriginal identities and cultures in the urban environment where they make their home.[13]

Sylvia, with her effective communication skills, her deep sensitivity to the importance of cultural roots, and her fierce determination that policies and institutions should recognize rather than seek to extinguish the Aboriginal world, has become a powerful voice on behalf of all Aboriginal people, but especially for those living in urban settings. In addition to her work with the federation, she sits on numerous boards and committees which are working to give substance to the concept of Aboriginal rights which has been recognized by the Ontario government.

Emily Jane Faries is Cree, born in 1952 in Moose Factory, Ontario, an island community located at the southern tip of James Bay. She is among the first Aboriginal women in Canada to earn a doctoral degree. She graduated in 1991 with a doctorate of education from the University of Toronto (Ontario Institute for Studies in Education). Her thesis[14] explores the role of Aboriginal languages in education; it makes a strong case for educating Aboriginal children in their native language in the primary grades of school, introducing English as a second language only when the children have established skills working with academic constructs in the language of home and community.

Emily believes firmly that Aboriginal people must pursue bicultural education, entrenching a strong sense of Aboriginal identity as a prerequisite for achieving competence in other spheres. She sees this balanced education as essential in regaining control of institutions like schools and governments which determine so much of peoples' lives and potential. Her work as an educator and consultant is directed to demonstrating how those dual goals can be achieved.

Like the other women profiled here, Emily reflects on her childhood and the influences that shaped her present character. Her mother and grandmother taught her the skills essential for a traditional Cree woman: preserving meat, sewing hides, making moccasins, and caring for children. Boys learned different skills from their fathers and uncles, but occasionally girls went out also with the men to learn how to set fish nets and rabbit snares. Her father was a war veteran who taught, mostly by example, the value of hard work, self-discipline, unselfishness, and respect for human dignity.

At the age of thirteen, Emily was sent out from her community to attend high school, first in Ottawa and later in North Bay. She lived in non-Aboriginal boarding homes, essentially isolated from her parents, her brothers and sisters, her people and her community. She was a shy person who drew strength from her parents through letters. Her mother had taught herself to read and write. Her father's horizons had been broadened by serving overseas in the Second World War, and this experience undoubtedly contributed to his strong commitment to education for his children. He encouraged Emily in every way possible to persist in school despite the loneliness and stress she experienced.

Emily thought a lot about why she was sent away to school. She rationalized that her parents would not have allowed this to happen unless there was some good to come of it; she trusted their judgment that education was important. Unlike the children who had been stripped of human support at the age of six or seven, Emily was able to integrate the pain of isolation, the assurance of her parents' care for her, and the necessity of assuming responsibility for setting her own life goals. She determined that she would persevere, that she would become an educator, and that she would use her gifts to help her people.

Having completed in succession the degrees of Bachelor of Arts, Bachelor of Education, Master of Education, and Doctor of Education, Emily is now applying herself to effecting change in educational institutions. She works as a consultant based in Moose Factory. She has assisted the Innu of Labrador to plan an education system that will reinstate community control, and to negotiate with the government of Newfoundland and Labrador. In 1994 she was awarded a contract by Trent University to research and write a text on the teachings of the elders from various Aboriginal nations throughout Canada.

Emily recognizes that not all Aboriginal children have the good fortune to be able to learn from their parents all they need to know about themselves and their culture. The institutions of church and school that have encouraged Aboriginal people to deny and neglect their heritage must play their part in restoring dignity to that heritage. She is motivated in her ongoing work by her son, who has been with her since her teen years, and her partner who shares her vision of helping to recreate vital, self-reliant First Nations. Her father, who has been a constant inspiration to her, died in an accident in 1992. As she emerged from a period of grieving her personal loss, she experienced a heightened sense of her responsibility to work for the realization of his dreams of a better world.

THEIR STORIES

In embarking on the writing of this article, the authors were motivated by several desires: to give visibility and show respect for Aboriginal women who have made and are making history; to share insights into what made them who they are; and to communicate powerfully what any well-informed Aboriginal woman knows already – that while these women are remarkable in terms of Canadian public life, they are also daughters and granddaughters, apprentices to elder women who model wisdom, courage, and grace of character.

Edna, Jeannette, Sylvia, and Emily agreed to participate in interviews reflecting on their origins, the experiences and relationships that influenced them, their perspectives on their accomplishments, and their hopes and concerns for the future. In each of the interviews, a sense of continuity, from the past through the present and into the future, came through. The women see themselves as inheritors of a tradition which gives meaning to their lives and which belongs to generations yet to come. The tradition is transmitted through family, but when this is interrupted, by separation or dysfunction or death, there are others to assume the teaching role.

My mom was a school teacher. She had been through teachers' college and everything. She had also been through the residential school system. On the other hand, my dad never went to school. To this day he doesn't read or write. He's always lived within our community; that is his total world. He speaks Ojibway, but he has also picked up English at the same time ...

When I was doing this [the court challenge to the Indian Act] there were some people at home in my own community that got very abusive and very insulting. That was when I felt my family being very supportive, telling me in the Ojibway language about our own beliefs. My dad especially urged me: 'Keep your mind on the goodness of what you are trying to do. Don't get sidetracked. You have to have respect for others. They do what they see as best. If you put out bad feelings they will come back to you.' Of course he was disappointed at the way people reacted, telling him to his face how wrong I was. He had to deal with that.

Jeannette Lavell

Edna followed a different path to find instruction:

The first time I heard that big drum, it was like coaxing your heart, because it sounded like your own heartbeat, and it felt so good. I just wanted to dance ...

In '74 [when we first attended Ojibway ceremonies in Michigan] there was a strong pull, and even on the way there you just felt something, like you were on the threshold of something. That night when we got there, I heard the sound of the water drum, the Little Boy water drum. It wasn't so much the heartbeat, it was more release. It was like that Little Boy water drum made me cry and cry and I didn't know why I was crying. It took me back to my dream experience, when I just sobbed and sobbed. Every time that drum sounded, tears would come, and I would go out of control. I think it was years and years of stuff that I held in, all the sadness, the loneliness, even the rage was just coming out. Whenever I heard the sound of the water drum, there was a feeling that I had come home. After that I started to listen to those teachings that Little Boy gave, and things really started to change for me. All the things about womanhood, Anishinabe way, started to emerge then.

An old man said to me once: 'You're a part of all of life, all of Creation. You're connected to all things. You're connected to all people.' After the experience in Michigan I started to fast, to meditate on those things, to find out about Creation, about the Earth.

Edna Manitowabi

The teachings which are so highly valued come often from elders and have the effect of establishing a link with the natural world. Sylvia speaks of her first encounter in her late teens with an elder Iroquois woman on the Six Nations reserve at Brantford to whom her grandparents sent her with a gift of tobacco. The old woman was apparently expecting her, offered her tea, and burned the tobacco in the stove. She agreed to help as best she could, but instead of sitting down and talking, she set the young woman to moving a woodpile. When the task was finished she had Sylvia move it again. By the end of the weekend Sylvia was tired and disappointed. When the old woman asked why she was upset, Sylvia blurted out: 'I came here to learn who I was, and all I've been is a slave all weekend, moving your wood around.' Sylvia describes the outcome in this way:

The old woman reached across the table, took my hand and said: 'You have had the most magnificent teachers in the world. The earth has watched everything that you have done. The wind has come to check on you and what's going on. The sun has shone and mixed his powers with yours so that there can be life. The birds have serenaded you and other animals, some so very small, have come around as well ...' She talked so eloquently, and made me feel so special that I felt awful for complaining that she hadn't paid attention to me. She went on: 'All those creatures are so much wiser than I am. I only know a little bit, but if you want to come back and spend time I'll teach you the little that I know.' And she did.

Sylvia Maracle

Teachings come not only from elders and nature, but from children too.

Another strong influence in my life is my son. I became a mother in my late teen years. From him, I learned the responsibility of raising a child. I took that responsibility very seriously, to raise him in the best way I could. To me, my son represented all Aboriginal children and he became a great motivator just by being with me.

Emily Faries

I take my nieces and nephews every summer for two weeks, sometimes a month, to give their parents a break. When I take them I try conscientiously to live as close to the traditional way as possible. We get up the very first thing in the morning and we smudge and offer our prayers. We're grateful throughout the day for the experiences that we provide each other. I try to speak softly to them. I try to tell them stories about who they are as a people. Those are some of the most fun times.

Sylvia Maracle

Children are so, so precious. They are the gift of life. They come, they are given to you for a reason. Not only to give them birth and to raise them up, but to give you life. They give you energy and reason to keep on with life. They give you that incentive. I really see my kids as beautiful, beautiful gifts. They are the ones that lifted me up at times when felt like I was sinking.

Edna Manitowabi

We asked the four women to speak about male-female relationships, as they learned about them early in life and as they understand them today. Without exception their early memories were of rural life in which men and women worked together in complementary but not rigid roles:

Both families were farmers and come haying time there was a lot of help. Women did the cooking; the men did the haying; but us kids were out there working, helping them. My good memory about that is a feeling of being safe because we were all there working. We used to have fields and fields of potatoes. It wasn't just for us. Other people would come and dig the potatoes. There would be piles, like a haystack, of potatoes and everyone would have potatoes for the winter.

Edna Manitowabi

Both of my parents worked in the store. My mom worked behind the counter. She was the cashier and took care of the books. My dad did all the other kinds of work, driving the truck to get flour and groceries and supplies in the nearby town. But they both shared in the selling as well ... If my mom wasn't around my dad was perfectly capable of taking care of us, and he was a good cook. In no time at all he'd have dinner ready. His father and mother used to be cooks in the big lumbering camps on the waterways around the Great Lakes, and my dad must have observed them because he certainly knew how to cook.

Jeannette Lavell

When I was growing up the women were always in the house and the men were always outside of the house. They would sit out on the porch or under the apple tree or they would be doing things. Even in the winter they managed to be somewhere else ... My brothers and cousins and I were all sort of allowed to run in a pack for a very long time. Then there was that magical time, about eight or nine years of age, when you didn't hang out any more; you were a part of the activities.

The boys were learning to split wood and haul water and help my grandfather. My grandmother had a quilt rack in her sunroom and she would roll down that quilt with chalk lines drawn on it and we girls would have to help her sew and everyone would be talking. And some of the things they talked about would make my face red.

When people came together at meal time that's when the men and the women would talk together. My grandmother talked about responsibility and how things were when she was a girl, and what was going right and what was going wrong with people in the family, so everyone could hear. If my grandmother felt that there were problems my grandfather would never say anything except at the end of when my grandmother spoke, he would support her.

I think that when I was growing up men and women sort of fit together, in terms of being a balanced unit. It made sense that inside the house was my grandmother's domain and outside of the house was my grandfather's domain. Traditionally, the fire of the people was inside the house and even now, when you come home you come home to the fire, the sense of comfort that's there. You come home to where your mother and grandmother and aunts are. It is a treat that your father and grandfather and uncles are there, but they are not the primary reason that we go home.

Sylvia Maracle

Changes in the relationships between male and female were described as changes in community life rather than in the relations of one man and one woman. Emily described the difference in value-neutral terms, though she has concern that Aboriginal people might go too far in adopting non-Aboriginal ways.

In my childhood days, responsibilities of men and women were in balance; each depended on the other; each needed the other, fulfilling their responsibilities, in order to survive. Today's world is different. It is important for both men and women to pursue professions. In today's world we are more influenced by white society and in order to survive we must have a balance between white ways and our own traditional ways. But it is important to ensure that we do not adopt too much of the white world so that we do not lose our own traditions, culture, language.

Emily Faries

Jeannette offered the analysis that Aboriginal women have been more successful than Aboriginal men in adapting to an education system that conflicts with Aboriginal learning styles. Also, she observed that it was easier for young women than it was for young men to stay in school because young men were expected at a certain age to go to work and contribute to the family, or at least to fend for themselves. When service jobs opened up in reserve communities, women were therefore better positioned to become counsellors, clerks, teacher aides, and teachers, even school bus drivers, almost setting up class differences between men and women. She sees Aboriginal men being caught in a bind between the expectations of their culture and the possibilities that exist in contemporary society for them to live out those expectations.

Even as people leave the communities to go outside to work it is often the women who find it easier to get into the non-Native work environment, in business or government. But it doesn't have anything to do with us as Native people and our own expectations of each other. It's how the system was set up, how people have been able to adjust or adapt. Maybe this is where, as Native women, we have that sense of being more flexible, where we can adapt just for survival. Perhaps Native men bump up against things and it's not in their character to bend. They will confront it more and if there is a confrontation they will back off. The value that Native men have, that they should be protectors, perhaps makes it more difficult for them to be flexible because it may be seen as being weak. And maybe this is why there are a lot of Native men who get into alcohol abuse and other abuses, just because of the frustration of events.

Jeannette Lavell

Sylvia makes similar observations, but she places her observations of contemporary gender roles in the framework of tradition and political analysis.

Today I think our men have moved away from their original instructions. At the very beginning of time, according to our traditions, women were given the responsibility to complete creation and women still do that. Men were given the responsibility to protect and provide. When a Mohawk society exists in an environment which is hostile to our ways, whether in economics, politics, criminal justice, social welfare or race relations, it becomes very hard for our men to fulfil their responsibilities. Often they swing over to the other side, where the male is supreme, and it's very difficult for them to do that in a matriarchal society. So as a consequence, I don't see the balance and harmony that I used to see with male and female roles fitting together. People of my generation are a lot more prone to violence, to separation, to having children from multiple partners, than they were in my parents' generation and certainly more than they were in my grandparents' generation. Attacks from the outside, whether you consider them spiritual attacks or cultural attacks, have wrought havoc in our communities and have very much wrought havoc in relationships between men and women.

Sylvia Maracle

These women are not simply passive observers of the social change swirling about them. Each of them has a vision of the role of women and their personal responsibilities in shaping the future. For Edna, discovering her connection with the Earth has been a powerful source of healing from the early hurts that troubled her so deeply. As a teacher of language and culture and as a ceremonialist in Ojibway tradition, she tries to share what she has discovered.

When those old women and those old men said 'You have to go home to your mother,' I took it literally. I tried to figure out what they meant. At first I thought they meant my biological mother, but she died when I was twenty-one. Then I thought that maybe they wanted me to go back to my reserve. Later on I figured out that it had to do with the Earth. It was when I started to ask myself questions about womanhood, that's when I realized I had to find it from the Earth. 'Go home to your mother. You need to be with your mother.' Those words clicked ...
    When I connected to the Earth, it was like a mirror, like seeing myself. And when I saw a crane or a bulldozer digging into the Earth it was like a form of rape; I just felt like that machine was scarring me. I began to realize that Earth is Woman and what happens to woman happens to her. It's like we're so connected as females that what happens to us as women happens also to Her. And she's feeling that. I really really feel that as woman comes into her own she finds that Spirit within her and she begins to stand up. I'm just coming to that. It's like I talked about it all along, but it's only now that I've really come to understand it.

Edna Manitowabi

Sylvia's greatest hope is that her people will return to their cultural roots, becoming stronger in spirit and responsible for practising and passing on traditional teachings. She worries how to slow down the pace of life which she sees her people caught up in, so that more people take time to learn who they are, and so that Aboriginal people themselves will look to ways to heal the injuries inflicted by colonial institutions and economic oppression. She sees the fragmentation of Aboriginal political organizations and asks: 'How do we tell our children on the one hand that our spirit as a people is holistic when we replicate how non-Indians do things, building a separate organization for every single element of our lives?' She feels a responsibility as a Mohawk woman to help reawaken consciousness of the spiritual and ethical foundations of Aboriginal cultures, especially among Aboriginal people living in urban centres who may find themselves cut off from their roots.

The fact that I am a Mohawk woman means to me that I have a licence to make changes in the world. I have my instructions from the beginning of time to look at the world we live in, to challenge and encourage people to return to our roots. Some of my great aunties, who are still alive, don't bat an eye in telling someone they know or someone they don't know: 'This is what has to be done.' I grew up that way, and now I get paid to do it ...

In trying to walk a traditional path there are four lifelong questions we ask ourselves: Who am I? In order to answer that I have to know: Where have I come from? And once I know where I come from, I have to know: Where am I going? And once I know where I am going, I need to know: What is my responsibility? We ask ourselves these questions and every time we think we know the answer to one, it changes all the other answers.

I have a personal sense of responsibility to give back to my people what they have given to me. And my people have given me an extraordinary life so far. Extraordinary! They have given me a great sense of worth, a feeling of belonging; they've even given me plaques and awards. Because of the way I was raised I need to make a contribution back. My grandmother was forever saying: 'What goes around, comes around.' So, if what's coming to me is so good, that's what I have to give back. That's what comes from being raised as part of this magnificent people.

Sylvia Maracle

Jeannette also sees cultural traditions as the source of respect in human relations, awareness of the environment, and a holistic understanding of health which encompasses wellness of body, mind, feelings, and spirit. She believes passionately that the collective rights of the First Nations must be built upon respect for individual human rights; otherwise, Aboriginal governments that assume power from federal and provincial orders of government could themselves become dictatorships, standing between Aboriginal citizens and the exercise of their human rights. She suggests that while certain leaders' motivations may be right, in many cases they lack the background and the spiritual guidance to be making those fundamental decisions about collective and individual rights on behalf of the people.

Native women will, I think, provide the buffer, that cushion so that abuses of power don't happen. Since obviously everyone recognizes that self-government is going to come about, must come about, Native women are going to have to take a more active role than they have in the past in political life. They have to ensure that (Aboriginal) governments which are established practise respect, fairness, equity.

Some leaders are buying into a European model of male dominance. We need to find how our communities used to function and restore harmony at the grassroots level. The work that all of us, including women, have to do in the next while is crucial. It is working for whole communities.

Jeannette Lavell

For Emily, the contemporary responsibilities of women involve their traditional roles as life givers, mothers, and teachers. By linking these traditional responsibilities with new skills, Aboriginal women can take on professional roles and build new community and governmental institutions rooted in Aboriginal languages and cultures. Aboriginal control of institutions is not an end in itself; it is a means of ensuring the ongoing transmission of a sense of connectedness with the Creator that Emily sees as an integral part of Cree life:

My greatest hope for my people is that as more Aboriginal people become educated, we will achieve self-determination and self-sufficiency. We will no longer depend on non-Native people to help us advance towards our goal of self-government. We ourselves will govern and administer our own institutions. We, as Aboriginal people, know what is best for ourselves and our communities.

Emily Faries

RESTORING THE BALANCE

Aboriginal cultures, in their diversity, were sustained into the mid-twentieth century by the social isolation of most Aboriginal communities, whether they were reserves recognized as administrative units by the Indian Act or Métis and Inuit settlements. Rural and remote communities were the centres for subsistence activities which, with settlement, began to include some small-scale farming even for previously mobile peoples. Those reserves and settlements near centres of population provided a reference point for Aboriginal people who moved away for shorter or longer periods so they could seek work in surrounding farms and logging operations or in more distant towns and cities.

Since the Second World War, and since the arrival of television, government services, roads and airplanes, the level of interaction between Aboriginal and non-Aboriginal societies has accelerated. This interaction had been given a generally unrecognized boost by the voluntary participation of hundreds of Aboriginal men in the war effort.

The changes in the lives of Aboriginal communities, and their women, which have taken place over the past two generations are similar to changes which occur in any society moving from a subsistence to an industrial, urban-oriented economy. Economic activity began to be separated from the home and the land, and the family was displaced as the primary unit of production. In regions remote from industrial and agricultural development, economic and social patterns based on harvesting persist into the present. However, with the establishment of reserves and permanent settlements, the depletion of the local game supply became a widespread problem, and the enforcement of provincial fish and game laws further undermined traditional economic activities. When Aboriginal people migrated to the cities, they experienced low employability, poverty, and cultural dislocation.

Institutions took over responsibilities that were formerly the domain of women: education, health, and community care of children. Elected band councils, which served to emphasize male roles, were imposed under the authority of the Indian Act, replacing decision-making councils that reflected family and clan organization and female contributions to community life. With the support and collusion of the Canadian government, Christian churches suppressed Aboriginal ceremonial practices. They forcibly denied children the opportunity to learn their spiritual traditions by removing them from their families, often for years at a time, and socializing them into a new, non-Aboriginal mould in residential schools.

Even though Aboriginal families and communities have been caught up in a whirlwind of change, whose pace and coercive nature have been enormously disruptive, our grandmothers still remember the old ways. They remember the languages that descibe the Aboriginal world, the relationships that helped to maintain balance in the whole of creation, the skills and responsibilites and capacity for hard work that placed them at the vital centre of family and community life.

In speaking about the social and cultural change experienced in the Aboriginal community, it is important to recognize that we are not talking about deculturation – that process by which Aboriginal people are alleged to lose their culture. The myth of the Vanishing Red Man is precisely that – a myth, a story that represents reality and compels belief because it mirrors a familiar view of the world. Colonial America wanted to believe that Aboriginal people were disappearing, perhaps because possession and exploitation of the continent would be more comfortable without awkward reminders of alternative political orders and competing claims to the land. Canadian policy, from the first Indian Act in 1876 until the Constitution Act of 1982, displayed a frankly assimilationist bent, looking to the day when Indians would become Canadians like any others.

As the stories of these four women show, it is possible to retain a strong Aboriginal identity while still mastering the skills required to walk in balance in two worlds. Edna, Jeannette, Sylvia, and Emily recognize that much work needs to be done to restore the physical, emotional, mental, and spiritual health of families and communities that have been ravaged by change. They make the analysis that dysfunction and pain are products of the powerlessness enforced by governments and institutions outside their communities. But they also speak powerfully of the obligations of individuals, communities, and nations to relearn and reclaim their responsibilities to themselves, to their relations, and to the Creator.

Aboriginal people in Ontario and across Canada are going through a process of revitalization,[15] recovering consciousness of who they are and strength to assert their distinctiveness. Renewal is seen in the restoration of ancient ceremonies in which young and not-so-young Aboriginal people discover the spiritual and ethical foundations of their cultures. It is paralleled by the recovery of health as Aboriginal people support one another in experiencing and going beyond the grief that stunted the growth of so many of our people; grief over overwhelming losses – of land, language and sustenance, of generations of children to residential schools, foster homes, and, too often, violent death. This renewal of Aboriginal cultures is symbolized in adoption of the term First Nations, identifying us as charter members of Canadian society and the family of nations worldwide. It gains momentum in negotiations to entrench legal and political recognition of inherent rights to self-government which have survived a lengthy history of denial and suppression. And, as the stories of the women in this article demonstrate, renewal is energized by women reclaiming their responsibilities, working to restore the balance in male-female relationships, and, in ways we can only apprehend by faith, contributing to the balance of the universe as a whole.

Niawen. That is all we have to say.

NOTES

1 For a discussion of Aboriginal relationship to the land, see Thomas Berger, *Northern Frontier, Northern Homeland: The Report of the MacKenzie Valley Pipeline Inquiry*, vol. 1 (Ottawa: Minister of Supply and Services Canada 1977). For a discussion of efforts to sustain this kind or relationship in face of settlement and shared use, see Richard Price, *The Spirit of Alberta Indian Treaties* (Edmonton: Pica Pica Press 1987).

2 James Frideres, *Native Peoples in Canada: Contemporary Conflicts*, 3rd ed. (Scarborough: Prentice Hall 1988), provides an introduction to the contemporary conditions of Indian communities and relations with Canadian society.

3 Marlene Castellano, 'Women in Huron and Ojibwa Societies,' *Canadian Woman Studies / Les Cahiers de la Femme* 10, 2 and 3 (1989): 45–9.

4 Harold Cardinal in *The Unjust Society: The Tragedy of Canada's Indians* (Edmonton: Hurtig 1969) made an eloquent argument for dismantling the colonial institutions that regulated the lives of Indian people under the Indian Act. J. Rick Ponting, ed., *Arduous Journey: Canadian Indians and Decolonization* (Toronto: McClelland and Stewart 1986), reviews the progress made in the two decades following the publication of Cardinal's provocative book.

5 For a fuller analysis of discriminatory aspects of the Indian Act see Kathleen Jamieson, *Indian Women and the Law in Canada: Citizens Minus* (Ottawa: Minister of Supply and Services 1978).

6 See Celia Haig-Brown, *Resistance and Renewal: Surviving the Indian Residential School* (Vancouver: Tillacum Library 1988), and Bridget Moran, *Stoney Creek Woman: The Story of Mary John* (Vancouver: Tillacum Library 1988). For further reading on residential schools, see Basil Johnston, *Indian School Days* (Toronto: Key Porter Books 1988); J.R. Miller, 'A Research Project on Residential Schools,' Royal Commission on Aboriginal Peoples 1992; Jean Barman, Yvonne Hebert, and Don McCaskill, eds, *Indian Education in Canada, The Legacy* (Vancouver: University of British Columbia Press 1986). Patrick Johnston, *Native Children and the Child Welfare System* (Toronto: James Lorimer 1983), was a landmark study of the misdirected interventions and devastating effects of child-welfare interventions in Indian families in the 1960s and 1970s.

7 See Barman, McCaskill, and Hebert eds, *Indian Education in Canada*, 1: *The*

*Legacy* and 2: *The Challenge*, for a review of historical and contemporary issues in Aboriginal education.

8  The *Canadian Woman Studies Journal / Les Cahiers de la Femme* 10, 2 and 3 (1989), devoted the issue to the stories and poems of Aboriginal women telling their lives in their own words.

9  For a more developed example of using life histories as an entrée to the study of regional history, see Julie Cruikshank, *Life Lived Like a Story: Life Stories of Three Yukon Native Elders* (Vancouver: University of British Columbia Press 1990).

10  Edna Manitowabi, 'An Ojibwa Girl in the City,' *This Magazine Is about Schools,* 1971.

11  See Kathleen Jamieson, 'Sex Discrimination and the Indian Act,' in *Indian Women and the Law in Canada: Citizens Minus*, for a historical and sociological review of the conflicts generated by Aboriginal women's action and the legislation of the Indian Act. See also Janet Silman, *Enough is Enough: Aboriginal Women Speak Out* (Toronto: Women's Press 1987), for a description of the experience of women of the Tobique Reserve in New Brunswick.

12  See Osennontion and Skonaganleh:Ra, 'Our World,' *Canadian Woman Studies* 10, 2 and 3 (1989): 7–19.

13  National Association of Friendship Centres, *The Friendship Centre Movement – 30th Anniversary* (Ottawa 1988).

14  Emily Faries, 'Language Education for Northern Native Children: A Case Study,' (PhD dissertation, University of Toronto 1991).

15  See Jeanne Perreault and Sylvia Vance, *Writing the Circle: Native Women of Western Canada* (Edmonton: Newest Publishing 1990).

NANCY ADAMSON

# Feminists, Libbers, Lefties, and Radicals: The Emergence of the Women's Liberation Movement

Between 1968 and early 1971 a few dozen political action groups of women calling themselves 'women's libbers' sprang up across Ontario.[1] After a brief hiatus in organizing during 1971, a new surge of activity began around 1972. Many other women came together in consciousness-raising groups in those early years to 'spill our guts,' as one participant remarked, 'look at the world, realize how we'd been taken in by men and say to hell with it.'[2]

What set these groups apart from earlier organizations, and marked the beginning of a new kind of women's organizing, were the decisions to organize autonomously as women and to define the group's issues as the concerns of women as defined by women. These traits were to be the hallmarks of feminist organizing. Collectively called the women's liberation movement, these groups of women were regarded both by themselves and by the media as a new phenomena. In fact, they were part of a long history of Canadian women struggling together to change the conditions of their lives. The political activities of women, the personal writings of authors such as Simone de Beauvoir and Betty Friedan,[3] and the changes in women's educational and work opportunities during the 1960s set the stage for the emergence of what is now called the second wave of the women's movement.

In 1966 a number of women who had been active in electoral politics and in women's organizations such as the Canadian Federation of University Women came together to form the Committee for Equality for Women in Canada (CEW). The representatives of the thirty national women's organizations who formed the CEW called on the federal government to establish a Royal Commission on the Status of Women. In February 1967 the RCSW was announced 'to inquire into and report upon the status of women in Canada, and to recommend what steps might be taken by the Federal Government to ensure for women equal opportunities with men in all aspects of Canadian society.'4 Women's issues were on the public agenda.

Against this backdrop, the women's liberation movement emerged. The goal of the movement was to make change. Women wanted to transform every aspect of society. In order to do that, it was necessary to theorize and to articulate a political position. More importantly, women had to translate those words into actions that would bring more women into the movement and change the world. The challenge for women's liberation was threefold: first, to draw women into the movement; second, to construct practices within organizations which would turn newcomers into activists; and, third, to persuade decision-makers to effect the kinds of changes women were calling for. Drawing women into the movement was not a problem; by the late 1960s women's liberation groups were springing up across the province (see table 1).5

The emergence of the women's liberation movement occurred in two spurts of political organizing and recruiting. The first began in Toronto in about 1966 and in most of Ontario in about 1968, and came largely from women active on the left. The motivation for developing a feminist analysis came, in the first instance, from a desire to critique and change left organizations and Marxist theory. That developed, very quickly in some women, more slowly in others, into a sense that the women's liberation movement was a movement unto itself. By organizing broadly into women's liberation movement groups, the late 1960s activists had a wide base from which to address a range of issues. Many of those groups also sponsored, or used as part of their own process, consciousness-raising (CR) groups or techniques.

In those small discussion groups, focused on women's own experiences, we can see the basis for the second burst of activity of the early women's liberation movement. After a brief hiatus following the Abortion Caravan in mid-1970, the women's liberation movement re-emerged led by a more diverse and less politically experienced group of women. Women's centres formed the base for their political organizing.

The women who began to speak their criticisms of the New Left and to separate themselves from it were usually called women's liberationists, or women's libbers for short, and as a group were referred to as the women's liberation movement. These women saw themselves as distinct, both politically and organizationally, from the established women's rights groups who had preceded them and who had called on the federal government to establish the Royal Commission on the Status of Women. Women's libbers felt that they were asking new questions, that they were seeing for the first time the extent

TABLE 1
Founding Dates of Some Ontario Women's Liberation Groups

Guelph
1969 Guelph Women's Liberation Movement
1972 Guelph Women's Centre

Hamilton
1969 Hamilton Women's Liberation Movement
1971 Group for Equal Rights at McMaster University
1971 Hamilton Committee on the Status of Women
1973 Hamilton Women's Centre

Kingston
1969 Kingston Women's Liberation
1970 Queen's University Community Co-op Day Care Centre
1970 Women's Union
1972 Women's groups meet weekly at Queen's University
1973 Kingston Women's Centre

Kitchener-Waterloo
1971 Kitchener-Waterloo Women's Caucus
1972 K-W Women's Coalition for the Repeal of the Abortion Laws
1973 K-W Women's Place

London
1970 Birth Control and Abortion Centre at the University of Western Ontario
1970 Abortion Action
1970 London Women's Liberation Movement
1973 London Women's Resource Centre

Niagara Region
1973 Niagara Region Action Committee on the Status of Women Ottawa

Ottawa
1969 Ottawa Women's Liberation Committee
1969 Carleton University Women's Liberation Committee
1971 Women's Resource Group
1971 Gays of Ottawa/Gais d'Ottawa
1972 Women's Centre

Peterborough
1970 Peterborough Women's Caucus
1974 Women's Place

St Catharine's
1974 Women's Resource Centre, YWCA

Sarnia
1969 Sarnia Women's Liberation

Sudbury
1970/71 Sudbury Women's Liberation

Thunder Bay
1969 Thunder Bay Women's Liberation

TABLE 1 (concluded)

---

1969 Lakehead University Day-Care Centre
1970 Birth Control & Counselling Centre at Lakehead University
1973 Women's Centre
1973 *The Northern Woman Journal*

Toronto[6]
1966 Toronto Women's Liberation Work Group, a University of Toronto student group
1967 SUPA Women's Liberation Work Group
1968 Toronto Women's Liberation Movement
1969 New Feminists
1970 Leila Khaled Collective
1970 Toronto Women's Caucus
1972 Women's Centre
1972 Women's Press
1972 *The Other Woman* begins publication
1972 Women for Political Action
1973 Interval House Shelter for Women
1973 Rape Crisis Centre

Waterloo
1973 Women's Collective

Windsor
1970 Windsor Women's Liberation Movement
1973 Windsor Women's Place

Woodstock
1973 Women's Centre and Shelter

---

and the depth of women's oppression, and that out of those questions and insights they would force Canadian society to reorganize itself.

The 1971 collective of women who edited *Women Unite!* the first Canadian book to explore the women's liberation movement, explained the differences between women's liberation and women's rights groups: 'Although the broad basis of both is the improvement of the quality of life for women in Canada, the philosophy of the women's rights groups is that civil liberty and equality can be achieved *within* the present system, while the underlying belief of women's liberation is that oppression can be overcome only through a radical and fundamental change in the structure of our society.'[7]

Within the women's liberation movement there gradually emerged two distinct approaches to women's liberation. Before about 1972, a group of women using a Marxist analysis struggled to understand women's oppression. In contrast to them, another group called feminists argued that 'the origins of sexism are based on biological differences rather than economic or structural conditions.'[8] The distinction between feminists and leftie or militant women's libbers was clear to those active in the women's liberation movement. To the public, however, women's liberationists were all the same: they called them radicals, radical feminists, consciousness raisers, feminists, bra-burners, libbers, leftie women, or women militants. By the mid-1970s all those organizing to change women's lives would fit loosely under the umbrella term 'women's movement.' But in the late 1960s, as the women's liberation movement defined and created itself, the differences mattered more than the similarities.

This article will examine the political strategies, size, organizational structure, and membership of the women's liberation movement in Ontario from the late 1960s to the mid-1970s. The article is based largely on two types of sources: contemporaneous writings and articles by participants in the women's liberation movement, and interviews done in 1992 with women who were active in those years in Thunder Bay and in Ottawa. Both sources reflect the experiences of women who lived in urban areas. Much more remains to be done about rural and small-town women and their response to the emerging women's liberation movement.

EMERGING FROM THE LEFT

Many scholars have identified the Canadian left as the site of the women's liberation movement. Angela Miles argues that the New Left's 'powerful vision of liberation for *all*' and its commitment to social transformation were important to the emergence of the women's liberation movement.[9] These women were moved to look at their position as women because, as a woman active in the Student Union for Peace Action (SUPA) remarked, they felt 'oppressed as women within an organization that was attacking oppression.'[9] That vision, combined with the inability of the male leaders of the New Left to incorporate the oppression of women into their politic, prompted many women to leave New Left organizations and form women's groups.

For a number of women that was a painful transition. Myrna Kostash, herself a participant in the women's liberation movement, suggests that many New Left women initially 'accepted that their projects were subsumed under the "larger" and "more important" one of student radicalism.'[11] Women, she suggests, tried very hard to find justification in the accepted texts of the period for 'their feminism and locate their female oppression not in the "patriarchy" or "male supremacy" ... but in capitalism and imperialism.'[12] Laurel Limpus, writing in 1971, commented on this struggle:

What happened in these meetings basically is that we laid down very heavy stuff about Marxism. And we were blowing our minds because we didn't understand how we could fit women's liberation into a Marxist perspective, although we still understood the primary contradictions between labour and capital. But we were also beginning to understand totally how being women had destroyed us. We were trying desperately to make those things fit together.[13]

They were trying to reconcile politics as they understood them with their new understanding of their oppression as women. One Ottawa woman remarked that for her the 'prominent pieces' were 'holding onto my Marxist framework, trying to fit my feminism into that Marxist framework and being involved in a CR group.'[13] Finally however, that did not prove possible for many New Left women.

Taking with them from the New Left a strong commitment to a vision of liberation for all, the political and organizing skills learned in their New Left groups, and their profound determination to work for the liberation of women, women created the women's liberation movement. The skills and political insights they brought enabled them to organize a new political movement quickly. These were, for the most part, skilled political women. Although their insights into their own oppression as women were new, they could place them within a larger political context and organize based on that analysis.

Not all women who were active in the women's liberation movement shared the attempts by New Left women to fashion an autonomous movement of women within the general sphere of left-wing politics.[15] Limpus has left us a description from 1971 of her first confrontation with different political analyses in the name of women's liberation:

The initial organizing around the question of women's liberation, the initial consciousness, came out of the women who were the Canadian left, in SUPA. That whole year, 1967–68, included a few meetings but there wasn't anything that you could call a movement. It was just a group of women in the left. During that year we wrote the Abortion Brief and went to Ottawa. The next year I remember there were some more of us – people were kind of springing up all around. A whole group of women, both from Ottawa and Toronto, went down to the Chicago Women's Liberation Conference. It was the first [US] national women's conference and I think it had a lot of effect on what happened in Toronto. There was a tremendous debate in that conference between the women who called themselves 'consciousness raisers' (we had never heard of consciousness raisers before at all) and women who said that the basic question of oppression was Marxism.[16]

The difference in analysis and approach of the 'consciousness raisers' and the Marxists was one that would surface in other Ontario cities in the 1970s, although not always in those terms. The former had no need to reconcile their new insights into the condition of women with a commitment to Marxism while the latter could not imagine a feminist politic without a critique of capitalism at its core. It did not take long for the two groups to clash. As Limpus described: '[One group] said "fuck you Marxist women, men are the enemy." And we said, "Oh how can you say that? Capitalism is the enemy."'[17]

This difference caused a group of women to leave the Toronto Women's Liberation Movement in 1969 and form the New Feminists. As the New Feminists described the split:

The philosophy of the [Toronto] Women's Liberation Movement was basically Marxist (until society changes women can't change – i.e. a revolution is necessary). The splinter group who formed the New Feminists were feminists essentially, rather than being primarily concerned with politics. In short, Women's Liberation said the revolution came first: New Feminists said feminism came first. We believe that the attitude of society that women are inferior to men is basic, that as long as women are considered inferior we will never really make it, no matter what kind of political system the country may have.[18]

This posing of women's liberation as distinctly different from feminism surfaced elsewhere in the province. In the 12 April 1970 issue of the *Thunder Bay Women's Liberation Newsletter*, an article entitled 'Women's Liberation vs The Feminists' appeared. It began: 'Recent literature seems to see Women's Liberation and the Feminist Movement synonymously. It becomes increasingly evident that we, of Women's Liberation, will have to be more emphatic. We will have to clearly and loudly state that we do not hate men, we do not want to be men, we do not blame men for our oppression.'[19]

In the following issue of the *Newsletter* an anonymous letter writer responded, calling on readers not to waste their time bickering with one another about the differences between groups and their various strategies for liberation. 'We have more important things to do,' she argued.[20] Her suggestion was heeded and the *Newsletter* contained no further posing of women's liberation in opposition to feminism.

Despite the brief surfacing of this issue in Thunder Bay, the New Feminists' analysis of women's oppression was virtually unique in Ontario in the late 1960s. Kostash argues that the New Feminists had a core membership of Americans who had recently moved to Canada and that their presence accounts for the rejection of the linking of women's liberation to a larger left agenda of the radical transformation of capitalism.[21] Certainly, women's liberation groups in this early period seem to have seen both their origins and their allies on the left.

While there was a fairly widespread belief among activist women that the women's liberation movement emerged from the left, they understood 'the left' in different ways. For some it referred to progressive organizing such as the peace movement or the student movement. For others it referred to the New Democratic Party, and to still others it meant the Communist Party or far-left political organizations. A woman's understanding of what constituted the left was at least in part a function of the size of the community in which she lived. Larger communities played host to a more diverse organized left, while small centres tended to offer fewer options for progressive political work.

Some Ontario communities also had a history of old left groups raising various women's issues and organizing as women. Kostash notes that the Canadian New Left was not alienated from its socialist roots and points to the Communist Party and the CCF–NDP as having raised, a generation earlier, the issues of women in the labour force, equal pay, and the right to abortion, birth control, and day care. In the Women's Labour Leagues and the Congress of Canadian Women, New Left activists could look to a model of women struggling against capitalism so that women could take their place as full human beings and citizens.[22] Thunder Bay was a city with just such a history. Although the extent to which the women in the New Left, and later in women's liberation, were conscious of that history is not clear, it was part of the communities they inhabited.[23]

In a number of Ontario cities with universities, women's organizing took place among those who were active in the student movement. In Canada the ideas of the New Left were articulated and acted upon by student organizations such as the Student Union for Peace Action, the Canadian Union of Students, Students for a Democratic University, and the Union générale des étudiants de Québec.[24] Women in Thunder Bay remember the women's movement as emerging from the Canadian Union of Students, whose pamphlets brought the first news of women's liberation to Thunder Bay:

My friend Laurie said, 'Let's start a women's group.' She had some articles from the Canadian Union of Students about women. It was a completely new idea to me. She had friends who were leftish – more Marxist. We were both NDPers ... We put up notices in the university for a 'women's liberation group.' I'd never heard the name before, but it sounded okay. I never knew where she got the name. So we went around the university putting up notices. I felt like [Martin] Luther putting up those notices.[25]

Although this group started at Lakehead University, it quickly moved to an off-campus location for meetings and ceased to be linked to the university.

In Ottawa, the left was also the site of the first women's organizing, in about 1969, although not solely in a university context. One activist remembers that 'the movement in Ottawa was spearheaded by women of the left – principally young NDP women.'[26] Women on the university campuses were also organizing and, by 1969, the Carleton University Women's Liberation Committee was in existence, though in Ottawa the university women seem to have remained more separate from the larger community than they did in other Ontario cities.

Leueen MacDonald, writing about the London Women's Liberation Movement, says that 'the women's movement in London originated in the left, the student movement of the university, specifically out of a concern among some people in the Student Christian Movement over the kinds of roles which men and women are forced to play.'[27] In Kingston the emergence of the women's movement was also clearly within a university context, and while there were some alliances made with male students on the left, there does not appear to have been a divisive debate over the politics of women's liberation.[28]

Women's liberationists clearly identified the left – defined variously, but always as left – as the place from which they emerged. These women contrasted themselves to the women's rights activists who came out of other political traditions.

'WOMEN'S LIBBERS'

Women's liberationists came together to talk about their personal experiences and to take action as a result of those discussions. This was unlike anything they had experienced before. It was the talking together *as women about women*, and their understanding that such talk was a political act, which that women found so exciting. Limpus described the excitement of a public meeting held in Toronto in 1969: 'There were about 20 or 30 women in the room, and we just sat there – there it was! A lot of women just showed up. There were women from around the university. I'd say it was pretty middle class ... So we just sat around for the first few months and we *talked*. And we all blew out our minds. For a lot of women, it was a really incredible period.'[29]

An Ottawa woman commented on this feeling of excitement at her first women's liberation movement meeting in about 1971: 'I was blown away by the notion of women coming together. It was beyond my imagination or my experience.'[30] Despite the fact that she had many years of political activism in organizations on the left of the political spectrum, this woman felt the experience of women talking together about women's issues was transformative. That sense of distinctiveness, of specialness, of discovering something new characterizes the memories of many women who became active in women's liberation in its early years. The sense of women sharing a common oppression developed into the notion of sisterhood.

The slogan 'sisterhood is powerful' was a rallying cry for the women's liberation movement. It linked all women together and suggested the strength of women both in their own lives and in the public world. Feminist scholars have reassessed the notion of sisterhood and come to understand its limitations as well as its strengths. In the emerging years of women's liberation, however, sisterhood was an uncomplicated notion that reflected the emerging political consciousness of women's oppression. It was a call to all women to come out of their isolation and to join with each other to make change. It was a political message which conveyed that, together, women had strength.[31]

Although most women who become involved in women's liberation in the 1968 period had already been politically active – in the NDP, the old or New Left, or the student or anti-war movements – they were not homogenous. Formed in mid-1969, the Thunder Bay Women's Liberation had a core of fifteen to twenty members, who were described as 'diverse.' They were old and young middle class and working class working women and women on welfare 'hippie and straight' university students and women from outside the university; while many had been politically active in other groups, a few were new to activism. Looking back, one of those women remarked, 'We did not realize at the time how unique that diversity was until we later learned that most of the early feminist groups were made up of university students.'[32] In retrospect, we can see that they were largely able-bodied and white, with few self-identified lesbians.

The Ottawa Women's Liberation Group, which also began in 1969 and met for about a year, had a core group of ten members made up mainly of women from the left with political experience, mostly in the NDP.[33] Women were also beginning to organize at Carleton University; that group was composed of women with political experience on the left and in the student and anti-war movements.

In Kingston, the early women's liberation activists were largely students at Queen's University, many of whom were active in the student movement. The London Women's Liberation Movement seems to have been more diverse than Kingston's in this period. Writing in the early 1970s, one activist remembers that the London movement consisted of women from the university and from high schools, mothers and working women.[34] In general, the women's liberation activists of the late 1960s were women who came out of the left. From the vantage point of the 1990s we can see that they were a fairly homogenous group, but they felt themselves to be fairly diverse. Many were probably involved with the most diverse group of women in their lives – groups that crossed class, age, and occupational lines at the very least.

Women's liberation groups generally had a loose structure. Since many of the women had come out of various left groups and were critical of male models of leadership and organization, these groups prided themselves on working collectively, making decisions (when they had to be made) by consensus, and incorporating women's experiences into their understanding of political issues and actions. Women took pride in the lack of structure or apparent organization in their groups.[35]

Consciousness raising groups were an important part of the women's liberation groups. CR groups were small discussion groups, usually about six to ten women, which focused on personal issues and experiences such as stereotyping, relationships with men, child-raising, work, sexuality, and politics. The focus of these groups was discussion and personal reflection, not political action. Many of the women involved in CR groups also belonged to a women's action group. The politicization of women in CR groups occurred because the focus on personal experience allowed women to develop an explicit understanding of their oppression as women.

Across the province, women's liberation groups targeted beauty pageants as prime examples of the stereotyping and exploitation of women. The first Ontario challenge to beauty pageants came in Toronto in 1968 when Toronto Women's Liberation organized a protest against a 'winter bikini' contest. 'The protesters displayed meat-cutters' charts to show that the contestants were involved in marketing their flesh.'[36] The Kingston Women's Liberation Movement followed suit in October 1969, when they decided to focus on the beauty queen contests held at Queen's University.

Not content with one sexist circus a year, the men decided to hold another queen contest in connection with Homecoming ... Unable to prevent the contest from happening, the Kingston Women's Liberation Movement decided to enter it ... six of the eight finalists were WLM sisters ... While the audience waited for the show to begin, several women dressed in black wrapped another sister up in a white sheet and, gobbing her with cosmetics and hair accessories, proclaimed her 'Miss Consumer Product,' as other sisters passed around flyers explaining our protest. Finally the contestants were introduced. One after the other our sisters rose up and addressed the audience. As each new speaker came out in turn for the WLM, the two male chauvinist MC's got more and more insulting. They had only expected three of us, and their behaviour was so disgusting at seeing so many of us that in fact they made our point for us ... That night Kingston WLM became a force to be reckoned with at Queen's University. There has never been another queen contest on this campus.'[37]

Actions such as this attracted media attention to the women's liberation movement and provided an opportunity to address the audience who attended such events directly. They also expressed in a concrete manner the anger activists felt at women's oppression and their determination to attack its signs whenever and wherever possible. In the late 1960s women were engaging and challenging men directly in public spaces. They understood the value and made good use of street theatre. Women's liberation activists were loud and demanding and determined to occupy part of the public terrain.

The Abortion Caravan is another example of late 1960s organizing. In April 1970 the Vancouver Women's Caucus issued a call to women across Canada to join them in a caravan that would travel from Vancouver to Ottawa via Kamloops, Edmonton, Regina, Winnipeg, Thunder Bay, Toronto, and Kingston and in a message to politicians: 'We consider the government of Canada is in a state of war with the women of Canada. If steps are not taken to implement our demands by Monday, May 11, 1970, at 3:00 p.m. we will be forced to respond by declaring war on the Canadian government.'[38] Ontario groups planned events to coincide with the arrival of the caravan in their cities. At the request of caravan organizers in Vancouver, Thunder Bay women decided to hold a public meeting on abortion with speakers from the caravan. The meeting was held in a packed hall at a local church. As it turned out, the audience included an organized group that planned to disrupt the meeting. One of the anti-abortionists called one of the organizers 'a gutter slut and a filthy hippie,' and the woman responded by slapping the name-caller. At that point 'all hell broke loose' and the minister of the church dispersed the group. The Thunder Bay Women's Liberation Movement's assessment of the event was that 'overall [it] was a success ... the meeting room was overflowing with people who were interested in our cause. I'm sure we gathered more supporters. The Vancouver girls said that Thunder Bay was their first trouble spot ... Perhaps it was good practice for them in case they encounter other 'Thunder Bays' along the way.'[39]

Kingston women were disappointed when a last-minute decision meant that the caravan could not participate in planned activities. The caravan did, however, drive a few blocks through downtown Kingston on its way to Ottawa. Throughout its journey across the country the caravan carried a coffin to symbolize 'all the women who have died from illegal abortions. We will place this coffin, and with it the responsibility for the death of our sisters, at the feet of the men who make the laws of this country.'[40]

To make this point, when the caravan reached Ottawa, women packed the gallery of the House of Commons, tried to speak to the members of parliament, and chained themselves to the seats. Kingston WLM announced proudly that 'of the five women who were detained ... four were from Kingston WLM.'[41]

The 1970 Abortion Caravan was an important organizing event for the early women's liberation movement, but one that was difficult to follow up on. A year after the caravan, Leueen MacDonald commented on its impact in London: 'Follow-up to the Abortion March was difficult. It had been a sympathetic march rather than part of any particular strategy for us. An organization "Abortion Action" was started after the March ... However, this group couldn't seem to get together enough to keep working and eventually died.'[42] In assessing organizing efforts in the period preceding the Abortion Caravan, Pat Noonan of Windsor wrote that 'our presentation was often angry and radical, coming from our newly discovered theory of women's oppression ... Our message was almost too strong for the 1000s of women trapped by conditions that would take years to change.'[43] Another Windsor activist remarked that 'from our involvement in women's liberation, we had come to learn that most women did not and would not identify with this group.'[44] In the period after the Abortion Caravan, many women's activists were facing the fact that women were not flocking to women's liberation groups in droves. They were also struggling with the various analyses of women oppression which were developing and the resulting different action strategies. The range of issues raised by women in CR groups and in women's liberation groups was enormous. No longer could one group address all aspects of women's oppression. The lack of clear structures and organizations also made it difficult to organize on a longer-term basis.

As activists struggled with these issues, there was a lull in organizing. Some women's groups disbanded, others became inactive; some turned inward to rethink their strategies and needs. This hiatus occurred between late 1970 and early 1972. The exact dates and length vary from city to city. During that period women noticed the lull and struggled to understand it. The authors of *Women Unite!* wrote about the 'virtual disintegration' of Toronto women's groups in mid-1971. In July 1972 a member of the Ottawa

Women's Centre visited the Toronto women's centre, A Woman's Place, and reported that the idea for the centre began in 1971 when 'the women's liberation group in Toronto had ceased to function ... or had lost its appeal for most women.'[45] Writing about the Kingston women's movement, one author commented that although women's liberation had existed in Kingston since 1969, 'the current history begins around the fall of 1972.'[46] And Eleanor McDonald, writing in May 1971, reported that 'the Sarnia [women's liberation] group is not exactly thriving.'[47] In Ottawa and Thunder Bay, thriving women's liberation groups slowly ceased to be active, and there was virtually no women's organizing activity in 1971.

THE RE-EMERGENCE

In Thunder Bay and Ottawa, as well as in other Ontario cities, the activist women's movement re-emerged in about 1972. Whereas in the earlier period a critique of capitalism was the starting point, in this period the focus shifted to the role of patriarchy in the oppression of women. As women came together to define their own needs, they looked beyond the inherent sexism of capitalism to the sexism that permeated their daily lives. Across Ontario the expression of this philosophy took the form of organizing women's centres. Both the work of the women's centre and the women who came out to do that work differed markedly from the earlier period.

In contrast to the very public and militant action of the late 1960s, women's-centre organizing was focused more on women themselves, on providing space for women, and on trying to figure out how to organize a world that would reflect women's needs and experiences. Many women were drawn into this kind of organizing because of its insistence that 'the personal [is] political.' This understanding broke down the traditional separation between public and private life and enlarged the political arena to include a wide range of heretofore 'personal' issues.[48]

In trying to understand the politics of this period, a Thunder Bay activist describes the impact of the new understanding of what constituted the political: 'Those who seriously accepted the new idea of women as independent agents soon began to question their own personal lives and ... many were the struggles at home around housework and independence and many were the marital splits ... Not what to do about day care or beauty contests but what to do about supper tonight ... Women's Liberationists did see bras as counter-revolutionary and girdles too.'[49] The re-examination of how one lived one's life was, as Baril has suggested, characteristic of the feminism of the 1970s.

Women's liberation activists took very much to heart the need to reorder one's life according to feminist politics. They tended to criticize those who focused their political work in more traditional areas. Limpus, commenting on a rival group of feminists in 1970, said they 'were really into being professional, CBC, middle-class, really lacking in politics.'[50] Despite the judgmental nature of such remarks, it is important not to dismiss what feminists were struggling to create – a new politic that challenged all the assumptions society had made about women. There were no blueprints; women made it up as they went along.

The women who organized the women's centres were unlike their sisters of the late 1960s. It was less necessary to have previous political experience; in fact, such experience was often viewed with suspicion. An Ottawa woman active in 1969 and again after 1972 remembers the women who got involved in the formation of the Women's Centre as 'women who were married, at home, had children, sometimes quite small children, limited if any interest in active politics (traditional parties, etc.) and very different from the 1969 Women's Liberation left, NDP, youth types.' She characterized the politics of the Women's Centre thus: 'I would say it was grass roots but it was certainly middle class. Some of the younger women who had not established careers were definitely poor but came from middle class homes ... It was also definitely heterosexual but began to be infiltrated (if that is the word) by openly lesbian women in 1973.'[51]

During this period of renewed activity, large numbers of women – some of them politicized through consciousness-raising groups – moved into the women's liberation movement. In writing about the founding of the Kitchener-Waterloo women's centre, Liz Willick commented: 'There was little organizational or movement experience among the original ten or twelve [founders]; but their need for a self-help centre for women was great enough for the project to move ahead.'[52] It was the focus on validating women's experience and extrapolating from that, as opposed to the political theories of women's liberation, which drew many women into the women's liberation movement of the 1970s.

Many of the women who were active in the late 1960s found their politics changing, and they participated eagerly in the founding of women's centres. These women did not abandon their left analysis, but continued to struggle with an integration of feminism and Marxism. Some remained in socialist organizations such as the NDP, the Communist Party, or far-left groups, while others turned to the autonomous women's movement. The result, later, was the development of a distinct socialist feminism. Many women's centres set up study groups to explore socialist feminism.

As women decided to form women's centres, they were forced to confront the fact that they needed a different kind of structure than had existed in the women's liberation groups. The Kingston group realized they could not conduct a business meeting, have general discussions on issues of interest to their members, and maintain the intimacy of small groups in one meeting a week with a membership that was slowly increasing. They also had to confront the fact that having no permanent physical location made it difficult to coordinate their activities and to meet the needs of women who could not attend evening meetings. After discussion, they decided to seek funding for a women's centre.[53]

In August 1973 the women in Kingston received a grant from the Department of the Secretary of State and opened the Women's Centre on 13 October 1973. The centre planned the following activities: CR groups, a study group on feminism as a philosophy, a rape action committee a study-action group on Kingston media's image of women, a study-action group on sexism in Kingston schools, a study group on women in literature, and an action group on the discrimination against women in the Kingston workforce.[54] The mixture of action with study groups was typical of early women's centres.

Most women's centres presented themselves as space for all women to use. When the Hamilton Women's Centre opened in the summer of 1973, they reported that 'although women's liberation has been in Hamilton for four years, this is the first time all women in the movement – houseworkers, workers, university and high school students, abortion activists, consciousness raisers, gay women, children's liberationists and socialists – have had a chance to get together in a central place, meet and work with each other.' They went on to declare that 'the centre itself takes no political positions.'[55] The Hamilton Women's Centre, like most across Ontario, saw itself as being able to bridge the gaps that had come to exist between various groups of women. To accomplish such bridging, many women's centres felt they had to avoid identifying themselves with a particular politic within the women's movement.

In contrast, the Windsor Women's Centre was begun in early 1973 by a group of socialist women who wanted a place that was explicit in having a class analysis. Originally a collective of six, these women came to realize that their socialist politic was alienating some women who wanted to be involved; with much trepidation, they opened the collective to other women who did not share their point of view. The enlarged collective came to understand that the centre's role would be one of working for change, but that members did not have to share a common analysis or strategy. In their Policy Statement for Windsor Women's Place they declared, 'The Women's Place is not an organization, but a co-ordinative force, an open movement tending to link together all ... women.'[56]

By 1972 the political focus had shifted from one of reconciling Marxism with the new insights into women's oppression to one of exploring women's oppression outside any male-defined political perspective.

There was a determined effort by some women to steer clear of traditional politics and focus on women politics (the personal is political). It was successful I believe. There were many tense moments when women with a traditional left political focus tried to steer the rest of the group their way, but no consensus ever developed and in fact this attempt was always rejected ... In Ottawa the women's liberation movement of the 70s was definitely focused on woman politics and not traditional politics and not Marxist.[57]

By February 1973 the Ottawa Women's Centre had made a decision not to associate itself with any particular political analysis, to the point of not assuming that women at the centre called themselves feminists. The centre's description of its atmosphere emphasized this stand: 'Women at the Centre have a commitment to maintaining a low-pressure atmosphere which permits one to be oneself. In general members resist being labelled in any way. However, feminist analysis is undertaken routinely by many of the members as an important part of their development. Regardless of whether or not a member accepts the term 'feminist,' the commitment of women at the Centre is to improving conditions and services for women in every aspect of life.'[58] In response to a letter from another local group in late 1972, the Ottawa Women's Centre proudly remarked on its openness to all women: 'The women who participate regularly in the running of the Ottawa Women's Centre feel that it is a unique endeavour. It is a place where any woman, regardless of her qualifications, can come and be herself.'[59] Like its Ottawa counterpart, the Thunder Bay Women's Centre saw itself as a 'central meeting place for Women of all groups to come to exchange ideas, cooperatively act on issues affecting them and to develop an overall sense of community among women regardless of class, religion, ethnicity, age, etc.'[60]

Although by 1973–4 the women's liberation movement had been transformed by the media into 'the women's movement,' and all types of feminists had been lumped together, feminists working in women's centres continued to see themselves as distinct from women's rights feminists. In 1980 the Ottawa newspaper *Upstream* looked back to the early years of feminism, discussing radical feminism in relation to women's rights, or reform, feminism:

We assume that the goal of the radical women's liberation movement is a socialist society of some form ... It aims to abolish the division of humanity on the basis of sex

... Reform feminists begin with the assumption that we have an egalitarian society ... They say that women have been handicapped by unequal pay, the double standard and confinement to a narrow role, but once these handicaps have been eliminated, women and men will be equally free.[61]

Two Ottawa groups reflected the separateness of the feminst activists and the women's rights groups in many Ontario cities. The Women's Resource Group (WRG), whose politics in retrospect would be labelled women's rights, began meeting sometime in 1971. One participant remembers that the group had a core of about ten women, the vast majority of whom were 'career women' in the public service, the media, and in politics. This group spent some time discussing a national advisory council on the status of women, but seems to have had difficulty finding a focus for its work. In assessing the group, one member said, 'I am sure valuable contacts were made.'[62] Another group of Ottawa women who were considered part of the women's movement began meeting in early 1972 to discuss women's liberation; those women decided to establish a women's centre in Ottawa. A description by a participant in both groups suggests that, unlike the WRG, women who became involved in the women's centre were, on the whole, married women with children who did not work outside the home. She remembers that 'generally the two groups consisted of very different types of women who just didn't mix.'[63]

In general, feminist activists were quite contemptuous of women's rights feminists, seeing them as women who had 'sold out' to the patriarchy. Occasionally that stereotype proved misleading, as the following example illustrates. One woman from Thunder Bay remembers being invited to a meeting of the Congress of Canadian Women to talk about the women's liberation movement.

When we arrived there it looked like any church tea or ethnic hall ... This was the Ukrainian Hall and it had little flowers on the table and everything and so we thought it was just another ethnic organization and we explained to the chairwoman what we were going to talk about and she said 'Oh, I don't think you should mention abortion, dear.' And all the women were older, like fifties or sixties. But we got a big shock when the chairwoman got up and she began to read the telegrams that they were sending to Trudeau to protest the Vietnam war. And the first one read 'Running dogs of American imperialist capitalism.' And it was like a complete mindshift, and you realized this wasn't the Ladies of the Whatever Society.[64]

What the women from the Thunder Bay Women's Liberation Movement had not realized was that the Congress of Canadian Women, founded in 1950, was a part of the old left and that these women had been political radicals long before some of their own members were born.

The strategy of a women's centre as an organizational headquarters for women's movement organizing necessarily focused women on funding issues. Many of the Ontario women's centres began with short-term government grants under the Opportunity for Youth and Local Initiatives Project initiatives. After those grants expired, women usually turned to the Women's Programme of the Secretary of State for funding. Funding and staff issues come to absorb much time and energy for those on women's centre collectives. As more decisions had to be made, women increasingly struggled to develop a feminist process for working together.

Women were not only grappling with new issues and trying to set up organizations for women, but also trying to run their meetings and their organizations in a new manner. Women understood that how they organized themselves would facilitate and/or limit their ability to make change. Those who came to the women's liberation movement with experience in organizations, whether on the left or in political parties and the church, spoke of feeling powerless in those organizations. Those who came to the women's movement as housewives, wives, and mothers also spoke of a feeling of powerlessness within the family. Wherever women came from they were determined that their new organizations would not recreate the inequalities they had previously experienced. The result was often a rejection of hierarchy, leadership, and theory. In their place, women substituted the idea that all women had 'an existing common consciousness, commitment and ability within the movement.'[65]

Women's liberation groups usually functioned with consensus decision-making, rotating all tasks among members to avoid a few members becoming the group leaders. Early in its life, the Thunder Bay Women's Centre noted that 'cooperation is the keynote of the organization and has worked perfectly to date.'[66] To make their point, the Women's Centre group decided to list more than fifty women's names when they applied for incorporation, instead of the usual hierarchy of president and other key office-holders. Women remember 'the excitement of working in new ways, of building collectives, not having leadership, hierarchy. There were lots of process discussions.'[67]

Two feminists who were trying to re-radicalize the women's movement in 1980 looked back over the earlier years and commented on the task women set for themselves: 'If our goal is a society in which power imbalances are not built into the relationships people have with one another, we cannot get there except by working toward it in groups that reflect as nearly as possible our

vision of what might be. We need a piece of the future action now.'[68]
Feminists in both the late 1960s and the 1970s were organizing for change. While many of the techniques and ideas were the same, there were differences in style among organizing practices of the women's liberation movement and differences in structure and membership. Overall, the late 1960s can be characterized as organizing in a very public, confrontational, theatrical manner. A few years later, feminists turned their focus to organizing spaces for themselves and events that reflected their own needs. Women also made a priority of how things were done; what would later be called 'feminist process.' The later women's movement would draw on both types of organizing.

FACING NEW CHALLENGES

As women's centres and other feminist organizations struggled to define a politic, develop strategy, and change Canada, they were facing some serious challenges from within the women's movement. The main challenges were to learn to deal with different views of women's oppression; to identify and organize around a range of issues, many of which were being named and explored; and, finally, to survive over the long term.

*Differing Political Analyses*

A common heritage in the left and the rallying cry of 'sisterhood' suggest a shared political analysis and strategy. In reality, however, women's political analyses and strategies varied widely. Feminists had to confront the fact that not all women understood issues in the same way and that they did not always agree on strategies for making change. Historians of the contemporary women's movement have identified three main types of political analysis in the women's movement – radical, liberal, and socialist. Although these labels are useful and necessary characterizations for scholars, they do not reflect the complexity of women's actual experiences as activists, especially in the women's liberation movement. While the labels reflect the different analyses of the origins of women's oppression, that theoretical understanding does not necessarily translate into different strategies or practices. In larger communities such as Toronto, the women's movement was broad enough to support a number of groups, and women could organize according to their different politics. In smaller centres, the number of women involved in the women's movement was fewer, and that contributed to a different understanding of how women organized around diverse political points of view.

Reflecting on this issue, a Thunder Bay woman remarked: 'We never labelled. I don't ever recall that. We didn't define ourselves as any particular branch of feminism. And the outside community just lumped us all together as "women's libbers."'[69]

In smaller communities women simply did not have the luxury of the numbers that would allow them to splinter into opposing political camps. In response to a question about different feminist currents, an Ottawa activist remembers that 'there weren't that many of us – we needed each other.'[70] A London feminist reflecting on this issue commented: 'When you try to work in a city like this with such a small number of people you are much less willing to alienate people than you might be in the large metropolis. You become extremely sensitive to the reactions you do get.'[71] Where feminists were few, they worked together and emphasized their solidarity against a larger, and usually hostile, community, rather than their different political analyses.

In large centres such as Toronto, women's liberation movement groups of this period broke apart over political disagreements. For example, women left the Toronto Women's Liberation Movement in 1969 to form the New Feminists because they were critical of the group's Marxist analysis. More women left in 1970 to form the Leila Khaled Collective because they wanted to work in a group with men and to focus on Third World solidarity. Also in 1970 a group of women left the New Feminists to form the Toronto Women's Caucus, because they felt abortion should be the central focus of organizing for women's liberation. Such splintering is not characteristic of smaller centres. Their lesser numbers made it imperative that women focus on the common political ground they shared and work from there. Perhaps the decrease in activity of women's liberation movement groups in 1971 was, in part, due to the difficulty of reconciling the different emerging political analyses.

Despite historians' fondness for currents, they had little practical meaning for most Ontario activists. Only those in large urban areas would have had experience with clearly labelled separate feminist politics. For most women's liberation activists, it was a case of 'us' – the feminists – versus 'them' – the rest of the world.

*Identifying the Issues, Expanding the Analysis*

In both the 1960s and the early 1970s, women were beginning to focus on the issues that would be central to the women's movement for years to come. Day care, abortion, and the politics of feminism dominated the newsletters of this period. Feminists brought their own personal experiences to CR groups, where they were explored and elaborated. They were often galvanized into action around a particular issues as a result of their own, or other women's, personal experiences. As one Thunder Bay activist explained:

I think a lot of us in Thunder Bay got involved in an issue, because at that stage we didn't have any analysis. I got involved in about 1971 because I worked for a group called Human and Welfare Rights. And what we started finding is that a lot of women would call just to find out what we were doing and then they would say 'I've got a problem and I need to talk to somebody.' And what it was, they were battered women. But it was not the same kind of identified problem; I had known the issue because of a neighbour who lived near me. What [our group] would do was put an ad in the paper that said something like 'are you being beaten by your husband, if so call this number.' At that time what we did, with our limited knowledge, was to get her out and if she wanted to stay, try to arrange a peace bond, which we didn't realize was ineffectual. That made me become involved in housing for women and what we know now as battered women. But I had no analysis of it, other than to think 'what a horrible thing to be married to a person who beats you.' I couldn't quite understand, I didn't even know if it was wrong, I just knew it must be awful. Because I was involved in that issue I went to a couple of conferences and I started to develop an understanding of the whys and the political and social and economic reasons around violence, but that was later.[72]

Her experience parallels that of many feminists. First they began with some kind of personal experience – their own or that of a friend – and added to that the realization that other women had similar experiences. They then took some kind of action to address the problem. As they met with success or resistance, women analysed what was happening and slowly began to build a bigger picture – an analysis – of the issue.

The issues addressed by the women's movement varied over time. In 1969–70 Thunder Bay women and others were, typically, working on birth control and abortion, day care, marriage and sex-role stereotyping. In addition, they were beginning to discuss women and work. By 1973–4 the issues had shifted somewhat, though all of the above were still on the feminist agenda. In its first few issues, the *Northern Woman Journal* covered crisis shelters, women in politics, Native women, equal pay, housework, women's studies, and lesbianism. While discussions of day care and abortion/birth control were still there, the articles suggest that sex-role stereotyping had moved off the agenda. Already by 1973–4 the women's movement was becoming more diverse in the issues it focused on, and more sophisticated in its understanding of what was needed.

Over time, we have come to see that the women's liberation movement voiced white, heterosexual, middle-class, and able-bodied assumptions and aspirations. That is not to say that the women who were active in those years were all white, heterosexual, middle class, or able-bodied. They were not. There were always lesbians, working-class women, women of colour, Native women, women with disabilities, older women, and others active in feminist organizations. However, these groups of women were not yet self-identified or organized autonomously as women with a double oppression, and hence were not in a position to voice their own needs, understandings, and aspirations in a coordinated manner within the context of the women's liberation movement.[73]

*Hanging in Together over the Long Term*

All women's organizations faced the challenge of trying to build a long-term movement. In communities such as Thunder Bay, there was much continuity of individuals and approaches as the women's liberation movement evolved into the women's movement of the 1970s. The Thunder Bay Women's Liberation Movement's key organizations, the Women's Centre and the *Northern Woman Journal*, have endured with many changes in membership, but have continued to the present. Other communities, such as Ottawa, have been marked by change. The women's centre and the newspaper lasted until 1980, and few if any local organizations have survived over the long term. Individual women have come and gone within the women's movement, with the net result that there is little sense of organizational and political continuity. Thunder Bay is the exception rather than the rule, but its experience offers some interesting insights into factors that contribute to successful organizing by women over the long term.

The women's liberation movement in Thunder Bay was always consciously and firmly anchored in a region – northwestern Ontario – and understood its own struggles and successes in terms of women in the whole region. In order to make those connections among women across northwestern Ontario, a group of Thunder Bay women received funding for a Northern Women's Conference held in April 1972. Organizers imagined that fifty or a hundred women would come; six hundred registered.[74] One activist who could not attend the conference, though she baked 'a million dozen butter tarts' for it, describes the impact on women: 'It was the first experience for women, they were just overwhelmed with other women's stories, other women's strength, it was a sense of celebration, of connecting, the very beginning of that connectedness and kind of groundswell. It has carried a lot of women for many years.'[75] Women and women's groups across the region of northwestern Ontario felt themselves linked. As one woman explained: 'These weren't artificial links ... When

we talk about Northwestern Ontario, I come from Northwestern Ontario,
I don't come from Thunder Bay, and there're real ties to communities in
terms of people's roots, so it wasn't ... an artificial or arbitrary reaching
out. People were reconnecting with towns in the regions. You felt a sense
of connection with these communities because you knew people who had
grown up there and are still connected to them.'[76] Another woman said,
'There's something about the geography; we're not part of Ontario, you
know.'[77] The region defined by women in northwestern Ontario was not
one constructed to get government grants; it represented an area where
women had roots and connections. Most knew what it was like to live in
very small communities – the isolation, the hunger for new ideas, the need
for support. The women's movement, through newsletters, newspapers,
conferences, and organizations, offered women across the region a means
to connect with each other, to network, to offer support, to build community, and to make change.

The Thunder Bay women's movement not only saw itself as part of a
regional community, but worked to translate that idea into concrete political
action. Women recount two stories that illustrate the depth of loyalty among
women in the northwest and the ways in which they translated that loyalty
into action:

The Violence Committee of [Northwestern Ontario Women's] Decade Council operated in a way which is truly a model. They got together and negotiated with the Province who wanted to give individual centres resources and said 'no, Red Lake needs it.
We are all giving our money to Red Lake.' And then the Province had to go along with
that. That committee set the agenda.

The other example is of Kenora Women's Place. The Province said, we have so
much money and we are going to divide it between the 7 existing shelters [in northwestern Ontario]. And so we met earlier that day and it took some persuading,
because there were some groups who really needed that money. But Kenora Women's
Place, who was not a shelter, was a woman's centre and a sexual assault centre and
they were going to close because they had no money. And by the time the bureaucracy walked in the entire group said, 'we don't want your money, give it all to
Kenora.' There was no program or anything for it and they got over $100,000 to buy
this building which now houses in Kenora the Women's Place and a resource library,
the Sexual Assault Centre and a variety of other programs.

I think it was the fact that the Violence subcommittee had worked together, there
was a real solidarity there and they said, 'yeah, we need that money, but Kenora needs
it most.' And so they were able to say 'you've got to give the money to Kenora.' There
is not a rational reason, other than the solidarity of the groups, for them to have the
money.[78]

The women's movement in Ottawa did not have a sense of itself as part of a region. As was the case in most cities, the women of Ottawa accepted the boundaries of the city and built their movement from those who were there, without a clear sense of the distinctiveness of their region. Ottawa differed from other Ontario cities in having a strong federal government presence. Records of the women's centre and other organizations do not indicate much focus on the federal government, though inevitably there was more than in other areas.

A sense of being different from Toronto may have linked women's liberation organizations in Ontario's medium-size cities more than any sense of regional solidarity. In a 1971 article on the London women's liberation movement, Leueen MacDonald commented:

I would like to say something about our relationship with Toronto, and what the Kingston women have referred to as Toronto imperialism. When women from Toronto come to visit, they often come in large numbers, which we did not ask for. The life-styles and responses which they have developed from living in Toronto where there are large numbers of people they can identify with are often very alienating to a small movement where every potential ally is crucial. Toronto women, perhaps unintentionally, often exhibit a kind of sophistication which tends to destroy our confidence, which seems to be telling us that no matter how far we have come, we haven't come far enough.[79]

MacDonald identified a key element in understanding the development of the women's liberation movement – size. As she stated, when there weren't many women, they learned to work together, around each other's differences. Whether that succeeded or not is likely determined by a number of factors, among them chance. In Thunder Bay, the sense of regional solidarity and the small size made working together a priority. Their success over the long term is a testament to the strength, determination, and generosity of the women themselves. In other Ontario cities, such as Ottawa, the women's movement has had no less impact and is still present, but the sense of continuity and community is different from Thunder Bay's.

CONCLUSION

The women's liberation movement emerged between 1966 and 1969 in Ontario, and quickly sprang up in cities and towns across the province. In the late 1960s it was a movement made up largely of women from the left who placed their understanding of feminism within a Marxist context. The tradition of organizing on the left influenced their approach to women's liberation and lent it a theatrical and very public character. After a brief lull in active organizing, the women's liberation movement re-emerged in late 1971 with a somewhat different character. No longer did women assume that in order to put forward a progressive politic it had to be within the context of Marxism. Women focused on *women's* liberation – they defined their politics from their own experiences as women. Organizing efforts were often focused on local women's centres, newspapers, and issue-specific women's groups. These are some differences in the two stages of the women's liberation movement; there were, however, also important continuities between the two stages. Organizations, newspapers, and individuals spanned the two periods, and many remained active into the 1980s and 1990s. The issues that were identified by the early women's liberation movement have since been clarified and put on the public agenda. The homogenous nature of the early women's liberation movement has also begun to be diversified.

The second wave of the women's movement did not emerge, as many second-wave feminists initially believed, spontaneously. Its roots reach back over the decades to the suffragists and beyond, to a rich history of strong women and women's organizations. There were certainly changes – in language, in issues, in ways of organizing – in the nature of the women's movements. It is important, however, to see those changes in light of the long history of women struggling to make change. The second wave of the women's movement built on that history and, at the same time, transformed it into a broad-based social and political movement.[80]

NOTES

Many women helped with this article. In particular, I would like to thank the women in Thunder Bay and Ottawa who agreed to be interviewed for this research; Women's Place/Place aux Femmes in Ottawa for sharing the records they hold with me; Anne Molgat for her support and careful editing; and Joy Parr for encouraging me to write this article.

1  The first clear instance in Ontario of women organizing *as women* in the manner that would come to be called women's liberation occurred in 1960 with the formation of the Voice of Women (VOW). Two of the goals of early VOW organizers were 'to unite women in concern for the future of the world' and 'to provide a means for women to exercise responsibility for the family of humankind.' See Nancy Adamson, Linda Briskin, Margaret McPhail, *Feminist Organizing for Change: The Contemporary Women's Movement in Canada* (Toronto: Oxford University Press 1988), 263–4).

2 Helen Levine, interview, 11 Aug. 1992.

3 Simone de Beauvoir's *The Second Sex* (New York: Alfred A. Knopf) had been available in French since 1949 and in English since 1952. Betty Friedan's *The Feminine Mystique* (New York: Dell Publishing) was published in 1963 and became the first widely read analysis of women's oppression in North America.

4 *Report of the Royal Commission on the Status of Women in Canada* (Ottawa: Information Canada 1970), vii.

5 See the files for the various groups at the Canadian Women's Movement Archives/Archives canadiennes du mouvement des femmes (CWMA/ACMF), Special Collections, Morriset Library, University of Ottawa; Adamson, Briskin and McPhail, *Feminist Organizing for Change*; Women's Press files (unpublished manuscripts), CWMA/ACMF; Isobel Lymbery, 'The Word of the New Feminists,' *Homemaker's Digest* 5, 4 (July/Aug. 1970), 6; A. Prentice et al., *Canadian Women: A History* (Toronto: Harcourt Brace Jovanovich 1988), 352–61; Sue Berlove and Liz Willick, *Building the Movement: From One Women's Centre to Another* (Waterloo: Kitchner-Waterloo Women's Place 1975); Moira Armour with Pat Staton, *Canadian Women in History: A Chronology* (Toronto: Green Dragon Press 1990); and *The Other Woman* 1, 2 (1972): 16.

6 There are too many Toronto groups to list them all; what appears here are the major groups.

7 *Women Unite!* (Toronto: Canadian Women's Educational Press 1971), 9.

8 Ibid., 10.

9 Angela Miles, *Feminist Radicalism in the 1980s* (Montreal: Culture Texts 1985), 4.

10 Ottawa *Upstream* 2, 4 (1978): 16.

11 Myrna Kostash, *Long Way from Home: The Story of the Sixties Generation in Canada* (Toronto: James Lorimer 1980), 186.

12 Ibid., 186.

13 Laurel Limpus, 'The History of the Toronto Women's Liberation Movement,' Feb. 1971, Women's Press file (unpublished manuscripts), CWMA/ACMF.

14 Levine interview.

15 Kostash, *Long Way from Home*, 182.

16 Limpus, 'History.'

17 Ibid.

18 Letter from Val Perkins to Dawn Haites, 27 Jan. 1971, New Feminists file, CWMA/ACMF.

19 *Thunder Bay Women's Liberation Newsletter*, 12 April 1970.

20 'Reaction,' ibid., 27 April 1970.

21 Kostash, *Long Way from Home*, 182.

22 Ibid.

23 See, for example, Varpu Lindstrom, *Defiant Sisters: A Social History of Finnish Immigrant Women in Canada* (Toronto: Multicultural History Society of Ontario

1992), and Joan Sangster, *Dreams of Equality: Women in the Canadian Left* (Toronto: McClelland & Stewart 1989).

24  'New Left,' *The Canadian Encyclopedia* (Edmonton: Hurtig 1985), 2: 1241.

25  Joan Baril, interview, 1 May 1992.

26  Shirley Greenberg, private correspondence, 18 Aug. 1992.

27  Leueen MacDonald, 'London Women's Liberation: A History,' Women's Press files (unpublished manuscripts), CWMA/ACMF.

28  'Women's Liberation Movement – Kingston, Ontario,' Women's Press files (unpublished manuscripts), CWMA/ACMF.

29  Limpus, 'History,'

30  Levine interview.

31  See Robin Morgan, ed., *Sisterhood Is Powerful: An Anthology of Writings from the Women's Liberation Movement* (New York: Random House 1970), for one of the earliest expressions of the notion of sisterhood. For a more recent reassessment, see Adamson, Briskin, McPhail, *Feminist Organizing for Change*, 217–27. Activists in this period did not naively believe that all women were the same. They were struggling to understand issues of race, class, and sexual orientation and how those intersected with gender. See, for example, Morgan, ed., *Sisterhood Is Powerful, Women's Unite!*, and many of the newspapers and newsletters of the 1968–1971 period.

32  Joan Baril, 'Some Herstory and a Goodbye,' *Northern Woman Journal* 7, 1 (1981): 11.

33  Greenberg correspondence.

34  MacDonald, 'London Women's Liberation.'

35  Lynne Teather, 'The Feminist Mosaic,' in Gwen Matheson, ed., *Women in the Canadian Mosaic* (Toronto: Peter Martin 1976), 324.

36  Prentice et al. *Canadian Women*, 353.

37  'Women's Liberation Movement – Kingston.'

38  Adamson, Briskin, McPhail, *Feminist Organizing for Change*, 46.

39  *Thunder Bay Women's Liberation Newsletter*, 11 May 1970, 1-2.

40  [Kingston] Women's Liberation, 'Abortion Caravan,' *This Paper belongs to the People* 1, 15 (29 April 1970): 4.

41  'Women's Liberation Movement – Kingston.'

42  MacDonald, 'London Women's Liberation.'

43  Pat Noonan, 'The Women's Movement, Windsor, May 1974,' Windsor Women's Place file, CWMA/ACMF.

44  Ibid.

45  'Report from Shirley Greenberg on her Visit to the Women's Place,' 1972, Ottawa Women's Centre files, Women's Place/Place aux femmes, Ottawa.

46  'Brief History of Women's Liberation in Kingston,' 13 Oct. 1973, Kingston Women's Centre file, CWMA/ACMF.

47  Eleanor McDonald, 'Women's Liberation Movement – Sarnia, Ontario' (May 1971), Sarnia Women's Centre file, CWMA/ACMF.

48 Adamson, Briskin, McPhail, *Feminist Organizing for Change*, 198–205.
49 Joan Baril, personal correspondence, 6 Dec. 1992.
50 Laurel Limpus, 'History.'
51 Greenberg correspondence.
52 Liz Willick, 'Introduction: The K–W Woman's Place,' in Berlove and Willick, *Building the Movement*, 3.
53 'Brief History of Women's Liberation in Kingston.'
54 Ibid.
55 'The Hamilton Page,' *The Other Woman* 1, 6 (July/Aug. 1973): 4.
56 Policy Statement and 'Windsor Women's Centre: A History,' Windsor Women's Centre file, CWMA/ACMF.
57 Greenberg correspondence.
58 Ottawa Women's Centre files, 1973, Women's Place/Place aux femmes, Ottawa.
59 Ibid., Correspondence, 2 Nov. 1972.
60 Northern Women's Centre files, Secretary of State Office, Thunder Bay.
61 *Upstream* 4, 3 (1980): 4–5.
62 Greenberg correspondence.
63 Ibid.
64 Baril interview.
65 Berlove and Willick, *Building the Movement*, 5.
66 Northern Women's Centre files, Secretary of State Office, Thunder Bay.
67 Margaret Phillips/Fiona Karlstedt, interview, 2 May 1992.
68 *Upstream* 4, 3 (1980): 5.
69 Phillips/Karlstedt interview.
70 Levine interview.
71 MacDonald, unpublished manuscript, Women's Press files, CWMA/ACMF.
72 Dawn St Amand, interview, 1 May 1992.
73 Separate organizing of groups of women based on racial, ethnic, or language identities existed. I am arguing that these groups had not yet chosen to organize *within* the context of the women's liberation movement.
74 Phillips/Karlstedt interview.
75 St Amand interview.
76 Phillips/Karlstedt interview.
77 Ibid.
78 Leni Untinen/Lisa Bengtsson, interview, 1 May 1992.
79 MacDonald, 'London Women's Liberation.'
80 Thanks to Judith Bennett for her insights into the fundamental continuities within women's history at the same time that many changes in women's lives are occurring. 'Change and Continuity in Women's History,' lecture given at Carleton University, 30 Oct. 1992.

LINDA CARDINAL

# Making a Difference: The Theory and Practice of Francophone Women's Groups, 1969–82

We are rooted in language, wedded, have our beings in words. Language is also a place of struggle. The oppressed struggle in language to recover ourselves – to rewrite, to reconcile, to renew.

bell hooks, *Talking Back*, 29

The Canadian women's movement includes organizations, ideologies, and groups of people that have, until recently, been ignored. Research on women's groups across Canada has begun to question this indifference within the predominantly white and Anglo woman's movement. However, women from minority groups – Black, Jewish, Mennonite, Ukrainian, Indian, Chinese, as well as women from Quebec and many more – have all, at one point or another in their development, addressed issues of how they related to the women's movement and its white, Anglo-Saxon, middle-class, and Protestant roots. In fact, feminists from the non-dominant groups have taken on the task of theorizing about the importance of nationalism and ethnicity, immigration, race, class, and language in relation to women.[1] Francophone feminists living in Ontario are part of that movement. Since its beginnings, feminism in French Ontario has been articulated around more than one form of domination – most importantly, language, ethnicity, and region, or what has been called women's status of double and/or triple inferiority. Feminists have also been torn between one form of oppression and another, as if they had to choose. Still, since the 1970s, Franco-Ontarian feminism has evolved predominantly as a discourse of *différance* within the *différence*.

My purpose in this article is to concentrate on the development of francophone feminism in Ontario during the second wave of the women's movement. I want to analyse and discuss its impact on traditional Franco-Ontarian women's groups for the period 1969–1982. Other contributors in this volume have attempted to theorize about women's situation in other gendered systems of social relations such as race and class. In this particular case, the study of francophone women's groups will force us to address, more specifically, the relationship between language and feminism, language and the women's movement.

I will begin by giving some background information on the Franco-Ontarian community, looking at its demography through the twentieth century, its geography, and its economic activities. I will also present some general historical information about the community's organizations, including the main women's groups, stating their goals, major activities, and membership. In the second part I will present a more in-depth discussion of Franco-Ontarian feminism – its political origins, practices, and impact on Franco-Ontarian women and society. I will provide a relatively intimate portrait of feminism in French Ontario by focusing on Carmen Paquette, a well-known activist in the community, and her work. She is probably the person who, with her friends and colleagues Lise Latremouille, Jacqueline Pelletier, and many more, made feminism a reality. I decided to write this article partly as an exercise in remembering her work. I will present the specific projects she made possible in the community and their impact on more mainstream organizations such as the Union culturelle des franco-ontariennes, the Association des fermières de l'Ontario, and the Association canadienne-française de l'Ontario. I will also look at some feminist organizations in which Paquette was active or in touch, such as the Regroupement des Ontaroises de l'Est in the Ottawa region, Franco-femmes in Hearst, and the Regroupement des femmes du Sud de l'Ontario. Paquette was active in founding a national group for francophone feminists, the Réseau national action éducation femmes, which I will also present briefly.

In the final section, I will attempt to theorize about gender and francophone rights and to look more specifically at the way in which they were discussed by Franco-Ontarian feminists. These feminists had to cope with the paradox of becoming political individuals in their own regions, theorizing and working to transform women's lives, while at the same time they were being ignored by the dominant, white, Anglo, middle-class women's movement.

Although I will try to address the specificity of francophone feminism, I am not looking at all the women's organizations or projects that came into being in this period.[2] I will concentrate on those that have contributed the most in defining feminism in French Ontario, that have proposed a vision, a politics, or a specific type of action. Unfortunately, little has been written on francophone women living outside Quebec.[3] In general, there are few documents, archives, articles, reports, or records of women's voices and experiences. This article attempts to relate, discuss, and understand what it meant to be a francophone woman and feminist in Ontario between 1969 and 1982.

## THE CONTEXT

### The Franco-Ontarian community

Historians relate that francophones settled in Ontario as early as the seventeenth century,[4] as a direct consequence of the fur trade and the colonization process. The first Franco-Ontarian communities were established in the Detroit-Windsor area. A group of sixty families settled in the Georgian Bay area, and seventy-five families founded Penetanguishene. Francophones from Quebec began to arrive in Ontario around 1850 and established communities along the Outaouais River, mostly in the area known today as Prescott and Russell. In 1883 other francophones from Quebec settled in the northern part of the province – a migration movement prompted by the Quebec clergy in its attempts to maintain the agricultural way of life, big families, and devotion to the church among the francophone population.

According to Choquette, Ontario's francophone population was approximately 4000 in 1819 and 158,671 by 1901.[5] The overall population of the province at the time increased from 120,000 in 1819 to 2,182,947 in 1901, when Franco-Ontarians represented 7.3 per cent of the total. The Franco-Ontarian population increased steadily, reaching 482,045 in 1971.[6] Thereafter, the French-speaking minority did not register any significant growth,[7] declining proportionaely to the Ontarian population even while increasing in absolute numbers. As Dallaire and Lachapelle write, 'the minority language group is therefore not evolving at the same pace as the rest of the population.'[8] Still, in 1981, francophones represented 5.5 per cent of the province's population, but in some regions they are five times more than their provincial average. They constitute the majority in counties such as Prescott and Russell, and 15.3 per cent of the population in eastern Ontario.[9] Francophones are an important group (25.6 per cent) in the north eastern part of the province, but they make up only 4.2 per cent of the north western region and 4.5 per cent in the southern part of the province. Major cities for Franco-Ontarians are Ottawa and Sudbury, and regional centres include Cornwall, Hawkesbury, Hearst, North Bay, Sturgeon Falls, and Timmins.

While the Franco-Ontarian population occupies specific geographical areas, it also has a distinct socioeconomic character – one that is marginalized from decision-making centres and from the economic heart of the province in southern Ontario. More specifically, during the 1960s and 1970s

Franco-Ontarians were workers or farmers with low levels of schooling, involved in declining sectors of the economy where there were few possibilities of social mobility. Franco-Ontarians, for the most part men, had small and medium farms, especially in the eastern part of the province, where only big farms survived the modernizing process, while others contracted large debts in an attempt to become more business-oriented. In the north, men worked in mines and in paper mills, while in the south they contributed to the branch-plant economy. Franco-Ontarians also had a lower middle-class population of teachers and service sector workers, as well as a small middle-class group of lawyers and physicians – professions highly valued in the community. A very small number of people, the most well known being Robert Campeau and Paul Desmarais, constituted the Franco-Ontarian business class.[10] This profile has not changed much in the 1980s and the 1990s.[11]

During the 1960s and the 1970s, francophone women mostly worked at home, where they still had large families, often six or more children.[12] When women did paid work, one out of three had a job in the lower strata of the service sector – for example as office and clerical workers, hairdressers, and waitresses. In 1981 they still represented 65 per cent of all francophone workers in those sectors. Francophone women also become teachers and nurses, the only professions that allowed them a relatively decent income.

Francophone women experienced a double or triple work day. Committed to their families, they remained the main person responsible for the household when they worked outside the home. Moreover, during the 1960s and the 1970s, francophone women were still devoted Catholics, collecting money for the parish, cooking for the priest, cleaning the church, and organizing community celebrations.

Thus, as a group, Franco-Ontarians were and are ordinary people, not wealthy, with distinct patterns of economic underdevelopment. The population is mostly based in areas where the economy relies on a declining agricultural sector and vulnerable natural resource-based industries. Rates of illiteracy are twice as high in the francophone community as in the non-francophone population, the result of a long history of discrimination. The impact on women was probably more significant than on men, who with less schooling than women, could still find relatively well-paying jobs in the forest or mine industries. Women were forced into very low-income jobs. Nevertheless, Franco-Ontarians also had their own elite, who were mainly active in the professions. Still, Franco-Ontarians were not participating in the more scientific and techological professions such as engineering, computer programming, and physics.

*Franco-Ontarian Organizations*

Notwithstanding their difficult economic situation, Franco-Ontarians had a well-established network of groups, most of which were dominated by the small middle class. Between 1969 and 1982 the most active mainstream groups were the Association canadienne-française de l'Ontario (ACFO), the Union des cultivateurs de l'Ontario, the Union culturelle des franco-ontariennes, the Association des fermières de l'Ontario, Direction-Jeunesse, and the Fédération des élèves des secondaires franco-ontariens. Women were also members of the Fédération nationale des femmes canadiennes-françaises and, as of 1975, ACFO took part in the newly founded Fédération des francophones hors Quebec.[13] The feminist groups mentioned earlier in the article also belong here, even though they were mostly founded between 1977 and 1982.

These organizations constitute what we might call the Franco-Ontarian legacy. Their main characteristics are those of struggle for francophone rights and involvement in the development of a community respecting the values of the Catholic Church. However, following the Second World War, mainly during the 1960s and 1970s, the community's organizations, like those in Canadian society generally, witnessed some important transformations. Strongly influenced by such national events as the Royal Commission on National Development in the Arts, Letters and Sciences (Massey Commission, 1949–51), the Royal Commission on Bilingualism and Biculturalism (Laurendeau-Dunton Commission, 1963–71), and Quebec's independance movement, a cultural awakening (backed by some financial support from the federal, Quebec, and Ontario governments) led to some important changes within the Franco-Ontarian community. Its population became active in the creation of francophone radio stations, theatre groups, community and cultural centres, new youth groups, and feminist groups.

Quebec's political and cultural awakenings also forced francophones to rethink who they were as a people. Quebec no longer wanted to identify with the traditional French Canada, including the million francophones living outside their province. Moreover, the French-Canadian identity was associated with submissiveness to Anglo rule, to traditionalism and elitism.[14] This situation led to an important identity crisis among French Canadians. As a consequence, Franco-Ontarians[15] decided to concentrate their energy on understanding their own provincial history of discrimination, thus developing a new sense of history. The latter became the locus of their 'new' identity – the Franco-Ontarian identity. The development of a specific Franco-Ontarian identity became an issue within most mainstream organizations, including women's groups.

*The Association canadienne-française de l'Ontario*

French Ontario's main organization has been the Association canadienne-française de l'Ontario (ACFO) since 1910, when it was founded as the Association canadienne-française des enseignants de l'Ontario. Its first president, Napoléon Antoine Belcourt, came from Toronto as a lawyer and was known for his work with the Ottawa Separate School Board. A friend of Sir Wilfrid Laurier, Belcourt is seen as one of the first Franco-Ontarian leaders.[16]

Briefly, ACFO was founded as a reaction to harassment from the Ontario government over the quality of the province's French schools. In fact, from 1886 to 1925, francophones in Ontario were the target of an anti-catholic and francophobic campaign initiated by the Orange Lodge and supported by conservatives in government who had espoused their views. Divisions between the Irish and the French bishops, both struggling for control of the church and the separate school boards in the province, also contributed to the growth of the organization.[17] When the newly elected Conservative government ruled in 1912 that English would, in future, be the only language allowed in Ontario schools (Bill 17), ACFO become involved in a bitter struggle against what it felt was an unjust treatment of francophones. The organization also founded *Le Droit*[18] to keep its population, and other francophones in the country, informed of the way Franco-Ontarians were being treated by their government. The Bill was modified in 1927 after much lobbying and mobilization by the community and the ACFO. However, only in 1944 was Bill 17 taken out of the government's statutes, and it was not until 1968 that Franco-Ontarians gained the right to have French high schools.[19]

From the start, the clergy did not encourage the participation of women in ACFO. It believed that gender-mixed organizations would cause problems by distracting men from their work![20] The association also had a youth wing, the Association des jeunes franco-ontariens.

In 1968 ACFO took the word *enseignants* out of its name, in order to commit itself to community development as well as to struggling for educational rights. It gave itself a decentralized structure, with regional committees in most centres in French Ontario and a central office in Ottawa. ACFO became fully funded through the federal government's citizenship program managed by the Secretary of State.[21] Cultural animators or community development officers, also financed by the federal government, were hired by ACFO across the province. At that time, ACFO also ran the first Franco-Ontarian festival in Vanier.

In short, ACFO focused on community development during the 1960s and the 1970s, while keeping its identity as an organization mainly concerned with francophone rights and with education. It was also primarily a male-dominated group with only superficial acknowledgment of women's issues. Although ACFO elected its first woman leader, Gisèle Richer, in 1976, it has done very little to attract women to participate. It has always taken women for granted, as volunteers and as unconditional supporters of the Franco-Ontarian struggle.[22]

### The Union catholique des cultivateurs franco-ontariens

The Union catholique des cultivateurs franco-ontariens (UCCFO) is another important association that contributed to the community's traditions of solidarity and struggle. Franco-Ontarian farmers were first active in the United Farmers Association of Ontario, founded in 1914, and the United Farmers Cooperative Company. In 1924 they organized their own group, in Ottawa, after the collapse of the United Farmers Association. With the support of the Quebec Catholic Union of Farmers, ACFO, and Le Droit, a group of four hundred men and women founded the Union catholique des cultivateurs franco-ontariens. The Quebec farmers' association also gave UCCFO a full page in its well-known newspaper, La Terre de Chez Nous, for a regular column.

The union's mandate was mainly concerned with promoting the agricultural sector through the establishment of cooperatives and credit unions. UCCFO wanted cooperative values to be taught in school and scientific knowledge disseminated widely to farmers. It also urged the government to approve a plan for a francophone agricultural college.[23] In 1936 the union started a local group in Sudbury and, in 1937, a women's section was founded in Ottawa, the Union catholique des fermières de l'Ontario (see below). In 1945 the association dropped the word catholic from its name.[24]

In 1947 UCCFO had twenty-seven cooperatives and 3094 members, with assets of more than $20 million.[25] During the 1960s and the 1970s, the organization became involved in the Canadian Institute for Adult Education in order to make adult education more accessible to Franco-Ontarian farmers. In 1981 the Franco-Ontarian community finally got its agricultural college, based in Alfred, in eastern Ontario.

### The Union catholique des fermières de l'Ontario, the Union culturelle des franco-ontariennes, and the Association des fermières de l'Ontario

The specific context of Franco-Ontarian women's groups starts in 1937, when farm women organized their own section in UCCFO, with its own secretariat and activities. Based in eastern Ontario, the section was led by Mrs Joseph Lacasse from Wendover[26] and had a mandate to support family life in rural areas, to teach women how to cook, and sew, and to break farm women's feeling of isolation. Its motto was 'Aime Dieu, la terre et ton foyer.'[27] In 1962 the women's section became the Union catholique des fermières de l'Ontario (Union) and organized its first provincial congress, to which women came from both the eastern and the northern parts of Ontario. Like its brother organization, the union wanted adult education for its members, especially training sessions in domestic science subsidized by the Youth and Recreation Ministry.[28] The union also became active in teaching domestic science in schools and, more generally, in promoting the education of young women living in rural areas.

In the late 1960s, it became difficult for the organization to recruit new members, and its name, with its Catholic and rural affiliations, became an issue. For some, the name was too restrictive and did not help to recruit women living in urban and semi-urban areas; for others, things were fine as they were. Consequently, in 1968, at what became the union's last annual general meeting, the organization split into two factions. Each went its own way to give birth to two new organizations: the Union culturelle des franco-ontariennes and the Association des fermières de l'Ontario.

*The Birth of the Union culturelle des franco-ontariennes*

In 1969, under the leadership of Estelle Huneault, the union officially changed its name to Union culturelle des franco-ontariennes (UCFO) with the hope of attracting more women from across the province. The union replaced the words 'catholic' with 'cultural,' and 'fermières' with 'Franco-Ontarian.' During the 1970s and the 1980s, UCFO leaders also realized that their new organization could not focus on the traditional family and community values as defined by Catholicism or on urging women to be devoted to the church. According to one of UCFO's leaders, Ethel Côté, the organization had to start addressing women's issues per se, thus recognizing that women were individuals and citizens with specific needs and not just mothers.[29]

Although the new organization was challenging its rural heritage, it remained firmly based in rural and semi-rural areas, with a membership of more than three thousand women. In 1989 UCFO had more than seventy groups based in six areas: Cochrane-Hearst-Kapuskasing, Sudbury-Nipissing, Timiskaming-Timmins, Windsor-Essex-Kent, Prescott-Glengarry, and Russell-Carleton-Stormont.[30]

*The Association des fermières de l'Ontario*

The Association des fermières de Ontario (AFO) also claims its origins in the union. It was founded by seven groups from eastern Ontario which decided not to join the movement led by UCFO. The association insisted on the rural affiliation of its members and adopted the *moissonneuse* as its symbol. Members were involved, for the most part, in promoting women's crafts and in displaying them at agricultural exhibitions. They also organized fund-raising activities, such as annual bingo games and fairs for the church. In the late 1970s AFO, like UCFO, became involved in organizing training sessions for its members, teaching them about farm management, leadership, and health as well as about such issues as the status of farm women.

*The Fédération nationale des femmes canadiennes-françaises*

The Fédération nationale des femmes canadiennes-françaises (FNFCF) was founded in 1914 by Almanda Walker-Marchand, a French-Canadian women of Irish descent living in Ottawa.[31] She was married to a relatively well-off French-Canadian with important connections in the federal government.

The FNFCF was based mostly in Ottawa, with an active Ontarian section. However, Walker-Marchand travelled regularly to the West to organize more sections and recruit more members. The FNFCF had no sections in Quebec, where the Société Saint-Jean Baptiste was active under the leadership of Marie Gérin-Lajoie, with women only as members.

During the Second World War the fédération was involved in war work. It engaged in charitable activities, sewing and knitting for French-Canadian soldiers, cooking pastries, and collecting books for them. The FNFCF also supported francophone linguistic and educational rights, becoming active in the struggle against Bill 17, and supported women in Quebec who were demanding the right to vote.

In the thirty years following the war the FNFCF became an Ontarian organization exclusively, centred in Ottawa. This focus created a lot of resentment among members living outside the province of Ontario, and eventually forced the organization to change its constitution to become more representative of groups from the Maritimes and the West.

From 1975 until the end of the 1980s, the fédération went through some important restructuring and ideological transformations, becoming more feminist, with younger leaders as president. At the time, the organization had seven hundred individual members, plus sixty-four sections and thirteen regional councils.[32] The FNFCF gradually became the speaker for francophone women living outside Quebec, as it represented women at the Fédération des Francophones hors Quebec and participated in a variety of women's events.

In all spheres of activities, then, Franco-Ontarian women's history is tied to the community's destiny as a minority group. Women's groups are part of a specific heritage based in an agricultural way of life, with family and religious values dominating while promoting adult education and training. This lifestyle taught women to be servants to their husband, their children, the clergy, and the community. Men also served the community, but in their capacity as leaders and prominent figures, while women submitted to male authority. Nevertheless, the changing pattern of economic development amd the cultural and political awakening of Franco-Ontarians served as important catalysts for a new female consciousness. It is within that context that Franco-Ontarian feminism confronted the agricultural and religious heritage of the community and made a difference.

MAKING A DIFFERENCE: FRANCO-ONTARIAN FEMINISM

*The Theory and Practice of Franco-Ontarian Feminism*

Traditional women's groups were an important constituency and ground for the development of Franco-Ontarian feminist practice. Feminism was brought into the community by a group of young francophone women, active in adult education and inspired by New Left ideas. From that group, Carmen Paquette, a well-known Ottawa feminist activist, was a key person for the dissemination of feminist ideas in the community. In the mid-1970s, she was a community development officer hired by Algonquin College to work in a Franco-Ontarian neighbourhood. In 1977–8 she became coordinator of the first feminist project in French Ontario, Pro-femmes. This project was meant to assist traditional women's groups across Ontario in their restructuring and reorganizing and in becoming involved in community action. In 1981 Paquette participated in the Regroupement des Ontaroises de l'Est (ROE), a group of feminists committed to consciousness-raising and organizing around women's issues. Simultaneously, she became active in founding the Réseau national action éducation des femmes, a national group for francophone feminists involved in adult education.

With other feminists, Paquette invited ACFO to become more sensitive to gender issues; they also asked Anglo feminists to recognize the specificity of francophone women's needs. She participated in meetings of the National Action Committee on the Status of Women, the Canadian Congress for Learning Opportunities for Women, and the Canadian Research Institute for the Advancement of Women, thus acting as an important link between the Anglo women's movement and francophone women. She also met feminists in Quebec and kept in touch with them. Given this impressive record of activities in such a short period of time (five years), it seems fair to say that Carmen Paquette was a key person in making feminism a reality in French Ontario.

Other well-known Franco-Ontarian feminists at the time were Lise Latremouille and Jacqueline Pelletier. Paquette used to call them 'La gang du chemin Montréal' (in Vanier), from the location of their work. Latremouille set up Ottawa's first Women's Credit Union,[33] while Pelletier became a well-known journalist and speaker and a founder of Le tablier déposé, francophone women's first feminist magazine.[34]

Feminists could also be found at the University of Ottawa, at the Collège universitaire de Hearst, at Glendon College in Toronto, and in government service. Groups that came out of those circles are Franco-femmes in Hearst and the Réseau des femmes du Sud de l'Ontario. Some feminists from the University of Ottawa participated in the Regroupement des Ontaroises de l'Est. Thus, the birth of a specific Franco-Ontarian feminism took place in community colleges, universities, and government bureaucracies. Francophone feminism, like most of the women's movement in Canada, has a white-middle-class base, with women coming from both rural and urban communities.

Franco-Ontarian feminism is also rooted in a tradition of consciousness-raising, coming as it does from the New Left and the adult education movement. It is important to recall that Algonquin College, like many other groups or institutions at the time, was receiving funds from the federal government's citizenship program to promote community development. In 1967 the Ontario government recommended that Algonquin College became bilingual, to better respond to the needs to the francophone population. It is in that context that Carmen Paquette and others were hired as community developers by the college.

Paquette worked, more specifically, with Ottawa's francophone community located in the lower part of the city (the Basse-ville). She had been trained in community development, and her work consisted mainly in politicizing people through consciousness-raising activities and locally based organizing around day-to-day issues and individual life-experiences. She encouraged people to be active citizens by recognizing that the personal was political.

As such, Paquette acknowledged being influenced by the Civil Rights and Black Power movements from the United States, as well as national liberation and popular movements from Africa and Latin America. Those movements

had a specific approach to social change: they politicized people through consciousness-raising about their lives. With Pro-femmes and, later on, the
Regroupement des Ontaroises de l'Est, Paquette devoted most of her time to
working with women. Her theory was still based on the axiom, the personal
is political, although her practice became feminist community development.[35]

## Pro-femmes

Pro-femmes was structured to promote community action by and for women
and to help women's groups consolidate and recruit members. It was this
project, as well as Carmen Paquette's commitment to feminism, that helped
organizations such as UCFO and AFO address contemporary challenges.

Pro-femmes's mandate was 'la formation, l'information et le regroupement' [training, resources, and organizing].[36] The training took place in
activities and conferences addressing gender issues. The main resource provided for women was a kit, used extensively by groups. The organizing
involved meeting with organizations such as UCFO and AFO to discuss how
to better recruit members.

### Organizing

Pro-femmes was primarily responding to a need identified by Franco-Ontarian women's groups for more efficiency and consolidation.[37] Groups such as
UCFO and AFO were going through important ideological changes. Pro-
femmes helped them implement those changes, and taught them how to
restructure their organizations and to recruit new and younger members. It
was not an easy task for Paquette, since their structures were dominated by
the priests.

The priest often attended meetings of traditional women's groups or
opened them with a small religious ceremony or prayer. Obviously, his presence would be felt as well as his authority. Paquette did not agree with this
practice. She was also convinced that organizations like UCFO could no
longer focus solely on supporting the family and the parish if they wanted
new members; women had to redirect their energy towards themselves and
other women. Consequently, Paquette urged UCFO and AFO leaders to
attend to concerns such as budgets, health, leadership, local politics, nutrition,
pensions, and pornography. In trying to help groups like the UCFO adapt to
the changing conditions within the community, Paquette faced resistance
from the clergy, whose ideology strongly influenced women's groups. This
resistance made Paquette look at her work as being revolutionary. Arch-

bishop Plourde, from the Ottawa-Carleton diocese, in turn was convinced that she and her colleagues were communists![38]

Resources
The main resource or tool developed by Pro-femmes was a kit to be used by women's groups.[39] It informed them of programs and services available to women in their area, neighbourhood, communities, and the province. It explored different ways for women to get more training and to define and express their needs to the concerned institutions. Thus, women's groups were informed about their rights and were invited to write to ministers or to civil servants for information on different programs in place for women. Paquette made sure that women knew that the government had money for development in issues such as training and recycling and in fund-raising for women's centres.

The kit also recommended that women get together to discuss leadership, training, continuing education, and self-esteem. It explained how to do workshops. In short, whatever the activities, Pro-femmes was playing a key role in encouraging women to speak about the reality of their lives and in urging them to organize around it, thus creating a demand for new groups or for the traditional ones to respond to new needs. Pro-femmes's kit could always serve as a point of departure for more discussion or consciousness-raising, thereby helping to address the personal as political.

Training
Pro-femmes had three working committees: one for information; another for political action; and the third and most active for adult education. This education committee provided women with information on retraining programs and on training more generally.[40] Pro-femmes encouraged women to seek paid work and to become re-entry students.

Training activities were organized around health issues, community action, and the economy.[41] In 1977 Paquette helped organize a meeting in Plantagenet, where 125 women discussed rural women's issues such as their status on the farm. Others meetings were held in Hawkesbury in 1979 and in Cornwall in 1980. In 1980 Paquette also organized sessions to interest women in municipal politics and to encourage them to run as candidates. In 1981 she worked with women from northern Ontario to plan 'La rencontre des femmes du Nord,' at which Pro-femmes attempted to organize young Franco-Ontarian women.[42] Such an event allowed discussions about the 'macho' attitudes of the men working in the mills and the mines, and about community life and its exlusion of single people or couples without children.

*Pro-femmes's Transformative Impact on Women*

Notwithstanding the fact that traditional women's groups would not identify explicitly with feminism, it is clear that they were not outside its influence. With the support of Pro-femmes, traditional groups did start addressing women's issues per se, thus recognizing that they were individuals and citizens and not only mothers committed to their families. In the early 1980s UCFO worked at translating this idea into action with a project called Nouveau départ. As well, AFO became active in two projects: first, the concerns of women in farm management and, second, the need for a resource centre for francophone women living in the Prescott-Russell and Glengarry counties – both being ways to implement the organization's new awareness of women's needs.

*Nouveau départ*

Of equal importance to Pro-femmes was the Nouveau-départ project to develop training sessions for housewives seeking work outside the home. The program already existed in Quebec, where it helped women at home learn how to evaluate their abilities and to use them in a new career. UCFO lobbied Algonquin College, the University of Ottawa, the Prescott-Russell Catholic School Board, and a variety of women's groups for support in setting up the program first in French Ontario and, then, in all the other francophone communities outside the province of Quebec. The program has been a success story, attracting in Ontario alone around eight hundred women to its sessions between 1982 and 1987.[43]

Nouveau départ served as a tool to evaluate 'women's work,' thus teaching women to recognize that their work was worth more than they thought. Women developed portfolios in which they listed their activities and learned how to evaluate them.[44] The project acted as a catalyst in a process of self-evaluation that could become painful, sometimes leading to a complete re-evaluation of their lives and, as was often the case, their marital relationships. In fact, Nouveau-départ prompted changes in women's lives. In a survey of the impact the program had on women, 90 per cent said that it changed something in their lives.[45] It also brought women more confidence in themselves.[46]

*AFO's Surveys*

Also inspired by Pro-femmes, younger AFO members like Laurence Cardinal and Louise Myner, both presidents of the organization at different times during the 1970s and early 1980s, urged farm women to become more aware of their rights within the family business. Myner coordinated a study of farming women who were managers of farms.[47] Women began to recognize their need to enlarge their scope of activity on farms and to gain more independance; they argued that women should seek co-ownership of farms with their husbands and that they had to learn to be more assertive.

In 1982 Myner, then AFO president, sponsored another study that was larger in scope than the first one. With a group of university students, she collected data about the social needs of Franco-Ontarian women living in Prescott and Glengarry counties, where most AFO members resided.[48] The survey led to the creation of a resource centre for francophone women in Hawkesbury, but also called for other services such as day-care centres, and information on health issues, sexuality, violence against women, and nutrition.

Inspired by Pro-femmes, Nouveau-départ and the AFO's surveys were other ways of doing consciousness-raising while making sure that women's work would get recognition. Programs such as Nouveau-départ would help women with a fragile sense of self go beyond a mere understanding of themselves as victims of a specific system. It would try to bridge the fact that they were victims with the necessity of individually doing something about it. Nouveau-départ concentrated on building women's strength and capacity to make decisions for themselves and encouraged them to be active in their community. AFO's projects were perhaps more collectively focused because they involved securing new resources for women.

*The End of Pro-femmes and the 'Coming Out' of the Feminist Community*

Pro-femmes ceased to exist in 1981. Its three main godmothers, the Fédération des femmes canadiennes-françaises, the Union culturelle des franco-ontariennes, and the Association des fermières de l'Ontario, claimed they were ready to be in charge of their own business, training, and self-management,[49] and ACFO stopped funding the program. Without Pro-femmes, it was difficult to see who would do the groundwork encouraging younger women to join organized groups. The feminist community from Algonquin College protested ACFO's action at a 1981 conference on the theme 'Savoir c'est pouvoir,' for which Latremouille was an organizer.[50] But their protest was not heard and Pro-femmes ceased to exist.[51]

The attempt to save the organization was part of a more ambitious project to rally Franco-Ontarian women from eastern Ontario, continuing Paquette's work in adult education, consciousness-raising, and organizing. The organizers of 'Savoir c'est pouvoir,' women from the Continuing Education division at Algonquin College, thought that women who had learned to act collectively 'could create services, improve their situation and increase their individual and collective power.'[52] The conference attracted more than four hundred women and produced sixty-three resolutions,[53] covering all the aspects of women's lives that had been discussed in the ten workshops organized for the event: day care, economics, education, feminism, health, politics, resources, sexism in publicity, violence, and work.[54] The conference also led to the creation of the Regroupement des Ontaroises de l'Est (ROE), to insure the implementation of the resolutions.[55] In doing so, 'Savoir c'est pouvoir' meant another step towards the development of a more women-centred politics in French Ontario.

However, ROE had a short, one-year existence, 1981–2.[56] It had a substantial program and obviously could not do everything it had on its agenda. Its members channelled their energies into three projects: a Centre d'accès francophone pour femmes (CAF–francophone Women's Access Centre) begun in March 1982; a Banque de ressources pour femmes (Women's resource centre); and the '25 heures du ROE,' an explicitly feminist conference also held in 1982. While no information seems to be preserved on the resource bank and the '25 heures du ROE,'[57] CAF, which still exists today, described itself as a group that provided feminist resources to Franco-Ontarian women as well as a place for political action.[58] More specifically, CAF wanted to give francophone women from eastern Ontario the tools necessary for their own personal and collective growth, thus continuing the work of Pro-femmes in a more autonomous form.[59] CAF also published a newsletter on issues related to women's economic reality.

To summarize, the ending of *Pro-femmes*, the organization of 'Savoir c'est pouvoir,' and the creation of ROE and of CAF together show that a Franco-Ontarian feminist community is developing its own organizations at the same time that it is working together with traditional women's groups. Even after the end of Pro-femmes, activists pressured ACFO to give priority to women's issues and to support women's groups publicly. ACFO agreed to provide its regional sections with resources to organize International Women's Day in 1983. It supported the creation of an Access Centre for francophone women and contributed to establishing shelters for women victims of violence.[60] These efforts at the 1982 ACFO annual general meeting led to the birth of the Mouvement rose (Pink Movement),[61] a group that acted as an informal component within ACFO to focus on seven issues of direct concern to women: the economy, adult education, health, violence, older women, pre-schooling, and work. It saw its role as keeping the board of directors of ACFO informed on those issues,[62] but it did not remain active for long.

The brief existence of the Mouvement rose seems to capture the difficulty of doing feminist work in a more or less supportive environment. Carmen Paquette next tried to rally francophone feminists in formulating a long-term vision for feminism in French Canada – this time working through the Réseau national action éducation des femmes. In the beginning, RNAEF concentrated on training for women who wanted to re-enter the paid workforce. At the same time, education was seen as a means by which women were individually and collectively bringing changes in their lives and their communities.[63]

RNAEF emerged from a confrontation between white anglophone and francophone feminists. It was in the aftermath of a conference held in 1980 in Halifax by the Canadian Congress for Learning Opportunities for Women that the idea of the RNAEF actually started germinating.[64] Although CCLOW was a national and bilingual organization, it had taken no special interest in the needs of francophone women. As Michelle Trottier, RNAEF's first coordinator, wrote in another context, 'if it is true that society has always considered that education was the means from which underprivileged individuals could seek a better situation, why is it that we speak so little of the education of francophone women living outside Quebec?'[65]

Two further groups remain to be analysed in light of these developments: Franco-femmes and the Réseau des femmes du Sud de l'Ontario (RFSO). Both were formed outside the Ottawa region, where most of the other activities took place. However, members of Franco-femmes, especially, were not out of touch with the work of Carmen Paquette and Pro-femmes. These groups held regional conferences, did local work, and attempted to get women together outside the realm of traditional groups.

*Franco-femmes*

Franco-femmes was founded in 1977 as one of the first francophone feminist consciousness-raising groups based in northern Ontario. Its structure was explicitly feminist in the Anglo-American tradition of consciousness-raising groups, with emphasis on small memberships and no formal organization. Franco-femmes had its centre in Hearst's Collège universitaire. In fact, the group consisted of four members – Agathe Camiré, Danielle Coulombe, Johanne Morin, and Michèle Trottier[66] – and it did no recruiting. 'The advancement of women, the possibility of fulfilling the need of its members to get together, the possibility for action ... these are the *raison d'être* of the group.'[67] Members met to share their experiences and ideas and to discuss women's activities and actions. They tested their ideas on the public, organizing information campaigns for housewives and for women in the workforce. Every second week, Franco-femmes's members wrote a column in the newspaper *Le Nord*.

In 1978 Franco-femmes participated in organizing 'Au féminin,' the first feminist meeting of Franco-Ontarian women from the north, which was sponsored by the FNFCF. In 1979 Franco-femmes was responsible for the organization of 'Au féminin II,' named the *Grande rencontre des Franco-Ontariennes* (Franco-Ontarian Women's Big Meeting).[68] For the first time in northern Ontario, francophone women were given the possibility to get together, as women. They gathered in small groups and in workshops to discuss all aspect of their lives: sexist advertising, single-parent families, family law, women and religion, the economy, sharing domestic chores with husbands, nutrition, sports, social change, adolescence, and how to live fully. More than 150 women of all ages attended.[69]

Members of Franco-femmes also participated in the meetings organized by Pro-femmes in the north, but, unfortunately, extant information about the group's work gives no indication of what really happened. As in all small groups, members leave for other activities or perhaps paid work,[70] and, without the urge to recruit other women, Franco-femmes ceased to exist. Clearly, however, Franco-femmes was part of the development of feminism in French Ontario.

## Réseau des femmes du Sud de l'Ontario

In 1982, later than in the northern and eastern parts of the province, women from southern Ontario decided to form their own group, which was not as small as in Hearst or as political as in Ottawa. The Réseau des femmes du Sud de l'Ontario (RFSO) was planned as a network. According to Colette Godin, the Réseau linked up approximately five hundred women living in Parry Sound, Niagara, Belleville, Windsor, and Toronto.[71] The issues they addressed were the constitution, violence against women, immigration, and women's financial independance. The Réseau had action committees on violence against women and they worked mainly in schools and with women's groups. RFSO has set up a number of projects that still exist today: L'arbre de vie, a housing cooperative for francophone women living in Toronto; SOS Femmes, a crisis phone line for depressed women and victims of violence; and a centre for research and resources for francophone women in cooperation with Glendon College in Toronto.[72] The group seems to have been less focused on consciousness-raising than the others, and it was more service ori-

ented. Nevertheless, it fits well in the portrait of Franco-Ontarian feminism.
Put in its broader context, Franco-Ontarian feminism has continued the community's traditions of solidarity. Just as in the 1940s when the Union des cultivateurs franco-ontariens insisted on having adult education accessible to francophone farmers, and in the early 1960s when the Union des fermières catholiques de l'Ontario pressed for the same services for rural women, Franco-Ontarian feminists worked for social change through adult education. Feminists however, did more than training. They were involved in a more in-depth process of social and cultural transformation, inspired by the New Left's critic of life experience as alienation and oppression. They emphasized that women lived in a specific context framed as much by patriarchy as by ethnic and class domination. Nevertheless, the continuity between the traditional agricultural solidarity movements and the work of Franco-Ontarian feminists is important. It is in their meeting that the theory and practice of francophone feminism seem to have found their specificity and originality.

To summarize, Franco-Ontarian feminism from 1969 to 1982 was mostly a form of regional activism that evolved out of different contexts. Feminists' main tool was consciousness-raising and it seems to have worked well in small groups, workshops, and educational activities. However, feminists eventually had to develop their own parallel groups, in part because they were not able to carry on their work institutionally, but also because they needed political autonomy. Thus, their priorities shifted from working within other groups to setting up their own groups and organizing explicitly as francophone feminists. Within that context, RNAEF became a space where feminists could formulate their priorities and politics. Yet, there were few institutional settings through which Franco-Ontarian feminism could work with women.

There is one more question that needs to be addressed before ending this discussion on Franco-Ontarian feminism – and it is theory. Although Franco-Ontarian feminists were influenced by the New Left and the adult education movement, it is important to acknowledge that they also tried to theorize women's experience. In doing so, they formulated a language that allowed them to mediate their life experiences with words – feminists' words. That language was obviously tied to consciousness-raising, but it also led to a discourse created by and for francophone women.

THEORISING WOMEN AND FRANCOPHONE RIGHTS

*Theorising Franco-Ontarian Women's Experience*

Although Franco-Ontarian feminism was action-oriented feminists were engaging in theoretical discussions with language by virtue of using words to mediate women's experiences. And if they did so in French it is because language, as bell hooks writes, 'is also a place of struggle.' Franco-Ontarian women's experiences had to be translated into French, with words that gave meaning to women's lives and with writings that could express difference. Feminists made this language possible in French-Ontario, while integrating ideas coming from the Anglo-American worlds. More specifically, the theorizing of Franco-Ontarian women's experiences took place in groups that were trying to rewrite Franco-Ontarian history from a women's point of view. Some of the more analytical work was done in the university, while another important part of the writing happened in feminist collectives.

The FNFCF contributed two important documents on the subject of francophone women's history: *La part des femmes, il faut la dire* (1980), and *Femmes et francophonie: double infériorité* (1981).[73] Both studies present women's contribution to the development of francophone communities and struggles as well as to gender equality. For example, it is through such work that women became more aware of their role in ACFO's struggles for francophone rights. The story of Diane and Béatrice Desloges, both sisters and teachers at the Guigues school in Ottawa in 1912, is quite telling here. The Desloges sisters refused to submit to the precepts of Bill 17 and decided to teach the students in private homes, where they were protected from the police by other women. Also, when the Ottawa Separate School Board was left with no judicial recourse to stop the government from banning French, women took over the Guigues school armed with hat pins to fight the police forces when they tried to come and arrest the teachers. Partly because of the activism of Franco-Ontarian women, the Guigues school was baptised the *Ecole de la Résistance.*[74]

Danielle Juteau, a professor of sociology at the University of Ottawa, was also important in promoting a language for and by francophone women.[75] Inspired by national liberation groups including Quebec's independence movement, Juteau, along with Yolande Grisé from the French literature department at the University of Ottawa, proposed the expressions *Ontaroises* and *Ontarois*, which encapsulated the idea that francophone women and men were involved in defining a modern vision of community life that would break with the pattern of domination imposed by the Anglo Ontario government since colonization.[76] Naming oneself Ontaroises also meant a total break with the mother, the farmwife, and the servant – the only roles for women as understood within the French community. It meant liberation from all systems of domination, including partriarchy, as well as the possibility of defining oneself as an autonomous person. The expression was used by the Regroupement des Ontaroises de l'Est, and it appeared regularly in women's writings.

A feminist language was also formulated in newspapers and magazines. Carmen Paquette had a regular column in *Le temps*, ACFO's newspaper, while in Hearst, feminists wrote in *Le Nord*. Also, in 1978 Franco-Ontarian feminists produced their own medium, a magazine entitled the *Tablier déposé* which became, in 1982, the *Nouveau tablier déposé* until 1984, when the publication was discontinued. The magazine was a tool of expression and experimentation as well as a way to encourage women, and more particularly Ontaroises, to act on their situation. The magazine was produced by a collective of Ontaroises coming from eastern Ontario, financed through subscriptions from their readership and distributed in francophone areas of Manitoba, Quebec, and New Brunswick.[77] The members of the collective who were most involved in *Le Tablier déposé* were Francine Drouin, Diane Henrie, Lise Huot, Jeanine Laurencin, and Jacqueline Pelletier. 'They would describe women's daily life, ask questions, express their feelings and emotions, address the new dimension "woman-man," and examine politics affecting women.'[78]

*Women and Francophone Rights*

If there is one text that translates feminism for Franco-Ontarian women it is Jacqueline Pelletier's article 'Les franco-ontariennes.'[79] This text provides one of the most accurate accounts of the terms in which Franco-Ontarian feminists discussed their situation. Pelletier's analysis focused on double discrimination or double inferiority, discrimination against women on the basis of their language and their gender. The 1971 and 1976 census confirmed such a double status of inferiority. Compared with anglophone women, francophone women living outside Quebec were generally more likely to stay at home, have more children, and be less educated and also poorer. They were living in small towns and mostly in environments hostile to the French fact. Danielle Coulombe from Hearst added that Franco-Ontarian women living in the northern part of the province were victims of a triple inferiority because of the region's economic underdevelopment.[80] Lise Latremouille also confirmed the importance of economic inequality in her attempt to analyse Franco-Ontarian women's status of inferiority.[81]

Pelletier situated Franco-Ontarian women's status of inferiority in the context of the historical domination of francophones by anglophones in Canada and Ontario, thus making assimilation a recurrent theme in her analysis. She stated that the continuing assimilation of the Franco-Ontarian people had to be understood as a direct consequence of that domination. Even in the workplace, where women have better chances today than before, Franco-Ontarian women had become 'the anonymous pillars of a superficial form of bilingualism that one finds in almost every work setting.'[82] She observed also that the majority of francophone women live in areas where employment is not available to them or where their degrees are not useful. Eastern Ontario, like the northern part of the province, has little to offer its women.

Pelletier also discussed women's status of inferiority in relation to their specific commitment to the francophone community. Politically, they were not recognized as actors in their own mixed organizations. Pelletier claimed that francophone women were being exploited by the 'ethnic' struggle and that they would not get any recognition whatsoever for their defence of francophone rights. Jacqueline Martin, another feminist and Franco-Ontarian leader, confirmed Pelletier's view in a speech delivered at the AFO's fortieth anniversary, where she also stated that Franco-Ontarian women were taken for granted in their support for linguistic issues. They were never acknowledged as women, while their organizations were becoming increasingly identified as places where one could find information, education, and resources.[83] They had become a necessity to community vitality.

Pelletier also referred to the way women did not feel respected as francophones in the mainstream feminist Anglo organizations that left them on their own. Carmen Paquette's experience in the Anglo women's movement confirmed this situation. She attended meetings of NAC, CRIAW, and CCLOW. She made sure that Franco-Ontarian women got whatever information about women's issues they needed to do their work. Yet, it is clear that the FNFCF had a marginal status in feminist circles, while the RNAEF had none.[84] Based on Paquette's experience, francophone women were rarely, perhaps never, consulted or invited to discuss the interconnection of systems of domination. Whenever francophone women raised their voices they became the token French and/or the unofficial translator of the group, making the issue one of translation instead of one of empowerment, as if Franco-Ontarian feminists were born bilingual! For Paquette, for example, it became important to refuse any tokenism by declining to be used as a translator.

This is not to say that bilingualism should not be important to the women's movement. On the contrary, it is a recognition that women want to promote a society where language should not be the basis of discrimination; if this recognition is not accompanied by concrete measures for assuring that francophone women are represented and that they can express themselves in their language, however, bilingualism becomes 'ethnic,' 'folkloric,' a way of keeping a category of women silenced.[85]

To summarize, it is this complex point where ethnicity, language, regionalism, and gender inequality and rights meet that feminists from the FNFCF, the University of Ottawa, and the *Tablier déposé*, as well as Jacqueline Pelletier's writings, tried to put into words. Pelletier also described francophone women's growing awareness of issues of concern to them: re-entering the labour force, training, single mothers, violence, and youth. She wrote, with others, about how Ontaroises wanted and tried to control their own lives, an issue that is embedded in language as much as in social action.

CONCLUSION

This article was about Franco-Ontarian women, the development of feminism, and its impact on Ontario's traditional francophone communities. I have discussed how the status of francophone women in Ontario was tied to their destiny as members of a minority group. Their situation was determined by who they were as women within that community and context – mostly as white women and mothers coming from Catholic, farming, and working-class backgrounds. This also meant that they were doubly or triply affected by how society and governments addressed their needs.

Although Franco-Ontarian or Ontaroises feminists were mostly active in their own local, regional, or provincial groups, they were also part of the women's movement or so they thought. But how they would participate in the women's movement nationally is an issue that will need more in-depth discussion. For now, the history of francophone feminist groups in Ontario will have to end here. During the late 1970s and all during the 1980s, francophone women's groups have been reclaiming their history, they have also been developing an original form of politics where the community's agricultural traditions and specific form of organizing meet with a politics of liberation coming from the New Left and the adult education movement. The main characteristics of Franco-Ontarian feminist groups can be found in their insistence on women's experiences and in their local, community, and regional community nature, with the Réseau adding a networking dimension to their small-group consciousness-raising approach. The impact of Ontarois feminism was minimal on francophone's main political organization, the ACFO. Feminists addressed the personal as political, but francophone women, perhaps like most Canadian women, were not sensitized then to use the public sphere to claim political representation. Perhaps when the woman question becomes one of citizenship and equity, francophone feminism may have more impact on society's political organizations. Nevertheless, francophone feminists became interested in politics during the 1982 constitutional reform, and at the municipal level, but not overwhelmingly.

Since 1985, Franco-Ontarian women have been attempting to form a provincial coalition. In 1992 they created the Table féministe de concertation provinciale (TFCP) in Sudbury. It was one of the first times in French Ontario that women identified openly with feminism. The TFCP consists of eighteen groups including the UCFO, CAF, and RFSO and newer organizations such as the Réseau des femmes noires francophones de l'Ontario and the Réseau des chercheures féministes de l'Ontario français. These groups show that Franco-Ontarian feminism is being transformed to address issues which are being raised in the communities and which are new to French Ontario. It is a sign that the community is witnessing changes once again. However, ACFO is still predominantly male-centred and has not made any significant overtures to incorporate women's issues within its structure. Perhaps when Franco-Ontarian women ask for half of their assets in ACFO, ACFO will start taking them seriously. In the meantime, Franco-Ontarian women within the women's movement have been paying the price for speaking another language. They are not getting support from other women's groups, while the men, whether they get support or not for Franco-Ontarian issues, still keep their base of power in their own organizations. Women, without support from the broader women's movement, end up having little political community and little impact. This is something the Anglo women's movement should reflect on.

If the dominant Anglo feminism had truly been one of equality and respect towards the 'Other' – the non-Anglo and the non-white – women would not have hesitated to promote their full integration into that movement. But being a francophone woman in Ontario means belonging to a minority group that the majority has attempted to eradicate on many occasions throughout its history. Even though the majority of francophone women are white, they live in an uncomfortable relationship with the majority. Still, today, it is that uneasiness that makes it impossible for Franco-Ontarian feminists to recognize the women's movement as being all-inclusive.

NOTES

I would like to thank Valérie de Courville Nicol and Valérie Maillot for their assistance with research for this article, Edith Smith and Caroline Andrew for their helpful comments, and Joy Parr for her insightful suggestions on organizing the text. Estelle Huneault gave me valuable information about traditional francophone women's groups. Carmen Paquette allowed me to go through her personal documents and answered my questions about a period in her life when she contributed to making feminism a reality in French Ontario.

1 For a summary of the area of study being developed around the more specific theme of women's issues from minority groups, see Billson, 'Interlocking Identities: Gender, Ethnicity and Power in the Canadian Context,' 49–69, and Labelle, 'Femmes et migration au Canada : Bilan et perspectives,' 67–83.

2 I will leave out many local groups that were more service-oriented than politically active, as well as the Fédération des femmes canadiennes-françaises de l'Ontario, which has to be understood more specifically in the context of the evolution of the Fédération nationale des femmes canadiennes-françaises (FNFCF). For more details, see *Les femmes de la diaspora*, prepared by Desjardins for the FNFCF.

3 For a broad view of francophone women living outside Quebec, see my article, 'La recherche sur les femmes francophones vivant en milieu minoritaire: un questionnement sur le féminisme,' 5–29.

4 This section will draw mainly on the historiographical material presented in Choquette, *L'Ontario français*, and Grimard and Vallières, *Travailleurs et gens d'affaires canadiens-français*.

5 These approximate numbers are based on the Canada census and on data collected by the Catholic Church. See Choquette, *L'Ontario français*, 78.

6 See Dallaire and Lachapelle, *Demolinguistic Profile, Ontario*, 4. While Choquette uses data describing the population of French origin in Ontario, Dallaire and Lachapelle present tables with data on French as a mother tongue. I will use the latter statistical category to present the more recent data.

7 Table 1 summarizes the evolution of the Franco-Ontarian population in the total Ontarian population since 1951.

TABLE 1
Proportion of the French-Language Minority Group in the Total Population, Ontario, 1951 to 1986

| Year | Total population | French-speaking minority | Per cent |
|---|---|---|---|
| 1951 | 4,597,542 | 341,502 | 7.4 |
| 1961 | 6,236,092 | 425,302 | 6.8 |
| 1971 | 7,703,105 | 482,045 | 6.3 |
| 1976 | 8,264,475 | 467,540 | 5.7 |
| 1981 | 8,625,105 | 475,605 | 5.5 |
| 1986* | 9,101,690 | 484,265 | 5.3 |

SOURCE: Dallaire and Lachapelle, *Demolinguistic Profiles, Ontario*, 3.
*The 1986 data, including institutional residents, were adjusted to allow for comparison with previous data.
According to the 1991 census, the total francophone population in Ontario was 492,300, while 1.2 million persons in the province (12 per cent of the population) claimed they could speak French. Statistics Canada-Cat. No. 93-315, 1, and Cat. No. 93-318, 1.

8  Table 2 summarizes the growth rate of the Franco-Ontarian population in the total Ontarian population since 1951.

TABLE 2
Mean Annual Growth Rate of the Total Population and the French Mother-Tongue Population, Ontario, 1951 to 1986 (%)

| Period | French-speaking minority | on-French population | Total population |
|--------|--------------------------|----------------------|------------------|
| 1951–61 | 2.2 | 3.1 | 3.0 |
| 1961–71 | 1.3 | 2.2 | 2.1 |
| 1971–76 | –0.6 | 1.5 | 1.4 |
| 1976–81 | 0.3 | 0.9 | 0.9 |
| 1981–86 | 0.4 | 1.1 | 1.1 |
| 1971–81 | –0.1 | 1.2 | 1 |
| 1971–86 | 0.0 | 1.2 | 1.1 |
| 1976–86 | 0.4 | 1.0 | 1.0 |

Source: Dallaire and Lachapelle, *Demolinguistic Profiles, Ontario*, 4.

9  Association canadienne-française de l'Ontario, *Les francophones tels qu'ils sont*, 10.

10  For more details, see Grimard and Vallières, *Travailleurs et gens d'affaires canadiens-français*, chapters 5–8.

11  For more details, see the special issue on the Franco-Ontarian economy, in *Revue du Nouvel-Ontario* 12 (1990).

12  The 1961 census revealed that 26 per cent of francophone families living in Ontario had six children and more, compared with 12 per cent for the non-francophone population. See Allaire and Toulouse, *Situation socio-économique et satisfaction des chefs de ménage franco-ontariens*, 36.

13  In 1990 this organization became the Fédération des communautés francophones et acadienne du Canada.

14  Juteau-Lee, 'Français d'Amérique, Canadiens, Canadiens-français, Franco-Ontariens, Ontarois: qui sommes-nous?' 21–43, gives a good description of the process by which the French minority in Canada and in Ontario developed its identity.

15  As well as Franco-manitobains, Fransaskois, Franco-albertains, etc.

16  Choquette, *L'Ontario-français*, 181.

17  For more details, see Choquette, *L'Ontario français*, and Gaffield, *Language, Schooling and Cultural Conflict*. It is depressing to read how ordinary people had to suffer and pay the consequences of the hatred, based on religious conflict, between the Anglo-Protestants and the French-Catholics, but also between the Irish and the French bishops. Intolerance and hatred towards Franco-Ontarian

Catholics was such that a series of measures were enacted abolishing all form of cohabitation among linguistic and religious groups in Ontario. We should reflect on this history as we speak of the Canadian people as a tolerant and generous population.

18 Now owned by Conrad Black.

19 It was only after the adoption of the Canadian Charter of Rights and Freedoms that Franco-Ontarians gained the right to manage their own schools and have their own school boards. However, it was not until 1987, with the Liberal government in power, that two school boards were created in Ottawa and one in Toronto. The other francophone areas are still without their own school systems.

20 Brunet, *Almanda-Walker Marchand.*

21 Choquette recalls that in 1968, when Gérard Pelletier was minister at the Secretary of State, the Liberal government played a key role in the development of francophone communities outside Quebec. This policy, however, was not easily reconciled with Trudeau's view of equality. Trudeau did not involve himself in the survival of francophone minorities through community development; his approach was institutional bilingualism, making federal services available to all in French and in English from coast to coast. It is also important to note that, before 1968, the Quebec government was the only one financing activities organized by francophones outside Quebec. See Choquette, *L'Ontario français,* 209–12.

22 A view held by Jacqueline Pelletier. See her article 'La situation de la franco-ontarienne,' 102–9.

23 Grimard and Vallières, *Travailleurs et gens d'affaires,* 210–15.

24 I found no explanation given for the change of name.

25 Grimard and Vallières, *Travailleurs et gens d'affaires,* 212.

26 I could not find her own name, since women then where identified by their spouse's name. Wendover is a small town located in Prescott County, east of Ottawa.

27 'Love God, the Earth and your Household.' Côté, *Plus qu'hier, moins que demain,* 17.

28 Ibid., 55–6.

29 Ibid.

30 From interviews with Gracia Lalande by Nicole Rozon, 28 July 1989.

31 The information for the Fédération nationale des femmes canadiennes-française comes from Desjardins, *Les femmes de la diaspora.*

32 In 1990 it had four thousand members and thirty-three group members, plus the sections and the regional councils.

33 Pelletier, 'Les franco-ontariennes,' 63.

34 In 1993 Pelletier was appointed president of the Ontario Advisory Council on the Status of Women.

35 For more personal information on Paquette's contribution to developing a progres-

sive politics, see her article 'Le lesbianisme féministe et la francophonie' in *Les cahiers réseau de recherches féministes* (Montreal: UQAM, Institut de recherches féministes 1995).

36 Document 2, Pro-femmes, 1980.

37 'Pro-femmes: projet d'animation auprès des franco-ontariennes,' 16.

38 Paquette recalls being told that the RCMP was watching her and other activists with the consent and collaboration of Archbishop Plourde.

39 'Communication sur Pro-femmes' by Carmen Paquette, Archives du CRCCF de l'Université d'Ottawa, Fonds UCFO, C67-3/19, Pro-femmes.

40 'Pro-femmes,' *Tablier déposé*, 1979, 16.

41 Ibid.

42 Archives du CRCCF de l'Université d'Ottawa, Fonds FFCF, Activités, Femmes dans les provinces canadiennes, Nord de l'Ontario, originaux et copies, sd, 1980–1, 17 pièces.

43 Goudreau, *Nouveau-départ et rapport*, 6.

44 For older women, the portfolio became a record they would give their grandchildren as a legacy of francophone women's life.

45 Goudreau, *Nouveau-départ et rapport*, 2.

46 Ibid., 3.

47 The study was done by Diane Farmer, during the summer of 1980. Her work consisted in distributing 600 questionnaires to francophone women living in eastearn Ontario. In her survey, Farmer tried to collect data giving information about women's training needs as well as their expectations as managers of the farm with their husband. She also informed women of their rights, as well as raising their consciousness about the fact that they were managers of the farm. See page 6 of the study Archives du CRCCF de l'Université d'Ottawa, Fonds FFCF, C53\47\9, Activités; Femmes dans les provinces Canadiennes; Ontario-Est, Prescott-Russell, Glengarry, Stormont, copies été 1980, 23 juillet 1982, 3cm. The study actually laid the foundations of a new group called Femmes et gestion de la ferme.

48 Cardinal, *Besoins sociaux de la franco-ontarienne de Prescott-Glengarry*. A similar study had been done with francophone women living in Manitoba. The study was published with some modifications. Altogether, 281 questionnaires were gathered, 204 of which came from women living in Prescott County and 74 from women in Glengarry.

49 Diane Desaulniers, 'Rapport: Pro-Femmes,' Archives du CRCCF de l'Université d'Ottawa, Fonds UCFO C67\B2B\6, Pro-femmes.

50 The coordinating committee was composed of Ethel Côté, Pierrette Dessaint, Martine Lafrance, Lise Latremouille, and Nycol Vinette. *Rapport d'évaluation*, 1981, 36 pages prepared by the organizing committee and sent to all participants to the conference.

51 Deslauniers, 'Rapport: Pro-Femmes,' 4.

52 My translation of 'Peut-être comprendront-elles qu'unies, elles aussi peuvent créer des services pour améliorer leur sort et accroître leur pouvoir individuel et collectif.' Document, 12 mars 1981, Archives du CRCCF de l'Université d'Ottawa, Fonds FFCF, C\53\47\5, Activités: Femmes dans les provinces canadiennes; Ontario, Originaux, copies et imprimés, sd, 1976–81, 1 cm.

53 Ibid.

54 The conference program was published in *Le Nouveau Tablier déposé*, 1981, 3.

55 For a complete list of the resolutions, see the special issue of *Le Tablier déposé*, April 1981.

56 There were groups working on issues about pre-schooling with Paulette Lebrun, Rita Cyr Hicks, and Carmelle Jérôme; work and unionism with Liette Perron and Lucie Brunet; health with Jocelyne Talbot; training and resources with Lyse Huot, Rita Cyr Hicks, Carmen Paquette, Monique Leblanc-Vincent, and Madeleine Beaulieu; politics with Claire Guillemette Lamirande, Jocelyne Talbot, Rita Cyr Hicks, Madeleine Beaulieu, Lise Latremouille, and Carmelle Jérôme; retirement with Denise Sarda; art, tradition, and culture with Claire Guillemette Lamirande, Paulette Lebrun, Madeleine Beaulieu, and Jocelyne Talbot; and feminist theory with Liette Perron, Jocelyne Talbot, Monique Leblanc Vincent, Martine Lafrance, and Lise Latremouille. Somehow, the committees dealing with sexist publicity and economic issues had no specific members.

57 The ROE was reborn in 1989 to become a single-issue group on abortion.

58 Centre d'accès francophone pour femmes, *Autonome! Autonome! Autonome!.*

59 'Le centre d'accès pour femmes,' *Le Nouveau Tablier déposé*, 1982, 8–10.

60 Archives du CRCCF de l'Université d'Ottawa, Fonds UCFO, C67-3\19, Mouvement rose, 1 chemise. 'L'assemblée générale de 1982, liste des résolutions adoptées,' *Le Temps*, nov. 1982, 4. Our adaptation from 1) 'Que l'ACFO donne priorité aux dossiers touchant la condition féminine et qu'elle appuie publiquement les revendications des groupes de femmes et dénonce les situations qui leur sont injustes'; 2) 'Que l'ACFO fournisse aux conseils régionaux les ressources humaines, financières et matérielles pour l'organization de tables rondes sur la femmes et la pauvreté dans le cadre des activités de la journée internationale de la femme, le 8 mars 1983'; 3) 'Que l'ACFO, en collaboration avec des groupes tel que le centre d'accès pour femmes, appuie et contribue à la mise sur pied de centres d'hébergements pouvant accueillir des Ontaroises victimes de violence.'

61 Archives du CRCCF de l'Université d'Ottawa, Fonds UCFO, C67\B2b\7, Condition féminine, 'Le Mouvement rose,' 1 page.

62 Members of the Mouvement rose were Claire Péladeau, Carmen Paquette, Suzanne Gagnon, Diane Henrie, Micheline Desjardins, and Carole Lepage-Ratté,

some of whom were already involved in women's groups. Procès-verbal de la 3e réunion du Mouvement Rose, Vanier, le jeudi 4 novembre 1982, 6 pages.

63  Document RNAEF, 8, date unknown.

64  Some of the ideas discussed here have already been presented in my article, 'La recherche sur les femmes francophones,' 8–13. See also Lacroix, 'Action-éducation-femmes,' 22.

65  Michelle Trottier, 'Action-éducation-femmes,' 3–4. Our translation of 'S'il est vrai que notre société a toujours proposé l'éducation comme le moyen idéal par lequel l'individu défavorisé accède à une meilleure situation, pourquoi parle-t-on si peu de l'éducation des femmes francophones hors Quebec?' Trottier was a founding member of the group Franco-femmes in Hearst.

66  Blight, 'Au féminin II,' Archives du CRCCF de l'Université d'Ottawa, Fonds FFCF, C53\63\4, Relation avec l'extérieur, Originaux et copies, Franco-Femmes, 1979–80, 12 pièces.

67  Ibid. Our translation of 'La promotion de la femme, une chance de répondre au besoins des membres de se rencontrer, une chance pour agir ... sont les raisons d'être du groupe F.F.'

68  Ibid.

69  Ibid.

70  Michèle Trottier, for example, became RNAEF's first coordinator.

71  Godin, 'Le Sud en action,' 30.

72  Ibid.

73  In 1991 the FNFCF published Les femmes de la diaspora, another important document telling the history of francophone women involved in the development of the organization.

74  For more details, see Dumont, 'Des épingles à chapeaux pour les soeurs Desloges,' 9–11. See also the story of Jeanne Lajoie who, on her own in Pembroke, started the first Franco-Ontarian school in that community.

75  Juteau was important in disseminating feminist ideas at the University of Ottawa. She introduced students to the work of French materialist feminists such as Christine Delphy, Colette Guillaumin, and Nicole-Claude Mathieu. But, interestingly, although not without explanation, those authors would not be referred to explicitly in the texts written by Franco-Ontarian feminists at the time.

76  For more details, see Juteau-Lee, 'Français d'Amérique, Canadiens, Canadiens-français, Franco-Ontariens, Ontarois, 41.

77  Vachon, 'Le nouveau tablier déposé,' 9.

78  Our translation of 'elles désirent ainsi décrire le quotidien des femmes, poser des questions, exprimer des sentiments, des émotions qu'elles ressentent, cerner la nouvelle dimension 'Femme-homme,' analyser les retombées politiques affectant la femme.' Ibid.

79  See Pelletier, 'Les franco-ontariennes,' 60–3 as well as her other article, 'La situation de la franco-ontarienne,' 102–9.

80  Coulombe, 'Doublement ou triplement minoritaire,' 31–136.

81  Latremouille, 'La population franco-ontarienne et la politique,' 22–3.

82  Our translation of 'Les franco-ontariennes constituent les piliers anonymes du bilinguisme de surface dans presque tous les milieux de travail.' Pelletier, 'Les franco-ontariennes,' 62.

83  In *L'association des fermières de l'Ontario (1937–1987)*, Vankleek Hill (1987), 21.

84  In 1980 NAC adopted a resolution saying that it accepted 'the principle of taking into account, in all their future recommandations, the five hundred thousand francophone women living outside of Quebec.' Our translation of 'NAC adopte le principe de tenir compte des cinq cent milles femmes francophones vivant en dehors du Quebec dans toutes les recommendations qu'il exprimera à l'avenir.' According to Paquette, nothing was done in light of that resolution. In Degarie, 'Au Comité national d'action sur le statut de la femme, des Franco-Ontariennes "visibles,"' *Le Droit* (1980).

85  The attitude of a majority of Anglo-Canadian feminists towards Quebec women during the Meech Lake accord is instructive. It provided one more example of the difficulty the dominant women's movement has in articulating a vision in which diversity is given the power it needs for its actors to be full participants of a transformational politics at the provincial as well as at the national levels. The trend is also to play one's difference in language against another – Native, colour, or immigrant. Is this not dividing to conquer? Or is this what it means to be politically correct?

APPENDIX

*Dates Groups*

1910   Association canadienne-française de l'Ontario (ACFO)

1914   Fédération nationale des femmes canadiennes-françaises (FNFCF)

1929   Union catholique des cultivateurs franco-ontariens (UCCFO)

1935   Union catholique des fermières de l'Ontario (UCFO)

1969   Association des fermières de l'Ontario (AFO)
       Union culturelle des franco-ontariennes (UCFO)
       Assemblée provinciale des mouvements de jeunes de l'Ontario français

1971   National Action Committee on the Status of Women (CACSW)

1972   Direction Jeunesse

1973   Canadian Advisory Council on the Status of Women (CACSW)

1975   Canadian Congress for Learning Opportunities for Women (CCLOW)

Fédération des Francophones hors Québec
Fédération des élèves des secondaires franco-ontariens
1977   Franco-femmes (FF)
       Pro-femmes
1978   *Le tablier déposé*
1981   Regroupement des Ontaroises de l'Est (ROE)
1982   Centre d'accès francophone pour femmes (CAF)
       Le mouvement rose
       Réseau des femmes du Sud de l'Ontario (RFSO)
       Réseau national action éducation femmes (RNAEF)
1969   Adoption of a policy on official languages in Canada
1970   Royal Commission on the Status of Women in Canada
1977   FFCF/AFO/UCFO sponsors Pro-femmes
       Conference on rural women in Plantagenet, 'Femmes et gestion de la ferme'
       Pépin-Robarts Commission on Canadian Unity
1978   Au féminin I in Hearst
1979   Conference on rural women in Hawkesbury, 'Femmes et gestion de la ferme'
       Au féminin II: 'La grande rencontre des Franco-ontariennes'
1980   Conference on rural women in Cornwall, 'Femmes et gestion de la ferme'
       AFO sponsors study, *Femmes et gestion de la ferme*
       CCLOW's meeting in Halifax
1981   'Savoir c'est pouvoir'
       'La rencontre des femmes du Nord'
1982   UCFO sponsors Nouveau-départ
       AFO sponsors study, *Les besoins sociaux des franco-ontariennes*
       Conference on Women and the Constitution

SELECT BIBLIOGRAPHY

ACTION-ÉDUCATION-FEMMES
    1982   *Document de travail* (Ottawa: AEF)
    1980   *Compte-rendu de la première rencontre du groupe Ad Hoc (CCLOW) fran-
           cophone à Halifax* (Ottawa: AEF)
ALLAIRE, Yvan, and Jean-Marie TOULOUSE
    1973   *Situation socio-économique et satisfaction des chefs de ménage franco-
           ontariens* (Ottawa: ACFO)
ASSOCIATION CANADIENNE-FRANCAISE DE L'ONTARIO
    1989   *350 ans de présence francophone en Ontario* (Ottawa: ACFO)
    1986   *Les francophones tels qu'ils sont* (Ottawa: ACFO)
ASSOCIATION DES FERMIÈRES DE L'ONTARIO

1987   L'association des fermières de l'Ontario (1937–1987): un avenir pour le
       passé (Vankleek Hill, AFO)
BLIGHT, Margot
1979   'Au féminin II, en fin de semaine,' Le Nord, 17 October.
BOIVIN, Louise
1983   'Regards sur l'avenir: un colloque national avec une histoire,' Femmes
       d'action 13:3–4
BRUNET, Lucie
1992   Almanda Walker-Marchand (Ottawa: L'Interligne)
BRUNET, Lucie, and Chantal CHOLETTE
1986   'D'un siècle à l'autre, la FNFCF,' Les cahiers de la femme 7, 3:52–3
BRUNET, Lucie, Chantal CHOLETTE, and Micheline PICHE
1988   'Des préoccupations paroissiales aux préoccupations féministes,' Femmes
       d'action 17, 4:17–18
BRUNET, Marie-Elizabeth, and Carmen PAQUETTE
1979   'Pro-femmes,' Le tablier déposé 1, 1:16
CARDINAL, Linda
1982   Besoins sociaux de la franco-ontarienne de Prescott-Glengarry (Ste Eugène:
       AFO)
1992   'La recherche sur les femmes francophones vivant en milieu minoritaire: un
       questionnement sur le féminisme,' Recherches féministes 5, 1: 5–29
CARDINAL, Linda, and Cécile CODERRE
1990   Pour ne plus être les oubliées (Ottawa: RNAEF)
CENTRE D'ACCES POUR FEMMES
1987   Autonome! Autonome! Autonome! (brochure)
CHOQUETTE, Robert
1980   L'Ontario français, historique (Montreal: Etudes vivantes)
CÔTÉ, Ethel
1986   Plus qu'hier, moins que demain (Ottawa: UCFO)
COULOMBE, Danielle
1985   'Doublement ou triplement minoritaires,' Revue de l'Université d'Ottawa
       2:131–6
CROWLEY, Terry
1986   'The Origins of Continuing Education for Women: The Ontario Women's
       Institute,' Les cahiers de la femme 7, 3:78–81
DALLAIRE, Micheline, and Réjean LACHAPELLE
1990   Demolinguistic Profiles, Ontario (Ottawa: Secretary of State)
DUMONT, Monique
1991   'Des épigles à chapeaux pour les soeurs Desloges,' Femmes d'action, 20,
       3:9–11

FÉDÉRATION DES FEMMES CANADIENNES-FRANÇAISES

1991 *Les femmes de la diaspora*, (Ottawa: FNFCF) (prepared by Micheline Desjardins)

1981 *Femmes et francophonie: double infériorité* (Ottawa: FFCF) (prepared by Pauline Proulx)

1980 *La part des femmes, il faut la dire* (Ottawa: FFCF)

GAFFIELD, Chad

1987 *Language, Schooling and Cultural Conflict: The Origins of the French-Language Controversy in Ontario* (Montreal: McGill-Queen's)

GODIN, Colette

1990 'Le Sud en action', *Femmes d'action* 19: 3

GOUDREAU, Diane

1988 *Nouveau départ et rapports sur ses répercussions sur la vie quotidienne des participantes de l'Ontario* (Ottawa: UCFO)

GOVERNMENT OF CANADA

1982 *Canadian Charter of Rights and Freedom* (Ottawa)

GRIMARD, Jacques, and Gäetan VALLIÈRES

1986 *Travailleurs et gens d'affaires canadiens-français en Ontario* (Montreal: Etudes vivantes)

HENRIE, Diane

1983 'L'implication des femmes de l'Est de l'Ontario, réflexion sur ce mouvement,' *Le tablier déposé* 4, 1:36–37.

HOOKS, bell

1988 *Talking Back* (Toronto: Between the Lines)

HUOT, Lyse

1982 'Le centre d'accès pour femmes,' *Le nouveau tablier déposé* 3, 1:8–10

JUTEAU-LEE, Danielle

1980 'Français d'Amérique, Canadiens, Canadiens-français, Franco-Ontariens, Ontarois: qui sommes-nous?' *Pluriel* 24:21–43

LABELLE, Micheline

1990 'Femmes et migration au Canada: Bilan et perspective,' *Canadian Ethnic Studies/Etudes ethniques au Canada* 22, 1:67–83

LACROIX, Suzanne

1988–9 'Action-éducation-femmes: un réseau national,' *Femmes d'action* 18, 2:22.

LAROCHELLE, Bernadette

1982 'Mieux orientés pour mieux vivre,' *Le nouveau tablier déposé* 3, 3 and 4:17–20

LATREMOUILLE, Lise

1979 'La population franco-ontarienne et la politique, in Barbara Roberts and Ceta Ramkhalawansingh, eds, *Ressources for Feminist Research*, 22–3

MANCINI BILLSON, Janet
1992   'Interlocking Identities: Gender, Ethnicity and Power in the Canadian Context,' *International Journal of Canadian Studies/Revue internationale d'études canadiennes* 3:49–69
MOUVEMENT ROSE
1982   Document I. (Newspaper articles, minutes, notes)
PELADEAU, Claire
1984–5   'Nouveau Départ en Ontario: une réalisation des plus chères,' *Action-éducation-femmes* (Ottawa: AEF)
PELLETIER, Jacqueline
1981   'La situation de la franco-ontarienne,' *Revue du Nouvel Ontario* 2:102–9.
1981   *Rencontre de deux jours: féminisme et ethnicité* (Ottawa: 14–15 May)
1980   'Les Franco-Ontariennes', *Canadian Women's Studies/Les cahiers de la femme* 11 2:60–3.
PRO-FEMMES
1980   *Document II* (Letter from Carmen Paquette to UCFO, 14 November)
1979   *Le tablier déposé* 1, 1:16
1978   *Document I* (Minutes, 4 November)
RESEAU DES FEMMES DU SUD DE L'ONTARIO
1990   *SOS Femmes* (February)
SYLVESTRE, Paul François
1985   *Le discours franco-ontarien* (Ottawa: L'Interligne)
LE TABLIER DÉPOSÉ
1981   *Savoir c'est pouvoir* (special issue)
TROTTIER, Michelle
1984   'Le colloque national,' *Action-éducation des femmes* (March)
1979   'Action-éducation-femmes: un dossier féministe,' *Le Tablier déposé* 3:3–4
VACHON, Jean
1982   'Le nouveau tablier déposé,' *Bonjour chez-nous* (17 March)

ARCHIVAL SOURCES

Centre de recherche en civilisation canadienne-française, Université d'Ottawa
Fonds FFCF, C52/52/3, Activités projets 'insertion dans les hebdos,' 1980–1, 81 pièces
Fonds FFCF, C53/54/4, Activités diverses, Pro-féminines, 1978–9, 3 pièces
Fonds FFCF, C53/53/3, Activités, rapports, mémoires, discours et textes divers, 1974–1980, 18 pièces
Fonds FFCF, C53/52/17, Activités projets, projet pilote 'Un 8 mars ensemble,' relations avec l'extérieur, 1978, 1983, 13 pièces
Fonds FFCF, C53/52/1, Projets Franco-Fam, 1976–1977, 20 pièces

Fonds FFCF, C53/47/9, Activités; Femmes dans les provinces canadiennes; Ontario-Est, Prescott-Russell, Glengarry, Stormont, copies été 1980, 23 juillet 1982, 3cm

Fonds FFCF, Activités femmes dans les provinces canadiennes, Nord de l'Ontario, originaux et copies, sd, 1980–1, 17 pièces

Fonds FFCF, C53/47/5, Activités: Femmes dans les provinces canadiennes; Ontario, Originaux, copies et imprimés, sd, 1976–81, 1 cm

Fonds FFCF, C53/19/11, Administration nationale, membres et organismes affiliées, Association des fermières de l'Ontario, SD, 1974–9, 31 pièces

Fonds UCFO, C67/B2A/21, Association des fermières de l'Ontario, 1980

Fonds UCFO, C67/B2B/6, Pro-femmes

Fonds UCFO, C67/B2B/7, Condition féminine, Le Mouvement rose, 1 page

Fonds UCFO, C67/3/19, Pro-femmes

# Picture Credits

Canadian Women's Movement Archives: Women painting a sign, Yana Scheuer, P-116; The Brown Breast Brigade, Laura Williams, P-531; The Women's Place, photograph by Kate Williams from *Building the Movement*, published by the Kitchener-Waterloo Women's Place; International Women's Day celebration, taken from the April-May 1973 issue of *The Other Women* newspaper, photograph by Holly; Cover of *The Other Woman* newspaper, July-August 1973 issue, photographer unknown

City of Toronto Archives, *Globe & Mail* collection: Bakery on Danforth Avenue, 118937; High school cheer-leader, 118955; The 'New Look' fashion reaction, 118919

Concerned Farm Women: Farm family at work, early 1980s; Women leaders, 1980s; Woman farmer working, 1980s; Woman working with farm machine, 1980s

Gerda Freiberg collection: Gerda Freiberg: Holocaust survivor and prominent Jewish community activist

Franca Iacovetta collection: Sisters-in-law together, 1957

National Archives of Canada: Modern Canadian living-room, 1956, C. Lund, PA 111484

Ontario Archives: Young Greek women; Woman staff worker with the International Institute of Metropolitan Toronto

Peterborough Centennial Museum and Archives: Bell Canada collection: Bell Canada Operators 79-018, PG 3-21-26; Westclox collection: Westclox clock assembly, c. 1950, 79-016

Vincenzo Pietropaolo: Pressing shirts in a Toronto laundry

Ester Reiter collection: October 1991 reunion of Lanark strikers

United Electrical Workers: Lanark strikers at the provincial legislature; Yvette Ward addressing the Lanark strikers in Dunnville, 1964

# Index